Two Sons of Charles Whitten

i

Two Sons of Charles Whitten

William B. Moore Jr.

HERITAGE BOOKS
2013

HERITAGE BOOKS

AN IMPRINT OF HERITAGE BOOKS, INC.

Books, CDs, and more—Worldwide

For our listing of thousands of titles see our website
at
www.HeritageBooks.com

Published 2013 by
HERITAGE BOOKS, INC.
Publishing Division
5810 Ruatan Street
Berwyn Heights, Md. 20740

Copyright © 2013 William B. Moore Jr.

Heritage Books by the author:

Letters to Rebecca

Two Sons of Charles Whitten

A likeness of the author's great-grandfather, Dr. Alfred Washington Whitten,
graces the cover. It was drawn by Jane Lauber, daughter of the author's first cousin.

International Standard Book Numbers
Paperbound: 978-0-7884-5511-7
Clothbound: 978-0-7884-6828-5

Table of Contents

Foreword

My book, *Letters to Rebecca*, based on letters collected by mother's great-great-aunt, was published in 1995. During my search to find and understand all those letters, I visited people and places while learning my way around old cemeteries, courthouses, and state archives and meeting a host of Whittens I had never known. I was having such fun that I continued to search after the book was published. Whitten lore poured in. I received more old letters and family genealogy from readers of the first book. Whitten information began to appear on the Internet, and more was found in newly published records. When the new millennium arrived I had enough material for another book, but old age prevented me from preparing it for publication. It has slept in my computer since then.

But, early in 2013 I sent a copy to my good friend Joanne Foster in Scottsville, Virginia, who has assisted so many budding authors. She graciously offered to help me. Without her, *Two Sons of Charles Whitten* would still be sleeping.

Too many family members contributed to this book for me to list, or at eighty-eight, even remember. Major contributors include: Arthur Reagan, my mother, Kristen Germany, Maralyn Bullion, Paulene Cunningham, Felece Dissmeyer, Penny Holsomback, Preston Holt, Ann Ohmsen, Presley Merritt Wagoner, Laura Barnwell, Jean Davis, Karen McCann Hett, Josephine McLure, Patrick Roten, Jim Ward, Andy Ward, Lorraine Almsted, Mrs. Robert Berkeley, Patricia Lynn Murff Cooley, Comer Ellis, Ellen Fletcher, Mrs. E. W. Gless, Irene McCommon, Anne K. McCuen, Kathy McDonald, Pat L. McDowell, Jo Ann McFarland, Margaret McRea, William C. Moran, Charles M. Percy, Eugene R. Perry, Harry L. Poe, Shirley Rhimer, Dora Whitten Rice, Roy C. Vance, James Simpson, Mary Louise Sterling, John Whitten Street, Mitch Vetusky, Carol Tillery Whitten, Elizabeth E. Whitten, Mrs. Elton B. Whitten, Henry A. Whitten, Hobert Judson Whitten, Mrs. Joseph Burford Whitten, Nathaniel Murry Whitten, Mrs. W. W. Whitten, Mary Martha Merritt, Jane Stam Miner, and Shirley Whitten Wilkinson.

As descendants of John and his brother, Charles Whitten Jr., were identified, I tried to discover their roles in the settlement of lands that became the South. Typically Europeans and Africans, coming ashore at East Coast ports, settled nearby, started families, and put down roots. Subsequent generations moved south and west seeking more and better land, leaving behind relatives, records, and real estate that can still be found by those who wish to find it. Our Whittens were among them, leaving the mountains of Virginia for the Carolinas, Georgia, Alabama, Kentucky, Tennessee, Mississippi, Louisiana, Arkansas, and Texas. In the process, four Whittens left South Carolina and become several thousand by the time I stopped searching.

While this material slept, things happened. The journey continued. People have been born, married, divorced, remarried, and moved on. Perhaps this book can aid future Whitten researchers as they continue the search.

TWO SONS OF CHARLES WHITTEN

Book I
EARLIEST OF THESE WHITTENS

Charles Whitten was a pewter caster, and the earliest yet identified member of his branch of the Whitten family. He was born about 1736; his wife, about 1740. Some think her name was Nancy. Although we do not know where either was born, they lived in Virginia before moving to South Carolina in about 1784, for early census records show the two sons who moved with them were born in that state. On 21 June 1784 Charles Whitten bought three hundred acres of land from Thomas Sexton and his wife, Elizabeth. It was located in the fork between Broad and Saluda Rivers, on a small branch of Ferguson's Creek, called Enochs Branch, in Spartanburg District, near the Greenville District line.

Typical families of the time had several children, and this was true of Charles and his wife. The 1790 census of Spartanburg District has them with three males and four females. Unfortunately, we can positively identify only sons John and Charles Jr., born 12 April 1762 and 18 January 1769, respectively, somewhere in Virginia. They married sisters, Mary and Millicent Reagan, who were born in 1766 and 1769, respectively, in Stafford County, Virginia. Both were daughters of James Reagan, veteran of the Revolution, and his first wife, Elizabeth Hayes. The marriages were performed at the Reagan family home in Rockingham County, North Carolina, so it is easy to speculate that the Whittens lived in a nearby Virginia county. Families bearing the names Southerland, Jernigan, and Graham were closely associated with the Charles Whittens and their descendants in censuses, land transactions, and church records, and may have been those of married daughters. Charles died in Spartanburg District about 1798, after deeding his land to James Southerland on 27 May 1797, and before 1800, when his wife was recorded living in the home of son Charles Jr. in Greenville District. She probably died before the 1810 census, for she did not appear with either son in that year.

Much speculation surrounds the ancestry of Charles Whitten. Theories abound. Regrettably, none are based on hard evidence. Annie Ard, a descendant of his son, Rev. James Whitten, and collector of Whitten lore, spoke of a Thomas Whitten as being a "grandfather way back." No Thomas connections have turned up. A daughter of Rev. Arphax Whitten, son of Reverend James, wrote that the early Whittens came down from Pennsylvania. That Charles and Nancy Smith Whitten almost certainly lived in western Virginia before moving to western South Carolina lends credence to this theory. Could our Whittens have entered the colonies at Philadelphia, moved inland, settled for a while around Charles County, Maryland, then traveled south through the Valley of Virginia, stopping for a time in the southwest section before settling in the Spartanburg and Greenville Districts of South Carolina? The Reagan family traveled this route, and they supplied the Charles Whittens with two daughters-in-law. The Whittens and Reagans are known to have reached South Carolina together. A story, told around 1800 to Talitha Emily Whitten Bell, a daughter of Reverend Arphax, by a Professor Whitten from a Louisville, Kentucky, college, claimed two Whitten brothers immigrated together, one moving north into Maine; the other south into Virginia, could be fact or fancy.

Several Whitten families arrived in South Carolina at about the same time. Surely some of them were related. Did they spring from a common ancestor in Virginia? Extensive research in that state has yielded no concrete evidence. Searches in the Maryland, Pennsylvania, and Virginia archives may someday yield clues to a connection.

Charles and Nancy Smith Whitten are known to have had two sons. This book is about them and their descendants. They were John and Charles Jr., who married Reagan sisters, Mary and Millicent, daughters of James Reagan. The following look at their family was assembled by Arthur Reagan of Alexandria, Virginia, who graciously allowed me to include it here.

FIRST REAGAN GENERATION
1. **James Reagan** emigrated, almost certainly from Ireland, in 1679. His wife's name was Joan. They lived in the

Nanjemoy Creek area of Charles County, Maryland, most of the last quarter of the seventeenth century. James was a bricklayer and died about 1697.

Their six children were:
Mary Reagan
John Reagan
Matthew Reagan
William Reagan
Charles Reagan
Margaret Reagan

SECOND REAGAN GENERATION
Children of James Reagan and Joan
Born in Charles County, Maryland

2. **Mary Reagan** was born 8 August 1683.

2. **John Reagan** was born 24 March 1685.

2. **Matthew Reagan** was born 24 April 1687 and died 30 March 1716 in St. Paul's Parish, Stafford County, Virginia.

2. **William Reagan** was born 31 January 1691, married Keziah, and died 21 November 1744 in St. Paul's Parish, Iowa.

2. **Charles Reagan** was born 20 May 1692 and married Elizabeth in Charles County, Maryland. They died in Stafford County, Virginia.

Their ten children were:
Elizabeth Reagan
Elizabeth Reagan
Katherine Reagan
Charles Reagan Jr.
Jemima Reagan
John Reagan
James Reagan Sr.
Elisha Reagan
Margaret Reagan
Jane Reagan

2. **Margaret Reagan** was born on 12 February 1694.

THIRD REAGAN GENERATION
Children of Charles Reagan and Elizabeth

3. **Elizabeth Reagan** was born before 1731 and died quite young in Stafford County, Virginia.

3. **Elizabeth Reagan** was born 20 October 1731 in Stafford, where she married William Powell on 2 April 1747.

3. **Katherine Reagan** was born and died on 25 July 1733 in Stafford County.

3. **Charles Reagan Jr.** was born about 1734 in Stafford County, and in about 1756 in Frederick County, Virginia, married Elizabeth Henry, who was born in 1740 in Virginia. He was an ensign in the Virginia militia. They lived in Shenandoah County, Virginia, in the late 1700s and moved into Blount County in East Tennessee about 1787, where Charles Jr. died in 1815. Elizabeth died before 1830.

Their eight children were:

William Reagan	Sarah Reagan
Charles Reagan III	Ahimas Reagan
Henry Reagan	Rebecca Reagan
John Reagan	Margaret Reagan

3. **Jemima Reagan** was born about 1735 in Stafford County, Virginia, where she married George Oliver on 1 August 1745. He was born in 1726 in Stafford and served in the Revolution as ensign, John Nelson's Militia, James Martin's Regiment, and had ten sons by Jemima, several of whom also served in the Revolution. They died in North Carolina; she, before 31 January 1772; he, in 1786 in Rockingham County. After the death of Jemima, he married Martha Whitworth, and they had two sons and a daughter.

Seven of the children of George Oliver and Jemima Reagan were:
John Oliver Sr.

William Oliver
George Oliver Jr.
James Oliver
Charles Oliver
Peter Oliver
Elijah Oliver

3. **John Reagan** was born 23 August 1736 in Stafford County, Virginia, married Rebecca Mary, and died in 1826 in Rockingham County, North Carolina.

Their three children were:
Sarah Reagan
Elizabeth Reagan
Sophia Reagan

3. **James Reagan Sr.** was born 9 April 1738 in Stafford County, Virginia, where about 1763 he married Elizabeth Hayes, who also was born in Virginia. Following her death he married Nancy Cook, daughter of Francis and Betty Cook, in about 1778 in Rockingham County, North Carolina. She died, and James then married, about 1790 in Rockingham, Rebeckah, who was said to be a Quakeress. James lived in Rockingham County, from 1770 until 1800 when he moved into Kentucky and finally into Knox County, Tennessee, where he died in 1827. He enlisted in 1771 in the colonial forces of North Carolina raised by Governor Tryon to suppress the Regulator movement, probably fought in the battle of Alamance Creek 16 May 1771, and was discharged on the 29th of the next month.

The five children of James Reagan Sr. and Elizabeth Hayes were:
Elizabeth Reagan
Mary Reagan
Millicent Reagan
John Reagan
Anna Reagan

The three children of James Reagan Sr. and Nancy Cook were:
James R. Reagan Jr.
Charles Reagan
Frances Reagan

The five children of James Reagan Sr. and Rebeckah were:
Henry Reagan
Peter Reagan
Rachel Reagan
Rebeckah Reagan
William Reagan

3. **Elisha Reagan** was born 19 April 1740 in Stafford. He lived in North Carolina and East Tennessee.

3. **Margaret Reagan** married Jacob Johnson 13 October 1748 in Stafford.

3. **Jane Reagan** married Samuel Evans 29 June 1746 in Stafford County, Virginia.

FOURTH REAGAN GENERATION
Children of Charles Reagan Jr. and Elizabeth Henry
Born in Frederick County, Virginia

4. **William Reagan** was born in 1758, and on 10 March 1780 in Shenandoah County married Leah, born about 1764 in Virginia. William served in the Virginia militia during the Revolution. In Blount County, Tennessee, he was murdered by John Keys before 25 November 1807. She died about 1835.

4. **Charles Reagan III** was born in 1760, married Winnie Harrell 14 May 1783 in Shenandoah County, Virginia, and died after 1807 in Knox County, Tennessee.

4. **Henry Reagan** was born 20 October 1762, and married Phoebe Harrison about 1785 in Shenandoah County. Henry also served in the Virginia militia during the Revolution. They died in Overton, Tennessee: he, 15 September 1829; she, 15 August 1825.

4. **John Reagan** was born in 1766, and married Martha Black in 1788 in Shenandoah County. She was born in 1771 in Virginia. John died 13 November 1843 in Dade, Missouri.

4. **Sarah Reagan** was born in 1767, and married Thomas Hardin.

4. **Ahimas Reagan** was born 30 July 1774, and married Rebecca Black, born 4 September 1774 in Virginia. They died in Cass County in northeast Texas: Ahimas, 28 October 1842; Rebecca, about 1850. Ahimas and Rebecca may have

reached the area before 1836 while it was still part of Mexico.

4. **Rebecca Reagan** was born 25 July 1776, and on 30 August 1798 in Blount County, Tennessee, married James Berry, who was born on 20 April 1773 in that state. They died in Cooper, Missouri: she, 18 July 1830; he, 11 September 1842.

4. **Margaret Reagan** was born 15 July 1779 and married Hugh Cochran.

Children of George Oliver and Jemima Reagan

4. **John Oliver Sr.** was born after 1750, married Mary, and died before 1830 in Lincoln, Tennessee.
Their seven children were:

    Rebecca Oliver
    William Oliver
    John Oliver
    George R. Oliver
    Mary Oliver
    Nancy Agnes Oliver
    James Oliver

4. **William Oliver**

4. **George Oliver Jr.** was born in 1760 in Prince Edward County, Virginia; married Susannah White 31 July 1805 in Rockingham County, North Carolina; and died 24 October 1844 in Lincoln, North Carolina.

4. **James Oliver**

4. **Charles Oliver**, who died in 1833 in Carter, Tennessee.

4. **Peter Oliver**

4. **Elijah OliverC**

Children of John Reagan and Mary

4. **Sarah Reagan** married Leonard Barker, who died in 1813 in Guilford, North Carolina. She died later.
Their child was:

    Thomas Barker

4. **Elizabeth Reagan** married Capt. Thomas Cook in 1776. He served with North Carolina forces during the Revolution and was a brother of Nancy Cook, second wife of James Reagan Sr.
Their ten children were:

Francis Cook	James Cook
Nancy Cook	Elizabeth Cook
Thomas Cook	Fenton Cook
David Cook	Samuel Cook
Rachel Cook	Jesse M. Cook

Children of James Reagan Sr. and Elizabeth Hayes

4. **Elizabeth Reagan** was born in 1764 in Stafford County, Virginia, and about 1786 married Joseph Cavin, who died in February 1805 in Spartanburg District, South Carolina. Elizabeth died before 23 July 1821 in either South Carolina or Kentucky. The Spartanburg census of 1790 shows them with four sons and six daughters. They were in the Greenville District in the census of 1800.
Five of their children were:

    Joseph Cavin Jr.
    Moses Cavin
    John Cavin
    Eli Cavin
    Elizabeth

4. **Mary Reagan** was born 4 August 1766 in Stafford, Virginia, and early in 1784 in Rockingham County, North Carolina, married John Whitten, son of Charles Whitten and Nancy Smith. John was born 12 April 1762 in Virginia. They died and are buried in Fayette County, Tennessee: Mary, 29 July 1836; John, 8 February 1837.
Their children are listed with the Whittens.

4. **Millicent Reagan** was born about 1769 in Rockingham County, and there about 1788 married Charles Whitten Jr., brother of Mary's husband, John. Charles Jr. was born 18 January 1769 in Virginia. Millicent probably died before 1820 in Pendleton District, South Carolina; Charles Jr., after 1850 in Cherokee County, Alabama. Charles Jr. is almost

certainly buried in an unmarked grave on his land near Leesburg in Cherokee County. William C. Whitten Jr., author of *Whittens and Allied Families*, 2nd ed., believed Millicent was buried at the Old Stone Church near Clemson in old Pickens District, South Carolina.

Their children are listed with the Whittens.

4. **John Reagan** was born 24 May 1770 in Rockingham, where he married, in 1794, Mary Hays, daughter of James Hays Sr. After Mary's death, he married, in Knox County, Tennessee, Mrs. Rebecca Hazelwood Moore on 6 November 1823. John died 25 January 1857 in Knox County and was buried in Lebanon Church Cemetery.

The three children of John Reagan and Mary Hays were:

> Gen. James Hayes Reagan
> Margaret Reagan
> Sarah Reagan

4. **Anna Reagan** was born in 1774 in Rockingham County, and married Eliakim Hamlin about 1792. She died about 1850 in Brevard, Transylvania, North Carolina.

Children of James Reagan Sr. and Nancy Cook

4. **James R. Reagan Jr.** was born 2 July 1780 in Rockingham County, North Carolina. In about 1800 he, with brothers Charles and Francis, moved to Elbert (previously Wilkes) County, Georgia, to live with their maternal grandfather, Francis Cook, who died there in 1812. In Elbert County, James Jr. married Martha Dandridge Morrison on 8 January 1805. She was the daughter of Joseph Higginbotham Morrison, and was born in 1784 in Amherst County, Virginia. They died in Georgia: she, 8 September 1839 in Elbert; he, 27 December 1855 in Pike County.

Their eleven children were:

> William Morrison Reagan
> John Reagan
> Martha Reagan
> Nancy A. Reagan
> Charles Reagan
> Joseph Reagan
> James Reagan
> Francis Washington Reagan
> Mary Dandridge Reagan
> Sarah Elizabeth Reagan
> Dr. Thomas Jefferson Reagan

4. **Charles Reagan** was born in 1784 and married Mary about 1806 in Franklin, Georgia. After Mary's death, he married Elizabeth Fincher on 19 September 1839 in Troup, Georgia, where he died in about 1850.

4. **Frances Reagan** was born about 1787 in Rockingham County, married Eli W. Narramore in 1814, and died about 1831 in Hall County, Georgia.

Children of James Reagan Sr. and Rebeckah

4. **Henry Reagan**, twin of Peter, was born about 1791 in Rockingham County, North Carolina. He fought in the War of 1812 and died before 23 July 1821.

4. **Peter Reagan** was born about 1791 in Rockingham, and married Nancy Cunnyngham, daughter of Jesse Cunnyngham, on 24 October 1811 in Knox County, Tennessee. Peter also served in the 1812 War and died 20 June 1839 in Rome, Floyd, Georgia.

Their two children were:

> Carrie Reagan
> Addie Reagan

4. **Rachel Reagan** was born in 1793 in Rockingham, and on 17 October 1816 in Knox County, Tennessee, married William Clinton McCall. Rachel died 8 July 1847 in Carroll, Indiana, and was buried in Pleasant Run Cemetery there.

4. **Rebeckah Reagan** was born 1 August 1796 in Rockingham, and on 5 July 1827 in Knox County married William Burns. They lived many years in Athens, McMinn, Tennessee. Rebeckah died 14 November 1878 in Sweetwater, Monroe, Tennessee.

4. **Judge William Reagan** was born 4 August 1798 in Rockingham County, North Carolina, and on 4 October 1825 in Knox County, Tennessee, married Matilda Caroline Tunnell, daughter of Robert and Elizabeth Johnson Tunnell, who was born 24 December 1805 in Anderson, Tennessee. William was reared in Knox County but moved to Floyd County, Georgia, after 1827. In March 1835 with their first four children they moved to Nacogdoches, in the Mexican state

of Tejas, where he was granted 4,428 acres of land in April of that year. They died in Rusk County, Texas: he, 8 October 1867; she, 5 February 1871, and were buried in Sulphur Springs, in that county. William and Matilda Caroline were ancestors of Arthur Reagan, who produced so much of this Reagan and Whitten family history.

Their nine children were:

> Eliza Adaline Reagan
> James H. Reagan
> Amanda Melvina Reagan
> Robert William Reagan
> Caroline Matilda Reagan
> Dr. Noble Marion Reagan
> Mary Emily Reagan
> Helen Jane Reagan
> Harriet Albina Reagan

FIFTH REAGAN GENERATION
Children of John Oliver and Mary

5. **Rebecca Oliver** was born about 1781, and married William Cunningham Jr.

5. **William Oliver** was born in 1784 in Rockingham County, North Carolina, and died in Lincoln, Tennessee, in 1841. He married Elizabeth Edging, who born about 1788 in North Carolina, on 23 October 1806. She died in Lincoln before 1812; and on 28 February of that year he married Nancy Painter, who died after 22 March 1856.

5. **John Oliver**, born about 1785; he married Lurena Frazier on 28 April 1814.

5. **George R. Oliver**, who was born in 1785 and died in 1863 in Carter, Tennessee.

5. **Mary Oliver**, born about 1794.

5. **Nancy Agnes Oliver**, born about 1796.

5. **James Oliver**, who was born about 1799, and married Mary White on 28 November 1799.

Child of Leonard Barker and Sarah Reagan

5. **Thomas Barker** was born before 1826 in Rockingham, North Carolina.

Children of Thomas Cook and Elizabeth Reagan

5. **Francis Cook** was born in 1782 in North Carolina and on 9 November 1809 married Anna Dent, who was born 18 August 1780 and died 4 May 1854.

5. **Nancy Cook** was born about 1785, and on 31 October 1807 married Peter Faulkner.

5. **Thomas Cook**

5. **David Cook**

5. **Rachel Cook**, who married a Mr. Henderson.

5. **James Cook**

5. **Elizabeth Cook**, who married John Hubbard on 17 November 1810.

5. **Fenton Cook** was born about 1794, and on 10 January 1819 married Emily Schofield.

5. **Samuel Cook** was born about 1795 and died about 1867. He married A. Williams and, on 11 April 1839, J. Askew.

5. **Jesse M. Cook** was born about 1802, and married Mary A. on 31 December 1836.

Children Cof Joseph Cavin and Elizabeth Reagan

5. **Joseph Cavin Jr.**

5. **Moses Cavin**

5. **John Cavin**

5. **Eli Cavin**

5. **Elizabeth Cavin**, who married James Ray, a widower about twice her age, on 13 February 1816, in Knox County, Tennessee. They had two sons and two daughters, who were born there.

Children of John Reagan and Mary Hayes

5. **Gen. James Hayes Reagan** was born 12 February 1800 in Greenville District, South Carolina, and in 1824 married Elizabeth Holt, daughter of the Reverend Irby Holt. Elizabeth died in 1829, and General Reagan married Mira Ann Lenoir in 1835. In July of 1864, while a hostage of the Union Army, in Knoxville, Tennessee, he died of jaundice. From

1822 until his death he lived in McMinn County, Tennessee.

The child of Gen. James Hayes and Elizabeth Holt Reagan was:

Sarah E. Reagan

The children of Gen. James Hayes Reagan and Mira Ann Lenoir included:

Julia Reagan and four others

5. **Margaret Reagan**, who married Andrew McMillan in 1814.

5. **Sarah Reagan**, who married Thomas McMillan.

Children of James R. Reagan Jr. and Martha Dandridge Morrison

5. **William Morrison Reagan** was born 10 January 1806, married Elizabeth Larrimore on 6 December 1835, and died 22 June 1862.

5. **John Reagan** was born 28 January 1808, married Nancy Brawner on 6 November 1833, and died 25 February 1858.

5. **Martha Reagan** was born 31 May 1810 and died 25 July 1825.

5. **Nancy A. Reagan** was born 15 May 1813, married David Abbott on 22 December 1842, and died 6 August 1872.

5. **Charles Reagan** was born 13 May 1815 and died 8 October 1874.

5. **Joseph Reagan** was born 29 March 1817 and married on 3 May 1843 Martha Ann Davis, who was born in 1823. She died in 1896; he, 28 February 1904. They lived in Conyers, Georgia.

Their child was:

Col. E. J. Reagan

5. **James Reagan** was born 26 July 1819 and died 5 September 1896.

5. **Francis Washington Reagan** was born 12 August 1821 in Elbert County, Georgia, and married Sarah Cecelia Refo on 14 December 1845 in Augusta, Georgia, where she was born on 17 November 1826. He died 25 May 1865 in Augusta; she, 25 July 1910 in Astoria, Long Island, New York.

Their child was:

Eugenia Octavia Reagan

5. **Mary Dandridge Reagan** was born 8 October 1823, married Reuben T. Hull on 12 January 1843, and died 22 January 1902.

5. **Sarah Elizabeth Reagan** was born 6 August 1825, married Needham Avery 17 December 1845, and died 30 October 1854.

5. **Dr. Thomas Jefferson Reagan** was born 21 March 1828, and on 7 June 1857 married Mrs. Rebecca DeLona Stanton-Neely, who was born in 1829 in Georgia. He died 9 May 1887; she, in 1916.

Their two children were:

Mary Elizabeth Reagan
Julia Neely Reagan

Children of Peter Reagan and Nancy Cunningham

5. **Carrie Reagan**
5. **Addie Reagan**

Children of Judge William Reagan and Matilda Caroline Tunnell

5. **Eliza Adaline Reagan** was born 4 October 1826 in Knox County, Tennessee, and married Francis Marion Rust in 1851. She died 26 March 1899 in Trickham, Coleman, Texas.

Their seven children were:

Elizabeth Alice Rust
Matilda E. Rust
Albert Rust
Robert William Rust
Alberta Rust
Noble Marion Rust
James Edwin Rust

5. **James H. Reagan** was born 8 December 1828, and married Sarah Elizabeth Frances Dodson on 8 January 1852 in Rusk County, Texas, where he died 14 June 1862.

Their four children were:

Clarence M. Reagan
Robert William Reagan
M. E. Reagan
Martha H. Reagan

5. **Amanda Melvina Reagan** was born 23 January 1831, and married Lucien Drayton Smith 11 July 1854 in Rusk County. He died 19 May 1898 in Eulogy, Somerville, Texas; she, 10 October 1908 in Cleburn, Texas. They were buried in Marystown, Johnson, Texas.

Their ten children were:
Talitha Helen Smith
Charles Byron Smith
Jessie Reagan Smith
Minnie Lee Smith
Nathaniel Wilson Smith
Louisiana Albina Smith
Adaline Melva Smith
Mary Kate Smith
Caroline Lavinia Smith
Annie Drayton Smith

5. **Robert William Reagan** was born 26 December 1833 in Floyd County, Georgia, and died 23 October 1855 in Rusk County, Texas, where he was buried in Sulphur Springs.

5. **Caroline Matilda "Carrie" Reagan** was born 4 September 1836 in Nacogdoches, Texas, and on 10 January 1859 in Rusk County married James J. Bagley, who was born in Alabama. On 19 May 1867 she married Robert Tunnell Cannon, who was born in 1836 in Hamilton, Tennessee. He was a Texas Ranger serving under General Baylor, joined the Army of the Confederacy, and died in 1916 in San Antonio, where Caroline Matilda had died on 28 February 1912.

The two children of James J. Bagley and Caroline Matilda Reagan were:
James Robert Bagley
Noble Reagan Bagley
The four children of Robert Tunnell Cannon and Caroline Matilda Reagan were:
Zachariah William Cannon
Ethel Matilda Cannon
Caroline May Cannon
Mary Cannon

5. **Dr. Noble Marion Reagan** was born 22 March 1839 in Rusk County, and died 8 May 1893 in Joshua, Johnson, Texas.

5. **Mary Emily Reagan** was born 28 February 1841 in Rusk, and married Douglas John Cater on 22 May 1866. She died 15 February 1877 in Corsicana, Texas, and was buried in Sulphur Springs, Rusk County.

Their three children were:
Clint Cater
Rufus Cater
Clyde Cater

5. **Helen Jane Reagan** was born 24 April 1845 in Rusk County, Texas, where she died 30 September 1854.

5. **Harriet Albina Reagan** was born 16 August 1849 in Rusk, married Capt. Charles Lewis Nunnally, and died 17 August 1900 in Jacksonville, Texas.

Their nine children were:
Guy Reagan Nunnally
Charles Lewis Nunnally Jr.
Carrie Estella Nunnally
Daisy Nunnally
Percy Nunnally
Robert Bruce Nunnally
Marion Diehl Nunnally
Edmund Lee Nunnally
Lawrence Nunnally

SIXTH REAGAN GENERATION

Two Sons of Charles Whitten

Child of Gen. James Hayes Reagan and Elizabeth Holt
6. **Sarah E. Reagan**

Children of Gen. James Hayes Reagan and Mira Ann Lenore
6. **Julia Reagan, two infants, and two other children** whose names are not known.

Child of Joseph Reagan and Martha Ann Davis
6. **Col. E. J. Reagan** was born in 1853 and died in April 1926. He lived in McDonough, Georgia.

Child of Francis Washington Reagan and Sarah Cecelia Refo
6. **Eugenia Octavia Reagan**, born 17 October 1846.

Children of Dr. Thomas Jefferson Reagan and Mrs. Rebecca DeLona Stanton-Neely
6. **Mary Elizabeth Reagan** was born 8 December 1858, and married Joseph Addison Jordon 28 June 1880.
6. **Julia Neely Reagan** was born 5 April 1860, and married Matthew Jeremiah Whitfield on 28 June 1880 in a double ceremony with sister, Mary Elizabeth.

Children of Francis Marion Rust and Eliza Adaline Reagan
6. **Elizabeth Alice Rust**
6. **Matilda E. Rust**
6. **Albert Rust**
6. **Robert William Rust**
6. **Alberta Rust**
6. **Noble Marion Rust**
6. **James Edwin Rust**

Children of James H. Reagan and Sarah Elizabeth Frances Dodson
6. **Clarence M. Reagan**, born 1853.
6. **Robert William Reagan**, bornN 1856.
6. **M. E. Reagan**, 1858.
6. **Martha H.**, born 1860.

Children of Lucien Drayton Smith and Amanda Melvina Reagan
6. **Talitha Helen Smith**
6. **Charles Byron Smith**
6. **Jessie Reagan Smith**
6. **Minnie Lee Smith**
6. **Nathaniel Wilson Smith**
6. **Louisiana Albina Smith**
6. **Adaline Melva Smith**
6. **Mary Kate Smith**
6. **Carolyn Lavinia Smith**
6. **Annie Drayton Smith**

Children of James J. Bagley and Caroline Matilda Reagan
6. **James Robert Bagley**, born in 1860.
6. **Noble Reagan Bagley**, born in 1862.

Children of Robert Tunnell Cannon and fReagan
6. **Zachariah William Cannon**   6. **Caroline May Cannon**
6. **Ethel Matilda Cannon**   6. **Mary Cannon**

Children of Douglas John Cater and Mary Emily Reagan
6. **Clint Cater**
6. **Rufus Cater**

      6. **Clyde Cater**

Children of Charles Lewis Nunnally and Harriet Albina Reagan
      6. **Guy Reagan Nunnally**
      6. **Charles Lewis Nunnally Jr.**
      6. **Carrie Estella Nunnally**
      6. **Daisy Nunnally**
      6. **Percy Nunnally**
      6. **Robert Bruce Nunnally**
      6. **Marion Diehl Nunnally**
      6. **Edmund Lee Nunnally**
      6. **Lawrence Nunnally**

Book II
JOHN WHITTEN AND HIS DESCENDANTS
SECOND GENERATION

Whitten researchers have discovered a great deal about the descendants of John and Mary Reagan Whitten. Married about 1784 in Rockingham County, North Carolina, John and Mary moved in that year to Spartanburg District, South Carolina, with his parents, Charles and Nancy Smith Whitten. In 1795 they bought land and moved, only a few miles, into adjacent Greenville District. The new home was on the upper South Pacolet River, up against Hogback Mountain, near the site of Gowensville. It was to become Pleasant Grove, the home of granddaughter Rebecca, who collected the letters contained in *Letters to Rebecca.* Her father, Silas Reagan Whitten, purchased it from his father, John, on 4 March 1832, and lived there with his family until late in 1850.

John and Mary were loyal Baptists, joining Tygar (*old spelling*) Baptist Church in 1802, two years after it was founded. Its records are liberally sprinkled with their names and those of other family members. Cross Roads Baptist Church, about a mile from the Whitten home, was organized in 1820, and John and Mary joined in May 1822. Much later Cross Roads was moved into the village, and its name changed to Gowensville Baptist Church. It remains a vibrant, active place of worship.

The following selected entries appear in the records of Tygar Baptist Church:

> The Tygar Church was established in 1800, as a branch of Reedy River Church.
>
> Aug. 21 1802, John Whitten offered by experience.
>
> Aug. 26th 1802, Sister Mary Whitten.
>
> January the 22nd, Brother David Forrest, Brother Joseph Barrett, and Brother Charles Whitten our messengers to hear the petitions to the sister churches.
>
> Feb. 26th 1803, came Nancy Barrett and offered and was received. Respecting Brother John Stanford's getting drunk twice, therefore nominated our Brothers Nathaniel Jackson and Charles Whitten to go to him.
>
> April the 25th, then came forward David Barrett.
>
> June 4 1803, nominated for Deacon, John Whitten.
>
> Aug. 26 1803, was received by experience, Milly Whitten.
>
> Sept. 24th 1803, appointed Brethren Nathaniel Jackson, Abner Cass, and John Whitten as delegates to the association.
>
> Nov. 26 1803, ordained minister and three deacons, (*including*) John Whitten.
>
> January 21st 1804, met in Church meeting. Also Brother Charles Whitten reported that Brother Stanford had been drunk and denied it, appointed Brothers Whitten and Dill to cite him to meeting and request those that saw him to come likewise.
>
> March 24th 1804 appointed Charles Whitten (and three other judges).
>
> Aug. 24th 1804, (*thinking Brother Charles Gosnell ripe for excommunication*) nominated Brother John Whitten, et al., to go out and settle it.
>
> March 23rd 1806, Brothers Jackson and John Whitten were appointed to search the church book and to instruct the clerk in his duty (*David Barrett was clerk and needed training*).
>
> Nov. 9 1805, called meeting, a matter brought forward against Brother John Tubb by Mrs. Prince, a charge of uncleanness. Appointed Brothers Abner Center and Charles Whitten to cite her to our next meeting with all her friends, white and black, to authenticate her charges.
>
> Dec. the 21st 1805, also the matter of Brother David Barrett's riding into Littleberry Holcombe's house and denied it, and afterward acknowledged it, laid over till next meeting, nominated Brethren Nathaniel Jackson and Charles Whitten to cite him to next meeting.
>
> Sept. 27th 1806, rose up Brother Charles Whitten and confessed he had got angry and bore with, and rose up Sister Mary Whitten and confessed she had got angry and bore with, also appointed Brother Nathaniel and John Whitten as delegates to the association.
>
> Feb. the 20th 1807, application was made for letter of dismissal by Brother Charles Whitten and wife, also

by David Barrett for Brother Joseph Barrett.

July the 25th 1807, rose up Brother Michel Pruet and lade in an allegation against Nicholas Gosnell for selling corn at one dollar per bushel, after some talk upon it the Church lade it off till third Saturday in August and appointed brethren to settle it, (*nine appointed, including John Whitten*), the majority of 7 or 5 to carry the pint (*point*).

Aug. 20th 1807, also took in consideration the gift of Brothers Abner Center and John Whitten.

Sept. the 26 1807, delegates to the association, (*including John Whitten*).

June 24th 1808, Brothers John Whitten and A Senter came forward and made a report of Sister Hannah Bellows present circumstances.

April 21st 1810, nominated a Presbytery to go and act for the church and their satisfaction should be the churches satisfaction (*John Whitten among 10*).

January 26th 1811, also Brother David Barrett applied for a letter of dismissal.

Feb. the 21 1812, then Brother Whitten made application to the Church to know what was to be done with Church members that neglect to pay their just debts, in answer says, deal with such members agreeable to the Gospel.

Nov. the 20th 1812, Brother Rueben Barrett rose and unfellowshipt himself for drinking too much liquor and gave satisfaction for the same, (*June 1813, Brother Rueben Barrett in identical condition*).

April the 22 1814, David Barrett and wife (*Elizabeth Whitten*) came forward and gave themselves to the care of the Church.

March 21 1817, received Priscilla Southerland.

April the 27th 1822, met in Church meeting after prayer by Brother John Whitten, then chose Brother Whitten moderator.

May the 24th 1822, (*plans made to ordain Brother Thomas Barton, messengers from other churches to assist*) Brothers John and James Whitten from the Cross Roads Church were present to assist.

October 25 1823, proceeded to deal with Brother Page for believing and practicing the cure of witchcraft and excommunicated him for the same, then received a petition from the Cross Roads Church for the Eldership of our Church to assist them in the licensing of James Whitten.

Nov. the 27th 1824, February 27 1825, and November 25 1825, received a petition from the Cross Roads Church for help to assist in the ordination of James Whitten if found ripe, and the Church granted the petition and sent the Eldership.

October the 22 1825, then came forward Nancy Southerland and joined by letter.

May the 15th 1831 Martha Southerland, joined by letter.

John Whitten held the rank of Matross in the Virginia Artillery during the Revolution (*Service Record #5751 National Archives*). He owned considerable land and was justice of the quorum in the early 1800s. He and his family moved to Hall County, Georgia, between 1832 and 1834, probably to be near their eldest son, James. Following the trail of daughter Elizabeth and her husband, David Barrett, who told of their trip from South Carolina in a letter written in 1827, they moved to Fayette County, Tennessee. Sons Alfred and Ranson with Mary Dalton, daughter of their late sister Nancy, soon joined them. John and Mary died and are buried there: he, 8 February 1837; she, 29 July 1836. Their home was on the north fork of Wolf River. Having been among the early settlers of upper South Carolina, they became pioneers in the opening of western Tennessee.

The nine children of John Whitten and Mary Reagan were:

Rev. James Whitten
Charles Whitten
Elizabeth Whitten
Nancy Whitten
Silas Reagan Whitten
Alfred Whitten
Dr. Isaac Smith Whitten
Mariam Whitten
Ranson Whitten

THIRD GENERATION
JAMES WHITTEN

1. **Rev. James Whitten,** first child of John and Mary Reagan Whitten, was born on 26 January 1785 in

Spartanburg District, South Carolina. He married on 5 October 1809, Elizabeth Ann Thompson, who was born 24 February 1788 in Greenville District and died on 23 February 1835 in Hall County, Georgia. Young James was a well-known surveyor. Maps bearing his signature still survive. In 1814, he served in the 21st General Assembly of South Carolina. James joined Cross Roads Baptist Church in 1817, was licensed to preach in March 1823, ordained in December 1825, and moved to Hall County, Georgia, the following year, becoming pastor of Yellow Creek Baptist Church on May 20. After the death of Elizabeth Ann, James Whitten moved to Whitesville, Harris, Georgia, and served for a time as pastor of Mountain Creek Primitive Baptist Church. On 8 September 1836 he married Sarah Little Hogan, who was born in March 1797 and died on 21 February 1853. After her death he moved to Columbus, Muskogee, Georgia, and lived with his daughter, Elizabeth Ann, dying there on 16 November 1859. A biographical sketch of Reverend Whitten, contained in *Georgia Baptists* by J. H. Campbell of Perry, Georgia, and published in 1874 by J. W. Burke and Company of Macon, Georgia, contains these words:

> Having accomplished his work, in accordance with a prayer which he frequently uttered, he was gathered as a shock of corn, fully ripe, and died in the sight of Heaven at peace with God and all mankind. He was a good man, and full of the Holy Ghost and of faith. By no act of his life did he ever bring reproach on the cause of Christ. On the contrary, he glorified Him in all things. Few men were more familiar with the sacred volume, or could wield the weapons of warfare which it furnishes, more effectively. Verily he was a good minister of Jesus Christ.

The eleven children of James Whitten and Elizabeth Ann Thompson were:
- Harriet Whitten
- Rev. Arphax Whitten
- Melicent Mazelle Whitten
- Emily Whitten
- Orpha Judson Whitten
- Calvin Thompson Whitten
- Eliva Edgel Whitten
- Unnamed child Whitten
- Unnamed twins Whitten
- Elizabeth Ann "Liza" Whitten

FOURTH GENERATION
Children of Rev. James Whitten and Elizabeth Ann Thompson

2. **Harriet Whitten** was born on 19 October 1810 in Spartanburg District, South Carolina, where she died on 21 August 1823.

2. **Rev. Arphax Whitten** was born on 5 March 1812 in Spartanburg District, and married on 8 January 1834 in Lee County, Alabama, Matilda Allen Bennett, daughter of Rev. Mitchell and Didaema Parrott Turner Bennett, born 17 November 1813. Matilda Allen died 27 November 1848 at Smith Station, Lee, Alabama, and was buried in Mount Zion Cemetery. Arphax married on 22 February 1851 in Georgia, Aurelia Priddy, born 6 November 1826. He died 15 October 1872 at Smith's Station, and was buried with Matilda Allen. After his death Aurelia moved with her children to Texas and settled near Tyler. Her church was Hopewell Baptist in Smith County, where she died 14 June 1888. Rev. Arphax Whitten was a well-known Baptist preacher. Alabama Baptist records of the time contain numerous references to him and his work. *The Alabama Historical Quarterly*, vol. 15, page 409, mentions that his cousin was Rev. M. L. Whitten of the North Alabama Conference, Methodist Episcopal Church. This was Moses L. Whitten, son of Mason and Nancy Whitten of Lauderdale County, Alabama. Mason's father was Charles Whitten, who was born before 1765 and died about 1827. Charles and his family moved from Newberry District, South Carolina, to Lauderdale County, Alabama, before 1820. Apparently one must identify earlier generations of both Whitten lines in order to establish this relationship, if, in fact, it exists. The Bible of Arphax Whitten contains birth, death, and marriage entries for his family and that of his father. It is in excellent condition and is in the possession of Andrew Ward of Atlanta, who also has the Bible of Rev. James Whitten.

The eight children of Rev. Arphax Whitten and Matilda Allen Bennett were:

Julia Ann Elizabeth Whitten	Orpha Judson Whitten
Doleska Fitzallen Whitten	Sarah Mitchell Whitten
Talitha Emily Whitten	Matilda Allen Whitten
Mary Didema Whitten	Georgia Ann Whitten

The three children of Rev. Arphax Whitten and Aurelia Priddy were:

Joanna E. Whitten	Harriette V. Whitten

James E. Whitten

2. **Melicent Mazelle Whitten** was born 1 January 1814 in Spartanburg District, South Carolina, and married on 10 January 1828 in Hall County, Georgia, Nathaniel Harbin Goss, who was born 13 September 1805 in Pendleton District, South Carolina. They died in Phelps, Lawrence, Missouri: she, 27 April 1900; he, 5 September 1888, and were buried in the Goss Cemetery there.

Their sixteen children were:

Benjamin Franklin Goss
Martha Elizabeth Goss
Malinda Eleanor Goss
James Whitten Goss
Louisa Caroline Goss
Calvin Benson Goss
Melicent Elvira Goss
Nathaniel Jackson Goss
Alfred Webb Goss
Robert Lewis Goss
Silas Washington Goss
Wilson Lumpkin Goss
Mary Irene Goss
Unnamed daughter Goss
Orpha Louisa Goss
Julian Melissa Goss

2. **Emily Whitten** was born on 14 January and died 18 December in 1816 in Spartanburg District.

2. **Orpha Judson Whitten** was born 21 November 1817 in Spartanburg District, and married on 7 December 1837, in Harris, Georgia, Col. Thomas M. Hogan, born in 1809 in Kershaw, South Carolina. They moved from Harris County to Columbus, Georgia, in 1840 where Colonel Hogan, a staunch Union supporter, introduced Georgia's first fractional currency. Orpha Judson died 18 March 1878 in Lee County, Alabama. Colonel Hogan lived thereafter with the niece of his wife, Doleska Fitzallen Whitten, in the Smith's Station home of Rev. Arphax Whitten, where he died on 23 January 1886.

Their nine children were:

James Hogan
Thomas M. Hogan
John L. Hogan
Eliza Hogan
Susan E. Hogan
Rebecca Hogan
Mary E. Hogan
Emily Hogan
Annie Hogan

2. **Calvin Thompson Whitten** was born on 23 January 1820 in Spartanburg District, and married Malinda Catherine Kinsey on 25 November 1841 in Lumpkin, Stewart, Georgia. She was a daughter of Elisha and Elizabeth Kinsey, and was born 23 February 1819 in South Carolina. They died in Belton, Bell, Texas: he, 21 February 1886; she, 4 February 1893, and were buried in North Belton Cemetery. Calvin Thompson lived in Hall County, Georgia, before marriage, after which the couple moved first to nearby Gilmer County, then to Columbus, Georgia, and on to Guntown, Lee, Mississippi, where they lived until the Civil War. His sister Eliza wrote of visits to Guntown. Ranson Edwin Whitten, his cousin, wrote in August 1863 that, because of the war, Calvin Thompson had scattered the family for their safety. Malinda Catherine and daughter Sarah Rebecca were near Birmingham with her father, Elisha Kinsey. Mary Clifford, who feared federal reprisal because she had informed Confederate agents of a Union spy in Mississippi, was in Columbus, Georgia, with her Aunt Eliza and Uncle Rev. Arphax Whitten, while Calvin Thompson was in Okolona, Mississippi. After the war Calvin and Malinda moved to Belton, Texas, and lived near, or with, daughter Mary Clifford.

Their two children were:

Mary Clifford Whitten   Sarah Rebecca "Sally" Whitten

2. **Elvira Edgel Whitten** was born on 15 May 1822 in Spartanburg District, and married 13 December 1843 in Gilmer County, Georgia, James Green Perry, born 17 November 1820 in Canton, Cherokee, Georgia. They died in Dawson County, Georgia, and were buried in Antioch Cemetery. Elvira died on 26 March 1901; James Green, 22 April 1892.

Their ten children were:
- William Washington Perry
- James Whitten Perry
- Millicent Louisa Malinda Perry
- Sarah Elvira Elizabeth Perry
- Artimissa Edgel A. Perry
- Nathaniel Lewis Perry
- Orpha Elvira Perry
- Benjamin Arphax Perry
- John Evans Green Perry
- Thomas Jackson Perry

2. **Unnamed infant Whitten**, who was born and died in December 1824.

2. **Unnamed twins Whitten**, who were born and died 22 May 1827.

2. **Elizabeth Ann "Eliza" Whitten** was born 9 August 1829 in Columbus, Georgia, and died there of diphtheria on 25 September 1864. She never married, although correspondence, much of which has been preserved in *Letters to Rebecca*, suggests that she and her cousin Ranson Edwin Whitten were smitten with each other. During the Civil War, until her death, they exchanged letters. What might have happened had she escaped her untimely death?

FIFTH GENERATION
Children of Rev. Arphax Whitten and Matilda Allen Bennett

3. **Julia Ann Elizabeth Whitten** was born 20 February 1835 in Georgia, died 1 January 1867 in Russell County, Alabama, and was buried in Mount Zion Cemetery, Lee County, Alabama.

3. **Doleska Fitzallen "Dolly" Whitten**, twin of Talitha Emily, was born 22 May 1837 in Georgia, died 13 December 1900 in Lee County, Alabama, and was buried in Mount Zion Cemetery. In 1885, while serving as postmistress, Smith's Station, Alabama, and living at the old home place, she wrote to Silas Reagan Whitten, brother of her grandfather, James. In it Dolly told of her family. Later she wrote her cousin the following letter:

Doleska Fitzallen Whitten to Ranson Edwin Whitten (*son of Silas Reagan Whitten*)—Smith's Station, Alabama, to Ripley, Mississippi, 11 January 1897

> Your grandfather was named John Whitten and he had one brother, Charles Whitten (*Jr.*), whose descendants are all about you in the West, and fine people, too. They lived in Spartanburg District, S.C. and the two brothers married sisters, Mary and Millie (*Millicent*) Reagan. Our (*her great*) grandfather married Mary.
>
> My father's sister, Mrs. Nathaniel Harbin Goss (*Melicent Mazelle Whitten*), who lives in Missouri, says she always heard her great-grandfather (*Charles Whitten*) came from Ireland; Any Scotch blood then must have come from the Smith side, his wife, I had never heard; that they first settled in Pennsylvania.

Dolly apparently was the first of these Whittens to actively search for family history.

3. **Talitha Emily Whitten**, twin of Doleska Fitzallen, was born 22 May 1837 in Georgia and married on 1 February 1872, E. Alonza Bell, after which they moved to Caldwell, Butler, Texas, where she died after 1918. She, too, yearned for Whitten family lore. Her letters and collection of family history survive.

Their three children were:
- Mary Susan Bell
- Clifford D. Bell
- Arthur Edgar Bell

3. **Mary Didema Whitten** was born on 8 July 1840 in Chambers County, Alabama, and married William H. Tarver. She died 15 December 1931 in Lumpkin, Stewart, Georgia. They also moved to Texas after marriage.

3. **Orpha Judson Whitten** was born on 7 March 1842 in Chambers County, married Alexander Lamb 16 July 1867, and died 23 May 1870 in Salem, Alabama.

Their two children were:
- Charles Lamb
- Edward Lamb

3. **Sarah Mitchell Whitten** was born 14 May 1843 in Heard County, Georgia, and married on 8 January 1867 in Smith Station, Alabama, George Washington Lafayette Ard, who was born 21 July 1833 in Early County, Georgia. They died in Stewart County: he, 30 July 1894; she, in November 1930.

George Washington Lafayette Ard served the Confederacy in Company K, 2nd Georgia Regiment. On 17 September 1862 he lost his right leg while defending the Stone Bridge during the battle of Antietam. He was captured by federal troops and later wrote of the kindness shown him by fellow Masons who were attached to the 9th New York Regiment, U.S. Army.

Their nine children were:

Annie Ard
Julia Clifford Ard
Charles Edgar Ard
Sarah Matilda Ard
George Fitzallen Ard
Mary Jane Ard
Georgia Agnes Ard
Thomas Arphax Ard
John Ard

3. **Matilda Allen Whitten** was born 17 May 1845 in Lee County, Alabama, and married Ira Crow on 12 December 1865. They died where they lived, in Lee County: Matilda Allen, 19 September 1927. Her 11 November 1909 letter to Annie Ard has been preserved.

Their four children were:

William Berry Crowe
Ira Bennett Crowe
Jacob Crowe
Julia Bennett Crowe

3. **Georgia Ann Whitten** was born on 26 February 1847 in Lee County, married John Duke Richardson 12 December 1871, and died 17 May 1928. They lived in Stewart County, Georgia.

Their four children were:

Edward Richardson
Samuel Richardson
Willard Richardson
Mary Whitten Richardson

Children of Rev. Arphax Whitten and Aurelia Priddy
Born in Smith Station, Alabama

3. **Joanna E. Whitten** was born 20 February 1852, and married on 23 February 1879, John W. McRae, who was born 18 November 1851 and died 31 December 1881.

Their two children were:

William Whitten McRae
Johnnie S. McRae

3. **James E. Whitten** was born 25 February 1866 and died 11 January 1913 in Texas.

3. **Harriette V. Whitten** was born 26 December 1867, married William H. Swann 27 July 1904 in Texas, and died 4 December 1915 in that state.

Children of Nathaniel Harbin Goss and Melicent Mazelle Whitten

3. **Benjamin Franklin Goss** was born 30 March 1829 in Hall County, Georgia, and married Louisa Perry there on 23 January 1851. She was born 26 October 1827 and died 18 June 1877. On 13 March 1879 he married Margaret Elizabeth Shaw Evans, who was born 25 March 1844 and died 14 December 1916. Benjamin Franklin had moved to Arkansas in 1870, where he was killed by a falling tree 7 December 1894.

3. **Martha Elizabeth Goss** was born 3 February 1831 in Hall County, and married 2 February 1847 in Dawson City, Georgia, Nathaniel Jackson Ayres, born 5 February 1823 in Greenville, North Carolina. She died 3 September 1864 in Elijay, Gilmer, Georgia; he, 12 April 1911 in Cartecay, Gilmer, Georgia.

Their eight children were:

Malinda C. Ayers	Sarah E. Ayers
Mary Melicent Ayers	Julia A. Ayers
Loucinda E. Ayers	Louvicie Caroline Ayers
Nathaniel Jackson Ayers Jr.	Reuben C. Ayers

3. **Malinda Eleanor Goss** was born 21 August 1832 in Lumpkin County, Georgia, and married 21 August 1851 in

Dawson, Georgia, Evan Pierson Perry, born in Georgia on 15 December 1829. Evan was a brother of Green Perry, who married Malinda's aunt Elvira Edgel Whitten. Malinda and Evan had moved to Indiana by 1864, into Missouri about 1871, and were in Vinita, Indian Territory, by 1894, where he died 30 August 1902 and is buried. On 5 May 1903 Malinda Eleanor married J. H. May, died 12 December 1907 in Carthage, Lawrence, Missouri, and was buried in the Goss Cemetery.

The nine children of Evan Pierson Perry and Malinda Eleanor Goss were:

Artamissa Millicent Perry
William Nathaniel Perry
Benjamin Franklin Perry
Lorinda Caroline Perry
Mary Josephine Perry
John Hamilton Perry
James Roy Perry
Lewis Devillo Perry
Alice Mille Perry

3. **James Whitten Goss** was born 29 January 1834 in Gilmer County, Georgia, and married 3 March 1853, Eunice West, who died 15 April 1870. On 23 December 1870 he married Malinda Caroline Payne, who was born 5 May 1848 and died 5 November 1870 in Texas. James Whitten died in September 1914 in Dallas, where he was buried in Old Soldiers Cemetery.

3. **Louisa Caroline Goss** was born 5 February 1836 in Gilmer County, married Rev. James M. West on 30 July 1854, and died in Dawson County, Georgia, 26 April 1864.

Their four children were:

Benjamin West
Jackson West
Nancy West
Elizabeth West

3. **Calvin Benson Goss** was born 9 December 1837 in Gilmer County, and married on 10 October 1858, Mary Ann Densmore. They lived in Dawson County, Georgia. He died 28 February 1863 in a Vicksburg, Mississippi, hospital from wounds received while serving the Confederacy as private, Company I, 52nd Regiment, Army of Tennessee, and was buried in the Confederate Cemetery there.

3. **Melicent Elvira Goss** was born 14 July 1840 in Gilmer County, and married 25 July 1858 there, Samuel Mercer Densmore, born 4 March 1838 in Dawson County. They died in Bluff Dale, Erath, Texas: she, 14 March 1912; he, 1 May 1921.

Their child was:

Melicent Rhoda Densmore

3. **Nathaniel Jackson Goss** was born 15 July 1842 in Gilmer County, and married 14 February 1865, Mary Elizabeth Roe, born 21 February 1843 in Dawson County, Georgia. She was a sister of Hannah Mancencella, who married Robert Lewis Goss, Nathaniel Jackson's brother. The couple moved to Platt County, Missouri, before 1870, and later to Lawrence County. Nathaniel Jackson was working as postmaster and merchant in Bowers Mills, Missouri, in 1907. They died there: she, 22 December 1887; he, 31 January 1918, and were buried in the Goss Cemetery.

3. **Alfred Webb Goss** was born 26 September 1844, died 5 March 1845, and was buried in Gilmer County, Georgia.

3. **Robert Lewis Goss** was born 11 December 1845 in Gilmer County, and married 28 December 1873 in Dawson County, Hannah Mancencella Roe, born there 21 June 1856. They moved to Missouri before 1870 and later settled in Texas. He died 19 March 1923 in Rogers, Benton, Arkansas. She died in Ft. Stockton, Texas, 14 November 1926.

3. **Silas Washington Goss** was born 2 February 1848 in Gilmer County, and married 24 November 1872 in Lawrence County, Missouri, Catherine Ellen Shelton, born 22 April 1853 in Kentucky. Before 1870 he left Georgia for Platt County, Missouri, moving to Lawrence County in 1870. Silas Washington died 18 November 1920 in Springfield, Missouri, and is buried there. She died 16 July 1926 in Miller, Missouri.

3. **Wilson Lumpkin Goss** was born 8 July 1850 in Gilmer, and married 19 September 1867 in Dawson County, Hulda Jane Wilkins, born 2 September 1851 in Georgia. They died in Humble, Texas: he, 22 October 1922; she, 16 November 1931.

3. **Mary Irene Goss** was born 20 August 1852 in Gilmer, died 1 April 1893 in Phelps, Missouri, and was buried in Goss Cemetery.

3. **A daughter Goss** was born 20 August 1852 in Gilmer, died 3 September 1854, and was buried in Dawson.

William B. Moore Jr.

3. **Orpha Louisa Goss** was born 18 February 1856 in Gilmer, died 21 September 1880 in Phelps County, Missouri, and was buried in Goss Cemetery.

3. **Juliann Melissa Irene Goss** was born 21 June 1858 in Dawson County, Georgia, and married 30 December 1877 in Phelps County, Missouri, John Franklin Morgan, who was born 26 November 1852 in Linn County, Iowa. They died in Colfax, Washington: he, 23 November 1933; she, 18 June 1934.

Their ten children were:

Charles Nathaniel Morgan
James Roy Morgan
Mary Ellen Elizabeth Morgan
Silas Franklin Webster Morgan
Melicent Mazelle Belle Morgan
John Daniel Morgan
Ruth Eliza Irene Morgan
Lewis Byron Hope Morgan
Lillian Myrtle Louise Morgan
Katrina Bernice Morgan

Children of Col. Thomas M. Hogan and Orpha Judson Whitten
Born in Columbus, Georgia

3. **James Hogan** was born 15 July 1844, and married Belle Wilson on 11 April 1868.

3. **Thomas M. Hogan** was born 10 September 1845 and died 13 April 1848.

3. **John L. Hogan** was born 1 December 1847, and married Minnie Rhinehardt.

3. **Eliza Hogan** was born 3 December 1850, married Charles Yorston, and lived in Atlanta.

3. **Susan E. Hogan** was born 15 February 1854, married Peyton E. Moore, and died in Norfolk, Virginia. They lived in Atlanta.

3. **Rebecca Hogan** was born 15 May 1856.

3. **Mary E. Hogan** was born 5 October 1860 and lived in Atlanta.

3. **Emily Hogan**

3. **Annie Hogan**

Children of Calvin Thompson Whitten and Malinda Catherine Kinsey

3. **Mary Clifford Whitten** was born 9 October 1842 in Columbus, Muscogee, Georgia, and married 10 January 1871 in Guntown, Lee, Mississippi, Capt. Rufus Young King, born 12 July 1828 in Florence, Lauderdale, Alabama. She was his second wife. Mary Clifford died 6 January 1892 in Belton, Bell, Texas, and was buried in North Belton Cemetery. He died 8 February 1911 in Caldwell, Bell, Texas, and was buried with her.

Capt. Rufus Young King married three wives. In 1849 he married Frances Virginia Martin, who was born in Tennessee. Among their grandchildren were George Rufus and Herman Brown, founders of the Brown and Root Company of Houston, Texas. His third was Amaryllis Woodlief, granddaughter of Harriett Earle Roddy. She was a sister to Eleanor Kee Earle, who married Silas Reagan Whitten, brother of Mary Clifford's grandfather, James Whitten. Harriett Earle Roddy wrote letters to her Whitten relatives from String Prairie, Burleson, Texas, where she and her husband, Maj. Ephriam Roddy, had settled after leaving South Carolina. In one she grieved that her eldest daughter had married a Mr. Woodlief and gone to live in Galveston, Texas, where they lost three sons to yellow fever. Amaryllis was of that marriage. What a coincidence!

Burleson, Lee, and Bell County, Texas, histories make frequent mention of Capt. Rufus Young King; lawyer, salesman, lay preacher, Texas state legislator, Mason, first county judge from Lee County. He was in Milan District, Burleson County, by 1839. During the Civil War he served in Company B, Terry's Texas Rangers, and lost an arm during the battle of Shiloh.

The four children of Capt. Rufus Young King and Mary Clifford Whitten were:

Sallie Florence King
Dr. Rufus Whitten King
Hugh Clarence Alwyn King
Joseph Sayers King

3. **Sarah Rebecca "Sallie" Whitten** was born 23 July 1844 in Gilmer County, Georgia, and married 15 February 1872 in Guntown, Mississippi, Wilson Marion Richey, born 12 December 1842. She died 20 May 1908 in Guntown and was buried in Campbelltown, Lee, Mississippi. He died 21 December 1894.

18

Their three children were:
Jettie Clifford Richey
Robert Calvin Richey
Linda Rilla Richey

Children of James Green Perry and Elvira Edgel Whitten

3. **William Washington Perry** was born 25 February 1845, married Louisa Lowman on 10 February 1867, and died 24 June 1905. They had moved to Missouri by 1871.

3. **James Whitten Perry** was born 6 October 1846, and married Leah Jane Fricks on 2 January 1870, after which he married Nancy Jane Waters and died 2 August 1924.

The child of James Whitten Perry and Leah Jane Fricks was:
Lula Thompson Perry

3. **Millicent Louisa Malinda Perry** was born 5 February 1849, and married John Stephen Holden on 14 February 1873. He was born 9 June 1831. She died 6 March 1916; he, 10 February 1911.

3. **Sarah Elvira Elizabeth Perry** was born 14 January 1851 in Georgia and married 15 May 1880, Benjamin Harrison Mearse, born in September 1861, there. She died 29 March 1897; he, 16 July 1938 in Wichita Falls, Texas. He was buried in Loraine, Mitchell, Texas.

Their six children were:
Emmet M. Mearse
James Bascomb Mearse
Homer Jackson Mearse
William Luther Mearse
Harley Dallas Mearse
Albert H. Mearse

3. **Artimissa Edgel A. Perry** was born 27 February 1853 and died 29 March 1887.

3. **Nathaniel Lewis Perry** was born 6 May 1855, and married 18 October 1874, Cynthia Bryant, born 27 November 1854. They lived in Marble Hill, Pickens, Georgia. He died 9 March 1937; she, 12 July 1920.

3. **Orpha Elvira Perry** was born 5 May and died 20 September in 1857.

3. **Benjamin Arphax Perry** was born 4 September 1858, and married in 1883, Martha L. Darnell. In 1909 he married Avarilla Theresa Dobbs and died 19 March 1927. They lived in Jasper, Pickens, Georgia.

The child of Benjamin Arphax Perry and Martha L. Darnell was:
May Perry

The child of Benjamin Arphax Perry and Avarella Theresa Dobbs was:
Amy Perry

3. **John Evans Green Perry** was born 2 September 1863, and married 3 August 1884, Sadie Carmack. His second wife was Mary Cochran "Sis" Thomas. He died 11 December 1917.

3. **Thomas Jackson Perry** was born 9 November 1865, and married 29 September 1887, Missouri Angeline Anderson, born 28 November 1863. She died 27 August 1921, and he married Rebecca Anderson. Thomas Jackson died 27 February 1934. They lived in Dawson County, Georgia.

The eight children of Thomas Jackson Perry and Missouri Angeline Anderson were:
James Vance Perry
Ina Ethel Perry
Millard Arphax Perry
Henry Clay Perry
Alma Edge Perry
Beulah Mae Perry
Emmett Stephens Perry
Clarence Bell Perry

SIXTH GENERATION
Children of E. Alonza Bell and Talitha Emily Whitten
Born in Caldwell, Texas

4. **Mary Susan Bell** was born 3 February 1874, and married Robert Eugene Glenn.
4. **Clifford D. Bell** was born 6 March 1876 and died 6 August 1877 in Florence, Alabama.
4. **Arthur Edgar Bell** was born 9 May 1880, married Jessie Stern, and died in Texas.

Children of Alexander Lamb and Orpha Judson Whitten
4. **Charles Lamb**, born 24 July 1868.
4. **Edward Lamb** was born 20 April 1870 and died in June 1871.

Children of George Washington Lafayette Ard and Sarah Mitchell Whitten
Born in Lumpkin, Stewart, Georgia
4. **Annie Ard**, postmistress of Lumpkin, Stewart, Georgia, born 1 October 1867 and died 16 December 1915, was, along with her Aunt Dolly (Doleska Fitzallen Whitten), interested in family history. Her records and collection of family letters survive. Much of this James Whitten family history is the work of these two ladies. The following are from her collection:

Mattie (*Martha Earle*) E. Whitten to Miss Dolly (*Doleska Fitzallen*) Whitten—Jonesborough, Mississippi, to Smith's Station, Alabama, 20 May 1890

Cousin Dolly,
Rev. Mr. Buck of Ala. who has been stopping over in Miss. on his return from the Southern Baptist Convention (in interest of his profession) was the honored guest of our family on the night of the 19th, and in conversation, we found that he was an acquaintance and friend of yours and could tell us about you and your interest. We are glad through him to know you, and I shall introduce myself to you as being the seventh child of Dr. and Mrs. Alfred Washington Whitten. Our home is in the Northern part of Tippah County, a very beautiful situation; it is a healthy country.
We are twelve in number, all living, and all members of the church except Maude (*Elliott*), the youngest. Mollie (*Mary Dora*), our eldest sister married a physician (*her first cousin Frank Adams Whitten*), whose home is at Poplar Springs, Miss. John (*Graves*), our oldest brother, is married and lives near us. Silas (*Ray, grandfather of W. B. Moore Jr.*), the fourth child is also married and is a merchant at, or near, Oxford, Miss. Hosea, (*Ransom*) the fifth child, is President of the Normal College at Pocahontas, Tenn. He is also editing a paper. Bedford (*Forrest*), the sixth brother is a preacher with a family of three. He also keeps a boarding house for the Poplar Springs School. The others of us are now at home.
Our Ripley relatives (*Ranson Edwin Whitten and family with the minor children of his brother Joseph John*) are doing well and seem to be enjoying life. After Grandpa's (*Silas Reagan Whitten*) death in the fall, Aunt Rebecca (*Rebecca Berry Whitten, collector of letters*) went to live with her nephew (*Frank Adams Whitten*) at Poplar Springs. I am your junior in age. My father and mother are getting old but so blessed are we in health that they are yet very lively.
Your Cousin,
Mattie E. Whitten

Silas Reagan Whitten to Annie Ard—Jackson, Mississippi, to Lumpkin, Georgia, 3 March 1909

My dear Miss Ard,
In reply to your favor, I beg to advise that I carry his full name, Silas Reagan Whitten. I know two of his boys, Joe B. Whitten and Ranson E. Whitten and then one died before I can remember, was familiarly known as Uncle Pluck. My father was named Alfred Washington Whitten. Miss Rebecca Whitten, now of Poplar Springs, Miss., is the only one of my Aunts I know. My grandfather had a brother named Ransom Whitten, and I have a faint recollection of hearing of Mrs. Davis, but I do not know her or any of her people. My father came from Charleston, S.C.
S. R. Whitten

This letter was in reply to Annie Ard's stating she had seen his name in the Christian Index *and asking if he was of her Whittens. It illustrates how quickly family members forget and how often vanity overcomes veracity when ancestry is described. His name was Silas Ray, not Silas Reagan, his father had never been in fashionable Charleston, but was born and raised near the tiny hamlet of Gowensville in the South Carolina mountains. The Joseph B. was Joseph John, who was sometimes called Berry Joe. Mrs. Davis was Marian Whitten, sister of Silas Reagan. Pluck was Silas Reagan Whitten Jr., who died while fighting for the Confederacy.*
Annie Ard to Silas Ray Whitten—Lumpkin, Stewart, Georgia, to Jackson, Mississippi, 17 March 1909

Your grandfather, Silas Reagan Whitten, and my great grandfather, James were brothers. My grandfather was Arphax Whitten. He had a brother, Calvin Thompson who lived in Guntown, Mississippi. Calvin's daughter, Mary Clifford was a beautiful and unusually charming girl. She gave information to Confederate soldiers that enabled them to capture a federal spy. Federals then tried to capture her and she refugeed to my grandfather's home and remained for some time which was the only acquaintance that my mother (*Sarah Mitchell Whitten Ard*) had with Calvin's family.

Cousin Clifford had a son, Dr. Rufus Whitten King, of Austin, Texas, who has a watch that is said to have been the property of Thomas Whitten, one of the grandfathers way back. I have heard one of my aunts say that Thomas Whitten was the father of John who married Mary Reagan, but none of them have family records so far back.

Cousin Clifford has a sister, Mrs. Sallie (*Sarah Rebecca*) Ritchie at Guntown if she is still living (*she died the previous year*). She has two children, one a son whose name is Robert Calvin Ritchie. (*The other was Linda Rilla.*)

My great grandfather, James Whitten resigned as a member of the South Carolina Legislature to become a Baptist minister. Grandfather Arphax was a Baptist minister, too.

Annie Ard

This letter has caused much confusion among Whitten researchers. Many believe the father of John Whitten was Thomas. Census and court church records clearly prove that Charles was John's parent. Perhaps Charles's father was Thomas. So far he has not been identified.

Walter Wood Whitten to Annie Ard—Blue Springs, Mississippi, to Lumpkin, Georgia, 26 May 1909

Miss Annie Ard,

I will answer your letter of April 6th. to my great aunt, Rebecca Whitten. Silas Reagan Whitten, your grandfather's (*great grandfather*'s) brother, and my great grandfather, born Feb. 19th. 1794, died October 27th. 1888. Eleanor Kee Earle, his wife, born January 6th. 1792 and died August 18th 1851. S.R. Whitten and E.K. Earle married Oct. 31st 1815.

(*Their children were*): James Wood Whitten, born Oct. 27th 1816; Joseph John Whitten, born Sept. 26th 1817; Narcissa Amaryllis Whitten, born July 8th 1824; Rebecca Berry Whitten, born August 18th 1826, died May 2nd 1909; Silas Reagan Whitten Jr., born June 2nd 1830; Ranson Edwin Whitten born July 9th 1832.

Walter Wood Whitten (*son of Frank Adams and Mary Dora Whitten*)

This letter answers Annie's 6 April 1909 query to Rebecca Berry Whitten asking for family information. It appears in Letters to Rebecca *with the wish that Rebecca's reply could be found. This is it. Rebecca died before answering Annie. Her nephew did it for her.*

Matilda Allen Whitten Crowe (*daughter of Rev. Arphax Whitten and Matilda Allen Bennett*) to Annie Ard—Lee County, Alabama, to Lumpkin, Georgia, 11 November 1909

Dear Annie,

I will enclose a little torn record of some of your forefathers and mothers. You will see that your great grandmother was a Thompson (*Elizabeth Ann Thompson, wife of Rev. James Whitten*), a sister of Mrs. Estes' great grandfather (*Charles Irby Thompson*). I was at the home of her great grandmother, Mrs. Nancy Thompson, whose plantation was on the Etowah River in 1861. You will see by this torn script that my great grandmother Thompson was a Motlow (*Drucilla Motlow Thompson, mother of Elizabeth Ann*). Now where does the Reagan come in? (*Rev. James Whitten's mother was Mary Reagan.*) I have forgotten exactly how Mrs. Estes explained her parentage, but suppose she was of the Thompson side. I wish you could get a copy of the obituary notice of Grandpa Whitten's death which is pasted in the Hogan (*Orpha Judson Whitten Hogan, daughter of Rev. James Whitten*) Bible.

Aunt Matilda

Postmaster C. L. Abbett to Annie Ard—Phelps, Missouri, to Lumpkin, Georgia, 4 November 1909

Miss Annie Ard,

William B. Moore Jr.

And you no doubt will be surprised to know the postmaster's wife is a great granddaughter of Mr. and Mrs. Goss (*Nathaniel Harbin and Melicent Mazelle Whitten Goss*). Their daughter, Malinda Eleanor, married Evan Perry. Her daughter, Artamissa Millicent Perry, married Benjamin Frank Miller and I married her daughter Ida, so you can see you are hearing from your forty-second cousin.

I understand Mr. and Mrs. Goss were the father and Mother of 16 children, most of whom are dead. Granny Goss (*Melicent Mazelle Whitten Goss, daughter of Rev. James Whitten*) lived 1 1/2 miles south of this place which is now one of the finest farms in this part of the country. Grandma Goss died at the age of 93 years, been dead 10 years. Grandma Perry (*Malinda Eleanor*), who was their elder daughter died two years ago. My wife's mother is living in this place and is mother of 8 children; 3 boys and 5 girls. Charles Miller is in the marble and monument business at Aurora, Missouri. Jim and George are contractors and builders in Carthage, Missouri. Minnie, who married a man by the name of Black, lives in Carthage. He is a machinist. Emma married a man by the name of H.H. Russell, proprietor of Russell Mercantile Co., Miller, Missouri. Ida, my wife, and Effie and Ethel, single daughters at home represent the family. My wife is visiting in North Missouri at present. Silas Goss lives near Springfield, Missouri, RFD #1. Jackson Goss is postmaster and merchant, Bowers Mills, Missouri. John Goss lives in Myrtle, Arkansas. So far as I know this is all the Goss family.

Silas, Jackson, and John all have large families, but I don't know the children well. Dr. Shelton's wife, I think, was Silas's daughter, of Mt. Vernon, Missouri. (*Silas Washington, Nathaniel Jackson and James Whitten Goss were sons of Nathaniel Harbin and Melicent Mazelle Whitten Goss; I have no record of a John.*)
C. L. Abbett

Mrs. George P. Estes to Annie Ard—Gainesville, Georgia, to Lumpkin, Georgia, 23 October 1909

Dear Miss Ard,

My oldest son brought your letter and when he got to the Whittens I said, "give it to me for they are my people". Cousin Elvira Perry (*Edgel Elvira Whitten Perry, daughter of Rev. James Whitten*) I knew well. She lived at the foot of the Blueridge Mountains. She raised a large family and had a son named (*Benjamin*) Arphax, both dead now. Cousin Theron Thompson spent his last days with his sister Mary at Ringold. My father was Dr. Henry Clay Thompson. His father was Charles Irby Thompson (*brother of Elizabeth Ann, spouse of Rev. James Whitten*) who was born in S.C. His father was Scotch-Irish.

My grandfather Thompson was a merchant for years at Clarksville and then moved to the Etowah River where he died several years before I was born. My father has been dead 12 years and my mother 3. I have only 1 sister, Mrs. W.H. Burt of Atlanta. She lives at 225 Forrest Ave. I have one brother Dr. C.I. Thompson who lives at the old homestead and is a bachelor. We have a cousin, Mrs. Amelia Caldwell in Atlanta who lives with her daughter, Mrs. Jim Walker, at 59 West 5th. St., who is a sister of Theron Thompson. If you will write her she can tell you so much more about the Thompsons and will be glad to do so. We have a cousin in N.Y., Mrs. Eliza Yorston at 56 W 58th. St. She also has two sisters with her, Mrs. Moore and a single sister, Mary Hogan. They run a large boarding house, known as the "Home For Southern People". She will be glad to tell you lots about our relatives.

I am sorry I know so little about our relatives but grandmother died when I was quite small. My father was the only one left in his family and he was such a busy man that he hardly ever referred to them. I have 4 children, my oldest boy is 19, my next son 18, and my little girl is 14, and I have a little boy 12.
Mrs. George P. Estes

Silas Washington Goss to the editor of *The Chiefton*—Phelps County, Missouri, 10 January 1878

As today was the 50th. anniversary of the marriage of Nathaniel Harbin and Melicent Mazelle Whitten Goss, their children and grandchildren decided to give them a surprise golden wedding. They met at Evan Pierson Perry's, formed into a line and marched over to the home of the aged couple with a flag floating at their head. On reaching the gates they gave them rousing cheers. After hitching their horses they went into the house, proceeded to spread the wedding dinner which they had brought with them, but as the old gentleman was not at home the dinner had to await his arrival.

When he came James Whitten, the eldest son, and Wilson Lumpkin, the youngest, met him at the gate and attempted to carry him in, but the old gentleman was full of his fun, and when they took hold of him, he tripped up the older one who made an impression on the soft ground. They got him however.

Then came dinner, and such a nice dinner it was, too, loaded with everything good to eat, which was

22

greatly enjoyed by all. There were 38 children and grandchildren present. They have 86 in all, 55 of whom live in Missouri. They have 16 children with 11 of them living. Mr. Goss was 72 last September and Mrs. Goss will soon be 64. Besides the other presents they received 2 gold pieces from Mrs. Goss's sister who lives in Columbus, Georgia.

Silas Washington Goss

4. **Julia Clifford Ard** was born 6 July 1869, and married 10 September 1891, Frederick Orlando Eustis Ward, born 8 September 1864. She died 30 May 1944; he, 20 January 1927 in Stewart County, Georgia.
Their five children were:
      Ida Agnes Ward
      George Walter Ward
      Rodney Ward
      Lewis Ward
      Frank Ward
4. **Charles Edgar Ard** was born 23 January 1871, married Annie Yates, and died 15 January 1922.
Their three children were:
      Ruth Ard
      Charles Edgar Ard Jr.
      Jessie Ard
4. **Sarah Matilda Ard** was born 17 August 1872 and died 26 November 1952.
4. **George Fitzallen Ard**, born 24 April 1874, died in 1876.
4. **Mary Jane Ard** was born 22 March 1876, married Wesley W. Stephens, and died 21 October 1924.
Their five children were:
      George Stephens
      Frances Stephens
      Alma Stephens
      Lillie Stephens
      Annie Stephens
4. **Georgia Agnes Ard** was born 14 November 1877, married Henry Richard Teal, and died 5 April 1907.
Their child was:
      Richard Teal Jr.
4. **Thomas Arphax Ard** was born 15 April 1881, married Lillian Atkinson, and died 11 June 1923 in Lyttle, Texas.
Their three children were:
      Elizabeth Ard
      George Ard
      Catherine Ard
4. **John Ard** was born 22 March 1883, married Lillian B. Garrett, and died 12 July 1923 in Lumpkin.
Their child was:
      Saradel Ard

Children of Ira Crowe and Matilda Allen Whitten

4. **William Berry Crowe** was born 1 September 1866, and married Matteel Rush.
4. **Ira Bennett Crowe**
4. **Jacob Crowe**, who married a musician named Marie.
4. **Julia Bennett Crowe** married a Mr. Perryman.

Children of John Duke Richardson and Georgia Ann Whitten

4. **Edward Richardson** was born about 1870, died in August 1874 in Florence, Alabama, where he was buried.
4. **Samuel Richardson** was born about 1874, died in December 1877 in Florence, where he was buried.
4. **Willard Richardson** was born about 1876, died in December 1877 in Florence, and was buried there.
4. **Mary Whitten Richardson**, who married Eugene L. Harvey.

Children of John W. McRae and Joanna E. Whitten
Born in Smith Station, Alabama

4. **William Whitten McRae** was born 18 April 1880 and died in Texas, 27 February 1903.

4. **Johnnie S. McRae**, born 1 February 1882 and died there 31 January 1884.

Children of Nathaniel Jackson Ayers and Martha Elizabeth Goss

4. **Malinda C. Ayres** was born 28 August 1848, married Manuel C. Redmond 2 September 1868, and died 5 June 1884.

4. **Mary Melicent Ayres**, born 24 November 1849 and died 12 July 1864.

4. **Loucinda E. Ayres** was born 7 January 1852, married Timon C. Rogers 19 February 1878.

4. **Nathaniel Jackson Ayres Jr.** was born 27 April 1855 in Elijay, Georgia, and married Harriett Turrell on 19 February 1878. Less than a year later, on 30 January 1877 in Spencer, Missouri, he married Sarah Frances Manley, born 7 September 1863 in Illinois. They died in Las Animas, Colorado: he, 26 January 1916; she, 3 February 1915.

The child of Nathaniel Jackson Ayres Jr. and Sarah Frances Manley was:

    Lucinda Ellen Ayers

4. **Sarah E. Ayres**, born 6 March 1887 and married Eleazar Clay 19 March 1884.

4. **Julia A. Ayres** was born 14 April 1859 and died 24 October 1867 in Gilmer County, Georgia.

4. **Louvicie Caroline Ayres** was born 7 May 1861 and died 24 October 1862 in Gilmer County.

4. **Reuben C. Ayres**, born 26 September 1863.

Children of Evan Pierson Perry and Malinda Eleanor Goss

4. **Artamissa Millicent Perry** was born 27 May 1853 in Dawson County, Georgia, married Benjamin Frank Miller 22 May 1873 in Mount Vernon, Missouri, and died 25 June 1933 in that state. She was buried in Goss Cemetery.

Their eight children were:

    Ida Miller
    Charles Miller
    Jim Miller
    George Miller
    Minnie Miller
    Ema Miller
    Effie Miller
    Ethel Miller

4. **William Nathaniel Perry** was born 23 June 1856 in Dawson, Georgia, and married Sarah Jane Weaver on 13 March 1881 in Mt. Vernon, Missouri. She died before 3 October 1898, when he married Mary Jane Spencer Crow in Vinita, Indian Territory, Oklahoma. William Nathaniel died 20 August 1936 in Lawrence County, and was buried in Goss Cemetery with both of his wives.

4. **Benjamin Franklin Perry** was born 28 June and died 25 November in 1858 in Dawson, Georgia.

4. **Lorinda Caroline Perry** was born 29 August 1862 in Dawson, married Robert Jonathon Spencer, and died 15 February 1912 in Missouri.

4. **Mary Josephine Perry** was born 23 April 1865 in Indiana, married Henry Schrum, died 13 April 1887 in Missouri, and was buried in Siloam Springs, Missouri.

4. **John Hamilton Perry** was born 27 January 1868 in Indiana, and married, about 1898 in Indian Territory, Oklahoma, Sylvia Amanda Carrico, who was born in Kansas. The family moved by wagon in 1903 to Idaho, and, from that state, in 1910, to Colorado, where John Hamilton died 15 July 1932 in Rush. He was buried in Kanza Cemetery there.

Their six children were:

    George Dewey Perry
    Walter Perry
    Lydia Emily Perry
    Laura Winifred Perry
    John Preston Perry
    Eugene R. Perry

4. **James Roy Perry** was born 30 March 1870 in Missouri and died ten days later.

4. **Lewis Devillo Perry** was born 17 August 1871 in Missouri, died 12 July 1900 in Oklahoma, and was buried in Fairview Cemetery, Vinita, Oklahoma.

4. **Alice Mille Perry** was born 28 May 1875 in Missouri, married William Ebinezer Johnson, and died in a fire 21 February 1953.

Children of Rev. James West and Louise Caroline Goss

4. **Benjamin West**, born in 1856.
4. **Jackson West**, born in 1856.
4. **Nancy West**, born in 1857.
4. **Elizabeth West**, born 12 February 1860.

Child of Samuel Mercer Densmore and Melicent Elvira Goss
4. **Melicent Rhoda Densmore** was born 26 September 1859 in Dawson, where on 2 February 1882 she married Richard Wilson Grogan, born 10 June 1860 in Johntown, Dawson, Georgia. She died 12 January 1930; he, 24 November 1929, both in Sisters, Deschutes, Oregon.
    Their nine children were:
        Eva Lucinda Grogan
        Cora Elvira Elizabeth Grogan
        Tomie Elizabeth Grogan
        Osha Viola Grogan
        Julia May Grogan
        Oscar William Grogan
        Homer Calvin Grogan
        Alice Melinda Grogan
        Dewey Grady Grogan

Children of John Franklin Morgan and Juliann Melissa Irene Goss
4. **Charles Nathaniel Morgan** was born 11 October 1878 and died 28 September 1879 in Missouri.
4. **James Roy Morgan** was born 2 May 1880 in Golden City, Missouri, and on 16 September 1914 in Spokane, Washington, married Katherine Louise Reynolds, who was born 14 September 1883 in Dayton, Washington. They died in Washington: he, 23 December 1954 in Auburn; she, 17 August 1967 in Colfax.
4. **Mary Ellen Elizabeth Morgan** was born 15 January 1883 in Walla Walla, Indian Territory. She married Arlie Day Oster 24 May 1901 in Colfax. He was born 18 September 1878 in Washington and died 28 July 1940 in Oregon. She died 20 May 1966 in Hollywood, California.
4. **Silas Franklin Webster Morgan** was born 29 April 1885 in Whitman County, Washington, and in Colfax 27 November 1909 married Jennie Urness, who was born 2 February 1882 and died 2 May 1943 in Spokane. They were divorced in 1932, and Silas married Bertha Bradley, born in 1892 and died in 1965. Silas died 2 April 1953 in Spokane.
4. **Melicent Mazelle Belle Morgan** was born 28 January 1887 in Phelps, Missouri, and married Levi Harry Price 7 February 1905. He was born 26 March 1885 in South Dakota and died 24 January 1964 in Spokane. They were later divorced, and Melicent died in Chewelah, Washington, 19 March 1968.
4. **John Daniel Morgan** was born 19 June 1888 in Lacrosse, Washington. He married three wives, the first, whose name is not known, on 21 October 1905. After a divorce he married Emma Von Wendt, born in 1888. They divorced, and he married Ruby Oster, who was born 1 June 1886 in Oregon and died 14 April 1972. John Daniel was murdered in Spokane 22 October 1961.
4. **Ruth Eliza Irene Morgan** was born 18 June 1890 in Whitman County, Washington, and on 14 February 1912 married Jerry Alonzo Simmons, who was born 16 April 1875 in Missouri and died 23 February 1946 in St. Marie, Idaho. Ruth Eliza died 11 May 1973 in Spokane.
    Their nine children were:
        Gary John Franklin Simmons
        Laurence Alonzo Simmons
        Roy Laverne Simmons
        Marjory Estel Simmons
        Julia Irene Simmons
        Jessie Lucille Simmons
        Patricia Jean Simmons
        Shirley Ruth Simmons
        Janie Lea Simmons
4. **Lewis Byron Hope Morgan** was born 14 August 1892 in Lacrosse, Washington, and on 23 November 1915 married Dottie Jorgenson, who was born 24 January 1889 and died 3 January 1979. They divorced, and Lewis died 20 January 1975 in Colfax.
4. **Lillian Myrtle Louise Morgan** was born 26 September 1895 in LaCombe, Edmonton, Canada, and on 9

October 1913 married Lester Brownfield, who was born 11 January 1888 in Missouri and died 2 November 1951 in Washington. After his death she married Ray Peterson, who was born 27 March 1911 and died 26 June 1970. She died 19 November 1982 in Chewelah, Washington.

4. **Katrina Bernice Morgan** was born 3 January 1900 in Wilcox, Washington, and married Cyril Rogers 13 January 1916. They divorced, and he died in 1980. Her second husband was Donald Crist, whom she married 20 September 1952. She died in Cheney, Washington, 6 April 1986.

Children of Capt. Rufus Young King and Mary Clifford Whitten

4. **Sallie Florence King** was born in January 1872 in Texas, and married about 1895 there, Henry W. Woodruff, born in August 1872 in Kentucky. They died in Texas: she, about 1918; he, after 1920.

Their two children were:

Whitten K. Woodruff

Helen Woodruff

4. **Dr. Rufus Whitten King** was born about 1875 in Texas where, about 1907, he married Zora, born in 1878 in Louisiana. He died 2 August 1915 in Travis, Texas, and was buried in North Belton Cemetery.

In a widely circulated letter dated 17 March 1909, Annie Ard told Silas Ray Whitten that Dr. King lived in San Antonio and had a watch that had once belonged to Thomas Whitten, "one of the grandfathers way back." Could Thomas be the elusive father of Charles Whitten, "pewter caster"?

4. **Hugh Clarence Alwyn King** was born in December 1878, died in 1948, and was buried in North Belton Cemetery.

4. **Joseph Sayers King** was born in February 1883, died in 1951, and was buried in North Belton Cemetery. He was an actor and performed in New York on the stage and in films in Hollywood. He and his wife divorced in New York.

Children of Wilson Marion Richey and Sarah Rebecca "Sallie" Whitten

4. **Jettie Clifford Richey**, who died in infancy.

4. **Robert Calvin Richey** was born in February 1876 in Lee County, Mississippi, where he married Elizabeth Morton Farrow on 3 November 1904. She was born 8 November 1874. He died in July 1955; she, 18 May 1970.

Their two children were:

Catherine Farrow Richey

Elizabeth Roberta Richey

4. **Linda Rilla Richey**, who married David Edward Smith.

Child of James Whitten Perry and Leah Jane Fricks

4. **Lula Thompson Perry**

Children of Benjamin Harrison Mearse and Sarah Elvira Elizabeth Perry

4. **Emmet M. Mearse** was born in March 1891 in Georgia, and married Mamie Clardy on 31 January 1904 in Dekalb, Alabama. He died 16 July 1938 in Wichita Falls, Texas, and was buried in Loraine.

4. **James Bascomb Mearse** was born in August 1884 in Georgia, married May, and died about 1965.

4. **Homer Jackson Mearse** was born in September 1885 in Georgia, married Eathel, and died 5 April 1962 in Nolan, Texas. He also was buried in Loraine.

4. **William Luther Mearse** was born 19 March 1889 in Dalton, Whitfield, Georgia, married Jessie Singleton 30 November 1912, and died 14 April 1963 in Snyder, Scurry, Texas, where he was buried.

4. **Harley Dallas Mearse** was born in October 1891 in North Carolina, married Maude, and died 27 May 1966 in Andrews, Texas, where he was buried.

4. **Albert H. Mearse** was born in September 1894 in Tennessee, and died 4 September 1966 in El Paso, Texas.

Child of Benjamin Arphax Perry and Martha L. Darnell

4. **May Perry**, who served as a missionary in Africa most of her life.

Child of Benjamin Arphax Perry and Avarilla Thorese Dobbs

4. **Amy Perry**

Children of Thomas Jackson Perry and Missouri Angeline Anderson

4. **James Vance Perry** was born 8 February 1889, married Gertrude Thacker, and died 15 May 1971.

4. **Ina Ethel Perry** was born 10 April 1891 in Dawson County, Georgia, married Roy Bray Floyd on 4 July 1911, and died 26 March 1978 in Buford, Hall, Georgia. Roy, a first cousin of "Pretty Boy Floyd," was born on 8 March 1885 in Little Prairie Community, Bartow County, Georgia, and died on 20 March 1960 in White, Bartow, Georgia.

Their five children were:

Nellie Kathryn Floyd
Georgia Felice Floyd
Jackson Clark Floyd
Robert Murphy Floyd
Rubye Dell Floyd

4. **Millard Arphax Perry** was born 18 August 1893, married Mineola Allen, and died 10 March 1966.

4. **Henry Clay Perry** was born 29 June 1895 and married Pauline Mauney.

4. **Alma Edge Perry** was born 27 June 1898, and married Walter Grady Worley.

4. **Beulah Mae Perry** was born 3 May 1900, and married Spurgeon Blankenship.

4. **Emmett Stephens Perry** was born 28 January 1903, and married Winnie Lucille Langston.

4. **Clarence Bell Perry** was born 5 October 1905, and married Eva Lou McGowan, born 29 July 1910.

Their child was:

Nancy Perry

SEVENTH GENERATION

Children of Frederick Orlando Eustis Ward and Julia Clifford Ard

5. **Ida Agnes Ward** was born in Lumpkin, Stewart, Georgia, and died in 1984, there. She was active in the DAR, and, like her brother George, a student of James Whitten family history.

5. **George Walter Ward** was born in Smyrna, Cobb, Georgia, and married Annie Smith. He died 17 February 1965 in Marietta, Georgia. Annie was in a nursing home in Smyrna in 1995. George spent his life collecting family records and shared his treasures generously.

Their two children were:

Andrew Ward
George Walter Ward Jr.

5. **Rodney Ward**

5. **Lewis Ward**

His child was:

James Ward

5. **Frank Ward**

Children of Charles Edgar Ard and Annie Yates

5. **Ruth Ard**, who married Chile Dougherty.

5. **Charles Edgar Ard Jr.**

5. **Jessie Ard**

Children of Wesley W. Stephens and Mary Jane Ard

5. **George Stephens**

5. **Frances Stephens**, who married a Mr. Hatlford.

5. **Alma Stephens**, who married a Mr. Gilbert.

5. **Lillie Stephens**, who married a Mr. Stewart.

5. **Annie Stephens**

Child of Richard Teal and Georgia Agnes Ard

5. **Richard Teal Jr.**, who lived in Oregon in 1995.

His child was:

Richard Teal III

Children of Thomas Arphax Ard and Lillian Atkinson

5. **Elizabeth Ard**, who died at age eighteen.

5. **George Ard**, who lived in Austin, Texas, in 1984.

5. **Catherine Ard**

Child of John Ard and Lillian B. Garrett
5. **Saradel Ard**, who lived in Anchorage, Alaska, in 1984. She was married and divorced.

Child of Nathaniel Jackson Ayers Jr. and Sarah Frances Manly
5. **Lucinda Ellen Ayres** was born 3 November 1889 in Miller, Missouri, and married James Slagle on 8 December 1907 in Bluejacket, Craig, Oklahoma. He was born 30 March 1886 in Afton, Indian Territory, Oklahoma. She died 13 October 1972 in Boulder, Colorado.
Their child was:
Marie Slagle

Children of Benjamin Frank Miller and Artamissa Millicent Perry
5. **Ida Miller**, who on 23 October 1809 married C. L. Abbett, postmaster at Gainesville, Georgia.
5. **Charles Miller**, who in 1909 had a monument business in Aurora, Missouri.
5. **Jim Miller**, who was a contractor in Carthage, Missouri, in 1909.
5. **George Miller**, who worked with brother Jim in Carthage in 1909.
5. **Minnie Miller**, who married a Mr. Black and lived in Carthage.
5. **Ema Miller**, who married H. H. Russell and lived in Miller, Missouri, in 1909.
5. **Effie Miller**
5. **Ethel Miller**

Children of John Hamilton Perry and Sylvia Amanda Carrico
5. **George Dewey Perry**, born about 1899 in Oklahoma.
5. **Walter Perry**, born about 1903 in Oklahoma.
5. **Lydia Emily Perry**, born about 1905 in Idaho.
5. **Laura Winifred Perry**, born about 1911 in Colorado.
5. **John Preston Perry**, born about 1915 in Colorado.
5. **Eugene R. Perry** was born 18 July 1918 in Yoder, El Paso, Colorado, and married Beatrice Katherine Meehan 6 May 1942 in Portland, Maine. He supplied much of this data on the Perry family.
Their three children were:
Alexis Perry
Eugene R. Perry Jr.
Stephen Lewis Perry

Children of Richard Wilson Grogan and Melicent Rhoda Densmore
5. **Eva Lucinda Matilda Grogan** was born 12 November 1882 in Dawson County, Georgia, married Charles Emmity Griffith on 27 June 1912, and died 13 January 1950 in Bend Deschutes, Oregon.
5. **Cora Elvira Elizabeth Grogan** was born in Dawson and died 28 January 1963 in Portland, Oregon. She married Charles A. Aronson on 5 January 1815 there, and later married Alfred R. Holt.
5. **Tomie Elizabeth Grogan** was born in Dawson 17 July 1886 and died in Portland 7 May 1937. She married William Andrew Arthur and Harrison Phelps.
5. **Osha Viola Grogan** was born in Dawson 19 December 1887, died 19 December 1951 in Vancouver, Washington, and married Solomon J. Frazier.
5. **Julia May Grogan** was born 14 August 1892 in Dawson, married James Henry Brown 2 September 1911, and died in Chehalis, Washington, on 18 January 1960.
5. **Oscar William Grogan**, her twin, died 16 April 1965 in Pendleton, Oregon.
5. **Homer Calvin Grogan** was born 15 February 1895 in Dawson and died 27 September in Walla Walla, Washington.
5. **Alice Melinda Grogan** was born 2 July 1899 in Johntown, Dawson, Georgia, and married 17 December 1923 in Bakersfield, California, Mile Nickola Dragicerie, born 29 September 1881 in Rudopolje, Croatia, Yugoslavia. They died in Prineville, Oregon: she, 30 May 1972; he, 2 April 1974. She also married Lawrence Griffith.
The three children of Alice Melinda and Mile Nickola were:
Hugh Michael Dragich
Dale Martin Dragich
Geirgia Ann Dragich

5. **Dewie Grady Grogan** was born 9 January 1904 in Bluff Dale, Erath, Texas, and died 29 April 1982 in Portland.

Children of Jerry Alonzo Simmons and Ruth Eliza Irene Morgan

5. **Gary John Franklin Simmons** was born 30 October 1912 in Benge, Washington, and married Alice Elizabeth Schierman 5 October 1934. After a divorce he married Louise Gray Dailey and died 31 January 1986 in Mesa, Arizona.

5. **Laurence Alonzo Simmons** was born 9 June 1914 in Benge, and married Hazel Groth 2 September 1938. Later he married Celine Marie Feught.

5. **Roy Lavern Simmons** was born 30 June 1916 in Pandora, Washington, and in St. Maries, Idaho, on 8 February 1946 married Doris Ann Sczenski. He died 29 March 1993 in Spokane.

5. **Marjory Estel Simmons** was born 2 October 1918 in Pandora, Adams, Washington. She married twice; John Peter Gray on 17 June 1940 in Moscow, Idaho, and Robert Martin in March 1965. Both marriages ended in divorce.

5. **Julia Irene Simmons** was born 21 August 1920 in Desmet, Idaho, and married Delbert Baker 16 September 1939. After divorcing Delbert, she married Merl Comer, divorced him, and remarried Delbert.

5. **Jessie Lucille Simmons** was born 21 November 1922 in Tensed, Benewah, Idaho, and married Henry DeWald in 1941. That marriage ended in divorce, and she married William Oscar Edwards.

5. **Patricia Jean Simmons** was born in Wilcox, Washington, 12 December 1924, and on 24 November 1942 married Harry Allen Burch in Moscow, Idaho.

5. **Shirley Ruth Simmons** was born 3 October 1928 in Colfax, Washington, and married three husbands. The first was Orville Glenn Bruce, whom she married 4 December 1944 in Libby, Montana. After a divorce she married William Ambrose Adams and, then, Robert Ellis Rhimer, who was born 16 October 1925 in Tekoa, Washington. She is a Goss family researcher, who in 1997 lived in Lacey, Washington, and supplied data for this genealogy.

5. **Janie Lea Simmons** was born 3 September 1930 in Colfax and died 22 August 1932 near Tekoa, Washington.

Children of Henry W. Woodruff and Sallie Florence King
Twins, born in Texas

5. **Whitten K. Woodruff**, born in 1908.

5. **Helen Woodruff**, born in 1908.

Child of Joseph Sayers King and unknown spouse

5. **Jolene King**

Children of Robert Calvin Richey and Elizabeth Morton Farrow

5. **Catherine Farrow Richey** was born 30 June 1907, and on 2 March 1937 married James Karr Hinton, who was born 26 February 1892 and died 21 December 1952. In 1986 she was living in Collierville, Tennessee.
Their child was:
Col. Robert Richey Hinton

5. **Elizabeth Roberta Richey** was born 19 February 1911, and on 16 June 1936 married Eugene Augustus Stansel, who was born 24 October 1902 and died 25 March 1965.
Their three children were:
Elizabeth Farrow Stansel
Eugene Augustus Stansel Jr.
Martha Alford Stansel

Children of Roy Bray Floyd and Ina Ethel Perry
Born in Bartow County, Georgia

5. **Nellie Kathryn Floyd** was born on 30 July 1912 and died in the same county on 28 November 1967. She married William Thomas Jordon, who was born on 7 April 1918 in Midway, Alabama, and died 12 April 1957 in Georgia. They were buried together in the Cartersville City Cemetery in Bartow County.
Their two children were:
William Thomas Jordon Jr.
Homer Gunn Jordon

5. **Georgia Felice Floyd** was born on 16 November 1913 in Folsom and died in July 1999 and was buried in Gwinneth County, Georgia. She married first Jake Lewis; then, on 3 November 1977, Quinton Mewborn.
The child of Jake and Georgia Felice was:
Hilda Doris Lewis

5. **Jackson Clark Floyd** was born on 14 October 1916 in White. He married Weta Jewell Tyson on 2 August 1937 in Tifton, Crisp, Georgia. She was born on 14 December 1912 in Willacoochie, Atkinson, Georgia.
Their five children were:
Jewel Felice Floyd
Ina Jacquelyn Floyd
Jackson Clark Floyd Jr.
Charles Allen Floyd
David Lewis Floyd
5. **Robert Murphy Floyd** was born 29 October 1918 in White and died in Marietta, Georgia. He was buried in the White City Cemetery. On 22 June 1941 in Marietta he married Mattie Lee Copeland, who was born on 23 October 1920 in Kingston, Georgia.
Their two children were:
Bobby Lee Floyd
Mary Patricia Floyd
5. **Rubye Dell Floyd** was born 20 July 1923 in White, and married Owen Brooks, who died in Jacksonville, Florida.
Their child was:
Leslie Brooks

Child of Clarence Bell Perry and Eva Lou McGowen
5. **Nancy Perry**, who married James Ernest Young Jr., a dentist. In 2004 they lived in Greenwood, South Carolina, where Nancy searches for Whitten roots.
Their three children were:
Nancy Elizabeth Young
Mary Grace Young
Margaret Ann Young

EIGHTH GENERATION
Children of George Walter Ward and Annie Smith
6. **Andrew Ward**, who inherited his father's records, including the Bibles of James and Arphax Whitten. He lived in Atlanta in 1995.
6. **George Walter Ward Jr.**

Child of Lewis Ward
6. **James Ward**, who lives in Copper Hill, Tennessee, collects and shares James Whitten family data.

Child of Richard Teal Jr.
6. **Richard Teal III**

Child of James Slagle and Lucinda Ellen Ayers
6. **Marie Slagle** was born 5 June 1909 in Bluejacket, Kansas, and on 15 June 1928 in Coffeeville, Kansas, married Glenn I. Cooke, who was born there 5 June 1909.

Children of Eugene R. Perry and Beatrice Kathrine Meehan
6. **Alexis Perry** was born 3 November 1943 in San Francisco, California, and, on 18 August 1962 in Salt Lake City, Utah, married James Kone, born 18 July 1941. They divorced, and she married Robert Douglas Murray Woods 23 May 1975 in San Diego, California.
The three children of James Kone and Alexis Perry were:
Heidi Jean Kone
James Jess Kone
Yvette Marie Kone
The child of Robert Douglas Murray Woods and Alexis Perry was:
David Stevens Murray Woods
6. **Eugene R. Perry Jr.** was born 16 January 1945 in Portland, Maine, and married Linda Jean Shull, who was born 4 May 1947. They divorced, and on 5 December 1976 he married Karen Lynn Richmond, born 26 July 1952 in

Alameda, California.

The child of Eugene R. Perry Jr. and Linda Jean Shull was:

Lisa Jeanne Perry

The two children of Eugene R. Perry Jr. and Karen Lynn Richmond were:

Lance Adam Perry

Nathan Alan Perry

6. **Stephen Lewis Perry** was born 4 October 1954 in Milwaukee, Wisconsin, and on 19 December 1981 in San Diego married Karen Ann Usher, born 25 October 1957 in Norfolk, Virginia.

Their child was:

John Christopher Perry

Child of James Karr Hinton and Catherine Farrow Richey

6. **Col. Robert Richey Hinton** was born 29 April 1940 and married, in April 1968, Sigrid Reisiger Reineiman, born 20 October 1938.

Their child was:

Robin Karr Hinton

Children of Eugene Augustus Stansel and Elizabeth Roberta Richey

6. **Elizabeth Farrow Stansel** was born 14 June 1939, and on 2 January 1962 married Shelby Duke Goza, who was born 16 July 1938.

6. **Eugene Augustus Stansel Jr.** was born 24 August 1942, and on 24 July 1965 married Jane Gilbert, who was born 23 January 1945.

Their three children were:

Julie Elizabeth Stansel

Martha Gilbert Stansel

Virginia Catherine Stansel

6. **Martha Alford Stansel**

Children of William Thomas Jordan and Nellie Kathryn Floyd
Born in Bartow County, Georgia

6. **William Thomas Jordan Jr.** was born on 3 November 1934 in White, and married Pauline Honea, who was born on 13 December 1940 in Pickens County, Georgia.

Their four children were:

Marcus Jordan

Lynn Jordan

Kathy Jordan

Stephanie Jordan

6. **Homer Gunn Jordan** was born on 20 May 1936, and married Andrea Fowler on 16 February 1965 in Atlanta. She was born on 18 November 1943 in Cumming, Forsyth, Georgia.

Their three children were:

Alana Marie Jordan

Diana Leigh Jordan

Laura Elizabeth Jordan

Child of Jake Lewis and Georgia Felice Floyd

6. **Hilda Doris Lewis** was born on 18 December in Georgia, and married Charles Noward Richards in Indianapolis on 7 August 1968. He was born there on 11 March 1938.

Their two children were:

Erick Von Richards

Heather Lynn Richards

Children of Jackson Clark Floyd and Weta Jewel Tyson

6. **Jewel Felice Floyd** was born on 26 March 1938 in Americas, Georgia, and, on 8 May 1964 in Fresno, California, married George Edward Dissmeyer, who was born on 4 June 1937 in Jackson, Michigan. Felice is a talented Whitten researcher.

Their two children were:
>Stacy Leann Dissmeyer
>Sharon Beth Dissmeyer

6. **Ina Jacquelyn Floyd** was born 19 September 1939 in Jesup, Wayne, Georgia, and married Richard Quigley Turnbow on 8 February 1963 in Montclair, New Jersey. He was born on 9 April 1935 in San Jose, California.

Their two children were:
>Lisa Ruth Turnbow
>Sheri Lynn Turnbow

6. **Jackson Clark Floyd Jr.** was born on 2 August 1941 in Cartersville, Georgia, and married Glenda Hall on 28 March 1964 in Columbus. She was born there on 22 December 1943.

6. **Charles Alan Floyd** was born on 30 October 1943 in Wetumpka, Elmore, Alabama, and died in 1999 in Mobile. There he married Peggy Allen on 19 February 1965. She was born on 19 November 1945 in Leakesville, Green, Mississippi.

Their child was:
>Charles Alan Floyd

6. **David Lewis Floyd**, born on 5 January 1949 in Wetumpka.

Children of Robert Murphy Floyd and Mattie Lee Copeland

6. **Bobby Lee Floyd** was born on 12 August 1942 in Cartersville, Bartow County, Georgia. He married Canadian Jocelyne Lefebure on 30 December 1967 and died in Marietta.

6. **Mary Patricia Floyd** was born on 9 July 1952 in Marietta, and married Thomas M. Sawyer on 29 June 1974. Later she married Evans Axen.

The child of Thomas and Mary Floyd was:
>Thomas Vincent Sawyer

Child of Owen Brooks and Rubye Dell Floyd

6. **Leslie Brooks** was born in Jacksonville, Florida, and married Marc Suskin in Gainesville.

Their two children were:
>Marc Suskin
>Sam Suskin

Children of William Thomas Jordan Jr. and Pauline Honea

6. **Marcus Jordan** was born on 29 June 1961.

6. **Lynn Jordan** was born on 14 January 1963.

6. **Kathy Jordan** was born on 3 July 1968.

6. **Stephnie Jordan** was born on 31 July 1971.

Children of James Ernest Young and Nancy Perry

6. **Nancy Elizabeth Young** married William Scott Smith.

Their child was:
>Marshall Attison Smith

6. **Mary Grace Young** married James Slack Malone.

6. **Margaret Ann Young** married Arvie Paul Bennett Jr.

Their two children were:
>Arvie Paul Bennett III
>Charles Caleb Bennett

NINTH GENERATION

Children of James Kone and Alexis Perry

7. **Heidi Jean Kone** was born 18 March 1963 in Salt Lake City, Utah.

7. **James Jess Kone** was born 10 July 1964 in Salt Lake City.

7. **Yvette Marie Kone** was born 13 August 1970 in Albuquerque, New Mexico.

Child of Robert Douglas Murray Woods and Alexis Perry

7. **David Stevens Murray Woods** was born 28 July 1977 in San Diego, California.

Child of Eugene R. Perry Jr. and Linda Jean Shull
7. **Lisa Jeanne Perry** was born 19 March 1972 in San Diego.

Children of Eugene R. Perry Jr. and Karen Lynn Richmond
7. **Lance Adam Perry** was born on 8 October 1979 in San Diego.
7. **Nathan Alan Perry** was born on 9 September 1985 in San Diego.

Child of Stephen Lewis Perry and Karen Ann Usher
7. **John Christopher Perry** was born on 5 June 1986 in San Diego, California.

Child of Col. Robert Richey Hinton and Sigfrid Reisiger Reineiman
7. **Robin Karr Hinton** was born 8 March 1972 in Tennessee.

Children of Eugene Augustus Stansel Jr. and Jane Gilbert
7. **Julie Elizabeth Stansel**, born 21 December 1968.
7. **Martha Gilbert Stansel**, born 18 February 1971.
7. **Virginia Catherine Stansel**, born 12 August 1979.

Child of Richard Quigley Turnbow and Ina Jacquelyn Floyd
7. **Lisa Ruth Turnbow** was born on 29 January 1964 in Philadelphia, and married Bob Frost.
Their three children were:
  Spencer Aaron Frost, born 17 July 1996.
  Connor Frost
  Nathan Frost, born 10 January 1999.

Child of Charles Allen Floyd and Peggy Allen
7. **Rev. Charles Allen Floyd Jr.** was born on 2 July 1967 in Mobile, and married Kathy Green there.
Their two children were:
  Christopher Alan Floyd, born 5 November 1994.
  Connor Floyd, born 23 April 1999.

THIRD GENERATION
CHARLES WHITTEN

1. **Charles Whitten**, second child of John Whitten and Mary Reagan, was born 7 April 1787 in Spartanburg District, South Carolina, and died 19 September 1804 in Greenville District, South Carolina. He was buried either in the Tiger Creek Baptist Church Cemetery or the old Whitten place on the face of Hogback Mountain near present day Gowensville, South Carolina. (I searched the Tiger Creek Cemetery in about 1995 but could not find Charles's grave.)

THIRD GENERATION
ELIZABETH WHITTEN

1. **Elizabeth Whitten**, third child of John and Mary Reagan Whitten, was born 8 May 1789 in Spartanburg District, South Carolina, and married David Barrett 16 August 1807 in Greenville District, where he was born on 22 February 1786. Their life together over the next twenty years included a very unpleasant suit by David's siblings, who accused him and his brother, John, of mismanaging their father's estate.

David and Elizabeth did not accompany the rest of the Barrett family when they migrated to Mississippi. Instead, in 1826, they moved to Fayette County, Tennessee, traveling most of the way by flatboat down the Tennessee River; disembarking at Brown's Ferry, Tennessee; and finally reaching their new home site eight miles above the "Indian line" (present Mississippi-Tennessee border) and sixty miles east of Chickasaw Bluffs, the early name for Memphis. Their letter describing the trip has been widely circulated and published in *Letters to Rebecca*. Relocating to Houston County, Texas, in about 1840, they settled in Mustang Prairie, between Crockett and Madisonville. After David's death there on 10 April 1845, Elizabeth married Barton Clark, a wealthy widower, born in 1800 in Vermont. She died in Houston County in October 1855.

Their four children were:
  Albert Gallatin Barrett

John Whitten Barrett
Mary "Polly" Barrett
Marian Hannah Barrett

FOURTH GENERATION
Children of David Barrett and Elizabeth Whitten

2. **Albert Gallatin Barrett** was born 7 October 1810 in Greenville District, South Carolina, and married Elizabeth D. Seaton on 16 April 1832 in Hardeman County, Tennessee. She was born 15 April 1812 in Fayette County, Tennessee. They moved to Houston County, Texas, in 1840 and settled near Mustang Prairie, just north of present day Austonio, where he was elected justice of the peace in 1844. They died in Houston County: he, 8 March 1847; she, 17 November the same year.

Their eight children were:
Polly Caroline Barrett
James Whitten Barrett
David William Barrett
Elizabeth Mariam Barrett
John George Barrett
Unnamed Barrett child
Joseph Albert Barrett
Sally Jane Barrett

2. **John Whitten Barrett** was born 20 May 1813 in Greenville District, South Carolina, and married Hulda Redding on 7 February 1837 in Crockett, Houston, Texas. She was born 20 August 1820 in Davidson County, Tennessee. They died in Madison County, Texas, and were buried in the Barrett Cemetery there: he, 6 May 1877; she, 8 January 1894. He traveled by wagon train from Fayette County, Tennessee, to Crockett, Texas, in 1836, was in Montgomery County before 1840, and later became one of the first settlers of Madison County.

Their twelve children were:
Stephan Reding Barrett
William Robert Barrett
Ann Elizabeth "Nancy" Barrett
Martha Elizabeth Barrett
Amanda Catherine Barrett
David Albert Barrett
Jonathon Collard Barrett
Thomas Barrett
Luther Monroe Barrett
Sarah Alice Iantha Barrett
James Silas David Barrett
James W. "Withers" Barrett

2. **Mary "Polly" Barrett** was born 30 January 1819 in Greenville District, South Carolina, and married Dean McCarley on 13 August 1838 in Fayette County, Tennessee. He died 31 August 1840 in Fayette. On 13 October 1841, also in Fayette County, she married John R. Parker, who was born in 1815 in Virginia. They moved to Houston County, Texas, by 1846, where John R. died about 1869. Mary died in 1860 in Madison County, Texas.

The child of Dean McCarley and Mary Barrett was:
James McCarley
The ten children of John R. Parker and Mary Barrett were:
David Henry Parker
Rebecca Elizabeth Parker
Marion Parker
James Parker
Sarah Parker
Richard Parker
Mary Parker
Lavina Parker
Louise Parker
William Parker

2. **Mariam Hannah Barrett** was born 25 April 1821 in Greenville District, South Carolina, and on 18 July 1839 in Fayette County, Tennessee, married Hansell Coburn, who was born in 1817 in North Carolina. They moved, prior to 1840, to Houston County, Texas, and were in the Prarie Community of Walker County in 1848, returning to Houston County by 1860. They died in Bell County where they settled in 1867: he, about 1875; she, about 1902.

Their five children were:
> Harriet L. Coburn
> Hannah Jane Coburn
> Margaret Coburn
> William B. Coburn
> Mattie Bell I. Coburn

FIFTH GENERATION
Children of Albert Gallatin Barrett and Elizabeth D. Seaton

3. **Polly Caroline Barrett** was born 12 April and died 24 May 1833 in Fayette County, Tennessee.

3. **James Whitten Barrett** was born 24 April 1834 and died 12 November the same year in Fayette.

3. **David William Barrett** was born 3 January 1836 in Fayette County, and on 12 May 1859 in Cherokee County, Texas, married Elizabeth Hill, who was born in 1840 in that state. He died 27 January 1863 in South Bend, Arkansas, while serving as corporal, CSA.

Their child was:
> Mary Barrett

3. **Elizabeth Mariam Barrett** was born 15 June 1837 in Fayette and died 11 June 1841 in Houston County, Texas.

3. **John George Barrett** was born 11 July 1839 in Fayette, and on 11 August 1859 in Cherokee County, Texas, married Mary Hill, who was born there about 1843. He died 10 May 1862 in Mississippi while serving as private, Company I, 10th Texas Cavalry, CSA. They had one child.

3. **Joseph Albert Barrett** was born 17 May 1844 in Grimes County, Texas, and on 21 March 1867 in Walker County, Texas, married Elizabeth Skelton, born about 1848. This marriage was her third; the first was to Warrent D. Edinburg, the second to Oresta Passera. Joseph Albert died before 1870. He served, during the Civil War, as private in the 11th Texas Infantry, CSA.

Their child was:
> Sarah Barrett

3. **Sally Jane Barrett** was born 20 May and died 4 August in 1846 in Grimes County, Texas.

Children of John Whitten and Hulda Reding Barrett

3. **Stephen Reding Barrett** was born 3 September 1840 in Montgomery County, and on 1 September 1858 in Madison County married Sarah L. Larrison, who was born 8 November 1837 in Plantersville, Grimes, Texas. He died of typhoid fever 8 December 1863 in Louisiana while serving in Company G, 7th Regiment, Texas Mounted Volunteers, CSA. She died 1 December 1895 in Madison County, and is buried in Larrison Cemetery, Fraley Pasture, Texas.

Their two children were:
> Jonathon Daniel Barrett
> Steven Franklin Barrett

3. **William Robert Barrett** was born 30 December 1842 in Montgomery County, Texas, and there on 14 February 1866 married Elizabeth E. Walters, who was born 30 July 1840 in Mississippi. They died in Madison County, Texas: he, 1 January 1903; she, 19 March 1921. They were buried in Madisonville.

Their seven children were:
> William Seymour Barrett
> John I. Barrett
> Florence Barrett
> Johnston Tolephus Barrett
> Hugh Hayes Barrett
> Henry Barrett
> Ima Osamae Barrett

3. **Ann Elizabeth "Nancy" Barrett** was born 6 February 1845 in Montgomery County, and on 5 December 1861 in Madison County married John Washington Jenkins, who was born 23 January 1812 in South Carolina. He died in February 1880 in Madison County; she, 28 February 1925 in Johnson County, Texas.

Their six children were:

> John W. Jenkins
> John Washington Jenkins Jr.
> Ophelia Jenkins
> Cyrene Jenkins
> Thomas Milton Jenkins
> Martie B. Jenkins

3. **Martha Elizabeth Barrett** was born 17 March 1847 in Montgomery County, and about 1869 in Madison County married William F. Bobo, who was born in 1848 in Bastrop, Morehouse, Louisiana, and died 3 January 1888 in Madison County, Texas. In 1894 she married, in Brown County, Texas, Albert Morton, who was born in September 1859 in Illinois. Martha died about 1917 in Brown County; Albert, 15 September 1932.

The eight children of William F. Bobo and Martha Elizabeth Barrett were:

> Asie Bobo
> Robert Bobo
> Bill Dugan Bobo
> Mattie Bobo
> Lucy Bobo
> Annette Bobo
> Charles Bobo
> Thomas Nathaniel Bobo

3. **Amanda Catherine Barrett**, twin of David Albert, was born 2 May 1849 in Montgomery, and married on 20 January 1869 in Madison, James Marion McCan, Civil War veteran, who was born 20 October 1834 in Lawrence, Alabama. They died in Madison in 1915: she, 12 January; he, 31 July; and are buried in the Barrett Cemetery.

Their ten children were:

> James Littleton McCan
> Hulda McCan
> Samuel Wooldridge
> Kenneth Nathan McCan
> Minnie Ola McCan
> Allie Angeline McCan
> William Walter McCan
> John Reuben McCan
> Benjamin Monroe McCan
> Hettie M. McCan

3. **David Albert Barrett**, twin of Amanda Catherine, was born 2 May 1849 in Montgomery County, and married Martha J. Tolbert on 7 December 1876 in Madison County. She was born 26 February 1856 in Montgomery. At age fifteen he left home for Louisiana where, on 4 January 1865, he enlisted in Company G, 7th Regiment, Texas Cavalry, Green's Brigade, CSA. His brothers Stephen and William were members of this Company. The couple died in Madison County, Texas: he, 28 December 1928; she, 24 August 1891; and were buried in the Barrett Cemetery.

Their eight children were:

> William Anthony Barrett
> Martha Elizabeth Barrett
> Connard W. Barrett
> Robert K. Barrett
> Amanda Barrett
> Roscoe Wiley Barrett
> Ida Barrett
> George Barrett

3. **Jonathon Collard Barrett** was born 22 November 1851 in Walker County, Texas, and about 1876, in Madison County, married Martha Shepherd, born in 1860 there. They died after 1890 in Harper Hill Community, near Midway in Walker County, where they are buried.

Their eight children were:

> Roy Franklin Barrett
> Ada Mae Barrett
> James Walter Barrett
> Walter Barrett

Samuel Shepherd Barrett
Hubert Redding Barrett
William Barrett
Guy Roland Barrett

3. **Thomas Barrett** was born 4 February and died 21 October in 1854 in Madison County.

3. **Luther Monroe Barrett** was born 26 July 1855 in Madison, and married on 8 October 1874, Sarah L. Laney. On 26 June 1877 he married Sarah Louisa Adams, born 28 November 1859 in Ellwood, Madison, Texas. Luther Monroe died 10 January 1894 in Madison County and was buried in the Barrett Cemetery. Sarah Louise died 13 September 1957 in Houston County and was buried in Madisonville.

The eight children of Luther Monroe Barrett and Sarah Louisa Adams were:

Amanda Annis Barrett
William Joseph Barrett
Minnie Ora Barrett
Maude Elizabeth Barrett
James David Barrett
Mollie Conner Barrett
Martha Alice Barrett
George Barrett

3. **Sarah Alice Iantha Barrett** was born 12 May 1858 in Madison County, and there married a Mr. Estahr. On 3 July 1878, also in Madison, she married James B. Manning, born 30 November 1856 in Texas. They died in Madison: Sarah Alice, 18 March 1923; James B., 10 January 1894, and were buried in the Barrett Cemetery in Midway, Madison, Texas.

The eight children of James B. Manning and Sarah Alice Iantha Barrett were:

John Iredell Manning
Hulda A. Manning
James B. Manning Jr.
Martha V. Manning
Lila Manning
Benjamin Franklin Manning
Nugent B. Manning
Exa Manning

3. **James Silas D. Barrett** was born 17 November 1860 in Madison County, where on 7 May 1882 he married Clara Viola Manning, who was born in 1863 and died 18 April 1883 in Madison. On 12 November 1883 he married Mattie C. Adams, born 21 October 1869 in Madison. She was a sister of Sarah Louisa, wife of Luther Monroe Barrett. James Silas D. died 12 June 1889 in Madison and was buried in the Barrett Cemetery. Mattie died 23 March 1941 in Leon County and was buried in Pleasant Grove Cemetery.

The child of James Silas D. Barrett and Clara Viola Manning was:

Silas Clarence Barrett

3. **James W. "Withers" Barrett** was born 9 May 1873 in Madison County, where he married Rosa Vaughn on 3 January 1896.

Child of Dean McCarley and Mary "Polly" Barrett

3. **James McCarley** was born in 1839 in Fayette County, Tennessee, and died in 1863 in St. Louis, Missouri.

Children of John R. Parker and Mary "Polly" Barrett
Born in Texas

3. **David Henry Parker** was born in 1842 in Houston County and died 18 February 1863 in St. Louis, Missouri.

3. **Rebecca Elizabeth Parker** was born in 1844.

3. **Marion Parker** was born in 1846.

3. **James Parker** was born about 1847.

3. **Sarah Parker** was born in 1849.

3. **Richard Parker** was born in 1853.

3. **Mary Parker** was born in 1855.

3. **Lavina Parker** was born in 1857.

3. **Louise Parker** was born in 1857.

3. **William Parker** was born in 1859.

Children of Hansell Coburn and Mariam Hannah Barrett

3. **Harriet L. Coburn** was born in 1847 and died 10 September 1864 in Houston County, Texas.

3. **Hannah Jane Coburn** was born about 1850 in Houston County, and in Bell County on 24 July 1867 married Thomas William Holcomb, who was born 6 October 1847 and died in Texas 6 October 1919. She died in 1928 in Bell County.

Their eight children were:

William Coburn Holcomb
William Alfred Holcomb III
Zetha Roberta Holcomb
Charles Andrew Holcomb
Eva Holcomb
Benton Rogers Holcomb
Barney Holcomb
Mary Willia Holcomb

3. **Margaret Coburn** was born about 1857 in Houston County, and in about 1873 married T. J. Graves in Bell County, Texas.

Their three children were:

Ida Lou Graves
Bessie Bell Graves
Katie Emma Graves

3. **William B. Coburn** was born in January 1860 in Houston County, and married Mary Ella White on 29 January 1880 in Bell County, Texas. She was born 10 April 1863 in Dalton, Georgia, and died 3 January 1937 in Weleetka, Okfuskee, Oklahoma.

Their five children were:

Lee Coburn
Nette Coburn
John Coburn
Bess J. Coburn
Wilburn D. Coburn

3. **Mattie Bell I. Coburn** was born 25 December 1860, in Houston County, and on 22 August 1877 married William Alexander McCreary in Bell County, and died in 1909. He was born in 1852.

Their child was:

Ada Bell McCreary

SIXTH GENERATION

Child of David William Barrett and Elizabeth Hill

4. **Mary Barrett**, born in April 1860.

Child of Joseph Albert Barrett and Elizabeth Skelton

4. **Sarah Barrett**, born in 1868.

Children of Stephen Reding Barrett and Sarah L. Larrison

4. **Jonathon Daniel Barrett** was born 21 March 1860 in Madisonville, Texas, and had six wives. The first, whom he married on 19 November 1883 in Madison County, was Mattie Cornelia Carson, born in 1867 in Midway, Texas. She died 24 November 1884 in Del Rio, Val Verde, Texas, and was buried in Train Depot, in that county. Next he married on 22 March 1885, in Madison, Laura Burke, born in 1866 there. She died in 1886. After 1887 he married Susie Hiffner, who died about 1890. On 8 October 1890 in Shelby, Texas, he married Mary Lillian Jones, born 10 February 1873. Mary Lillian died 16 February 1911 in Antlers, Pushmataha, Oklahoma, and was buried there. Next he married Effie Hale, then Essie Marcum. He died 22 April 1945 in Antlers, and was buried with Mary Lillian.

The child of John Daniel Barrett and Mattie Cornelia Carson was:

Mattie Cornelia Barrett

The child of John Daniel Barrett and Laura Burk was:

Finias Barrett

The two children of John Daniel Barrett and Susie Hiffner were:
    Maggie Barrett
    David Barrett
The eight children of John Daniel Barrett and Mary Lillian Jones were:
    Ida Lee Barrett
    Etta Maud Barrett
    Daniel Alton Barrett
    Nevada Ethyl Barrett
    Edgar Lee Barrett
    Sarah Lillian Barrett
    John William Barrett
    Julius Marion Barrett
The child of John Daniel Barrett and Effie Hale was:
    Ruthie Barrett
The three children of John Daniel Barrett and Essie Marcum were:
    Lois Barrett
    Celil Barrett
    Willard Barrett

    4. **Steven Franklin Barrett** was born 19 April 1863 in Madison County, where he married Molly Agnes Bobo on 5 June 1882. She was born 17 August 1854 in Bastrop, Morehouse, Louisiana. They died and are buried in Madison County, Texas: he, 17 March 1903; she, 8 August 1913.
    Their five children were:
    Steven Robert Barrett
    William John Barrett
    Hattie Lee Barrett
    Frankie Lucille Barrett
    Henry Barrett

Children of William Robert Barrett and Elizabeth E. Walters

    4. **William Seymour Barrett** was born 30 January 1867 in Madison County, Texas, where he married on 26 December 1889 Loula Gracie McDonald, who was born 15 February 1870 in the same county. They divorced, and she died 30 August 1950 in Ardmore, Carter, Oklahoma. On 26 June 1889, in Madison, William Seymour married Maud Wright Randolph, who was born 30 April 1868 in Bell County, Texas. They died in Texas: William Seymore, 15 September 1929 in San Antonio; Maude, 1 May 1959 in Odessa, Ector County, where she was buried. William Seymore and his first wife were buried in Madisonville.
    The four children of William Seymour Barrett and Loula Gracie McDonald were:
    Beulah Barrett
    Sallie Barrett
    Clemmons Carmon Barrett
    Della Barrett
    The four children of William Seymour Barrett and Maude Wright Randolph were:
    Eldra Barrett
    Henry Hugh Barrett
    Velma Barrett
    Oce Mae Barrett

    4. **John I. Barrett** was born 8 January 1870 in Madison County, and married Minnie Cook, born in August 1875 in Texas. He died 12 February 1955 in Lubbock; she, 1974, in Albuquerque.
    Their two children were:
    Tommie Mae Barrett
    Fannie Florence May Barrett

    4. **Florence Barrett** was born 6 February 1873 in Madison County, married Jim Jones, and died 2 September 1896 in Huntsville, Walker, Texas.
    Their child was:
    Ercel Jones

    4. **Johnston Tolephus Barrett** was born 20 April 1875, and, on 24 April 1895, married Ariah Carolyn Adams,

born 17 March 1878. He died 24 April 1935; she, 19 March 1937 after living their entire lives in Madison County, Texas.

Their twelve children were:

    Eddie C. Barrett
    William Talmage Barrett
    Lizzie Florence Barrett
    William Robert Barrett
    Arie Lena Barrett
    Jake Herring Barrett
    Johnston Tolephus Barrett Jr.
    Martha Barrett
    George T. Barrett
    Alvis C. Barrett
    Mack Bennett Barrett
    Bracil C. Barrett

4. **Hugh Hayes Barrett** was born 14 December 1877 in Madison County, and married Virginia Isabel Runnelson on 17 December 1900 in Broaddus, San Augustine, Texas. She was born 3 September 1879. He died 13 May 1950 in Madison; she, 12 July 1962 in Huntsville, Walker, Texas.

Their seven children were:

    Hugh Hays Barrett Jr.
    Lora Minnie Barrett
    Ottie Eugene Barrett
    John Lee Barrett
    Mary Lizzie Barrett
    William Robert Barrett
    H. Richard Barrett

4. **Henry Barrett** was born 3 December 1882 and died 6 September 1884 in Madison County, where he is buried.

4. **Ima Osamae Barrett** was born 6 December 1887 in Madison, and married John Mims, Ben Barton, Claude Manning, and Jim Bryan.

Children of John Washington Jenkins and Ann Elizabeth "Nancy" Barrett

4. **John W. Jenkins** was born 2 August 1862 and died in April the following year in Madison County.

4. **John Washington Jenkins Jr.**, born in March 1870.

4. **Ophelia Jenkins**, born in 1873.

4. **Cyrene Jenkins**, born in 1875.

4. **Thomas Milton Jenkins** was born 17 November 1876 and died before 1880 in Madison.

4. **Martie B. Jenkins**, born in 1879.

Children of William F. Bobo and Martha Elizabeth Barrett

4. **Asie Bobo**, born about 1869.

4. **Robert Bobo**, born about 1871.

4. **Bill Dugan Bobo**, born about 1873.

4. **Mattie Bobo** was born in 1877, and married W. M. Stapp on 28 April 1894.

4. **Lucy Bobo** was born in 1877, and married L. D. Armentrout Jr.

4. **Annette Bobo** was born 25 December 1879, and married David Thomas on 24 March 1895.

4. **Charles Bobo**, born in September 1884.

4. **Thomas Nathaniel Bobo** was born 9 April 1887 and died 6 July 1944.

Children of James Marion McCan and Amanda Catherine Barrett

4. **James Littleton McCan** was born 27 May 1870 in Madison County, and married on 24 September 1890 in Dickey, Leon, Texas, Sarah Ida Dickey, born 14 May 1873 there. They died in Houston: he, 8 November 1923; she, 10 June 1954. He was buried in Hollywood Cemetery, Houston, Texas.

Their eleven children were:

    Maggie L. McCan
    Clemmie McCan
    James Matthew McCan

Georgia McCan
Kenneth Kyle McCan
Hallie McCan
Ione Zefa McCan
Andrew Buron McCan
Carroll McCan
Connie Ford McCan
Mossie McCan

4. **Hulda McCan** was born 16 November 1872 in Texas, and married James Monroe Winborn about 1892. He was born in March 1868 in Alabama. Hulda died 19 March 1966.

Their six children were:
Kenneth Edward Winborn
James Ethel Winborn
John Winborn
Minnie Gladys Winborn
Sarah Ross Winborn
Amanda Winborn

4. **Samuel Wooldridge McCan** was born 11 February 1875 in Texas, and on 21 November 1900 married Alice Blanche Dickey, who was born in 1876 in Texas. He died 9 March 1962 in Palestine, Texas.

Their seven children were:
Icely Aline McCann
Lockie Blanche McCann
Miner Dickey McCann
Ed Sloan McCann
Donnell Earl McCann
Bell Field McCann
Jane Kate McCann

4. **Kenneth Nathan McCan** was born 17 March 1877 in Madison County, Texas, married Annie Bell Duncan, and died 11 January 1899 in Montgomery County.

Their child was:
Lottie Bell McCan

4. **Minnie Ola McCan** was born 22 August 1879 in Madison County, and died 26 October 1880.

4. **Allie Angeline McCan** was born 8 March 1881 in Texas, and married Eugene Henry Golden, born in 1877. She died 27 September 1962 in Baytown, Texas.

Their eleven children were:
Talitha Amanda Golden
Virgil Littleton Golden
James Joseph Golden
Sadie Mae Golden
Hulda Eugene Golden
Annie Bell Golden
Connie Ola Golden
Winnie Viola Golden
Minnie Lucille Golden
George Woodburn Golden
Effie Wynonia Golden

4. **William Walter McCan** was born 6 November 1884 in Texas, married Alma Mcree Rhodes, and died in Houston in November 1967.

Their two children were:
Kenneth Gale McCann
Josephine McCann

4. **John Reuben McCan** was born 6 May 1886 in Texas, and married Debra June Stowe. He then married Rosa Lynch and died 6 April 1965 in Dallas.

The nine children of John Reuben McCan and Debra June Stowe were:
Johnie Mae McCann

Walter Stanley McCann
Claudia Irene McCann
Edgar Kahle McCann
Charles Keith McCann
Mildred Louise McCann
Hettie Vernal McCann
Harold Floyd McCann
Darrell Lloyd McCann

The four children of John Reuben McCan and Rosa Lynch were:

Franklin McCan
James Earl McCan
Charles Edward McCan
Paul McCan

4. **Benjamin Monroe McCan** was born 29 November 1889 in Texas, married Maggie E. Stowe, and died in 1949 in Drumwright, Oklahoma.

Their ten children were:

James Elmer McCann
Lola Faye McCann
Charles Edgar McCann
Martha Bessie McCann
Viola Mae McCann
Amanda Elizabeth McCann
Earl David McCann
Benny Star McCann
Bobby Gene McCann
Bluford Wesley McCann

4. **Hettie M. McCan** was born 11 August 1892 in Madison County, married Hartwell Hale, and died in 1918.

Their four children were:

Marvin Hale
Annie Hale
Ruby Jewell Hale
Jack Carl Hale

Children of David Albert Barrett and Martha J. Tolbert

4. **William Anthony Barrett** was born 14 December 1877 in Madison County, Texas, where he married Annie Seales in 1904. Annie was born 2 November 1886 in Robinson, Texas. William Anthony died 17 February 1941 in Madison County, where he was buried; she, 2 June 1962.

Their ten children were:

Lena Estelle Barrett
Ora Gertrude Barrett
James Luther Barrett
Ida Pearl Barrett
Annie Laura Barrett
Glenn Andrew Barrett
Wilbert Barrett
William Ernest Barrett
Mildred Barrett
Bessie Barrett

4. **Martha Elizabeth Barrett** was born in July 1879 in Madison County, where she married John Driver in December 1899. He was born in March 1875 somewhere in Texas.

4. **Connard W. Barrett** was born in September 1881 in Madison, where he married Lillie Bell Douglas in 1911.

Their child was:

Alma Crystal Barrett

4. **Robert K. Barrett** was born in November 1883 in Madison, and married Mattie Pearl Seales, born 14 November 1894. They died in Madison County: Robert, in 1953; Mattie Pearl, 11 December 1971. Both were buried in

Midway, Madison, Texas.

> Their three children were:
>> Vivian Claud Barrett
>> Margie Katherine Barrett
>> Robert K. Barrett Jr.

4. **Amanda Barrett**, born in February 1885 in Madison County.

4. **Roscoe Wiley Barrett** was born in August 1889 in Madison, where he married Lillie Cook in 1911.

> Their two children were:
>> Roland D. Barrett
>> Rueal Barrett

4. **Ida Barrett** was born in March 1891 in Madison, where she married Elijah J. Seals in 1909.

4. **George Barrett**

Children of Jonathon Collard Barrett and Martha E. Shepherd

4. **Roy Franklin Barrett** was born 4 April 1872 in Walker County, and married Tom Nolie Cravy.

> Their child was:
>> Thelma Barrett

4. **Ada Mae Barrett** was born in March 1876 in Texas, and married Tom Shuck in Madison County.

4. **James Walter Barrett** was born 11 December 1879 in Madison County, where on 6 March 1901 he married Eldra Randolph, who was born in August 1882 in Huntsville, Texas.

> Their three children were:
>> Essie Eula Barrett
>> J. C. Barrett
>> Lee Roy Barrett

4. **Walter Barrett**, born 28 September 1881 in Madison County.

4. **Rev. Samuel Shepherd Barrett**, Walter's twin, married Bertha Ohlenberger in Madison County. His second wife was Mrs. Edith Hill Davis.

> The three children of Rev. Samuel Shepherd Barrett and Bertha Ohlenberger were:
>> Vera Lee Barrett
>> Florence Barrett
>> James Barrett

> The four children of Rev. Samuel Shephard Barrett and Edith Hill Davis were:
>> Mildred Barrett
>> Alice Barrett
>> Ava Rae Barrett
>> John Barrett

4. **Hubert Redding Barrett** was born 19 February 1884 in McCulloch County, Texas, and on 11 June 1907 married Maggie Louanna Allphin, born 16 January 1886 in Huntsville. They were divorced, and in Madison County he married Mattie Shepard. Hubert Redding died 26 March 1965; Maggie Louanna, 2 October 1977 in Spring, Harris County. Both are buried in McAdams Cemetery, Huntsville, Texas.

> The ten children of Hubert Redding Barrett and Maggie Louanna Allphin were:
>> John Wallace Barrett
>> Mattie Addie Barrett
>> Hugh Roland Barrett
>> Marion Otis Barrett
>> Ora Ina Barrett
>> Henry Allphin Barrett
>> Altha Mae Barrett
>> Bobbie O'Nell Barrett
>> Roy Barrett
>> Billie Jo Barrett

4. **William Barrett** was born about 1887 in Madison County, and married Icy.

4. **Guy Roland Barrett** was born 3 March 1889 in Walker County, and married Edna Hines, who was born 13 April 1889. He died 24 November 1938 in Harris County; she, 14 January 1963 in Walker County. They are buried in McAdams Cemetery, Huntsville, Texas.

Their six children were:
Gayle Barrett
Vernon Barrett
Blanche Barrett
Bernice Barrett
Guy Roland Barrett Jr.
John Barrett

Children of Luther Monroe Barrett and Sarah Louise Adams

4. **Amanda Annis Barrett** was born 1 July 1879 and died 20 September 1885 in Madison County.

4. **William Joseph Barrett** was born 26 May 1881 in Madison, and married Alice Lynch on 2 July 1904 in Groveton, Texas. She was born 22 June 1885. William Joseph died in Ft. Worth.

Their two children were:
Louie Monroe Barrett
Marion Lynch Barrett

4. **Minnie Ora Barrett** was born 1 January 1883 in Madison, and married George Oscar Faulkner on 26 November 1899. He was born 7 November 1880. Minnie Ora's second husband was William D. Alford.

The two children of George Oscar Faulkner and Minnie Ora Barrett were:
Iola Mae Faulkner
Leo Faulkner

4. **Maude Elizabeth Barrett** was born 7 April 1885 in Madison County, and married John O. Lloyd on 5 December 1910. He was born in Robertson, Texas, and died in 1931 in Houston; she, 7 March 1908.

Their two children were:
Elmer Lloyd
Lois Lloyd

4. **James David Barrett** was born 24 March 1887 in Madison County, and married Della Ilene Lloyd on 3 July 1910 in Houston. She was born 20 October 1889 in Robertson, Texas. They died in Houston: he, 27 November 1956; she, 20 January 1970; and were buried in Woodlawn Cemetery, Harris County.

Their three children were:
James Ray Barrett
Lloyd Barrett
Sarah Helen Barrett

4. **Mollie Connor Barrett** was born 28 July 1889 in Madison County, and on 16 August 1918 married Henry Clay Wright. She died 28 January 1972; he, 21 July 1946.

Their two children were:
Henry Clay Wright Jr.
Jack Ledford Wright

4. **Martha Alice Barrett** was born 7 December 1891 in Madison County, and on 3 August 1912 married Matthew Sidney Clark, who was born 28 September 1888. She died 7 September 1927 in El Campo, Texas; he, 29 December 1969.

Their three children were:
Elsie Dell Clark
Martha Sidney Clark
William Sidney Clark

4. **George Barrett** was born 28 December 1893 and died 3 January 1894 in Madison County.

Children of James B. Manning and Sarah Alice Iantha Barrett
Born in Madison County, Texas

4. **John Iredell Manning** was born 21 August 1879, and married Prudence Polk, born 30 May 1878. He died 23 February 1961; she, 28 November 1943. They were buried in the Barrett Cemetery, Madison County.

Their four children were:
Florence Manning
Jewell Ona Manning
Melvin Iredell Manning
Billy Boy Manning

4. **Hulda A. Manning** was born in March 1881, and married Dempsey B. McDonald about June 1899 in Madison

County. He was born in January 1875 in Mississippi, died in 1936, and lies in the Barrett Cemetery, Madison County, Texas.

4. **James B. Manning Jr.** was born 8 January 1884, died 17 September that year in Madison, and was buried in the Barrett Cemetery, Madison, Texas.

4. **Martha V. Manning** was born 22 September 1885, died 14 October 1885 in Madison County, and was buried in Barrett Cemetery.

4. **Lila Manning** was born in January 1886, and married Walter Randolph.

4. **Benjamin Franklin Manning** was born 22 December 1889 and died on 15 April 1958 in Carlisle, Texas. He married Maude Bell Barrett on 9 May 1910.

Their four children were:
Anne May Manning
Ruby Elizabeth Manning
Sadie Augusta Manning
Lilla Juanita Manning

4. **Nugent B. Manning** was born 12 June 1892, died 27 January 1896 in Madison County, and was buried in Barrett Cemetery.

4. **Exa Buchannon Manning** was born 22 February 1894, and married William R. Anthony. Her second husband was a Mr. Moore. She died 29 March 1965 and was buried in Barrett Cemetery. Her entire life was spent in one Texas county.

The two children of William R. Anthony and Exa Manning were:
Donald Manning Anthony
L. B. Anthony

Child of James Silas David Barrett and Clara Viola Manning

4. **Silas Clarence Barrett** was born 13 April 1883 in Madison, and married on 9 April 1911 Lucy Elizabeth Brooks, born 17 April 1889. They died in Houston: he, 13 November 1978; she, 15 February 1968; and are buried in Brookside Cemetery.

Their two children were:
Clarence Brooks Barrett
Vera Faye Barrett

Children of Benjamin Franklin Harmon and Louise Parker
All born in Belton, Bell, Texas

4. **Edward Francis Harmon** was born 22 March 1878 and died 7 June 1938 in Elmore City, Oklahoma. In 1901 he married Mary Lee Barrett and, in 1909, Ethel Gordon.

4. **Thomas Franklin Harmon** was born 18 July 1880, married Anise Lindsay in 1903, and died in Graham, Texas, in March 1973.

4. **Mary Nancy Harmon** was born 30 December 1882, and married Tom Thigpen on 22 October 1902.

4. **Lydia Lovella Harmon** was born 20 April 1885, married O. G. Steen in 1904 and Enos Teel in 1909, and died 31 August 1955 in Long Beach, California.

4. **Lila Kate Harmon** was born 5 October 1887, married Joseph Nicholas Farber on 14 May 1905, and died 20 February 1934 in Walters, Oklahoma. He was born 19 September 1887 in Weatherford, Texas, and died 5 November 1966 in Duncan, Oklahoma.

Their ten children were:
Avery Farber
Benjamin Oscar Farber
Thomas Jefferson Farber
LaVern Farber
James Edward Farber
Josephine Nick Farber
Clyde Grant Farber
Claud Lee Farber
Mary Louise Farber
Donna Faye Farber

Children of Thomas William Holcomb and Hannah Jane Coburn

4. **William Coburn Holcomb**, who married Anna Miller.
4. **William Alfred Holcomb III**, who married Mary James.
4. **Zetha Roberta Holcomb**, who married Fred Brown.
4. **Charles Andrew Holcomb**, who was born in 1880 and married Minnie Lou Puckett.
4. **Eva Holcomb**, who married William Z. Reynolds.
4. **Benton Rogers Holcomb**, who married Mayme Locke.
4. **Barney Holcomb**
4. **Mary Willia Holcomb**, who married Perry W. Mitchell.

Children of A. J. Graves and Margaret Coburn
4. **Ida Lou Graves**, born in 1874.
4. **Bessie Bell Graves**, born in 1876.
4. **Katie Emma Graves**, born in 1878.

Children of William B. Coburn and Mary Ella White
4. **Lee Coburn** was born in Bell County, Texas, in July 1881.
4. **Nette Coburn**, born in Bell County in April 1883.
4. **John Coburn**, born in Bell County in February 1885
4. **Bess J. Coburn**, who was born 24 June 1893 in Graham, Young, Texas. She married Joe Clarence Camburn and died 12 August 1943 in Ganado, Arizona, where she was buried.
Their child was:
Clarence Camburn
4. **Wilburn D. Coburn**, born in Graham, Young County, Texas, in February 1895.

Child of William Alexander McCreary and Mattie Bell I. Coburn
4. **Ada Bell McCreary** was born in 1879 in Bell County, Texas.
Her child was:
Doris McCreary

SEVENTH GENERATION
Child of John Daniel Barrett and Mattie Cornelia Carson
5. **Mattie Cornelia Barrett** was born 20 November 1884 in Del Rio, and on 18 May 1905 married William Richard Morgan, who was born 15 March 1860 in Courtland, Cass, Texas. They died and are buried in Antlers, Oklahoma: she, 20 March 1980; he, 3 May 1929.
Their seven children were:
Richard Daniel Morgan
Orval V. Morgan
Etta Maude Morgan
Clyde Aaron Morgan
Ima G. Morgan
Oma G. Morgan
Rose Lee Morgan

Child of Jonathon Daniel Barrett and Effie Hale
5. **Ruthie Barrett**, who died in Hugo, Oklahoma.

Child of Jonathon Daniel Barrett and Laura Burk
5. **Finias Barrett** was born and died about 1886 in Madison County, Texas.

Children of Jonathon Daniel Barrett and Susie Hiffner
5. **Maggie Barrett** was born about 1888 in Texas.
5. **David Barrett** was born about 1890 in Texas and died about 1892 in Shelby, Texas.

Children of Jonathon Daniel Barrett and Mary Lillian Jones
5. **Ida Lee Barrett** was born 11 October 1892 in Shelby, Texas, married Bud Plumley, died 29 July 1970 in

Tishomingo, Johnston, Oklahoma, and was buried in Antlers, Oklahoma.

5. **Etta Maud Barrett** was born 16 January 1895 and died in 1915.

5. **Daniel Alton Barrett** was born 18 August 1899, married Willie Ring, and died in Bakersfield, California.

5. **Nevada Ethyl Barrett** was born 30 January 1900, died in 1981, and was buried in Wapanucka, Oklahoma.

5. **Edgar Lee Barrett** was born 11 April 1902 in Cass, Texas, married Madel Sandes, died 20 November 1977 in Oklahoma City, and was buried in Antlers.

5. **Sarah Lillian Barrett** was born 5 October 1904, married a Mr. Faulkner, and died in San Diego, California.

5. **John William Barrett** was born 13 February 1907, married Cleo Ferrel, and died in California.

5. **Julius Marion Barrett** was born 16 February 1911 and died in 1986 in Randelett, Oklahoma.

Children of Jonathon Daniel Barrett and Essie Marcum

5. **Lois Barrett**

5. **Cecil Barrett**

5. **Willard Barrett**

Children of Steven Franklin Barrett and Molly Agnes Bobo

5. **Steven Robert Barrett** was born in September 1883 in San Saba, Texas, and on 21 November 1904 in Madison County married Mary Matilda Ferrell, who was born in 1878 in Alabama. He died 16 September 1922 in Weldon, Houston, Texas, after which she married a Mr. Hosier. Her daughter, Lois Elizabeth Hosier, married Steven Robert's brother, William John. Mary Matilda died in 1946.

The two children of Steven Robert Barrett and Mary Matilda Ferrell were:

Earl M. Barrett

Madie Barrett

5. **William John Barrett** was born 26 August 1885 in San Saba, Texas, and on 10 April 1912 in Madison County married Lois Elizabeth Hosier, who was born in 1897 in Texas. They died in Trinity, Texas: he, 10 April 1976; she, the next day.

Their eight children were:

Lula Agnes Barrett

Robert Dan Barrett

Louie Franklin Barrett

Mary Evelyn Barrett

Lottie Mae Barrett

Steve William Barrett

James Paul Barrett

John Ferrell Barrett

5. **Hattie Lee Barrett** was born 21 January 1888 in Madison County, where she married, on 2 December 1903, John Carl William, who was born 12 January 1887 in Madison. He died in September 1955 in Baytown, Harris, Texas: she, 3 March 1976 in Midway. Hattie Lee was buried in Madisonville.

Their four children were:

Steve Jethro William

Mary Jane William

Dolly Mae William

Johnny William

5. **Frankie Lucille Barrett** was born 17 September 1894 in Larrison Praire, Madison County, and, there, on 6 April 1910, married Mitchell Lewis Vetuski, who was born 28 September 1889 in New Waverly, Walker, Texas. She died 11 November 1926 in Midway; he, 25 April 1962 in Baytown, Texas. They were buried in Midway.

Their eight children were:

Steven William Vetuski

Lee Tensley Vetuski

Lottie Odell Vetuski

Harold Eugene Vetuski

Woodrow Felix Vetuski

Edward Lewis Vetuski

Mitchell Glenn Vetuski

Mary Grancis Vetuski

5. **Henry Barrett** was born 18 September 1896 and died 6 November 1897 in Madison County, Texas, where he is buried.

Children of William Seymour Barrett and Loula Gracie McDonald

5. **Beulah Barrett** was born 2 January 1890 and died 19 October 1891 in Madison County.

5. **Sallie Barrett** was born 19 December 1891 in Madison, married C. A. Loughridge in 1909, and died on 21 June 1975 in Ardmore, Carter, Oklahoma.

Their child was:

Clemmons Asbury Loughridge

5. **Clemmons Carmon Barrett** was born 24 September 1895 in Madison County, and on 3 July 1923 in Sweetwater, Nolan, Texas, married Lora Francis Carwile, who was born 11 April 1900 in Gorman, Texas. She died 4 October 1949 in Crane, Texas; he, that same year in Odessa, where they are buried.

Their three children were:

Margaret Faye Barrett
Dorothy Elaine Barrett
Peggy Diane Barrett

5. **Della Barrett** was born 19 April 1898 and died 5 February 1986 in Madison County.

Children of William Seymour Barrett and Maud Wright Randolph

5. **Eldra Barrett** was born 18 April 1900 in Madison, and married Ira Telotte, who was born in San Antonio. Her second husband was Jack Smith and her third, Buster Stitts. She died 12 January 1979 in the county of her birth.

The child of Ira and Eldra Telotte was:

Dorothy Helen Telotte

5. **Henry Hugh Barrett** was born 6 January and died 29 May in 1902 in Madison County.

5. **Velma Barrett** was born 18 September 1903 in Lufkin, Texas, and married Corbett Cretsinger on 26 November 1964.

5. **Oce Mae Barrett** was born 22 November 1905 in Nacogdoches, Texas, and on 26 May 1929, married George Herman Bierschwale.

Their three children were:

George Eugene Bierschwale
Velma Ruth Bierschwale
William Ray Bierschwale

Children of John I. Barrett and Minnie Cook

5. **Tommie Mae Barrett** was born in November 1897, and died 26 February 1907 in New Mexico.

5. **Fannie Florence May Barrett** was born after 1900 in New Mexico, where she married Leon Henderson.

Child of Jim Jones and Florence Barrett

5. **Ercel Jones** was born about 1894 in Walker County, Texas, and married A. Carl Straley, who died 7 September 1976 in Lubbock, Texas.

Their child was:

A. Carl Straley Jr.

Children of Johnston Tolephus Barrett and Ariah Carolyn Adams
Born in Madison County, Texas

5. **Eddie C. Barrett** was born 6 September 1897 and died 29 November 1898.

5. **William Talmage Barrett** was born 20 September 1899, married Louise Elizabeth Battiss on 29 November 1928, and died 14 January 1970.

Their four children were:

Ellwood Talmage Barrett
Melvin Harold Barrett
Carolyn Louise Barrett
Ariebeth Alma Barrett

5. **Lizzie Florence Barrett** was born 24 November 1900 in Madison and married Lee Worsham and a Mr. Wolf.

5. **William Robert Barrett** was born 27 February 1904 in Madison County, and married Elma Blanche Henley on

29 December 1926 in Harris County. He died 4 August 1976 and was buried in Giddings, Texas.

Their five children were:
Billie Jean Barrett
Ollie Dean Barrett
Robert Johnson Barrett
Glenda Ann Barrett
Linda Jo Barrett

5. **Arie Lena Barrett** was born 29 March 1905 in Madison and married Jason Floyd.

5. **Jake Herring Barrett** was born 3 June 1906 and married Edna Pearl Carroll, born about 1906. They died in Houston: he, 7 August 1961; she, 5 February 1974, and are buried in Madisonville.

Their two children were:
Doris Barrett
Martha Barrett

5. **Johnston Tolephus Barrett Jr.** was born 30 May 1908 and died 14 January 1970 in Midway, Madison, Texas.

5. **Martha Barrett** was born 16 February 1910.

5. **George T. Barrett** was born 6 May 1912 in Madison County, and married a Miss Baxley and Lucille Schatte.

5. **Alvis C. Barrett** was born 12 December 1914 in Normagee, Madison, Texas, and died 16 June 1933 in that county.

5. **Mack Bennett Barrett** was born 12 February 1916 in Normagee and died 9 April 1971. He married Vertie Mae Wilson.

Their child was:
Avalon Bennett Barrett

5. **Bracil C. Barrett** was born 21 January 1919 in Normangee, and married Glenda Jo Ward in 1954. They divorced.

Their two children were:
Patrick Talmage Barrett
Brenda Ann Barrett

Children of Hugh Hayes Barrett and Virginia Isabel Runnels

5. **Hugh Hays Barrett Jr.** was born 30 October 1902 in Madison, and married Mary Jones on 24 December 1924 in Huntsville. She was born 4 October 1905 in Oletha, Limestone, Texas. The couple died in Madison County: he, 25 September 1974; she, 24 August 1980. They were buried in Madisonville.

Their two children were:
Mary Jo Barrett
Juanita Kathryn Barrett

5. **Lora Minnie Barrett** was born 12 April 1905 in Madison, and married Augastachn Prasatik on 2 June 1936.

Their two children were:
Virginia Ann Prasatik
Thomas Barrett Prasatik

5. **Ottie Eugene Barrett** was born 25 February 1908 in Madisonville. On 2 June 1936 in Huntsville he married Annevieve Fraser, who was born 21 September 1909, and died in 1936. Ottie died in Huntsville 22 February 1956 and is buried in Oakwood Cemetery.

Their four children were:
Ottie Eugene Barrett Jr.
Joan Kathleen Barrett
Jane Ann Barrett
Mary Elizabeth Barrett

5. **John Lee Barrett** was born 19 January 1911 in Madison and on 12 January 1928 married Jocie Martha Winborn, who was born 1 January 1912. He died 25 March 1988 and is buried in Madisonville.

Their two children were:
John Lee Barrett Jr.
Male Barrett

5. **Mary Lizzie Barrett** was born 16 October 1912, died 18 June the following year, and was buried in Madisonville.

5. **William Robert Barrett** was born 25 September 1914 in Madison, and married Harriett Reggio in La Marque,

Texas. His second wife was Anne Mae Brazelton.

The two children of William Robert Barrett and Harriett Reggio were:

Barbara Barrett

William Robert Barrett Jr.

The two children of William Robert Barrett and Annie Mae Brazelton were:

Hugh Hays Barrett

Charlene Barrett

5. **H. Richard Barrett** was born in 1915.

Child of Thomas Nathaniel Bobo

5. **Albert Roy Bobo**, born in 1911 in Texas.

Children of James Littleton McCan and Sarah Ida Dickey

5. **Maggie L. McCan** was born 7 December 1891, died 23 February 1892 in Leon County, and is buried in Pleasant Grove Cemetery.

5. **Clemmie McCan** was born 21 November 1894 in Rosebud, Milam, Texas, and married Dan Frazier, Charles Meyers, Jimmie Wood, and O. L. Shadoan. She died in Corpus Christi, Texas.

5. **James Matthew McCan** was born 6 February 1897 in Leon County and died in 1954. His first wife was Laverne Palen; his second, Agnes.

5. **Georgia McCan** was born in August 1899, died in 1902, and was buried in Pleasant Grove, Leon County.

5. **Kenneth Kyle McCan** was born 14 December 1902 in Leon, and married Audrey Faye Hicks, Lorene Zastro, and Jean Fortson.

The child of Kenneth Kyle McCan and Audrey Faye Hicks was:

Douglas Glenn McCann

5. **Hallie McCan** was born in 1904, died about 1907, and was buried in Pleasant Grove Cemetery, Leon County.

5. **Ione Zefa McCan** was born 27 December 1907 in Leon, and married Carl Cranfield Dixon on 15 November 1924. He was born 25 March 1895 in Livingston, where he died 12 March 1981.

Their two children were:

Shirley Jane Dixon

James Ray Dixon

5. **Andrew Buron McCan** was born 11 August 1909 in Leon County, died 13 November 1925 in an oil refinery fire, and was buried in Hollywood Cemetery, Harris County, Texas.

5. **Carroll McCan** was born 25 March 1912, died 9 January 1919, and was buried in Oakwood Cemetery in Leon County.

5. **Connie Ford McCann** was born 4 December 1914 in Dickey, Leon, Texas, and, on 5 January 1938 married Leona Ellen Wilbeck, who was born 24 June 1914 in Pierce, Wharton, Texas. She died in January 1986 in El Campo and is buried in Garden of Memories Cemetery. His second wife was Sylvia Smith.

The two children of Connie Ford McCann and Leona Ellen Wilbeck were:

Karen Penelope McCann

Connie Michael McCann

5. **Mossie McCan** was born 8 November 1916 in Texas, and married Vincent Keith Bova.

Their four children were:

Donald Byron Bova

Joseph Keith Bova

Kenneth Paul Bova

Mark Robin Bova

Children of James Monroe Winborn and Hulda McCan

5. **Kenneth Edward Winborn** was born 6 March 1893, married Eral Morrison, and died in 1978.

Their child was:

Kenneth Edward Winborn Jr.

5. **James Ethel Winborn** was born 20 August 1895, married Lena Franke on 14 May 1919, and died 28 January 1978 in Madison County, Texas. She was born 10 September 1894 in Austin.

Their three children were:

Ethel Mae Winborn

Juanice Winborn

Irene Winborn

5. **John Winborn** was born about 1897 in Madison County.

5. **Minnie Gladys Winborn** was born 23 March 1898, married Harry Ford Brooks, and died 27 November 1979.

Their two children were:

Ford Lamar Brooks

Mildred Ellena Brooks

5. **Sarah Ross Winborn** was born 28 December 1902 in Madison County, and died 8 April 1947 in Houston.

5. **Amanda Winborn** was born 22 February 1905, and married Odell Robinson, born 31 December 1900 in Midway, Texas. He died 10 March 1972 in Madison County.

Their child was:

James William Robinson

Children of Samuel Wooldridge McCan and Alice Blanche Dickey

5. **Icely Aline McCann** was born 5 April 1902 in Leon County, and married Leonard Carl Travis in Coleman County.

Their three children were:

Don Forrest Travis

Wooldridge Leon Travis

Kenneth Carl Travis

5. **Lockie Blanche McCann** was born 20 October 1904, and married Thomas Oscar Lowe.

Their child was:

Hallie Blanche Lowe

5. **Miner Dickey McCann** was born 28 May 1907, and married Anne Willis.

Their two children were:

Richard McCann

Joel McCann

5. **Ed Sloan McCann** was born 8 December 1909 in Centerville, Texas, and on 10 November 1928 in George West, Texas, married Ann Mary Pohoresky, who was born 15 December 1908 in Dime Box, Texas. She died 13 April 1977 in Houston and was buried in Brookside Cemetery, Harris, Texas.

Their two children were:

Carl Preston McCann

Stacie Aliene McCann

5. **Donnell Earl McCann** was born 1 April 1912, and married Annie Nora Collins on 20 June 1934 in Conroe, Montgomery, Texas.

Their four children were:

Frances Earl McCann

Donnel Wayne McCann

Larry Wooldridge McCann

Sherry Lynn McCann

5. **Bell Field McCann** was born 31 October 1914, and on 21 November 1942 married Evelyn Francis Boehler, who was born on 10 September 1923.

Their three children were:

Madeline McCann

Bell Field McCann Jr.

Gary Lee McCann

5. **Janie Kate McCann** was born 13 September 1918, and on 10 May 1942 in Conroe, Texas married Roland William Ray, who was born on 7 July 1915 in Lubbock.

Their five children were:

Marlin Evans Ray

Roland Wooldridge Ray

Virgil Floyd Ray

Carolyn Gayle Ray

Robert Eugene Ray

Child of Kenneth Nathan McCan and Annie Bell Duncan

5. **Lottie Bell McCan** was born 29 November 1897, and married Wiley Byron Knight.
Their five children were:
>Alvis Byron Knight
>Frank Marshall Knight
>Roland Thomas Knight
>Mildred Ferolene Knight
>Wiley Byron Knight Jr.

Children of Eugene Henry Golden and Allie Angeline McCan

5. **Talitha Amanda Golden** was born 27 April 1900 in Madison County, and married William Harris on 19 April 1922 in Magnolia, Texas. He died in 1924. Later she married George W. Stowe, who was born in 1892 and died in 1971. She died 18 December 1944. All three were buried in Mt. Zion Cemetery, Montgomery County, Texas.
The two children of William Harris and Tabitha Amanda Golden were:
>Hazel Harris
>Juanita Harris

The three children of George W. Stowe and Tabitha Amanda Golden were:
>Harold E. Stowe
>Oddis Stowe
>Clyde Stowe

5. **Virgil Littleton Golden** was born 4 December 1901 in Madison County, and in January 1924 married Ethel Cronnin in Conroe, Texas. Virgil died on 17 June 1957 in Baytown; Ethel, in 1983.
Their four children were:
>Edward Golden
>Virgil Golden
>Olen Golden
>Ethel Byron Golden

5. **James Joseph Golden** was born 13 November 1903 in Spring, Harris County, and married Alice Dikeman on 6 September 1926 in Conroe, Texas.
Their five children were:
>Ann Golden
>Verla Golden
>Maxine Golden
>Marie Golden
>James Golden

5. **Sadie Mae Golden** was born 29 October 1905 in Middleton, Leon, Texas, and on 30 October 1921 in Conroe, married George Hartford Harper, who was born 8 July 1905 in Newton County, Texas.
Their five children were:
>Dorothy Lee Harper
>Sadie Inez Harper
>George Hartford Harper Jr.
>Allie Sonoma Harper
>Donald Raymond Harper

5. **Hulda Eugene Golden** was born 11 January 1908 in Middleton, Leon, Texas, and on 3 April 1926 in Conroe, Montgomery, Texas, married R. D. Blair, who was born 10 December 1902. She died 4 January 1972 in Houston; he, 21 November 1937 in Conroe.
Their five children were:
>Beatrice Blair
>Betty Blair
>Joyce Blair
>Jo Doris Blair
>John Morris Blair

5. **Annie Bell Golden** was born 9 August 1910 in Spring, Harris, Texas, and married Alton O. Simmons on 30 October 1926 in Conroe. Annie Bell died 29 September 1945 in Houston, and was buried in Mt. Zion Cemetery, Montgomery County.
Their six children were:

        Alton O. Simmons Jr.

        Timmie Jean Simmons

        Lawson Simmons

        Lucille Simmons

        Tommy Simmons

        Tobie Simmons

    5. **Connie Ola Golden** was born 29 November 1912 in Leon County, and married Charlie McGee, who was born 14 August 1902. She died on 19 March 1975; he, 4 January 1972. They were buried in Mt. Zion Cemetery.

    Their child was:

        Jerry McGee

    5. **Winnie Viola Golden** was born 4 February 1915 in Montgomery, and on 27 January 1931 in Conroe married Wilford Mason, who was born on 4 August 1913 in Ratcliff, Texas.

    Their three children were:

        Josephine Ruth Mason

        Edwin Earl Mason

        Raymond Leon Mason

    5. **Minnie Lucille Golden** was born 4 February 1915 and died in September the same year in Montgomery County, where she was buried in Mt. Zion Cemetery.

    5. **George Woodburn Golden** was born 8 April 1917 in Willow, Harris, Texas, died 8 February 1935 in Spring, Harris, Texas, and was buried in Mt. Zion Cemetery.

    5. **Effie Wynonia Golden** was born 8 May 1920 in Wilmont, Montgomery, Texas, and married Ernie S. Vacula.

Children of William Walter McCan and Alma McCree Rhodes

    5. **Kenneth Gale McCann** was born 2 August 1907 in Leon County, and married Anna Ruth Turner.

    Their four children were:

        Kenneth Gale McCann Jr.

        Gerald Wayne McCann

        Michael Turner McCann

        John Douglass McCann

    5. **Josephine McCan** was born about 1909 and married C. W. Stevens.

Children of John Reuben and Debra June Stowe McCann

    5. **Johnie Mae McCann** was born 20 November 1911 in Grapevine, Texas, and married on 12 May 1930, August Leo Martin, who was born 29 August 1900 in Arcadia, Oklahoma, and died 4 December 1978.

    Their six children were:

        Bonnie Jean Martin

        Frances Dorene Martin

        Marcus Leo Martin

        Otis Carl Martin

        Glenn Dale Martin

        Barbara Elaine Martin

    5. **Walter Stanley McCann** was born 23 March 1916, and married Dorothy Landers. His second marriage occurred on 22 December 1951 when he married Lois Virginia Davis Dollgener. She was born 23 July 1920.

    Their five children of Walter Stanley McCann and Dorothy Landers were:

        Shirley Jean McCann

        Leuna Frances McCann

        Patsy Jo McCann

        Betty Lou McCann

        Sandra Kay McCann

    The six children of Walter Stanley McCann and Lois Virginia Davis Dollgener were:

        Walter Stanley McCann Jr.

        Debra Lois McCann

        Donald Wayne McCann

        Robert Leon McCann

        Norman Lee McCann

Billy Eugene McCann

5. Claudia Irene McCann was born 12 March 1918 in Drumwright, Oklahoma, and on 2 July 1935 in Lewisville, Texas, married Walter Jackson Malone, who was born 8 March 1914 in Wharton, Texas, and died 19 March 1979 in Dallas.

Their seven children were:

James Arthur Malone

Joy Ruth Malone

Walter Jackson Malone Jr.

Thomas Allen Malone

Lawrence Duane Malone

Larry Gene Malone

Gary Wayne Malone

5. Edgar Kahle McCan was born 20 May 1920 in Drumwright, Oklahoma, married Mildred Bennett, and died in 1971. They had three children.

5. Charles Keith McCann was born 20 May 1920 in Drumwright, Oklahoma, and married Elsie Mae Bennett. His second wife was Carol Joyce Sharp, and his third, Buena Lorene Hayhurst.

The child of Charles Keith McCann and Elsie Mae Bennett was:

Pat McCann

The child of Charles Keith McCann and Carol Joyce Sharp was:

Sharon Annette McCann

The child of Charles Keith McCann and Buena Lorene Hayhurst was:

Charlotte Lorene McCann

5. Mildred Louise McCann was born 2 April 1923 and married R. C. Newton. With three children, they lived in California.

5. Hettie Vernal McCann was born 10 April 1926 in Drumwright, Oklahoma, and married Charles Shelby Gibson. Her second marriage was to Wilmot Augustus Sowers.

The six children of Charles Shelby Gibson and Hettie Vernal McCann were:

Charles Wayne Gibson

Jerry Lee Gibson

John Tillman Gibson

Carla Mae Gibson

Linda Kay Gibson

Randy Paul Gibson

5. Harold Floyd McCann was born 20 December 1927 in Drumwright, Oklahoma, and on 4 July 1949 married Shirley Faye Rogers. On 23 October 1963 he married Sherry Jean Cowherd.

The three children of Harold Floyd McCann and Shirley Faye Rogers were:

Patricia Ann McCann

Deborah Lynn McCann

Danny Floyd McCann

The two children of Harold Floyd McCann and Sherry Jean Cowherd were:

Kathy Jean McCann

Lori Jane McCann

5. Darrell Lloyd McCann was born 20 December 1927 in Drumwright, Oklahoma, and married Dixie Nadine Whisenant, who was born in 1933 in Buda, Texas.

Their three children were:

Elizabeth Gaye McCann

Ronald Allen McCann

Steven Eugene McCann

Children of John Reuben McCan and Rosa Lynch

5. Franklin McCan

5. James Earl McCann

5. Charles Edward McCann was born 28 December 1940, and married Mae Bell Newton.

5. Paul McCann

Children of Benjamin Monroe McCann and Maggie E. Stowe

5. **James Elmer McCann** was born 22 September 1913 in Lewisville, Texas, and died 4 October 1913.

5. **Lola Faye McCann** was born 11 July 1915, and on 15 June 1940 married Leonard Ray Tracy, who died 14 July 1954 in Snyder, Texas. Her second husband was a Mr. Spayd.

The four children of Leonard Ray Tracy and Lola Faye McCann were:

      Mary Elizabeth Tracy
      Donald Ray Tracy
      Margaret Ellen Tracy
      Howard Eugene Tracy

5. **Charles Edgar McCann** was born 22 December 1917, and married Maurine Bookout, who died in January 1950 in California.

Their three children were:

      Edward Lee McCann
      Ronald Carl McCann
      Linda Jean McCann

5. **Martha Bessie McCann** was born 8 April 1920, and in March 1944 married Clinton Oliver Turner, who died in 1958. In 1962 she married Herb Needham.

The five children of Clinton Oliver Turner and Martha Bessie McCann were:

      Janice Marie Turner
      Carolyn Turner
      Frederick Benjamin Turner
      Clinton Oliver Turner Jr.
      Peggy Turner

5. **Viola Mae McCann** was born 7 January 1923, and married John LeRoy Thompson, who died 12 December 1981 in Idaho.

Their five children were:

      Mary Jo Thompson
      Denny LeRoy Thompson
      John Thompson
      Oila Louise Thompson
      James Thompson

5. **Amanda Elizabeth McCann** was born 22 February 1925, and on 26 February 1943 married Jesse Benjamin Tabler.

Their five children were:

      Barbara Elaine Tabler
      Charles Monroe Tabler
      Russell Lee Tabler
      Richard Albert Tabler
      Sandra Kay Tabler

5. **Earl David McCann** was born 10 May and died 19 October in 1927.

5. **Benny Star McCann** was born 21 January 1930, and married Joyce Smith.

Their four children were:

      Cheryl Ann McCann
      David Earl McCann
      John Fitzgerald McCann
      Benjamin Monroe McCann

5. **Bobby Gene McCann** was born 23 March 1932 and died 8 October 1932.

5. **Bluford Wesley McCann** was born 21 July 1933, and married Bonnie Minnie.

Their four children were:

      Doyle Ray McCann
      Judy McCann
      Tracy Ellen McCann
      Darrell Wayne McCann

Children of Hartwell Hale and Hettie M. McCann

5. **Marvin Hale** was born in 1910 and died in 1918.

5. **Annie Mae Hale** was born in 1913 in Madison County, Texas, married James A. Turpin, and died before 1983. Their three children were:

James Hartwell Turpin

Barbara Ann Turpin

John Turpin

5. **Ruby Jewell Hale**

5. **Jack Carl Hale** was born 8 June 1916, and married first, Margaret Winter, and later, Helen Briggs. The two children of Jack Carl Hale and Margaret Winter were:

Robin Arnold Hale

Shirley Jean Hale

Children of William Anthony Barrett and Annie Seales

5. **Lena Estelle Barrett** was born 19 November 1904 in Madison County, and married a Mr. Black.

5. **Ora Gertrude Barrett** was born 7 March 1907 in Madison, and married Zaney Gunn.

5. **James Luther Barrett** was born 24 June 1908 in Madison and died before 1983.

5. **Ida Pearl Barrett** was born 16 October 1909 in Madison and died before 1983.

5. **Annie Laura Barrett** was born 14 March 1911 in Madison, and married James Hopkins.

5. **Glenn Andrew Barrett** was born 6 February 1913 in Madison, and married Pauline Bowen. Their children were:

Glen Law Barrett

Raymond Lee Barrett

Betty Jean Barrett

Glenne Ruth Barrett

5. **Wilbert Barrett**, born 16 November 1915.

5. **William Ernest Barrett** was born 27 June 1918. His wife died 21 November 1981.

5. **Mildred Barrett** was born 24 June 1921.

5. **Bessie Barrett** was born 25 January 1924 in Madison County.

Child of Conrad Barrett and Lillie Bell Douglas

5. **Alma Crystal Barrett** was born 22 July 1912 in Madison County, Texas.

Children of Robert K. Barrett and Mattie Pearl Seales
Born in Madison County, Texas

5. **Vivian Claud Barrett** was born 21 September 1913 and died 10 January 1976. He married Mina Jewell Vaughn.

Their two children were:

Charles Robert Barrett

Robert Ray Barrett

5. **Margie Katherine Barrett** was born 20 June 1926.

5. **Robert K. Barrett Jr.** was born 22 August 1928.

Children of Roscoe Wiley Barrett and Lullie Cook
Born in Madison County, Texas

5. **Roland D. Barrett** was born 14 October 1912. He married Beatrice Little. Their child was:

David Earl Barrett

5. **Rueal Barrett** was born 30 December 1920.

Child of Roy Franklin Barrett and Tom Nolie Cravy

5. **Thelma Barrett**

Children of James Walter Barrett and Eldra Randolph
Born in Madison County, Texas

5. **Essie Eula Barrett** was born 21 December 1901.

5. **J. C. Barrett** was born on 15 September 1905 and died the same day.

5. **Lee Roy Barrett** on 17 August 1911 and died 19 September 1959.

Children of Samuel Shepherd Barrett and Bertha Ohlenberger

5. **Vera Lee Barrett**, who married Jack Smith. They lived in Huntsville, Texas. Her second husband was a Mr. Duke.

The three children of Jack Smith and Vera Lee Barrett were:

       Jack Smith Jr.

       Bertha Smith

       James Smith

5. **Florence Barrett**

5. **James Barrett**

Children of Samuel Shepherd Barrett and Edith Hill Davis

5. **Mildred Barrett**

5. **Alice Barrett**, who married a Mr. Carter.

5. **Ava Rae Barrett**

5. **John Barrett**

Children of Hubert Redding Barrett and Maggie Louanna Allphin

5. **John Wallace Barrett** was born 17 April 1908, died 3 December 1909, and was buried in McAdams Cemetery, Huntsville, Texas.

5. **Mattie Addie Barrett** was born 4 August 1909 in Walker County, and on 11 August 1928 in Midway, Madison, Texas, married Louis B. Starns, who was born 9 February 1909. He died 29 November 1973 and was buried in Midway.

Their three children were:

       Mary Alice Starns

       Margaret Ann Starns

       Hazel Louise Starns

5. **Hugh Roland Barrett** was born 14 June 1910 in Walker County, and on 1 October 1933 in Huntsville married Myrtle Lillie Bennett, who was born 11 June 1908 in Katy, Harris, Texas. She died in Houston 9 February 1981 and was buried in Huntsville.

Their five children were:

       Nancy Arlene Barrett

       Gerald Elmer Barrett

       Donald J. Barrett

       Hugh Redding Barrett

       Theda Rae Barrett

5. **Marion Otis Barrett** was born 17 January 1913 in Walker County, and married Delma Lee Walls.

Their six children were:

       Marion Otis Barrett Jr.

       Lou Ann Walls Barrett

       John Marion Barrett

       Lee Bruce Barrett

       Rita Gail Barrett

       Rhonda Elaine Barrett

5. **Ora Ina Barrett** was born 15 October 1917.

5. **Henry Allphin Barrett** was born 9 February 1918, and married Bobbie Marigold and Ruby Wilson. He died 7 June 1973 and was buried in McAdams Cemetery, Huntsville, Walker, Texas.

The child of Henry Allphin Barrett and Bobbie Marigold was:

       Barbara Barrett

The three children of Henry Allphin Barrett and Ruby Wilson were:

       Karen Lee Barrett

       Linda Kay Barrett

       Monte Burton Barrett

5. **Altha Mae Barrett** was born 12 March 1920 in Walker County, and married Burl Thomas Johnston on 25 July 1946.

Their child was:

Burl Thomas Johnston

5. **Bobbie O'Nell Barrett**, who married Winston Baines Jolly.

5. **Roy Barrett** was born 3 November 1924 in Walker County, and on 30 December 1948 married Evelyn Roland, who was born 8 August 1921 in Blairo, Virginia.

5. **Billie Joe Barrett** was born 6 May 1927 in Madison County, and on 1 January 1958 married James H. Gray, who was born 16 February 1932. Her second husband was a Mr. McDonald.

The two children of James H. Gray and Billie Joe Barrett were:

James Robert Alexander Gray

Patricia Ann Gray

The two children of Mr. McDonald and Billie Joe Barrett were:

Seth Tracy McDonald

Mason Everett McDonald

Children of William Joseph Barrett and Alice Lynch

5. **Louie Monroe Barrett** was born 12 November 1907 in El Campo, and married Hattie Louise Furlow on 14 December 1929 in Dallas. He was born 19 November 1909 in Kenedy, Texas, and died 24 March 1964 in Ft. Worth.

Their four children were:

Andrienne Louise Barrett

Andre Barrett

Donald Louis Barrett

Ronald Monroe Barrett

5. **Marion Lynch Barrett** was born 19 April 1911 in Wharton, Texas, and married Bessie Lee Wells, born 3 November 1908.

Their two children were:

Joe Bruce Barrett

Carolyn Barrett

Children of Guy Roland Barrett and Edna Hines

5. **Gayle Barrett**

5. **Vernon Barrett**, who married Rachael Simington.

Their child was:

Maurice Barrett

5. **Blanche Barrett** was born in 1914, died in 1919, and was buried in McAdams Cemetery, Huntsville.

5. **Bernice Barrett**, who married a Mr. Powers.

5. **Guy Roland Barrett Jr.**

5. **John Barrett**

Children of George Oscar Faulkner and Minnie Ora Barrett

5. **Iola Mae Faulkner** was born 10 November 1901 in Madison County, Texas, and married first, Lawrence Parker Young, and later, Jack Spangler. She died 12 July 1967.

The child of Lawrence Parker Young and Iola Mae Faulkner was:

Lawrence Perry Young

5. **Leo Faulkner** was born in 1902 in Madison County.

Children of John O. Lloyd and Maude Elizabeth Barrett

5. **Elmer Lloyd**

5. **Lois Lloyd**

Children of James David Barrett and Della Ilene Lloyd

5. **James Ray Barrett** was born 16 July 1911 in Houston, and married Emma Ardel Collins on 18 May 1930 in Lake Charles, Louisiana. She was born 20 October 1914 in Orange, Texas. They died in Houston: he, 30 July 1979; she, 20 March 1974, and were buried in Woodlawn Cemetery, Harris County.

Their child was:

James Ray Barrett Jr.

5. **Lloyd Barrett** was born 6 February 1914 in Houston, where he married on 14 September 1935 Catherine Delbert Haley, who was born on 30 January 1917 in Hot Springs, Arkansas. She died 6 November 1992 in Houston.

Their three children were:

Lloyd Frederick Barrett

James Bruce Barrett

David Lee Barrett

5. **Sara Helen Barrett** was born 21 December 1922 in Houston, where she married on 24 December 1941 Kenneth Ray Batson, who was born 8 January 1922 in Oklahoma. They died in Houston: Sara Helen, 27 October 1974; Kenneth Ray, 3 November 1972. Both were buried in Woodlawn Cemetery.

Their child was:

Kenneth Ray Batson Jr.

Children of Henry Clay Wright and Mollie Conner Barrett

5. **Henry Clay Wright Jr.** was born 20 June 1921, and married Cory Ann Snowdon and Dorothy Lee Holmes McCary.

The two children of Henry Clay and Cory Ann Wright were:

Matisa Ann Wright

Michael Clay Wright

5. **Jack Ledford Wright** was born 30 December 1923, and married Alney Dora Sheldon.

Their two children were:

Philip Henry Wright

Mollie Frances Wright

Children of Matthew Sidney Clark and Martha Alice Barrett

5. **Elsie Dell Clark** was born 24 March 1915, and married Paul Suttles Willingham on 18 January 1942.

Their two children were:

Clark Suttles Willingham

Beverly Sue Willingham

5. **Martha Sidney Clark** was born 10 December 1918, married Willis William Armistead on 17 September 1938, and died 21 June 1964.

Their three children were:

Willis William Armistead Jr.

Jack Murray Armistead

Sidney Merrill Armistead

5. **William Sidney Clark** was born 15 November 1920, and on 3 January 1953 married Margaret Johana Read.

Their child was:

William Sidney Clark Jr.

Children of John Iredell Manning and Prudence Polk

5. **Florence Manning**

5. **Jewell Ona Manning** was born on 11 January 1909, and married William Hayes Rhodes, who was born on 27 April 1910 and died 12 November 1970.

5. **Melvin Idie Manning** was born 11 August 1907, died 30 July 1983, and married Decy Ozelle Taylor, born 8 September 1908 and died 19 November 1930.

Their five children were:

Joyce Rae Manning

Billie Earlene Manning

Lloyd Melvin Manning

James Buchannan Manning

Ruby Aileen Manning

5. **Billy Boy Manning** was born on 5 January 1915, and married Robbie Orine Rhodes on 25 June 1938.

Their three children were:

Charles Ira Manning

Harold Elwin Manning

Lanell Manning

Children of Benjamin Franklin Manning and Maude Bell Barrett

5. **Anna Mae Manning**, born 19 February 1910 in Carlisle, Trinity, Texas.

5. **Ruby Elizabeth Manning** was born on 19 December 1912 in Madison County, Texas, married Archie Jordy, and died on 8 December 1997 in Houston. He was born on 25 July 1908 and died 20 October 1956.

Their five children were:

Bennie Martin Jordy
Donald Irwin Jordy
Mildred Arlene Jordy
Luthur Hilton Jordy
Luke Milton Jordy

5. **Sadie Augusta Manning** was born 21 October 1915, and married Currie Atmal Skains on 21 June 1934.

Their five children were:

Shirley Anita Skains
Billie Atmal Skains
Mary Alice Skains
Joyce Adell Skains
Edward Allen Skains

5. **Lilla Juanita Manning** was born on 2 November 1918 in Ballinger, Texas, married Elmer Leon Williams on 19 December 1937, and died on 12 January 1985 in Galveston, Texas.

Their two children were:

Wanda Williams
Virginia Belle Williams

Children of William R. Anthony and Exa Buchannon Manning

5. **Donald Manning Anthony**

5. **L. B. Anthony**, who married a Miss Moore.

Children of Silas Clarence Barrett and Lucye Elizabeth Brooks

5. **Clarence Brooks Barrett** was born 14 August 1912 in Madison County, and married Louise Burnch on 2 December 1936. They divorced, and on 26 July 1948 he married Mildred Lyons and died in March 1975.

The child of Clarence Brooks Barrett and Louise Burnch was:

Sandra Louise Barrett

5. **Vera Fay Barrett** was born 20 December 1914 in Madison, and on 19 February 1936 married Roland Pitts, who was born 4 July 1903.

Their three children were:

Gwendolyn Pitts
Wanda Janell Pitts
Milton Eugene Pitts

Children of Joseph Nicholas Farber and Lela Kate Harmon
Born in Elmore City, Oklahoma

5. **Avery Farber** was born on 22 March 1906 and died on 21 April 1906.

5. **Benjamin Oscar Farber** was born 29 May 1907, married May Harrison in 1956, and died in McAlister, Oklahoma, 23 August 1975.

5. **Thomas Jefferson Farber** was born on 14 November 1909 and died 29 October 1910.

5. **Laverne Farber** was born on 5 October 1911, married Frank Owen Romine on 27 August 1927, and died 29 January 1985 in El Paso, Texas. Frank was born on 23 June 1910 and died 29 December 1989 in Dallas.

Their five children were:

Herman Oliver Romine
Billy O. Romine
Karl Anton Romine
Lela Eulene Romine
Patrick Ray Romine

5. **James Edward Farber** was born 23 June 1914, married Virginia Hale in December 1934, and died on 4

September 1975 in Glendale, California.

    5. **Josephine Nick Farber** was born 12 April 1917, and married Hassell Harvey 4 June 1939.

    5. **Clyde Grant Farber** was born 28 November 1919, and married Clara Faye Thompson 18 January 1941.

Their child was:

        J. W. Farber

    5. **Claud Lee Farber** was born 31 August 1931 and died in the North Sea on 15 November 1943.

    5. **Mary Louise Farber** was born on 6 May 1925, and married Arthur C. Jones in December 1940.

Their child was:

        Donna Faye Jones

Child of Joseph Clarence Camburn and Bess J. Coburn

    5. **Clarence Camburn** was born 21 January 1911 in Bear Creek, Texas, and married Fern Elsworth on 6 November 1934. He died 15 November 1981 in Duncan, Arizona.

Their child was:

        Marjorie Camburn

Child of Ada Bell McCreary

    5. **Doris McCreary**, who married a Mr. McKee.

EIGHTH GENERATION

Children of William Richard Morgan and Mattie Cornelia Barrett

    6. **Richard Daniel Morgan** was born 1 April 1906 in Antlers, Oklahoma, and died 20 July 1918 in Gillam, Arkansas, where he was buried.

    6. **Orval V. Morgan** was born 9 February 1908 in Antlers, and married Leona Lemons.

    6. **Etta Maud Morgan** was born 11 April 1910 in Gillam, Arkansas, and in Broken Bow, McCurtain, Oklahoma, married Bill McKeever. She died 15 July 1973 in Broken Bow, and was buried in Gillam.

    6. **Clyde Aaron Morgan** was born 25 February 1912 in Gillam, and in August 1932 married Lois Wilson in Antlers.

    6. **Ima G. Morgan** was born 20 July 1914 in Gillam, and in 1929 married Leonard Speaks in Antlers.

    6. **Oma G. Morgan** was born 14 November 1919 in Gillam, and married Raymond Splawn on 11 November 1939 in Hugo, Oklahoma.

    6. **Rose Lee Morgan** was born 31 July 1922 in Eagletown, McCurtain, Oklahoma, and married Dink Burgess on 27 December 1937 in Antlers.

Child of Bud Plumley and Ida Lee Barrett

    6. **Lee Plumley**, who married Mr. Lane

Children of Dell Wilson and Nevada Ethyl Barrett

6. **Delbert Wilson**

6. **Darlene Wilson**

Children of Edgar Lee Barrett and Mable Sands

6. **Homer Lee Barrett**, who married Ruby Ellen.

Their four children were:

        Lee Barrett

        Janice Barrett

        Jimmy Barrett

        Leon Barrett

6. **Frieda Adel Barrett**, who married Roy Weidel and Troy Cummings.

The child of Frieda Adel Barrett and Roy Weidel was:

        Royceanne Weidel

The child of Frieda Adel Barrett and Troy Cummings was:

        Ronnie Lee Cummings

6. **Jearldene Barrett** married Earnest Herman Cummings.

Their two children were:

William B. Moore Jr.

Patricia Kay Cummings
Karen Cummings
6. **Jewell Edward Barrett**, who married Linda.
Their two children were:
Julie Barrett
John Daniel Barrett

Children of John William Barrett and Cleo Ferrell

6. **Christine Barrett**
6. **Billie Barrett**

Children of Julius Marion Barrett and Ellen Johnson

6. **Marion Barrett**
6. **Helen Barrett**

Children of Steven Robert Barrett and Mary Matilda Ferrell

6. **Earl M. Barrett**
6. **Maddie Barrett** was born in April 1905 in Texas, and married Earl McCaffety.
Their six children were:
Bob McCaffety
Marie McCaffety
Earl McCaffety Jr.
Johnnie Mae McCaffety
Eugene McCaffety
Mary Beth McCaffety

Children of William John Barrett and Lois Elizabeth Hosier

6. **Lula Barrett** was born 24 January 1915 in Houston, married W. T. Parker Jr. in Midway, Madison County, in 1931, where she died on 24 August 1933.
6. **Robert Dan Barrett** was born 22 October 1918 in Houston, married Fannie Mae Johnson in Trinity, Texas, in January 1940, and died on 15 June 1950 in Freeport, Texas.
Their three children were:
Robert Wayne Barrett
David Roscoe Barrett
Ronald Troy Barrett
6. **Louie Franklin Barrett** was born 6 August 1921 in Weldon, Houston, Texas, married Alice Mae Gerston in September 1940 in Marlin, and died 24 October 1987 in Silsbee, Texas, where he was buried.
Their four children were:
Katherine Louise Barrett
Billy Ray Barrett
Evelyn Marie Barrett
Bobbie Jean Barrett
6. **Mary Evelyn Barrett** was born 3 April 1924 in Madison County, and in 1948 married Arthur A. Sullivan in Houston.
Their three children were:
Dan Arthur Sullivan
Sandra D. Sullivan
James Vick Sullivan
6. **Lottie Mae Barrett** was born 14 October 1926 in Midway, and married Robert Earl Guynes on 18 November 1944 in Houston.
Their four children were:
Robert Guynes
Linda Guynes
John Guynes
Larry Wayne Guynes

6. **Steve William Barrett** was born 16 October 1929 in Midway, and married Syble Yates in June 1947 in Trinity. Their three children were:

> Wanda Lourine Barrett
> Steve William Barrett Jr.
> Clarence Randall Barrett

6. **James Paul Barrett** was born 12 February 1933 in Midway, and married Helen Coles on 13 August 1955 in Beaumont.

Their five children were:

> Mary Elaine Barrett
> Paul Ray Barrett
> Lois Norene Barrett
> John Louis Barrett
> James David Barrett

6. **John Ferrell Barrett** was born 18 January 1941 in Stafford, Fort Bend, Texas, and died 22 December 1959 in Silsbee.

Children of John Carl William and Hattie Lee Barrett

6. **Steve Jethro William** was born 22 October 1905 in Elwood, Madison County, where in October 1923, he married Artie Lenord, and died on 5 December 1963 in Galveston.

6. **Mary Jane William** was born 21 November 1910 in Madison, and on 19 September 1928 in Midway married John I. Lenord, who died in 1962.

Their child was:

> John I. Lenord Jr.

6. **Dolly Mae William** was born 1 November 1916 in Madison, and married Dick Strickland, who was born 28 April 1921 and died 16 July 1983.

6. **Johnny William** was born 21 November 1920 in Madison and died in 1984 in Texas.

6. **Steven William Vetuski** was born 2 January 1911 in New Waverly, Walker, Texas, and married Sally Coleman. Later he married on 31 August 1937 in Huntsville, Walker County, Ruby Marie Weaver, who was born 10 April 1909 in Austin. Steven William died 22 March 1973 in Houston, where he was buried.

6. **Lee Tensley Vetuski** was born 4 March 1913 in New Waverly, and married Ethel Woods on 23 January 1932 in Madison County, where she was born on 30 December 1910. They died in Madison County: he, 19 August 1986; she, 3 May 1991. She was buried in Midway.

Their three children were:

> James Lee Vetuski
> Billie June Vetuski
> Mitchell Lewis Vetuski Jr.

6. **Lottie Odell Vetuski** was born 16 November 1915 in New Waverly, Walker, Texas, and on 31 December 1952 in Rosenburg, Fort Bend, Texas, married Gregory Columbus Forrester,. She subsequently married John Ackerman, and John Fritz. The latter was born 23 June 1912 in Philadelphia, Pennsylvania, and died 21 August 1974 in Houston.

The child of Lottie Odell and Gregory Columbus was:

> Leroy Forrester

The child of John and Lottie Odell was:

> Donald Ackerman

The two children of John Fitz and Lottie Odell were:

> Twins Fitz

6. **Harold Eugene Vetuski** was born 31 October 1917 in Madison, married Denna Twain, died 9 October 1957 in Houston, and was buried there.

Their child was:

> Sandra Anna Vetuski

6. **Woodrow Felix Vetuski** was born 4 August 1919 in Madison, married Millie Lorrine Higgs, who was born 27 July 1930. He later married a Mrs. Higgans and died on 26 January 1975 in Houston.

The five children of Woodrow Felix Vetuski and Millie Lorrine Higgs were:

> Michael Vetuski
> Walter Wayne Vetuski
> Adonna Rose Vetuski

Paul Mark Vetuski

Denise Carol Vetuski

The child of Woodrow Felix Vetuski and Mrs. Higgans was:

Rayford Vetuski

6. **Edward Lewis Vetuski** was born 15 October 1921 in Madison, and on 29 December 1951 in Chapel Hill, Washington, Texas, married Eva Krolezyk, who was born there on 25 October 1922. They died in Houston: he, 3 August 1987; she, 6 June 1970.

Their child was:

Frankie Lucille Vetuski

6. **Mitchell Glenn Vetuski** was born 12 November 1922 in Madison County, and on 20 February 1943 in Spokane, Washington, married Alice Mary Wassem, who was born 7 January 1920 in Clarkston, Asotin, Washington. He died 14 April 1965 in Glendale, Maricopa, Arizona, and was buried in Houston.

Their four children were:

Rena Lucille Vetuski

Mitchell Glenn Vetuski Jr.

Michael Lynn Vetuski

Millicent Helaine Vetuski

6. **Mary Francis Vetuski** was born 16 February 1925 in Madison County, Texas, and married Tom Ford.

Their child was:

Laveral Ford

Child of C. A. Loughridge and Sallie Barrett

6. **Clemmons Asbury Loughridge** was born 15 September 1918, and married Olga.

Their child was:

Richard Loughridge

Children of Clemmons Carmon Barrett and Lora Francis Carwile

6. **Margaret Faye Barrett** was born 13 May 1925 in Ranger, Eastland, Texas, and on 19 November 1944 in McCamey, Upton, Texas, married Lonzo Quitman Rudicil, who was born 19 June 1922 in Big Spring, Howard, Texas. He died there 6 May 1974, after which she married Paul Ervin Gathings. Margaret Fay was accepted for membership by The Daughters of the Republic of Texas.

The three children of Lonzo Quitman Rudicil and Margaret Faye Barrett were:

Margaret Kaye Rudicil

Wanda Carol Rudicil

Brenda Diane Rudicil

6. **Dorothy Elaine Barrett**

6. **Peggy Diane Barrett**

Child of Ira Telotte and Eldra Barrett

6. **Dorothy Helen Telotte** was born 21 January 1920 in San Antonio, and on 2 June 1944 married Fred A. Beer, who was born 1 August 1922 in St. Paul, Minnesota.

Their two children were:

Fred A. J. Beer

Shelly Ann Beer

Children of George Herman and Oce Mae Barrett Bierschwale

6. **George Eugene Bierschwale** was born in 1930.

6. **Velma Ruth Bierschwale** was born in 1932, and married Lawrence Long.

6. **William Ray Bierschwale** was born in 1936, and married Glenda Gail.

Their three children were:

Charles Randolph Bierschwale

William Ray Bierschwale Jr.

George Glenn Bierschwale

Child of A. Carl Straley and Ercel Jones

6. **A. Carl Straley Jr.** was born about 1925 and died in 1960. He had two daughters.

Children of William Talmage Barrett and Louise Elizabeth Battiss

6. **Ellwood Talmage Barrett** was born 14 September 1930 in Houston, and on 3 July 1952 in Madison County married Ennis Marie Whitley, who was born there on 14 November 1932.

Their two children were:
Ellie Marie Barrett
Ellwood Talmage Barrett Jr.

6. **Melvin Harold Barrett**, who married Gayle Gordon Rhea.

Their four children were:
Tammy Ann Barrett
Tina Louis Barrett
William Harold Barrett
Raymond Basye Barrett

6. **Carolyn Louise Barrett**, who married Joel D. Guedry.

Their child was:
Mark Dean Guedry

6. **Ariebeth Alma Barrett** married Harry Atwood Stanley II on 14 June 1958. He was born 16 August 1936 and died 17 March 1959. Following his death she married Ronald E. Bott.

The child of Harry Atwood and Aribeth Standley was:
Harry Atwood Stanley III

The child of Ronald E. and Aribeth Bott was:
Ronald Creston Bott

Children of William Robert Barrett and Elma Blanche Henley

6. **Billie Jean Barrett** was born 21 December 1927 in Houston, and married Maurice Lemdy Heck on 11 November 1946.

Their three children were:
Carol Jean Heck
Jay Howard Heck
Donna Lou Heck

6. **Ollie Dean Barrett** was born 9 February 1931 in Houston, and married Jimmie Dale Siegeler on 5 March 1949.

Their three children were:
William Dale Siegeler
Michael Thomas Siegeler
Theresa Lynn Siegeler

6. **Robert Johnson Barrett** was born 25 February 1940 in Giddings, Lee, Texas, and married Rebecca Willard.

Their two children were:
Robert Stephen Barrett
Shannon Lamar Barrett

6. **Glenda Ann Barrett** was born 4 May 1945 in Brenham, Washington, Texas, and married Ronald Meryl Spate on 4 March 1967.

Their two children were:
Shari Lynn Spate
Ronald Timothy Spate

6. **Linda Jo Barrett** was born 4 May 1945 in Brenham, and married Robert James Nitsche on 26 November 1964.

Their two children were:
Robert Kevin Nitsche
Jamin Barrett Nitsche

Children of Jake Herring Barrett and Edna Pearl Carroll

6. **Doris Barrett**, who married Gerhard Frings.
6. **Martha Barrett**, who married Harland Davie Jr.

Child of Mack Bennett Barrett and Vertie Mae Wilson

6. **Avalon Bennett Barrett**, born on 10 October 1939.

Children of Bracil C. Barrett and Glenda Jo Ward

6. **Patrick Talmage Barrett** was born on 25 February 1956, and married Diana.

Their three children were:

    Kelly Barrett

    Jeremy Barrett

    Kayla Barrett

6. **Brenda Ann Barrett** was born 8 December 1957, and married Mark Thompson in 1980.

Their two children were:

    Brandon Thompson

    Kyle Thompson

Children of Hugh Hays Barrett Jr. and Mary Jones

6. **Mary Jo Barrett** was born 11 August 1926 in Oletha, Limestone, Texas, and on 21 April 1946 married Harold Dean Griffin, who was born 11 October 1922 in El Paso.

Their two children were:

    Walter Lewis Griffin

    David Barrett Griffin

6. **Juanita Kathryn Barrett** was born 2 August 1927 in Madison, and on 15 April 1950 married Bill David Wakefield, who was born on 9 November 1924 in that county.

Their two children were:

    Kay Wakefield

    Karen Wakefield

Children of Augastachn Prasatick and Lora Minnie Barrett

6. **Virginia Ann Prasatik** was born 29 May 1938, and married Paul Russell Coleman on 3 July 1956 in Corpus Christi.

Their three children were:

    Paul Russell Coleman Jr.

    Virginia Kay Coleman

    Lora May Coleman

6. **Thomas Barrett Prasatik** was born 31 October 1945.

Children of Ottie Eugene Barrett and Annevieve Fraser

6. **Ottie Eugene Barrett Jr.** was born 19 May 1934 in Huntsville, and married Carole Ann Klapperich on 27 July 1958 in Houston. She was born 14 September 1937 in McAllen, Texas.

Their four children were:

    Amy Elizabeth Barrett

    Lisa Ann Barrett

    Julia Kathleen Barrett

    Daniel Eugene Barrett

6. **Joan Kathleen Barrett** was born 28 May 1937 in Huntsville, Texas, and married Robert Earl Davis on 14 May 1958. He was born 21 February 1933 in Hearne, Texas.

Their two children were:

    Kay Lynn Davis

    Joanna Lee Davis

6. **Jane Ann Barrett** was born 18 November 1942 in Huntsville, where on 24 August 1962 she married Charles Andrew Durbin III, who was born 4 February 1942 in San Antonio.

Their two children were:

    Charles Andrew Durban IV

    Christina Lynn Durban

6. **Mary Elizabeth Barrett** was born 21 September 1946 in Huntsville, where she married Roger Dale Mercer on 1 June 1968. He was born 25 November 1946 in Sherman, Texas.

Their child was:

Michael Barrett Mercer

Child of John Lee Barrett and Jocie Martha Winborn
6. **John Lee Barrett Jr.** was born 2 April 1929 in Madison.
His child was:
John Lee Barrett III

Children of William Robert Barrett and Harriett Reggio
6. **Barbara Barrett** was born about 1939.
6. **William Robert Barrett Jr.** was born about 1944.

Children of William Robert Barrett and Annie Mae Brazelton
6. **Hugh Hays Barrett** was born after 1944.
6. **Charlene Barrett** was born after 1945.

Child of Kenneth Kyle McCan and Audrey Faye Hicks
6. **Douglas Glenn McCann** was born 7 July 1923, and married Lois Allmond on 31 May 1946.
Their child was:
Douglas Glenn McCann Jr.

Children of Carl Cranfield Dixon and Ione Zefa McCan
6. **Shirley Jane Dixon** was born 25 October 1926, and in 1945 married Lingo Brown. In 1952 she married Mac Turner, and in 1962, Bill Jay.
The two children of Lingo Brown and Shirley Jean Dixon were:
Terry Lee Brown
Jane Ann Brown
The child of Mac Turner and Shirley Jane Dixon was:
Carl Alton Turner
6. **James Ray Dixon** was born 1 August 1928, and on 28 February 1953 married Mary Ellen Finley.
Their five children were:
Maya Elaine Dixon
James Ray Dixon Jr.
Tana Arlene Dixon
Dawn Ione Dixon
Toby Dixon

Children of Connie Ford McCann and Leone Ellen Wilbeck
6. **Karen Penelope McCann** was born 28 October 1939 in El Campo, Texas, where she married Arthur Roger Hett on 10 October 1964. He was born 23 March 1935 in Alexander, McKenzie, North Dakota. Karen is a well-known genealogical researcher, who assembled and edited most of the sections of this book that refer to Elizabeth and Alfred Whitten and their descendants.
Their three children were:
Mari Michal Hett
Tobin McCann Hett
Christian Rogers Hett
6. **Connie Michael McCann** was born 18 December 1942 in Wharton, Texas, and married Ana Caso.
Their child was:
Anna Celeste Caso McCann

Children of Vincent Keith Bova and Mossie McCann
6. **Donald Byron Bova** was born 24 September 1939 in Houston, and on 11 August 1961 married Linda Parchmont. Later he married Diane Smith.
The two children of Donald Byron Bova and Linda Parchmont were:
Donna Bova
Steven Bova

6. **Joseph Keith Bova** was born 1 June 1942 in Houston, and married Antoinette Keuhn on 27 December 1966.
Their two children were:
> Emile Bova
> Joseph Paul Bova

6. **Kenneth Paul Bova** was born 30 May 1953 in Houston, and married Janet Sue Jordan on 26 May 1974 in Coldspring, Texas.

6. **Mark Robin Bova** was born 6 January 1955 in Houston, and married Susan Niccoli.
Their child was:
> Susan Nicole Bova

Child of Kenneth Edward Winborn and Eral Morrison
6. **Kenneth Edward Winborn Jr.**
His two children were:
> Gregory Winborn
> Kenneth Edward Winborn III

Children of James Ethel Winborn and Lena Franke
6. **Ethel Mae Winborn** was born 2 October 1925, and married Dr. Samuel R. Turner on 10 June 1946 in Houston.
Their three children were:
> LeAnne Turner
> James Winborn Turner
> Andrew Roland Turner

6. **Juanice Winborn** was born 29 October 1927, and married Leslie W. Hatcher on 15 February 1952 in Harris County, Texas.
Their three children were:
> David Rich Hatcher
> Hollis Jan Hatcher
> Alexander H. Hatcher

6. **Irene Winborn** was born 16 November 1929, and married Warren P. Castle Jr. on 23 March 1947 in Ft. Bend County, Texas. On 10 April 1965 she married Phillip R. Miller.
The two children of Warren P. Castle Jr. and Irene Winborn were:
> Ronald Bryan Castle
> Kay Lanette Castle

Children of Harry Ford Brooks and Minnie Gladys Winborn
6. **Ford Lamar Brooks** was born 13 January 1917 in Madison County, and on 15 October 1940 married Norene Janice Franzel, who was born on 13 February 1924. He later married Winefred Edwards.
The two children of Ford Lamar Brooks and Norene Janice Franzel were:
> Samuel Young Brooks II
> John Redding Brooks II

6. **Mildred Ellena Brooks** was born 5 May 1918, and married Carl Ralph Hull, who was born 26 December 1914.
Their child was:
> Carl Ralph Hull Jr.

Child of Odell Robinson and Amanda Winborn
6. **James William Robinson** was born 18 April 1942 in Alvin, Texas, and on 19 August 1961 married Carolyn Bond, who was born in Baytown, Texas.
Their two children were:
> James William Robinson Jr.
> Susan Annette Robinson

Children of Leonard Carl Travis and Icely Aline McCann
6. **Don Forrest Travis** was born 22 September 1922 in Santa Anna, Coleman, Texas, and married Sue Blough.
6. **Wooldridge Leon Travis** was born 19 March 1926 in Oakville, Leon, Texas, and married Patricia Ritchey.
6. **Kenneth Carl Travis** was born 8 June 1934 and died in April 1936.

Child of Thomas Oscar Lowe and Lockie Blanche McCann
6. **Hallie Blanche Lowe** was born 7 May 1939 in Conroe, Montgomery, Texas, and on 11 February 1961 in Palestine, Texas, married Larry Bert Johnson, who was born on 4 January 1938 in Austin.
Their two children were:
      Gary Thomas Johnson
      Bert Lanier Johnson

Children of Miner Dickey McCann and Anne Willis
6. **Richard McCann**
6. **Joel McCan**

Children of Ed Sloan McCann and Ann Mary Pohoresky
6. **Carl Preston McCann** was born 24 June 1930 in Giddings, Lee, Texas, and on 11 October 1952 in Houston married Mary Jeanette Stringer, who was born 14 October 1933.
Their four children were:
      Carl Steven McCann
      Catherine Susanna McCann
      Thomas Edward McCann
      Janet Marie McCann
6. **Stacie Aliene McCann** was born 6 October 1934 in Houston, and on 18 January 1958 in Richmond, Texas, married James Hale, who was born 19 January 1934 in Wheeler, Texas.
Their two children were:
      James Hale Jr.
      Lizabeth Ann Hale

Children of Donnel Earl McCann and Annie Nora Collins
6. **Frances Earl McCann** was born 3 April 1936, and on 10 August 1953 married Delbert Spencer Ray.
Their four children were:
      Timothy Nelson Ray
      Deborah Frances Ray
      Terry Phillip Ray
      Todd Stephen Ray
6. **Donnel Wayne McCann** was born 14 May 1938, and on 23 July 1972 married Judith Inez Froelich.
Their two children were:
      Heather Norene McCann
      Kerwin Heath McCann
6. **Larry Wooldridge McCann** was born 20 June 1946, and married Alice Jean Williams on 23 December 1970.
Their child was:
      Jennifer Mechell McCann
6. **Sherry Lynn McCann** was born 27 September 1927.

Children of Bell Field McCann and Evelyn Francis Boehler
6. **Madeline McCann** was born 6 September 1941, and married Don H. Cook on 21 November 1964.
Their two children were:
      Stephen Allen Cook
      Angela Kay Cook
6. **Bell Field McCann Jr.** was born 18 January 1947 and died 12 October 1970.
6. **Gary Lee McCann** was born 25 December 1950, and on 8 July 1973 married Martha Lynn Goodwin.
Their child was:
      Brandy Marie McCann

Children of Roland William Ray and Janie Kate McCann
6. **Marlin Evans Ray** was born 27 February 1942, and on 18 August 1976 married Barbara Jeanne Lemm, who was born 30 May 1948. They were missionaries to Japan.

6. **Roland Wooldridge Ray** was born 17 December 1944 and died 27 February 1967.

6. **Virgil Floyd Ray** was born 6 November 1947, and married Cathy Rena Caraway on 2 July 1970. She was born on 4 April 1950.

Their child was:

Kevin Bruce Ray

6. **Carolyn Gayle Ray** was born 5 August 1949, and on 16 August 1966 married Jimmy Glynn Lewis, who was born 25 August 1949.

Their three children were:

Nancy Gayle Lewis

Jimmy Glynn Lewis Jr.

Jennifer Lynn Lewis

6. **Robert Eugene Ray** was born 27 October 1951, and on 12 January 1974 married Mellany Gay Adams, who was born on 6 April 1952.

Their child was:

Megan Geneal Ray

Children of Wiley Byron Knight and Lottie Bell McCan

6. **Alvis Byron Knight** was born 9 March 1915, married Minnie Bert Garner, and died 13 January 1977.

Their five children were:

Alvis Byron Knight Jr.

Charlotte Knight

Barbara Ann Knight

Shirley Marie Knight

Jimmy Wayne Knight

6. **Frank Marshall Knight** was born 27 September 1917, and married Hazel Ophelia Owen.

Their two children were:

Frankie Ann Knight

John Roland Knight

6. **Roland Thomas Knight** was born 18 July 1919, married Loretta Mills, died 15 March 1944, and was buried at Ft. Bliss, El Paso, Texas.

6. **Mildred Ferolene Knight** was born 23 February 1923, and married Norman Franklin Fannin.

Their two children were:

Robert Byron Fannin

Beverly Fannin

6. **Wiley Byron Knight Jr.** was born 8 December 1928, and married Martha Mae Heron.

Their three children were:

Jean Knight

Wiley Byron Knight III

Don Roland Knight

Children of William Harris and Talitha Amanda Golden

6. **Hazel Harris** was born 23 March 1923.

6. **Juanita Harris** was born 31 January 1925 in Conroe, Texas.

Children of George W. Stowe and Talitha Amanda Golden

6. **Harold E. Stowe**

6. **Oddis Stowe**

6. **Clyde Stowe**

Children of Virgil Littleton Golden and Ethel Cronnin

6. **Edward Golden**

6. **Virgil Golden**

6. **Olen Golden**, who died before 1983.

6. **Ethel Byron Golden**

Children of James Joseph Golden and Alice Dikeman

6. **Ann Golden**
6. **Verla Golden**
6. **Maxine Golden**
6. **Marie Golden**
6. **James Golden**

Children of George Hartford Harper and Sadie Mae Golden
6. **Dorothy Lee Harper** was born 22 January 1923 in Conroe.
6. **Sadie Inez Harper** was born 4 April 1926 in Montgomery County, and on 24 May 1947 married Clarence Hubert Allen, who was born on 23 July 1924.
Their three children were:
Larry Hubert Allen
Janis Lynn Allen
Alwyn Lea Allen
6. **George Hartford Harper Jr.** was born 15 October 1930 in Goose Creek, Harris, Texas, and on 8 April 1953 in Dallas married Dolores Clara Morton, who was born on 10 May 1930 in Mexico. She died on 25 August 1966 in Conroe, and was buried in Mt. Zion Cemetery, Montgomery County, Texas.
Their two children were:
Michael Neal Harper
Mark Edward Harper
6. **Allie Sonoma Harper** was born 2 February 1933 in Conroe, Texas.
6. **Donald Raymond Harper** was born 17 October 1935 in Dickenson, Texas, and on 27 May 1960 married Fatima Ann Stroud, who was born on 1 February 1941 in San Angelo.
Their four children were:
Ty Lynn Harper
Nile Raymond Harper
Colin Dean Harper
Cole Patrick Harper

Children of R. D. Blair and Hulda Eugene Golden
6. **Beatrice Blair**
6. **Betty Blair**
6. **Joyce Blair**
6. **Jo Doris Blair**
6. **John Morris Blair**

Children of Alton O. Simmons and Annie Bell Golden
6. **Alton O. Simmons Jr.**
6. **Timmie Jean Simmons**
6. **Lawson Simmons**
6. **Lucille Simmons**
6. **Tommy Simmons**
6. **Tobie Simmons**

Child of Charlie McGee and Connie Ola Golden
6. **Jerry McGee**

Children of Wilford Mason and Winnie Viola Golden
6. **Josephine Ruth Mason** was born 11 December 1933 in Montgomery County, Texas, and married on 24 June 1955 in Baytown, Harry Edward Prebble, who was born on 17 December 1930 in San Antonio.
Their four children were:
Harry Edward Prebble Jr.
Malinda Ann Prebble
John Freeman Prebble
Amy Jo Prebble

6. **Edwin Earl Mason** was born 31 July 1937 in Baytown, and married on 20 December 1957 in Memphis, Tennessee, Alice Estelle Arrington, born 6 July 1938 in Clinton, Kentucky.

6. **Raymond Leon Mason** was born 11 June 1940 in Baytown, Texas, where he married Ja Kay Warren 24 June 1955. She was born 6 May 1942 in Fort Meade, South Dakota.

Their three children were:
Marguerite Ann Mason
Tracy Lynn Mason
Raymond Leon Mason Jr.

Children of Kenneth Gale McCann and Anna Ruth Turner

6. **Kenneth Gale McCann Jr.** was born 5 July 1931, and married Dolores Willets and Robin Johnson.
The child of Kenneth Gale McCann Jr. and Dolores Willets was:
Katherin Gale McCann

6. **Gerald Wayne McCann** was born 22 November 1936, and married Sandra Wells. They were divorced.
Their two children were:
Delyse McCann
Kelly McCann

6. **Michael Turner McCann** was born 15 April 1942, and married Carole Owens.
Their three children were:
Michelle McCann
Kristi McCann
Monty McCann

6. **John Douglass McCann**, born 12 November 1952.

Children of August Leo Martin and Johnie Mae McCann
Born in Paden, Oklahoma

6. **Bonnie Jean Martin** was born 4 January 1932 and died 8 December 1935.

6. **Frances Dorene Martin** was born 6 April 1934, and on 12 January 1953 married Gerald William Rhyner, who was born in March 1930 and died 2 September 1953. She also married Walter Arnold Tapp, who was born on 20 August 1930 in Crescent, Oklahoma.

The two children of Walter Arnold Tapp and Frances Dorene Martin were:
Terry Lynn Tapp
Frances Arlene Tapp

6. **Marcus Leo Martin** was born 16 November 1935, and on 18 November 1956 married Mavis Louise Thompson, who was born on 27 March 1935 in Davenport, Oklahoma.

Their two children were:
Edna Louise Martin
Marcus Leo Martin Jr.

6. **Otis Carl Martin** was born 8 October 1937, and married Donna Jones in March 1968. His second wife was Tina Selfridge Long; his third, Gwen Case, who was born 17 June 1943.

The child of Otis Carl Martin and Donna Jones was:
Karla Dorene Martin

6. **Glenn Dale Martin** was born 12 December 1940, and married on 17 April 1959, Freeda Yvonne Bailey. His second wife was Martha Evelyn Sands Siebel.

The three children of Glen Dale Martin and Freeda Yvonne Bailey were:
Glenda Joyce Martin
Glenn Dale Martin Jr.
Karen Elaine Martin

6. **Barbara Elaine Martin** was born 6 January 1943, and married on 26 May 1961 Oscar Bryne Stone Jr., who was born on 29 June 1939 in Cartersville, Oklahoma.

Their two children were:
David Bryne Stone
Jonathon Martin Stone

Children of Walter Stanley McCann and Dorothy Landers

6. **Shirley Jean McCann**, who married J. D. Hix.

6. **Leuna Frances McCann** was born 24 August 1941 in Lewisville, Texas, and married Clint Norman in January 1969.

Their three children were:
  Christi Norman
  Leah Norman
  Clint Norman Jr.

6. **Patsy Jo McCann**
6. **Betty Lou McCann**
6. **Sandra Kay McCann**

Children of Walter Stanley McCann and Lois Virginia Davis Dollgener

6. **Walter Stanley McCann Jr.** was born 8 August 1952, and married twice; first in 1973, and on 11 May 1976, to Laurie Ferry.

The child of Walter Stanley McCann Jr. and his first wife was:
  Lori Elizabeth McCann

6. **Debra Lois McCann** was born 7 October 1953, and married on 18 December 1971 David B. Platts, who was born on 11 July 1952.

Their child was:
  Michael David Platts

6. **Donald Wayne McCann** was born 23 January 1956, and on 18 October 1974 married Jeanie Ray Gutzman, who was born on 14 May 1959.

Their two children were:
  Tiffany Michele McCann
  Nicky Kay McCann

6. **Robert Leon McCann** was born 17 February 1957.
6. **Norman Lee McCann** was born 16 November 1958.
6. **Billy Eugene McCann** was born 29 August 1961.

Children of Walter Jackson Malone and Claudia Irene McCann

6. **James Arthur Malone** was born 12 May 1936 in Lake Dallas, Texas, and on 16 October 1965 married Rose Marie Cox, who was born on 2 July 1944 in Mabank, Texas.

Their four children were:
  James Arthur Malone Jr.
  Nannette Marie Malone
  Donald Ray Malone
  Wendy Renee Malone

6. **Joy Ruth Malone** was born 8 August 1938 in Woodsboro, Texas, and on 11 August 1956 in Dallas married Dennis Earl Johnson, who was born on 11 August 1936 in Lewiston City, Illinois.

Their two children were:
  Pamela Joy Johnson
  Dennis Earl Johnson Jr.

6. **Walter Jackson Malone Jr.** was born 30 April 1940 in Ashdown, Arkansas, and on 26 August 1960 in Dallas married Patricia Ann Nethery, where she was born on 6 December 1941.

Their three children were:
  Barry Dean Malone
  Robby Lynn Malone
  Regina Gail Malone

6. **Thomas Allen Malone** was born 19 February 1943 in Corpus Christi, and on 23 September 1963 in Alabama married Sheila Ann Fowler, who was born on 17 June 1945 in Milton, Florida.

Their two children were:
  Thomas Allen Malone Jr.
  Desmond Lee Malone

6. **Lawrence Duane Malone** was born 26 December 1944 in Paden, Oklahoma, and married, on 18 August 1967 in Long Beach, California, Margaret Ann Groover, born on 5 June 1950 in Pensacola, Florida.

Their four children were:
>   Debra Jane Malone
>   Cinthia Ann Malone
>   Carol Lynn Malone
>   Lawrence Duane Malone Jr.

6. **Larry Gene Malone** was born 3 March 1951 in Port Lavaca, Texas, and married on 13 December 1969 in Dallas, Trenie Diane Brimer, where she was born on 8 August 1952.

Their twins were:
>   Larry Dean Malone
>   Carry Gene Malone

6. **Gary Wayne Malone** was born 11 May 1961 in Dallas.

Child of Charles Keith McCann and Elsie Mae Bennett

6. **Pat McCann**, who married Jodie Harrell.

Child of Charles Keith McCann and Carol Joyce Sharp

6. **Sharon Annette McCann** was born on 20 May 1962.

Child of Charles Keith McCann and Buena Lorene Hayhurst

6. **Charlotte Lorene McCann**, who married Jimmie Lee Hanniford on 9 January 1961.

Their child was:
>   Teresa Jane Hanniford

Children of Charles Shelby Gibson and Hettie Vernal McCann

6. **Charles Wayne Gibson** was born 7 April 1945, married Shirley Deanna Hathaway on 21 January 1963 in Burley, Idaho, and died before 1983.

Their three children were:
>   Charles Wayne Gibson Jr.
>   Marsha Deanna Gibson
>   Christine Carlene Gibson

6. **Jerry Lee Gibson** was born 4 February 1947, and on 27 December 1977 married Shelia Tracy Tafoya.

6. **John Tillman Gibson** was born 4 December 1948, married Caroline Narthe on 31 May 1968 in Pocatello, Idaho, and died on 8 May 1973.

Their two children were:
>   John Dominic Gibson
>   Toby Scott Gibson

6. **Carla Mae Gibson** was born 15 April 1952, and on 4 June 1976 married Dan Martsch, who was born on 11 September 1951.

Their child was:
>   William Lee Gibson Martsch

6. **Linda Kay Gibson** was born 11 December 1955, and married on 15 February 1975 Terry Lee Ketterling, who was born on 12 March 1952.

6. **Randy Paul Gibson** was born 23 September 1960.

Children of Harold Floyd and Shirley Faye Rogers McCann

6. **Patricia Ann McCann** was born 23 June 1950.

6. **Deborah Lynn McCann** was born 23 December 1954, and married Tom Muckenthaler on 5 June 1976.

Their two children were:
>   Jason Muckenthaler
>   David Muckenthaler

6. **Danny Floyd McCann** was born 29 February 1957.

Children of Harold Floyd McCann and Sherry Jean Cowherd

6. **Kathy Jean McCann** was born 13 June 1965.

6. **Lori Jane McCann**

Children of Darrell Lloyd McCann and Dixie Nadine Whisenant
6. **Elizabeth Gaye McCann** was born 13 December 1956 in Dallas, and married Richard Baker.
6. **Ronald Alan McCann** was born 26 July 1959 in Weatherford, Parker, Texas, and married Tert Sue Bankston on 5 October 1991. Ronald was adopted.
6. **Steven Eugene McCann** was born 6 June 1969 in Kerrville, Texas, and married Shelia Lynn Melguard. He, too, was adopted.

Children of Leonard Ray Tracy and Lola Faye McCann
6. **Mary Elizabeth Tracy**, who on 10 May 1958 married Leonard Wesley Risenhoover.
6. **Donald Ray Tracy**, who married Kathryn Cleveland on 5 November 1975.
6. **Margaret Ellen Tracy**, who married Fred F. Foster on 29 December 1966.
6. **Howard Eugene Tracy**, who on 18 December 1979 in Cahokia, Illinois, married Della Ann Mace, who died there on 18 December 1979.

Children of Charles Edgar McCann and Maurine Bookout
6. **Edward Lee McCann**
6. **Ronald Carl McCann**
6. **Linda Jean McCann**

Children of Clinton Oliver Turner and Martha Bessie McCann
6. **Janice Marie Turner**
6. **Carolyn Turner**
6. **Frederick Benjamin Turner**
6. **Clinton Oliver Turner Jr.**
6. **Peggy Turner**

Children of John LeRoy Thompson and Viola Mae McCann
6. **Mary Jo Thompson**
6. **Denny LeRoy Thompson**
6. **John Thompson**
6. **Oila Louise Thompson**
6. **James Thompson**

Children of Jesse Benjamin Tabler and Amanda Elizabeth McCann
6. **Barbara Elaine Tabler** married Louis Dyer and, in 1969, Carl Beaver.
The two children of Louis Dyer and Barbara Elaine were:
    Timothy Dyer
    Curtis Dyer
The child of Carl Beaver and Barbara Elaine was:
    Tammy Beaver
6. **Charles Monroe Tabler** married Barbara B.
Their child was:
    LeWayne Tabler
6. **Russell Lee Tabler** was born on 8 May 1947 in Drumwright, Oklahoma, and married Sydney Lynn Bergon 7 June 1967 and Connie Baker in August 1970.
The child of Russell Lee and Sidney Lynn was:
    Melissa Bobette Tabler
The two children of Russell Lee and Connie were:
    Angela Tabler
    Diedra Tabler
6. **Richard Albert Tabler** was born 5 December 1948 in Drumright, and married Judy and Susie.
The child of Richard and Judy was:
    Jessie Tabler
The two children of Richard and Susie were:

William B. Moore Jr.

Annie Tabler
Lori Tabler
6. **Sandra Kay Tabler**

Children of Benny Star McCann and Joyce Smith
6. **Cheryl Ann McCann**
6. **David Earl McCann**
6. **John Fitzgerald McCann**
6. **Benjamin Monroe McCann**

Children of Bluford Wesley McCann and Bonnie Minnie
6. **Doyle Ray McCann**
6. **Judy McCann**
6. **Tracy Ellen McCann**
6. **Darrell Wayne McCann**

Children of James Arthur Turpin and Annie Mae Hale
6. **James Hartwell Turpin** married Sally Mae Grabow.
Their child was:
    James Edward Turpin
6. **Barbara Ann Turpin**
6. **John Turpin**

Children of Jack Carl Hale and Margaret Winter
6. **Robin Arnold Hale**, born in 1939.
6. **Shirley Jean Hale**, born in 1942.

Children of Glenn Andrew Barrett and Pauline Bowen
6. **Glen Law Barrett**, born 6 February 1913 in Madison County, Texas.
6. **Raymond Lee Barrett** was born on 7 April 1942 in Harris County, Texas.

Children of Glenn Andrew Barrett and Ruby Marie Hilderbrant
6. **Betty Jean Barrett**, born 29 February 1940.
6. **Glenda Ruth Barrett** was born on 12 February 1945 in Harris, Texas.

Children of Vivian Claud Barrett and Mina Jewell Vaugn
6. **Charles Robert Barrett**, born on 3 September 1943.
6. **Donald Ray Barrett** was born on Christmas day 1940 in Madison Texas, and married Joyce Crippens on 25 August 1981.

Child of Roland D. Barrett and Beatrice Little
6. **David Earl Barrett** was born on 13 January 1945.

Children of Jack Smith and Vera Lee Barrett
6. **Jack Smith Jr.**
6. **Bertha Smith**
6. **James Smith**

Children of Louis B. Starns and Mattie Addie Barrett
6. **Mary Alice Starns** was born 14 July 1929 in Madison County, and married twice: first, Raymond Jessie Janicke; and second, Donald Robertson.
The three children of Raymond Jessie Janicke and Mary Alice Starns were:
    Lou Ann Janicke
    Mary Catherine Janicke
    Jessie Raymond Janicke

The child of Donald Robertson and Mary Alice Starns was:

> George Arthur Robertson

6. **Margaret Ann Starns** was born 17 August 1931 in Madison County, and on 6 August 1950 married Vernon Patrick Villars, who was born on 13 November 1929.

Their seven children were:

> Patrick Louis Villars
> Margaret Ann Villars
> Mary Kelly Villars
> Mark Steven Villars
> Debra Lynn Villars
> Peter Matthew Villars
> Elizabeth Joan Villars

6. **Hazel Louise Starns** was born 27 September 1935 in Madison County, and married Billy Thomas Malone. On 19 February 1954 she married Clyde Frederick Grady.

The three children of Billy Thomas Malone and Hazel Louise Starns were:

> Louanna Jane Malone
> Jimmie Mattie Malone
> Billy Thomas Malone Jr.

The child of Clyde Frederick Grady and Hazel Louise Starns was:

> Dennis Leon Grady

Children of Hugh Roland Barrett and Myrtle Lillie Bennett

6. **Nancy Arlene Barrett**, who married Robert Ray Foylds.

Their two children were:

> Barbara Lynn Foylds
> Peggy Diane Foylds

6. **Gerald Elmer Barrett** was born 2 July 1937, and married Tommie Lewise Fields, who was born on 4 April 1935 in Dayton, Texas. He died 31 March 1965 and was buried in Rosewood, Harris, Texas.

Their three children were:

> Jacqueline Ruth Barrett
> Terrie Kay Barrett
> Gerald Mark Barrett

6. **Donald Joe Barrett** was born in Sherman, Texas, on 15 May 1938, and married Dolfaliene Von Raby on 29 May 1958. She was born on the fourth of July 1941 in Stockton, California. He married Betty Spake in January 1983.

Their six children were:

> Darla Sue Barrett
> Michael Shane Barrett
> Robert Ray Barrett
> Theda Gay Barrett
> Dana Renee Barrett
> Roy Hubert Barrett

6. **Hugh Redding Barrett** was born 11 March 1942, and on 8 February 1964 in Houston married Vivian Klodsinski, who was born on 5 December 1947.

Their five children were:

> Hugh Wesley Barrett
> Jason Wade Barrett
> Denise Orlean Barrett
> Jonathan Gay Barrett
> Deborah Kay Barrett

6. **Theda Rae Barrett** was born after 1942, and married Wayne Stevenson.

Their two children were:

> Scott Stevenson
> Alan Stevenson

Children of Marion Odious Barrett and Delma Lee Walls

6. **Marion Otis Barrett Jr.**, born 20 April 1941.
6. **Lou Ann Walls Barrett** was born 22 May 1942, and married Robert Clark.
Their four children were:

    Robert Spencer Clark
    Richard Winfield Clark
    Karen Stephen Clark
    Christine Noel Clark

6. **John Marion Barrett** was born 15 December 1945, and married Margaret.
Their two children were:

    Melody Barrett
    Steven Barrett

6. **Lee Bruce Barrett** married first, Ann, then, Cherie.
The child of Lee Bruce Barrett and Ann was:

    Kimberly Ann Barrett

6. **Rita Gail Barrett** was born 8 November 1955, and married Edward Kenner.
Their child was:

    Edward Barrett Kenner

6. **Rhonda Elaine Barrett** was born 10 August 1959, and married Marty Mertes.

Child of Henry Allphin Barrett and Bobbie Marigold

6. **Barbara Barrett**

Children of Henry Allphin Barrett and Ruby Wilson
Born in Harris County, Texas

6. **Karen Leigh Barrett**, born 21 May 1946.
6. **Linda Catherine Barrett**, born 7 July 1948.
6. **Monte Barrett**, born 12 September 1949.

Children of Mason Everett McDonald and Billie Jo Barrett

6. **Seth Tracy McDonald** was born 13 October 1948 in Galena Park, Harris, Texas, died 6 June 1974, and was buried in McAdams Cemetery, Huntsville.
His child was:

    Mason Everett McDonald

Child of Mr. Alexander and Billy Joe Barrett

6. **James Robert Alexander** was born 28 August 1955 in Dallas.

Child of James S. Grey and Billy Jo Barrett

6. **Patricia Ann Gray** was born 17 October 1958 in Houston, and on 27 December 1977 in Conroe, Texas, married Michael C. Baust.
Their two children were:

    Elisabeth Anne Baust
    Benjamin Alexander Baust

Child of Vernon Barrett and Rachael Simington

6. **Maurice Barrett**

Children of Louie Monroe Barrett and Hattie Louise Furlow

6. **Andrienne Louise Barrett** was born 26 September 1931 in Austin, and on 30 June 1951 in Honolulu married Richard Dean Rabe, who was born on 3 December 1923 in North English, Iowa.
6. **Andre Barrett** was born 17 July 1944 in Ft. Worth.
His child was:

    Micah Sue Barrett

6. **Donald Louis Barrett** was born 19 March 1948 in Los Angeles, and on 21 July 1973 in LaJolla, California, married Jennifer Best Hunter, who was born on 21 September 1953 in Los Angeles.

6. **Ronald Monroe Barrett** was born 19 March 1948 in Long Beach, California, and on 7 April 1971 in Nevada married Georgianna Rose Redican.
Their three children were:
Travis Monroe Barrett
Alyse Caroline Barrett
Ann Louise Barrett

Children of Marion Lynch Barrett and Bessie Lee Wells
6. **Joe Bruce Barrett** was born 3 April 1937, and married Linda O'Neal.
Their seven children were:
Tammy Lea Barrett
Christy Ann Barrett
Donna Jean Barrett
Susan Rene Barrett
Sabrina Carol Barrett
Bruce O'Neal Barrett
Jason Bryan Barrett
6. **Carolyn Barrett** was born 26 July 1945, and married Morris Randall Nelson.
Their three children were:
Morris Randall Nelson III
Carrie Lynn Nelson
Denise Nanette Nelson

Child of Lawrence Parker Young and Iola Mae Faulkner
6. **Lawrence Perry Young** was born 12 February 1932 in Houston, and on 21 February 1952 married Evanell Gibson, by whom he had a son. Later he married, on 2 July 1960, Pearl Dell Weaver. They had two children.

Child of James Ray Barrett and Emma Ardel Collins
6. **James Ray Barrett Jr.** was born 17 May 1931 in Houston, where he married on 7 July 1950 Barbara Cunningham, who was born 28 October 1933. He died 16 July 1989 in Houston and was buried in Woodlawn Cemetery.
Their three children were:
James Ray Barrett III
Linda Ann Barrett
Keith William Barrett

Children of Lloyd Barrett and Catherine Delbert Haley
6. **Lloyd Frederick Barrett** was born 25 September 1938 in Houston, where he married on 24 August 1957 Wrenda Wray Oxspring, who was born on 8 October 1938 in Houston.
Their three children were:
Dana Lynn Barrett
Laura Ann Barrett
Lloyd Frederick Barrett Jr.
6. **James Bruce Barrett** was born 24 June 1948 in Houston, where he married on 3 April 1970 Elizabeth Ann Comer, who was born on 25 October 1949 in El Paso, Texas.
Their two children were:
Kristina Ann Barrett
Joshua Brandon Barrett
6. **David Lee Barrett** was born 19 December 1951 in Houston, and married Patricia Ann Billings.

Children of Kenneth Ray Batson and Sara Helen Barrett
6. **Kenneth Ray Batson Jr.** was born 4 July 1943 in Houston, and married on 7 June 1964 Elizabeth Ann Hauk, who was born on 24 October 1942 in Houston.
Their two children were:
Kenneth Ray Batson III
Jennifer Lynn Batson

Children of Henry Clay Wright Jr. and Cory Ann Snowdon
6. **Matisa Ann Wright** was born 19 July 1957, and married Donald Dickey on 30 May 1975.
6. **Michael Clay Wright** was born 1 March 1960.

Children of Jack Ledford Wright and Alney Dora Sheldon
6. **Philip Henry Wright** was born 22 August 1953, and married Dinah K. Osburn on 4 April 1974.
6. **Mollie Frances Wright** was born 28 June 1958.

Children of Paul Suttles Willingham and Elsie Dell Clark
6. **Clark Suttles Willingham** was born 29 November 1944, and on 16 August 1969 married Jane Joyce Hitch.
Their two children were:
    Meredith Moores Willingham
    James Barrett Willingham
6. **Beverly Sue Willingham** was born 10 July 1951.

Children of Willis William Armistead and Martha Sidney Clark
6. **Willis William Armistead Jr.** was born 23 September 1940, and married Marianne Ferris on 24 December 1969.
Their two children were:
    Eugene Francis Armistead
    Cassidy Clark Armistead
6. **Jack Murray Armistead** was born 7 March 1943, and married Jane Theresa Barber on 3 July 1971.
Their child was:
    Emily Murray Armistead
6. **Sidney Merrill Armistead** was born 14 October 1945, and married Robert Livingston Dixey on 27 June 1970.

Child of William Sidney Clark and Margaret Johana Read
6. **William Sidney Clark Jr.** was born 8 October 1954, and married Kathryn Fulton on 8 October 1954 in Madison, Texas.

Children of Billy Boy Manning and Robbie Orene Rhodes
Born in Madison County, Texas
6. **Charles Ira Manning** was born on 27 June 1939, and married Delores A. Horton.
6. **Harold Elwin Manning** was born on 4 July 1942, and married Peggy Lee Nabb.
6. **Lanell Manning** was born 12 June 1947, and married George Ray Kipp.

Children of Melvin Idie Manning and Dezy Ozelle Taylor
Born in Madison County, Texas
6. **Joyce Rae Manning** was born on 13 October 1931, and married Arthur Ross Grantham.
6. **Billie Earlene Manning** was born on 4 August 1933, and married Loys Lyle Hall on 12 February 1953.
6. **Lloyd Melvin Manning** was born on 3 October 1934, and married Wanda Stuts on 16 June 1956.
6. **James Buchannon Manning** was born 1 April 1936, and married Evelyn Janice Moore on 6 June 1958.
6. **Ruby Aileen Manning** was born on 24 May 1938, and married Bobbie Jones Nesmith on 9 August 1958.

Children of Archie Jordy and Ruby Elizabeth Manning
6. **Bennie Martin Jordy** was born on 1 June 1932, and married Carolyn Masso in 1956.
Their four children were:
    Irving Jordy
    Janet Marie Jordy
    Jennifer Louise Jordy
    Jacquelyn Denise Jordy
6. **Donald Irwin Jordy** was born on 16 November 1933, and married Irene.
Their four children were:
    Jill Marie Jordy

           Jeffrey Don Jordy

           Suzie Jordy

           Donnie Jordy

6. **Mildred Arlene Jordy** was born 4 February 1937, and married Donald Lee Hoke on 18 August 1956.

Their four children were:

           David Lee Hoke

           Danny Lynn Hoke

           Donna Louise Hoke

           Dennis Lloyd Hoke

6. **Luthur Hilton Jordy** was born 30 June 1940 in Crosby, Texas, and married Roselie Julia Yenter on 10 June 1967.

Their two children were:

           Debra Ann Jordy

           Darrell Thomas Jordy

6. **Luke Milton Jordy** was Luthur's twin, who married Lydia Louise Froehlich on 3 August 1963.

Their three children were:

           Lisa Louise Jordy

           Laura Lynette Jordy

           Larry Michael Jordy

Children of Currie Atmal Skains and Sadie Augusta Manning

6. **Shirley Anita Skains** was born on 8 October 1935, and married Rell Welden Gamblin on 28 December 1955.

Their three children were:

           Darwin Glenn Gamblin

           Deborah Gail Gamblin

           Tina Lynette Gamblin

6. **Billie Atmal Skains**, Shirley's twin, was born two days later and, in March 1956, married Jeanne Ardell Stenzel.

Their two children were:

           Jolitta Ann Skains

           James Atmal Skains

6. **Mary Alice Skains**, born 26 July 1939.

6. **Joyce Adell Skains**, born 13 October 1940.

6. **Edward Allen Skains**, born 4 December 1946.

Child of Clarence Brooks Barrett and Louise Kathryn Burnch

6. **Sandra Louise Barrett** was born 2 July and died 27 July 1937.

Children of Roland Pitts and Vera Fay Barrett

6. **Gwendolyn Pitts** was born 6 December 1937, and, in 1954, married LeRoy Koska.

Their two children were:

           Gregory Lee Koska

           Kellye Lynn Koska

6. **Wanda Janell Pitts** was born 29 May 1940, and married Robert Ernest Rice.

Their child was:

           Paula Ann Rice

6. **Milton Eugene Pitts** was born 23 January 1954.

Children of Frank Owen Romine and LaVerne Farber

6. **Herman Oliver Romine** was born on 11 July 1928 in Walters, Oklahoma, and married Mary Earnestine Lee on 28 August 1955. She was born on 13 June 1929 in San Francisco.

Their five children were:

           Robert William Romine

           Ellen Patricia Romine

           Cheryl Dianne Romine

James Glen Romine
Karen Lee Romine
6. **Billy O. Romine** was born on 7 March 1930, and married Grace.
6. **Karl Anton Romine** was born on 4 February 1932, married Josephine, and died in November 1991.
6. **Lele Eulene Romine** was born on 12 March 1934 in Pernell, Oklahoma, and married Billy Lee Walker on 25 July 1948.
6. **Patrick Ray Romine** was born on 10 August 1936, and married Gladys.

Child of Clyde Grant Farber and Clara Fay Thompson
6. **J. W. Farber**, who married M. A. Frink.

Child of Arthur C. Jones and Mary Louise Farber
6. **Donna Faye Jones** was born on 21 November 1932 in Walters, Oklahoma, and married Garland David Kopple on 25 May 1966.

Child of Clarence Camburn and Fern Elsworth
6. **Marjorie Camburn** was born 23 July 1937 in Arizona, and married Henry Beckham Latimer.

NINTH GENERATION
Child of Lee Plumley and Mr. Lane
7. **Jay C. Lane**, who married John DeWitt.

Children of Homer Lee Barrett and Ruby Ellen
7. **Lee Barrett**
7. **Janice Barrett**
7. **Jimmy Barrett**
7. **Leon Barrett**

Child of Roy Weidel and Freida Adel Barrett
7. **Royceanne Weidel**, who married Mr. Faggins.
Their two children were:
Shayla Faggins
Brandon Faggins

Child of Troy Cummings and Frieda Adel Barrett
7. **Ronnie Lee Cummings**, who married Linda Heatherington.
Their two children were:
Shawn Cummings
Shiela Cummings

Children of Earnest Herman Cummings and Jearldene Barrett
7. **Patricia Kay Cummings**
7. **Karen Cummings**, who married David Wayne Fowler.
Their two children were:
Heather Lynn Fowler
David Wayne Fowler

Children of Jewell Edward Barrett and Linda
7. **Julie Barrett** married Mr. McDonald.
Their child was:
Kyle McDonald
7. **John Daniel Barrett**
His two children were:
Devin Barrett
Hunter Barrett

82

Children of Earl McCaffety and Madie Agnes Barrett
7. **Bob McCaffety** married Eva Mae.
7. **Marie McCaffety** married Mr. Tumlinson.
7. **Earl McCaffety Jr.** married Polly.
7. **Johnnie Mae McCaffety** married Mr. Bishop.
7. **Eugene McCaffety** was born in 1935, and married Shirley.
7. **Mary Beth McCaffety**

Children of Robert Dan Barrett and Fannie Mae Johnson
7. **Robert Wayne Barrett**
7. **David Roscoe Barrett**
7. **Ronald Troy Barrett**

Children of Louie Franklin Barrett and Alice Mae Gerston
7. **Katherine Louise Barrett** was born on 13 December 1942 in Houston, Texas, and married Rev. Elbert Kinard on 30 June 1959. He was born in Silsbee, Texas, on 29 January 1940.
Their two children were:
Debra Louise Kinard
Terrie Lynn Kinard
7. **Billy Ray Barrett** was born on 11 June 1942 in Sugarland, Texas, and married Carolyn Joyce Tribe on 23 November 1948. She was born on 23 January 1940 in Houston. They were divorced, after which he married and divorced Mary Vivian Eason, Peggy Gross, and Phyllis, then married Mary Vivian Barrett.
The six children of Billy Ray and Carolyn Joyce were:
Billy Ray Barrett Jr.
Janet Darlene Barrett
Daniel Louie Barrett
David Russell Barrett
John Charles Barrett
Karen D'Anne Barrett
7. **Evelyn Marie Barrett** was born 20 August 1944 in Houston, and married Edward Nichols on 18 July 1964. He was born on 8 July 1945 in Silsbee.
Their three children were:
Rebecca Ann Nichols
Edward Carl Nichols
Kristi Lynn Nichols
7. **Bobbie Jean Barrett** was born in Houston on 30 April 1946, and married Henry Clemmon Lowe, born 24 September 1941 in Sabine, Texas, on 19 February 1966.
Their three children were:
Tammy Jean Lowe
Trudella Mae Lowe
Henry Lowe

Children of Arthur A. Sullivan and Mary Evelyn Barrett
7. **Dan Arthur Sullivan** was born in 1950, and married Janet.
7. **Sandra Darlene Sullivan** was born in 1952, and married Rick Brady.
7. **James Vick Sullivan** was born in 1954, and married Jenny Morlen.

Children of Robert Earl Guynes and Lottie Mae Barrett
7. **Robert Guynes** was born on 22 August 1946, and married Shirley Jones.
Their two children were:
Timothy Guynes
Shannon Guynes
7. **Linda Guynes** was born on 19 November 1947, and married Kenneth Charles Tims and Mr. Kellerman.
The child of Kenneth Charles and Linda was:

William B. Moore Jr.

Kenneth Charles Tims II
The three children of Mr. Kellerman and Linda were:
Katie Elizabeth Kellerman
Lori Grace Kellerman
Robert Casey Kellerman
7. **John Guynes**, born on 9 September 1949.
7. **Larry Wayne Guynes** was born on 28 January 1955, and married Janet Hutchinson.
Their child was:
Laurin Mikayla Guynes

Children of Steve William Barrett and Syble Lourine Yates
7. **Wanda Lourine Barrett** was born 6 August 1948 in Huntsville, and married David Miller on 3 October 1967. He was born 6 March 1946.
Their child was:
Russell Miller
7. **Steve William Barrett** was born in Houston on 29 June 1951, and married Debbie Simmons, born 3 February 1954 in Arkansas, on 29 December 1973.
Their three children were:
Natalie Nachelle Barrett
Daniel William Barrett
Kelli Jannette Barrett
7. **Clarence Randall Barrett**, born on 8 August 1957 in Kountz, Texas, married Phyllis Simmons on 4 October 1976. She was born on 18 September 1958 in Arkansas.
Their two children were:
Andrea Barrett
Weslie Randall Barrett

Children of James Paul Barrett and Helen Coles
7. **Mary Elaine Barrett**, born 2 September 1953 in El Paso.
7. **Paul Ray Barrett**, born 2 May 1956 in Beaumont, and married June Emily.
Their two children were:
Jessica Dawn Barrett
Jeremy Paul Barrett
7. **Lois Norene Barrett** was born on 20 November 1959 in Sacramento, California, and married Phillip Andrew Jones, Mr. Stanley, and Mr. Massa.
The child of Phillip Andrew and Lois Norene was:
Phyllis Amanda Jones
The child of Mr. Stanley and Lois Norene was:
Aaron Michael Stanley
The child of Mr. Massa and Lois Norene was:
Louis Anthony Massa
7. **John Louis Barrett**, born 19 April 1961 in Sacramento, married Barbara Ann Craig.
Their two children were:
Savannah Nichelle Barrett
John-Michael Louis Barrett
7. **James David Barrett**, born 13 February 1963 in Washington, D.C., married Tammy Marie Munson.
Their child was:
Melissa Alice Barrett

Child of John I. Lenord and Mary Jane William
7. **John I. Lenord Jr.**

Children of Lee Tensley Vetuski and Ethel Woods
7. **James Lee Vetuski** was born 6 January 1933 in Madison County, Texas, and married Dixie Walker on 21 June 1955.

84

7. **Billie June Vetuski** was born 10 March 1935 in Baytown, Texas, and married a Mr. Habib in 1966.

7. **Mitchell Lewis Vetuski Jr.** was born 8 July 1937 in Crocket, Houston, Texas, married Patricia Ann Hilton in November 1957, and died 10 May 1981.

Child of Gregory Columbus Forrester and Lottie Odell Vetuski
7. **Leroy Forrester** was born on 24 August 1933 in Houston, and married Norma Mae Satterwhite and Wanda Davis.

Child of John Ackerman and Lottie Odell Vetuski
7. **Donald Ackerman** was born on 21 June 1934 in Houston, and married Judith Wagner on 30 April 1952. She was born on 13 April 1934 in LaPort, Texas.

Child of Harold Eugene Vetuski and Denna Twain
7. **Sandra Anna Vetuski** was born 29 October 1953 in Houston, and married Jack Sterling.

Children of Woodrow Felix Vetuski and Millicent Rose Caletka
7. **Michael Vetuski** was born in 1949 in Baytown, Texas, died 10 May 1949.
7. **Walter Wayne Vetuski** was born 18 January 1950 in Houston.
7. **Adonna Rose Vetuski** was born 31 July 1951 in Houston, and married Albert Glenn Goodwin on 26 June 1970. He was born on 5 December 1949 in Trinity, Texas.
7. **Paul Mark Vetuski** was born 18 October 1955 in Houston.
7. **Denise Carol Vetuski** was born 25 December 1957 in Houston.

Child of Woodrow Felix Vetuski and Higgans
7. **Rayford Vetuski**

Child of Edward Lewis Vetuski and Eva Krolezyk
7. **Frankie Lucille Vetuski** was born 2 October 1952 in Houston, and married Mr. Law.

Children of Mitchell Glen Vetuski and Alice Mary Wassem
7. **Rena Lucille Vetuski** was born 10 September 1945 in Lewiston, Nez Perce, Idaho, and on 2 March 1964 in Reno, California, married Jerrold Lee Robbins, who was born 10 April 1943 in Springfield, Ohio.
Their two children were:
Jerrold Lee Robbins Jr.
James Glen Robbins
7. **Mitchell Glen Vetuski Jr.** was born 24 August 1947 in Fort Crook, Sarpy, Nevada, and on 17 April 1970 in Houston married Stephanie Lois Garrison, who was born 19 May 1949 there. He and his cousin Karen McCann Hett supplied most of the information on the families and descendants of Elizabeth and Alfred Whitten.
Their five children were:
Glenna Michele Vetuski
Mollie Elizabeth Vetuski
Micah Andrew Vetuski
Benjamin Michael Vetuski
Emily Marie Vetuski
7. **Michael Lynn Vetuski** was born 2 February 1949 in Enid, Garfield, Oklahoma, and on 11 May 1975 in Maricopa, Arizona, married Sandra Arlene Deburger, who was born on 17 September 1946 in Selma, California.
7. **Millicent Helaine Vetuski** was born 24 May 1960 in Chandler, Arizona, married David Belcher in Las Vegas, and on 6 June 1981 married Andrew Porter.
The two children of David Belcher and Millicent Helaine Vetuski were:
Wayne Austin Belcher
Michael Dillon Belcher
The child of Andrew Porter and Millicent Helaine Vetuski was:
Joshua Daniel Porter

Child of Tom Henry Ford and Mary Frances Vetuski

William B. Moore Jr.

7. **Laveral Ford**, who married James Allen Wheeler on 8 October 1971 in Houston.

Child of Clemmons Asbury Loughridge and Olga
7. **Richard Loughridge**

Children of Lonzo Quitman Rudicil and Margaret Faye Barrett
7. **Margaret Kaye Rudicil**, who married Charles Smith.
7. **Wanda Carole Rudicil** was born 12 January 1950 in Odessa, and married Thomas Claude Canon. She was accepted for membership in The Daughters of the Republic of Texas.
7. **Brenda Diane Rudicil** was born 15 November 1955 in Odessa, married George Eric Sivertson, and became a member of The Daughters of the Republic of Texas.
Their child was:
Katrina Sivertson

Children of Fred A. Beer and Dorothy Helen Telotte
7. **Fred A. J. Beer II** was born in 1951 and died in 1974.
7. **Shelly Ann Beer** was born in 1954.

Children of William Ray Bierschwale and Glenda Gail Barrett
7. **Charles Randolph Bierschwale**
7. **William Ray Bierschwale Jr.**, who married Dee Ann.
7. **George Glenn Bierschwale**

Children of Ellwood Talmage Barrett and Ennis Marie Whitley
7. **Ellie Marie Barrett** was born 1 October 1954 in Huntsville, Texas, and on 14 April 1983 in Houston, married Wendall Royce Smith.
7. **Ellwood Talmage Barrett Jr.** was born 31 July 1957 in Houston.

Children of Melvin Harold Barrett and Gayle Gordon Rhea
7. **Tammy Ann Barrett**
7. **Tina Louise Barrett**
7. **William Harold Barrett**
7. **Raymond Basye Barrett**

Child of Joel D. Guedry and Carolyn Louise Barrett
7. **Mark Dean Guedry**

Child of Harry Atwood Stanley II and Ariebeth Alma Barrett
7. **Harry Atwood Stanley III**

Child of Ronald E. Bott and Ariebeth Alma Barrett
7. **Ronald Creston Bott**

Children of Maurice Lemdy Heck and Billie Jean Barrett
7. **Carol Jean Heck** was born 6 April 1948, and married Jerry Pearson.
Their two children were:
Michele Lee Pearson
Laura Diane Pearson
7. **Jay Howard Heck** was born 26 November 1950, and married Patricia McGee.
Their child was:
Jay Howard Heck Jr.
7. **Donna Lou Heck** was born 14 October 1951, and married Arthur Thomas Traill.
Their two children were:
Tamara Lynn Traill
Jennifer Traill

86

Children of Jimmie Dale Siegeler and Ollie Dean Barrett
7. **William Dale Siegeler** was born 30 September 1949, and married Peggy Jane Kiesnick.
Their child was:
Dixie Leann Siegeler
7. **Michael Thomas Siegeler** was born 19 July 1953, and married Catherine Ruth Urban.
Their child was:
Michael James Siegeler
7. **Theresa Lynn Siegler** was born 22 January 1955, and married Thomas Harold Sump.
Their child was:
William Ray Sump

Children of Robert Johnson Barrett and Rebecca Willard
7. **Robert Stephen Barrett**, born 6 August 1966.
7. **Shannon Lamar Barrett**, born 17 August 1971.

Children of Ronald Meryl Spate and Glenda Ann Barrett
7. **Shari Lynn Spate**, born 19 September 1971.
7. **Ronald Timothy Spate**, born 10 January 1974.

Children of Robert James Nitsche and Linda Jo Barrett
7. **Robert Kevin Nitsche**, born 17 December 1970.
7. **Jamin Barrett Nitsche**, born 22 October 1973.

Children of Bracil C. Barrett and Glenda Jo Ward
7. **Kelly Barrett**
7. **Jeremy Barrett**
7. **Kelly Barrett**
7. **Kayla Barrett**

Children of Mark Thompson and Brenda Ann Barrett
7. **Brenda Thompson**, born in 1982.
7. **Kyle Thompson**, born in 1985.

Children of Harold Dean Griffin and Mary Jo Barrett
7. **Walter Lewis Griffin** was born 23 June 1947 in Madison, and on 6 July 1968 in Huntsville married Louise Suggs, who was born 3 November 1946 in Groveton, Texas.
Their child was:
Stephen Anthony Griffin
7. **David Barrett Griffin** was born 14 January 1952 in El Paso, and on 27 May 1973 in Galveston married Rebecca Lynn Curry, where she was born on 9 September 1951.
Their child was:
Christian Michele Griffin

Children of Bill David Wakefield and Juanita Kathryn Barrett
Born in Madison County, Texas
7. **Kay Wakefield** was born 19 March 1952, and married Bradley Mathewson on 16 November 1976 in Madison County.
7. **Karen Wakefield**, born 1 September 1957.

Children of Paul Russell Coleman and Virginia Ann Prasatik
7. **Paul Russell Coleman Jr.**, born 11 October 1957 in Corpus Christi.
7. **Virginia Kay Coleman** was born 16 January 1959 in Corpus Christi, where she married Timothy Johnson on 24 January 1976.
Their child was:

Timothy Johnson Jr.
7. **Lora May Coleman**, born 20 June 1960 in Corpus Christi.

Children of Ottie Eugene Barrett Jr. and Carol Ann Klapperich
7. **Amy Elizabeth Barrett**, born 16 May 1959 in Houston.
7. **Lisa Ann Barrett**, born 15 May 1960 in Elk City Oklahoma.
7. **Julia Kathleen Barrett**, born 5 November 1961 in Huntsville, Texas.
7. **Daniel Eugene Barrett**, born 5 April 1964 in Huntsville.

Children of Robert Earl Davis and Joan Kathleen Barrett
7. **Kay Lynn Davis**, born 3 October 1961 in Houston.
7. **Joanna Lee Davis**, born 13 April 1966 in Beaumont.

Children of Charles Andrew Durban and Jane Ann Barrett
7. **Charles Andrew Durbin IV**, born 10 August 1965 in Sinton, Texas.
7. **Christina Lynn Durbin**, born 18 November 1969 in Conroe, Montgomery, Texas.

Child of Roger Dale Mercer and Mary Elizabeth Barrett
7. **Michael Barrett Mercer**, born 17 November 1972 in Sherman, Texas.

Child of John Lee Barrett Jr.
7. **John Lee Barrett III** was born 30 April and died 3 May in 1958 in Madison County, Texas.

Child of Douglas Glenn McCann and Lois Allmond
7. **Douglas Glenn McCann Jr.** was born 27 May 1947, and married Janice Patton.
Their three children were:
    Rebecca Allison McCann
    Douglas Glenn McCann III
    David Gregory McCann

Children of Lingo Brown and Shirley Jane Dixon
7. **Terry Lee Brown** was born 15 October 1946, and married Irene.
7. **Jane Ann Brown** was born 6 April 1948, and married Michael Yarbrough on 10 August 1968 in Abilene, Texas.
Their child was:
    Rebecca Yarbrough

Child of Mac Turner and Shirley Jane Dixon
7. **Carl Alton Turner** was born 2 August 1953, and married Rose.
Their child was:
    Alliecia Turner

Children of James Ray Dixon and Mary Ellen Finley
7. **Maya Elaine Dixon** was born 31 August 1955, and married Dohn Banks, who was born 20 November 1952.
Their child was:
    Dallas Alaina Banks
7. **James Ray Dixon Jr.** was born 5 July 1957, and married Lanore Mannon Johnson, who was born 11 June 1957.
Their child was:
    Lauren Camille Dixon
7. **Tana Arlene Dixon** was born 10 September 1959, and married Daniel Stewart. On 17 January 1981 she married Jack Harrington.
The child of Daniel Stewart and Tana Arlene Dixon was:
    Dylan Anthony Stewart
The child of Jack Harrington and Tana Arlene Dixon was:
    Keegan Earl Harrington

88

7. **Dawn Ione Dixon** was born 28 July 1961, and on 19 December 1981 married Billy Ray Gaston, who was born on 18 July 1953.

7. **Toby Dixon**, born 26 June 1968.

Children of Arthur Roger Hett and Karen Penelope McCann

7. **Mari Michal Hett** was born 22 December 1966 in Edna, Texas, and married David Oscar Ferrell on 4 March 1995 in Austin. He was born 20 September 1966 in Amarillo, Texas.

Their child was:

Lila Tate Ferrell

7. **Tobin McCann Hett**, born 24 March 1968.

7. **Christian Rogers Hett**, born 1 October 1969.

Child of Connie Michael McCann and Ana Caso

7. **Ana Celeste Caso McCann**, born 9 January 1995 in Wharton, Texas.

Child of Connie Michael McCann and Catherine Haynes

7. **Celeste McCann**, born 9 January 1995 in Wharton, Texas.

Children of Donald Byron Bova and Linda Parchmont

7. **Donna Bova**, born 16 August 1963.

7. **Steven Bova**, born 13 September 1966.

Children of Joseph Keith Bova and Antoinette Keuhn

7. **Emile Bova**, born 19 December 1972.

7. **Joseph Paul Bova**, born 20 September 1977.

Child of Mark Robin Bova and Susan Niccoli

7. **Susan Nicole Bova**, born 23 July 1982 in Houston.

Children of Kenneth Edward Winborn Jr.

7. **Gregory Winborn**

7. **Kenneth Edward Winborn III**

Children of Dr. Samuel R. Turner and Ethel Mae Winborn

7. **Le Anne Turner** was born 4 March 1949 in Nashville, Tennessee, and married John Burnett.

Their three children were:

May Burnett

Amanda Burnett

Justin Cain Burnett

7. **James Winborn Turner** was born 10 August 1951 in Nashville, Tennessee, and married Susan Strange.

Their two children were:

Jason Turner

Joshua Turner

7. **Andrew Roland Turner**, born 4 February 1956 in Tulsa.

Children of Leslie W. Hatcher and Juanice Winborn

7. **David Rich Hatcher** was born 4 March 1953 in Houston, and married Jo Ann Ochoa on 16 June 1973.

Their child was:

Monica Renee Hatcher

7. **Hollis Jan Hatcher**, born 3 December 1954 in Houston.

7. **Alexander H. Hatcher**, born 21 January 1968 in Nicaragua.

Children of Warren P. Castle Jr. and Irene Winborn

7. **Ronald Bryan Castle** was born 11 December 1947 in Houston, and married Pam Dodd in Oklahoma City.

Their four children were:

Shannon Castle
Kristan Irene Castle
Marc Andrew Castle
Rebecca Jane Castle
7. **Kay Laynett Castle**, born 18 November 1952 in Houston, and married Phillip R. Miller on 10 April 1965.

Children of Ford Lamar Brooks and Norene Janice Franzel
7. **Samuel Young Brooks II** was born 25 July 1942 in Houston, and married Sandra Sue Harris, who was born on 18 August 1943 in Alexandria, Louisiana.
Their two children were:
Samuel Young Brooks III
Harris Wycoff Brooks
7. **John Redding Brooks II** was born 23 January 1944 in Houston, and married Beverly Samsa, who was born 30 April 1944 in Euclid, Ohio.
Their two children were:
John Redding Brooks III
Jeffrey August Brooks

Child of Carl Ralph Hull and Mildred Ellena Brooks
7. **Carl Ralph Hull Jr.**, born 23 March 1948.

Children of James William Robinson and Carolyn Bond
7. **James William Robinson Jr.**, born 17 January 1963.
7. **Susan Annette Robinson**, born 21 August 1965.

Children of Larry Bert Johnson and Hallie Blanche Lowe
Born in Arlington, Texas
7. **Gary Thomas Johnson** was born 23 July 1963, and married Linda Diane Newland, who was born 10 October 1960.
Their three children were:
James Thomas Johnson
Casey Alan Johnson
Andrea Danae Johnson
7. **Bert Lanier Johnson** was born 19 March 1965, and married Donna Ellen Bradley, who was born 31 August 1966.
Their child was:
Cooper Bradley Johnson

Children of Carl Preston McCann and Mary Jeanette Stringer
Born in Houston, Texas
7. **Carl Steven McCann**, born 16 June 1954.
7. **Catherine Susanna McCann**, born 14 August 1955.
7. **Thomas Edward McCann** was born 12 September 1956, and on 18 September 1976 married Brenda Wilson, who was born 17 September 1956.
7. **Janet Marie McCann**, born 18 July 1958.

Children of James Hale and Stacie Aliene McCann
7. **James Hale Jr.**, born 4 December 1958 in Great Falls, Montana.
7. **Lizabeth Ann Hale**, born 1 May 1961 in Chicopee Falls, Massachusetts.

Children of Delbert Spencer Ray and Frances Earl McCann
7. **Timothy Nelson Ray**, born 25 December 1955.
7. **Deborah Frances Ray**, born 26 March 1958.
7. **Terry Phillip Ray**, born 15 August 1963.
7. **Todd Stephen Ray**, born 16 March 1965.

Children of Donnel Wayne McCann and Judith Inez Froelich
7. **Heather Norene McCann**, born 3 March 1974.
7. **Kerwin Heath McCann**, born 7 December 1975.

Child of Larry Wooldridge McCann and Alice Jean Williams
7. **Jennifer Mechell McCann**, born 14 December 1976.

Children of Don H. Cook and Madeline McCann
7. **Stephen Allen Cook**, born 17 August 1967.
7. **Angela Kay Cook**, born 22 May 1971.

Child of Gary Lee McCann and Martha Lynn Goodwin
7. **Brandy Marie McCann**, born 18 February 1974.

Child of Virgil Floyd Ray and Cathy Rena Caraway
7. **Kevin Brice Ray**, born 15 March 1973.

Children of Jimmy Glynn Lewis and Carolyn Gayle Ray
7. **Nancy Gayle Lewis**, born 3 October 1969.
7. **Jimmy Glynn Lewis Jr.**, born 20 June 1973.
7. **Jennifer Lynn Lewis**, born 12 February 1977.

Child of Robert Eugene Ray and Mellany Gay Adams
7. **Megan Geneal Ray**, born 1 March 1977.

Children of Alvis Byron Knight and Minnie Bert Garner
7. **Alvis Byron Knight Jr.**
7. **Charlotte Knight**
7. **Barbara Ann Knight**
7. **Shirley Marie Knight**
7. **Jimmy Wayne Knight**

Children of Frank Marshalla Knight and Hazel Ophelia Owen
7. **Frankie Ann Knight**
7. **John Roland Knight**

Children of Norman Franklin Fannin and Mildred Ferolene Knight
7. **Robert Byron Fannin**
7. **Beverly Fannin**, who married Horace A. Davis.

Children of Wiley Byron Knight Jr. and Martha Mae Heron
7. **Jean Knight**, who was born and died in 1953.
7. **Wylie Byron Knight III**
7. **Don Roland Knight**

Children of Clarence Hubert Allen and Sadie Inez Harper
Born in Houston, Texas
7. **Larry Hubert Allen** was born 23 March 1948, and married Blythe Loreen Brudnick in July 1973 in Huntsville,
Texas.
Their child was:
John Ashley Allen
7. **Janis Lynn Allen**, born 20 October 1950.
7. **Alwyn Lea Allen**, born 26 July 1952.
Children of George Hartford Harper Jr. and Dolores Clara Morton

Born in Houston, Texas

7. **Michael Neal Harper**, born 24 May 1955.

7. **Mark Edward Harper**, born 29 May 1963.

Children of Donald Raymond Harper and Fatima Ann Stroud

7. **Ty Lynn Harper**, born 28 October 1961 in San Angelo, Texas.

7. **Nile Raymond Harper**, born 16 December 1963 in San Angelo.

7. **Colin Dean Harper**, born 1 February 1965 in Edinburgh, Scotland.

7. **Cole Patrick Harper**, born 28 November 1965 in Hitchen, England.

Children of Harry Edward Prebble and Josephine Ruth Mason

7. **Harry Edward Prebble Jr.**, born 20 June 1957 in Dallas, Texas.

7. **Melinda Ann Prebble**, born 8 October 1959 in Philippi, West Virginia.

7. **John Freeman Prebble**, born 10 May 1961.

7. **Amy Jo Prebble**, born 3 December 1968.

Children of Raymond Leon Mason and Ja Kay Warren
Born in Baytown, Texas

7. **Marguerite Ann Mason** was born 11 November 1961, and on 19 February 1977 married Charles Warren Morris, who was born 10 May 1954 in Kansas City, Missouri.

Their child was:

John Charles Morris

7. **Tracy Lynn Mason**, born 9 November 1962.

7. **Raymond Leon Mason Jr.**, born 9 October 1971.

Child of Kenneth Game McCann Jr. and Dolores Willets

7. **Katherine Gale McCann**, born 6 June 1962.

Children of Gerald Wayne McCann and Sandra Wells

7. **Delyse McCann**, born 10 February 1962.

7. **Kelly McCann**, born 2 April 1964.

Children of Michael Turner McCann and Carole Owens

7. **Michelle McCann**, born 6 June 1963.

7. **Kristi McCann**, born 17 July 1970.

7. **Monty McCann**, born 16 September 1972.

Children of Walter Arnold Tapp and Frances Dorene Martin
Born in Prague, Oklahoma

7. **Terry Lynn Tapp**, born 8 December 1956.

7. **Frances Arlene Tapp**, born 11 February 1959.

Children of Marcus Leo Martin and Mavis Louise Thompson

7. **Edna Louise Martin**, born 24 December 1957 in West Warwick, Rhode Island.

7. **Marcus Leo Martin Jr.**, born 8 November 1961 in Fort Lee, Virginia.

Child of Otis Carl Martin and Donna Jones

7. **Karla Dorene Martin**, born in March 1969 in Shawnee, Oklahoma.

Children of Glenn Dale Martin and Freeda Yvonne Bailey
Born in Prague, Oklahoma

7. **Glenda Joyce Martin**, born 27 April 1960.

7. **Glenn Dale Martin Jr.**, born 25 May 1962.

7. **Karen Elaine Martin**, born 12 January 1964.

Children of Oscar Bryne Stone Jr. and Barbara Elaine Martin

7. **David Bryne Stone**, born 30 August 1967 in Ponca City, Oklahoma. David was adopted.
7. **Jonathon Martin Stone**, born 6 December 1967 in Prague, Oklahoma.

Children of Clint Norman and Leuna Frances McCann
7. **Christi Norman**
7. **Leah Norman**
7. **Clint Norman Jr.**

Child of Walter Stanley McCann Jr. and his first wife
7. **Lori Elizabeth McCann**, born 22 May 1973.

Child of David B. Platts and Debra Lois McCann
7. **Michael David Platts**, born 19 May 1972.

Children of Donald Wayne McCann and Jeanie Ray Gutzman
7. **Tiffany Michele McCann**, born 18 May 1975.
7. **Nicky Kay McCann**, born 19 November 1976.

Children of James Arthur Malone and Rose Marie Cox
Born in Dallas, Texas
7. **James Arthur Malone Jr.**, born 27 June 1967.
7. **Nannette Marie Malone**, born 24 October 1969.
7. **Donald Ray Malone**, born 1 May 1972.
7. **Wendy Renee Malone**, born 14 December 1974.

Children of Dennis Earl Johnson and Joy Ruth Malone
7. **Pamela Joy Johnson** was born 18 September 1958 in Burley, Idaho, and in Dallas married David Lee Herron, who was born 27 May 1957.
Their two children were:
Kyle Douglas Herron
Tricie Gail Herron
7. **Dennis Earl Johnson Jr.**, born 5 May 1961 in Dallas.

Children of Walter Jackson Malone Jr. and Patricia Ann Nethery
Born in Dallas, Texas
7. **Barry Dean Malone**, born 12 July 1961.
7. **Robby Lynn Malone**, born 21 November 1962.
7. **Regina Gail Malone**, born 27 June 1964.

Children of Thomas Allen Malone and Shelia Ann Fowler
Born in Dallas, Texas
7. **Thomas Allen Malone Jr.**, born 7 December 1957.
7. **Desmond Lee Malone**, born 7 April 1972.

Children of Lawrence Duane Malone and Margaret Ann Groover
Born in Dallas, Texas
7. **Debra Jane Malone**, born 5 August 1958.
7. **Cinthia Ann Malone**, born 11 August 1970.
7. **Carol Lynn Malone**, born 6 October 1972.
7. **Lawrence Duane Malone Jr.**, born 30 June 1973.

Twins of Larry Gene Malone and Trenie Diana Brimer
Born in Dallas, Texas
7. **Larry Dean Malone**, born 21 June 1970.
7. **Carry Gene Malone**, born 21 June 1970.

Child of Jimmie Lee Hannaford and Charlotte Lorene McCann
7. **Teresa Jane Hannaford** who was born 5 March 1963 and married Ralph H. Keen II.
Their two children were:
> Desiree Keen
> Matthew Keen

Children of Charles Wayne Gibson and Shirley Deanna Hathaway
7. **Charles Wayne Gibson Jr.**, born 2 September 1963.
7. **Marsha Deanna Gibson**, born 30 August 1964.
7. **Christine Carlene Gibson**, born 16 November 1971.

Children of John Tillman Gibson and Caroline Narthe
7. **John Dominic Gibson**, born 9 December 1968.
7. **Toby Scott Gibson**, born 20 August 1970.

Child of Dan Martsch and Carla Mae Gibson
7. **William Lee Gibson Martsch**, born 23 June 1971.

Children of Tom Muckenthaler and Deborah Lynn McCann
7. **Jason Muckenthaler**, born 7 January 1978.
7. **David Muckenthaler**, born 15 June 1980.

Children of Louis Dyer and Barbara Elaine Tabler
7. **Timothy Dwyer**
7. **Curtis Dwyer**

Child of Carl Beaver and Barbara Elaine Tabler
7. **Tammie Beaver**, born 26 February 1943.

Child of Charles Monroe Tabler and Barbara B.
7. **LeWayne Tabler**

Child of Russell Lee Tabler and Sydney Lynn Berg
7. **Melissa Bobette Tabler** was born on 4 January 1969 in Carmel, California, and married Morgan Franklin Sloan.
Their child was:
> Austin Richard Sloan

Children of Russell Lee Tabler and Connie Baker
7. **Angela Tabler**, who was born on 27 January 1971, and married Paul Barnes on 19 November 1988.
Their child was:
> Derek Michael Barnes
7. **Diedra Tabler**, born 25 January 1972.

Child of Richard Allen Tabler and Judy
7. **Jesse Tabler**, born in April 1969.
His two children were:
> Christopher Tabler
> Tristan Tabler

Children of Richard Allen Tabler and Susie
7. **Annie Tabler** was born in 1971, and married Glenn Spiginer.
Their child was:
> Sidney Alexis Spiginer

7. **Lori Tabler** was born in 1972, and married Mr. Rodney.
Their child was:
> Quinton Rodney

Child of James Hartwell Turpin and Sallie Mae Grabow
7. **James Edward Turpin**, who married Alice Marie Pior.
Their child was:
> Laura Marie Turpin

Children of Raymond Jesse Janicke and Mary Alice Starns
7. **Lou Ann Janicke**, who married a Mr. Lane.
7. **Mary Catherine Janicke**, who married a Mr. Ogg.
7. **Jessie Raymond Janicke**

Child of Donald Robertson and Mary Alice Starns
7. **George Arthur Robertson**

Children of Vernon Patrick Villars and Margaret Ann Starns
7. **Patrick Louis Villars** was born 1 March 1951 in Panama City, Florida, and married Pamela Sue Garrett, who was born 12 September 1955. His second wife was Kristi Lee Campbell, who was born 7 July 1951.
The child of Patrick Louis Villars and Pamela Sue Garrett was:
> Nathan Joseph Villars

The two children of Patrick Louis Villars and Kristi Lee Campbell were:
> Melisa Ann Villars
> Matthew Joseph Villars

7. **Margaret Ann Villars** was born 26 February 1952 in Panama City, Florida, and married Donald Peter Abodie, who was born 28 September 1948 in New Orleans, Louisiana.
Their two children were:
> Donald Peter Abodie Jr.
> Georgiana Villars Abodie

7. **Mary Kelly Villars** was born 10 February 1953 in Munich, Germany, and married Isam Omar Tuguz, born 26 March 1945 in Amman, Jordan.
Their two children were:
> Natasha Isam Omary Tuguz
> Nadia Omar Tuguz

7. **Mark Steven Villars** was born 11 March 1953 in San Antonio, and married Sherry Yvonne McCarter, born 3 November 1952 in Opelika, Alabama.
Their child was:
> Joshua Steven Villars

7. **Debra Lynn Villars** was born 16 January 1959 in Big Spring, Texas.
7. **Peter Matthew Villars** was born 23 September 1962 in Little Rock, Arkansas, and married Debra Lynn Dale, born 29 May 1964.
7. **Elizabeth Joan Villars** was born 15 July 1965 in Shreveport, Louisiana.

Children of Billy Thomas Malone and Hazel Louise Starns
7. **Louanna Jane Malone** was born 2 June 1950 and married George Rector.
Their two children were:
> David Lee Rector
> Brandy Rector

7. **Jimmie Mattie Malone**, who married Ronnie Hennis.
Their four children were:
> Ronnie William Hennis
> Richard Louis Hennis
> Sherman Wayne Hennis
> Todd Elton Hennis

7. **Billy Thomas Malone Jr.**, born 20 July 1953.

Child of Clyde Frederick Grady and Hazel Louise Starns
7. **Dennis Leon Grady**, born 23 May 1958.

Children of Robert Ray Foylds and Nancy Arlene Barrett
7. **Barbara Lynn Foylds** was born 21 October 1955, and married John Sparks.
Their child was:
    John Robert Sparks
7. **Peggy Diane Foylds**, who married Scott Gaskill on 14 July 1976 in Big Spring, Texas.
Their two children were:
    Staci Diana Gaskill
    Steven Gaskill

Children of Gerald Elmer Barrett and Tommie Lewise Fields
7. **Jacqueline Ruth Barrett** was born 29 June 1955, and on 18 March 1978 married Larry Wayne Patton, born 10 October 1951.
Their four children were:
    Matthew Roland Patton
    Terrie Kay Patton
    Gerald Mark Patton
    Lindsey Michelle Patton
7. **Matthew Roland Barrett**, born 10 June 1960 in Houston.
7. **Terrie Kay Barrett**, born 10 February 1963 in Houston.
7. **Gerald Mark Barrett**, born 1 September 1965 in Houston.

Children of Donald Joe Barrett and Dolfaliene Von Raby
7. **Darla Sue Barrett** was born in Houston on 20 April 1959 and died 15 June 1959.
7. **Michael Shane Barrett** was born in Houston 25 September 1960.
7. **Robert Ray Barrett** was born in Houston on 15 February 1963, and married Darla Tiel, Penny Marie Alfred, Kimberli Faye Dunlap, and Betty Spake.
The child of Donald Joe and Penny Marie was:
    Robert Ray Barrett Jr.
The child of Robert Ray and Kimberli Faye was:
    Kailyn Danee Barrett
7. **Theda Gay Barrett** was born on 29 April 1964 in Houston, and on 7 May 1982 married David Brian Aiken, born 10 February 1963.
Their two children were:
    Brian David Aiken
    Nathan Allen Aiken
7. **Dana Renee Barrett** was born 6 April 1969, and married William Kyle Grant on 7 November 1992. He was born in Baytown on 12 August 1968.
Their two children were:
    Ryann Nichole Grant
    Brooklyn Renee Grant
7. **Roy Hubert Barrett** was born in Baytown on 29 May 1970, and married Kelly Dawn Edmonds on 21 November 1992. She was born in Alamogordo, New Mexico, on 21 December 1961.

Children of Hugh Redding Barrett and Vivian Klodsinski
Born in Houston, Texas
7. **Hugh Wesley Barrett**, born 11 September 1962.
7. **Jason Wade Barrett**, born 30 October 1964.
7. **Denise Orlean Barrett**, born 16 November 1965.
7. **Jonathon Gay Barrett**, born 8 February 1970.
7. **Deborah Kay Barrett**, born 30 April 1971.

Children of Wayne Stevenson and Theda Rae Barrett

7. **Scott Stevenson**
7. **Alan Stevenson**

Children of Robert Clark and Lou Ann Walls Barrett

7. **Robert Spencer Clark**, born in March 1961.
7. **Richard Winfield Clark**, born in March 1962.
7. **Karen Stephen Clark**, born 27 November 1963.
7. **Christine Noel Clark**, born 31 December 1964.

Children of John Marion Barrett and Margaret

7. **Melody Barrett**
7. **Steven Barrett**

Child of Lee Bruce Barrett and Ann

7. **Kimberly Ann Barrett**

Child of Edward Kenner and Rita Gail Barrett

7. **Edward Barrett Kenner**, born in 1983.

Children of Michael C. Baust and Patricia Ann Gray
Born in Houston, Texas

7. **Elisabeth Anne Baust**, born 6 August 1981.
7. **Benjamin Alexander Baust**, born 3 May 1983.

Child of Ardre Barrett

7. **Micah Sue Barrett** married Robert Earl Colby on 3 June 1963. He was born in San Francisco on 19 January 1942.

Children of Ronald Monroe Barrett and Georgianna Rose Redcan

7. **Travis Monroe Barrett**, born 3 May 1972.
7. **Alyse Caroline Barrett**, born 14 March 1976.
7. **Ann Louise Barrett**, born 30 June 1978.

Children of Joe Bruce Barrett and Linda O'Neal

7. **Tammy Lea Barrett**
7. **Christy Ann Barrett**
7. **Donna Jean Barrett**
7. **Susan Rene Barrett**
7. **Sabrina Carol Barrett**
7. **Bruce O'Neal Barrett**
7. **Jason Brian Barrett**

Children of Morris Randall Nelson Jr. and Carolyn Barrett

7. **Morris Randall Nelson III**
7. **Carrie Lynn Nelson**
7. **Denise Nannette Nelson**

Child of Seth Tracy McDonald

7. **Mason Everett McDonald** was born 15 October 1969 in Oceanside, California.

Children of James Ray Barrett Jr. and Barbara Cunningham

7. **James Ray Barrett III**, born 25 July 1955 in Houston.
7. **Linda Ann Barrett** was born 30 March 1956, and married Mr. Lammers.

7. **Keith William Barrett**, born 22 August 1961 in Houston.

Children of Lloyd Frederick Barrett and Wrenda Wray Oxspring
7. **Dana Lynn Barrett** was born 15 August 1958 in Houston, where she married Jeff Fincher on 8 January 1977. Jeff was born on 18 August 1956 in Downey, California.
Their five children were:
Caleb Frederick Fincher
Amanda Wray Fincher
Rachael Maree Fincher
Jesse David Fincher
Catherine Lynn Fincher
7. **Laura Ann Barrett** was born 17 December 1961 in Houston, where she married Bret Laughter on 14 February 1981 and where he was born on 2 December 1958.
Their two children were:
Laura Ashley Laughter
Bret Colman Laughter
7. **Lloyd Frederick Barrett Jr.** was born 9 September 1963 in Houston, where he married Pearl Padilla on 5 August 1989. She was born 8 August 1963 in San Diego, California.

Children of James Bruce Barrett and Elizabeth Ann Comer
7. **Kristina Ann Barrett**, born 28 May 1971 in Houston.
7. **Joshua Brandon Barrett**, born 27 July 1979 in Houston.

Children of Kenneth Ray Batson Jr. and Elizabeth Ann Hauk
7. **Kenneth Ray Batson III**, born 27 October 1967 in Houston.
7. **Jennifer Lynn Batson**, born 26 July 1971 in Houston.

Children of Clark Suttles Willingham and Jane Joyce Hitch
7. **Meredith Moores Willingham**, born 22 September 1972.
7. **James Barrett Willingham**, born 12 September 1973.

Children of Willis William Armistead Jr. and Marianne Ferris
7. **Eugene Francis Armistead**, born 17 June 1972.
7. **Cassidy Clark Armistead**, born 6 January 1975.

Child of Jack Murray Armistead and Jane Theresa Barber
7. **Emily Murray Armistead**, born 4 February 1975.

Children of Bennie Martin Jordy and Carolyn Masso
7. **Irving Jordy**
7. **Janet Marie Jordy** was born on 5 September 1960, and married Michael Shepard Newton on 27 June 1987.
7. **Jennifer Louise Jordy** was born on 22 March 1964, and married Thomas Francis Woods on 27 March 1993.
7. **Jacquelene Denise Jordy**, born 8 July 1966.

Children of Donald Irwin Jordy and Irene
7. **Jill Marie Jordy**
7. **Jeffery Don Jordy**
7. **Suzie Jordy**
7. **Donnie Jordy**

Children of Donald Lee Hoke and Mildred Arlene Jordy
7. **David Lee Hoke** was born 1 July 1957, and married Sandra Joyce McLemore on 21 January 1979.
7. **Danny Lynn Hoke** was born on 20 November 1959, and married Jana Lynn Creighton on 3 July 1985.
7. **Donna Louise Hoke** was born on 13 February 1961.
7. **Dennis Loyd Hoke** was born on 26 October 1969, and married Tabitha Armstrong on 12 February 1994.

98

Children of Luthur Hilton Jordy and Roselie Julie Yenter
7. **Debro Ann Jordy** was born on 24 January 1968 in San Diego, California, and married Andrew Negevesky on 3 October 1987.
7. **Darrell Thomas Jordy** was born on 7 January 1972 in Great Lakes, Illinois.

Children of Luke Milton Jordy and Linda Louise Froehlich
7. **Lisa Louise Jordy** was born on 5 August 1965, and married Cary Lynn Ditzman on 7 May 1994.
7. **Laura Lynette Jordy** was born 10 September 1968, and married Phil Erstz Hanusch on 4 December 1993.
7. **Larry Michael Jordy**, born 15 June 1976

Children of Rell Weldon Gamblin and Shirley Anita Skains
7. **Darwin Glen Gamblin**, born 22 May 1959.
7. **Deborah Gayle Gamblin** was born on 27 April 1961, and married Joel Carr Gotcher on 31 August 1961.
7. **Tina Lynette Gamblin** was born on 27 November 1965, and married Jim Parker on 24 July 1984.

Children of Billie Atmal Skains and Jeanne Ardell Stenzel
7. **Jolitta Anne Skains** was born on 16 November 1959, and married Bobby Bessel.
7. **James Atwal Skains** was born on 4 November 1960, and married Tina.

Children of LeRoy Koska and Gwendolyn Pitts
7. **Gregory Lee Koska** was born in March 1955 and died 17 May 1978.
7. **Kellye Lynn Koska**, born 10 July 1960.

Child of Robert Ernest Rice and Wanda Janell Pitts
7. **Paula Ann Rice**, born 17 December 1965.

Children of Hermon Oliver Romine and Mary Earnestine Lee
Born in Glendale, California
7. **Robert William Romine**, born 3 June 1957.
7. **Ellen Patricia Romine** was born on 30 January 1960, and married Christopher Frass in November 1998.
7. **Cheryl Diane Romine** was born on 12 November 1961, and married Valentin Usle on 12 December 1981.
7. **James Glen Romine** was born on 29 August 1964, and married Donna Richardson on 30 April 1994.
7. **Karen Lee Romine**, born 25 October 1970.

THIRD GENERATION
NANCY WHITTEN
1. **Nancy Whitten**, fourth child of John and Mary Reagan Whitten, was born on 10 September 1791 in Spartanburg District, South Carolina, and married John Bradley Dalton Jr. Nancy died on 25 September 1831; John, before July 1847, in Fayette County, Tennessee.
Their child was:
Mary E. Dalton

FOURTH GENERATION
Child of John Bradley Dalton Jr. and Nancy Whitten
2. **Mary E. Dalton** was born about 1830 in Hall County, Georgia, and married on 25 May 1848 in Fayette County, Tennessee, John J. Boyd, born in 1825 in North Carolina.
Their child was:
Martha E. Boyd

FIFTH GENERATION
Child of John J. Boyd and Mary E. Dalton
3. **Martha E. Boyd** was born about 1849 in Fayette County, Tennessee.

THIRD GENERATION

SILAS REAGAN WHITTEN

1. **Silas Reagan Whitten**, fifth child of John and Mary Reagan Whitten, was born on 19 February 1794 in Spartanburg District, South Carolina, and on 31 October 1815 in Rutherford County, North Carolina, married Eleanor Kee Earle, who was born on 6 January 1792 in Earle's Fort, in that county. Silas Reagan and Eleanor Kee died in Ripley, Tippah, Mississippi: she, 18 August 1857; he, 27 October 1888. They are buried in the Ripley Cemetery.

The family of Elinor Kee is an old and distinguished one whose members have served England, her Virginia colonies, and the states of Virginia, the Carolinas, and Kentucky with honor. John Earle, founder of the American line, was born in Dorsett, England, around 1612, a son of Sir Richerd Earle. He married Mary Symmonds, also born in England about 1630. The Earles, with three children, came to the Americas in about 1640, landing in St. Mary's, Maryland, and moving shortly thereafter across the Potomac River to Northumberland County, Virginia, in what was to become Westmoreland County. John Earle received extensive land grants from the English king, which the Earles retained for nearly 120 years. The family then moved west to nearby Frederick County, from which many migrated to the Carolinas and Kentucky. Their histories and genealogy have been well documented elsewhere. The Whittens and the Earles were closely associated from the time that Charles Whitten Sr., Col. John Earle, and his brother Judge Baylis Earle moved into close proximity along the North-South Carolina border well before 1800.

Silas Reagan Whitten served in the War of 1812, holding the rank of ensign, and was elected a Union delegate to the 1832 Nullifying Convention of South Carolina, where he voted against secession. He farmed, made fine whiskey, and held public office in South Carolina and Mississippi. Addressed as "Esquire" and "Captain" in South Carolina, and "Colonel" in Mississippi, he was a census taker, tax collector, and could perform marriages. We know from letters saved by daughter Rebecca that he was frequently consulted in matters of the law. From the same source it is learned that he was elected to public office in Tippah County, Mississippi, running on the Know-Nothing ticket.

Silas Reagan and his family were the last of John and Mary Reagan's children to leave South Carolina, setting out for Mississippi during the latter months of 1850 and settling near Ripley, Tippah County, by mid-January 1851. It is now apparent that he considered a westward move for many years before he made one, for he advertised his land in the *Greenville Mountaineer* on 24 September 1831. This was about the time that his father moved with his family to Hall County, Georgia. Perhaps he thought of joining them and changed his mind when he found no buyer. This is his ad:

FOR SALE

The undersigned proposes to sell his tract of land, of 7 or 800 acres, lying on the South Pacolet, in Greenville, near the Hogback Mountain. The advantages of a proportion of bottom, good upland, and plenty of timber, with several excellent waterfalls, are combined in this tract, on which there is now three comfortable settlements. I might further add, it is in the gold vicinity, and shews indication of being enriched with that precious metal.- Those wishing such a settlement are invited to call and view the premises. Terms will be made easy.

Silas R. Whitten

Sept. 10 1831

On 3 September 1847 Silas Reagan again advertised in the same newspaper the sale of his land, now said to comprise "near 1,400 acres." This time he proposed to offer it at public auction on 22 September 1847. The "near 1,400 acres" must have included 310 acres bought from his father, John, on 4 March 1832. John Whitten bought those acres, in Greenville District, South Carolina, on Morgan's Creek, waters of Tygar River, from John Roebuck of Greenville. Both father and son purchased much land over the years. Of this auction, we know nothing further. Greenville District land records show that on 27 November 1848 Silas recorded the sale of 50 acres (*believed to include his home place*) to Maurice "Mo" Vaughn, and on 18 November 1851, 1,250 acres on both sides of Green's Creek to James McMakin. The latter transaction necessitated a return trip to South Carolina from Mississippi. The site of his Carolina home, Pleasant Grove, adjoined lands owned by Theron Earle and David Mc. Davis.

That this family was active and well respected in the community is illustrated by the following article, which appeared in the *Greenville Mountaineer* on 19 June 1844:

The anniversary of American Independence was celebrated in a spirited manner at S. R. Whitten's, Esq., 25 miles North of Greenville C.H. The weather was unusually fine and by 10 o'clock, from 400 to 500 persons had assembled to participate in the festivities of the day. At 11 o'clock a procession was formed by the Marshall, Maj. William Fuller, preceded by two volunteer companies in uniform, commanded by Captains Jackson and Taylor, and a good band of music, which marched to the stand prepared for the speakers, where an appropriate and impressive prayer was offered up by the Rev. William Hannon, the Declaration of Independence read by Mr. A. N. Lankford (*soon to marry Harriett Earle, daughter of S. R. Whitten*), and an eloquent and interesting oration delivered by T. J. Earle (*cousin of Eleanor Kee Earle Whitten, and only nineteen years of age*). About 2 o'clock the company sat down to a sumptuous dinner prepared by S. R. Whitten, Esq. (*I wager he prepared none of it.*) After doing ample justice to the viands set before them, T. C. Carson, Esq. was requested to act as President upon the occasion, when the following toasts were read:

The report described eleven formal toasts and more than fifty offered from the floor. Many referred to the current battle to annex the Republic of Texas, the forthcoming presidential election between Polk and Clay, local elections, the ladies, temperance, and other causes receiving community attention. Sons Joseph John and Alfred Washington offered toasts, as did Elias Holcombe, husband of daughter Narcissa Amaryllis. One hundred and fifty years later, a well-known South Carolina Historian Anne K. McCuen wrote of this event, describing many of those named.

Whether the Independence Day observance was an annual event in the life of our Whittens we do not know. That a similar celebration was held 4 July 1832 is revealed in an article, titled "Celebration at Capt. Whitten's muster ground," appearing in the 30 July 1832 *Greenville Mountaineer*. The event was similar to one described in the later article. Silas R. Whitten read the Declaration of Independence; Rev. William Hannon led in prayer; Capt. John C. Hoyt delivered the oration; Col. W. T. Green furnished the meal; Dr. A. R. Laster was nominated president; and many offered toasts, among them Silas Reagan's father, John, and brothers, Alfred and Ranson.

Their eight children were:
> James Wood Whitten
> Joseph John Whitten
> Harriet Earle Whitten
> Alfred Washington Whitten
> Narcissa Amaryllis Whitten
> Rebecca Berry Whitten
> Silas Reagan Whitten Jr.
> Ranson Edwin Whitten

FOURTH GENERATION
Children of Silas Reagan Whitten and Eleanor Kee Earle

2. **James Wood Whitten** was born in Greenville District, South Carolina, 27 October 1816, and died 15 November the same year. Perhaps he was buried in the Tygar Baptist Church Cemetery in Greenville District, South Carolina. If so, the grave was not marked, or the marker has fallen victim to time.

2. **Joseph John Whitten** was born 25 September 1817 in Gowensville, Greenville District. He lived close to his father all his life. In South Carolina and Mississippi, their farms adjoined. "Berry Jo" married three wives, the first, 3 February 1842 in Greenville District, was Masina "Sina" Deborah Adams, born 1 May 1824 there and died 17 October 1851. On 15 December 1853 he married, in Ripley, Mary Jane White, born 4 March 1830 in Mississippi, and died 11 January 1864. On 5 October 1871, Joseph John married Mrs. Maggie Davis Doyle, who was born 18 May 1841 in Mississippi and died 12 February 1873. He died 18 November 1885. The four deaths occurred in Ripley, Tippah, Mississippi, where all are buried together.

The five children of Joseph John Whitten and Masina Deborah Adams were:
> Mary Eleanor Whitten
> Harriet Earle Whitten
> Baylis Earle Whitten
> Walter Wood Whitten
> Dr. Frank Adams Whitten

The five children of Joseph John Whitten and Mary Jane White were:
> Dr. William Andrew Whitten
> Narcissa Amaryllis Whitten
> Elliot Kee Whitten
> John Dayton Whitten
> Hester Virginia Whitten

The child of Joseph John Whitten and Maggie Davis Doyle was:
> Maggie Medora Whitten

2. **Harriet Earle Whitten** was born 4 February 1820 in Gowensville, where she married on 4 September 1845 Nathan Alexander Lankford, born 20 May 1819 in Greensboro, North Carolina. Harriet Earle died 17 October 1908 in Cameron, Texas, and was buried in Oakwood Cemetery, McLennan, Texas. He died 16 May 1872 in Lee County, Mississippi, and was buried there. They moved to Pontotoc County, Mississippi, late in 1845 and lived near Palmetto, which later was to become part of Lee County. She, with some of her children, settled near Waco, Texas, after Nathan Alexander died. Their story, told by her many letters, describes her homesickness after moving into the wilderness of Mississippi, and the life of a pioneer.

Their nine children were:

> Rebecca Eugenia Lankford
> William Henry Lankford
> Anna C. Lankford
> Thomas Earle Lankford
> Charles Alexander Lankford
> Sallie Florence Lankford
> Mary Kee Lankford
> Dr. John Silas Lankford
> James Dwight Lankford

2. **Dr. Alfred Washington Whitten** was born 1 March 1822 in Gowensville, South Carolina, and married on 26 February 1853 in Chalybeate, Tippah, Mississippi, Elliott Ann Ray, daughter of Rev. Ambrose Ray II and Mary Garrett Ray. She was born 22 November 1834 in South Carolina. Alfred Washington died 9 March 1897 in Jonesborough, and was buried in Union Cemetery there. Elliott Ann died 31 August 1920 at the home of her daughter, Martha Earle "Mattie" Flynn, in Olive Branch, DeSoto, Mississippi, and was buried with her husband. Alfred Washington studied medicine under Doctors Mooney and M. Baylis Earle in South Carolina, at Transylvania College in Lexington, Kentucky, and the University of Pennsylvania in Philadelphia. Upon graduating from Penn he walked home to Greenville District, South Carolina. Dr. Whitten practiced medicine in Gowensville, Pickensville, and Pendleton, South Carolina. After moving in 1850 to Mississippi, he practiced in Ripley, married, moved to Chalybeate in Tippah County, and opened an office in nearby Jonesborough. Alfred Washington practiced medicine and farmed there for the remainder of his life.

Their ten children were:

> Mary Dora "Molly" Whitten
> Sarah "Sallie" Kee Whitten
> John Graves Whitten
> Silas Ray Whitten
> Hosea Ransom Whitten
> Bedford Forrest Whitten
> Martha Earle "Mattie" Whitten
> Joseph Brooks Whitten
> Jesse June Whitten
> Maude Elliott Whitten

2. **Narcissa Amaryllis Whitten** was born 8 July 1824 in Gowensville, and married Elias Holcombe on 15 September 1842 in the home of her grandfather, Col. John Earle, in Rutherford County, North Carolina. Elias was born about 1821 in South Carolina. Narcissa died 22 January 1852 in Charleston, South Carolina, where she was buried in the churchyard of the First Baptist Church, the first Baptist Church in the South. Her burial is recorded in the church records, but her grave was covered by a building and her stone not found. "Cissa" was a prolific letter writer. Many of those she wrote were saved by her sister, , and appear in this author's book *Letters to Rebecca*. She took in sewing to augment the family income.

Their child was:

> Isabelle Tominson "Bell" Holcombe

2. **Rebecca "Becca" Berry Whitten**, collector of letters, was born 18 August 1826 in Gowensville, South Carolina, and died 2 May 1909 in Poplar Springs, Pontotoc, Mississippi. Rebecca spent her life with her father until 1883, when she moved to Poplar Springs, and lived with niece, Mary Dora, and nephew, Frank Adams Whitten. She was buried in the Poplar Springs Cemetery, which, in 1995, was all but lost to kudzu and the forests.

2. **Silas Reagan Whitten Jr.** was born 2 June 1830 in Gowensville, and married 12 October 1855 in Tippah County, Mississippi, Frances Medora Ray, daughter of Rev. Ambrose II and Mary Garrett Ray. She was born 3 April 1837 in South Carolina. Her sister, Elliott Ann, was the wife of Silas Jr.'s brother, Dr. Alfred Washington Whitten. Silas, a defender of Vicksburg, died 22 July 1863 in Newton Station, Mississippi, where he was buried in the Doolittle Confederate

Cemetery. Frances Medora died 29 June 1917 in Jonesborough, Tippah County, and was buried in Union Cemetery. Her nickname was "Duck"; his, "Pluck" and "Colonel."

Silas Jr. served in Company G, 7th Mississippi Cavalry, and Company C, 23rd Mississippi Infantry, CSA, enlisting 27 May 1861. He was wounded and captured during the battle of the Big Black about 5 July 1863. After escaping, he died of measles or pneumonia at the Newton Station Army Hospital 13 July 1863 (according to service record #W-1949-2069). On his gravestone is inscribed "died 22 July 1863."

Their four children were:

Carrie Isabel Whitten
Effie Berry Whitten
William Pendleton Whitten
Ranson Hosea Whitten

2. **Ranson Edwin Whitten**, youngest child of Silas Reagan and Eleanor Kee Earle Whitten, was born 9 July 1832 in Gowensville, South Carolina, and on 12 December 1865 in Tippah County, Mississippi, married Pochontas Medora Rogers, who was born 4 March 1849. She died 11 June 1878 in Ripley and was buried in the Ripley Cemetery with "three little ones," perhaps children who were stillborn or died shortly after birth.

After the death of Pocahontas, Ranson E. married on 17 April 1883 in Tippah County, Sarah "Sally" Moran, daughter of Willis John and Martha Portis Moran, who was born 7 February 1844 in Benton County, Mississippi. Her father's second wife was Harriett M. Whitten, a daughter of Ranson Whitten, Ranson Edwin's uncle. Sally died 25 June 1907 in Ripley, and was buried in Benton County, with her first husband, Charles W. Rowland.

Ranson served with the Army of Northern Virginia, Longstreet's Corps, throughout the Civil War, enlisting 27 May 1861, with Company G, 17th Regiment, Mississippi Infantry. He fought at Leesburg, Savage Station, Malvern Hill, Fredericksburg, Chickamauga, the Wilderness, and Belle Grove, where he was wounded. Returning to the Army, he was at Petersburg and Appomattox. Ranson's Confederate service record number is #W-2489. He wrote many letters both during and after the war. Several are contained in *Letters to Rebecca.*

There has long been confusion among Whittens concerning the spelling of Ranson. Many have believed that properly spelled the name ended with m. Rebecca's letters cleared this up. Letters exist where the various Ransons signed their names, clearly ending it with n rather than m. Other letters written by close relatives consistently address or refer to the various Ransons in this way. Only Hosea Ransom, son of Alfred Washington Whitten, used the m spelling. Why he did so is unknown to this writer. Surely, living near and knowing well his uncle Ranson Edwin, cousin Ranson Hosea, and great-uncle Ranson, he was aware of the spelling the family preferred.

In later life Ranson Edwin suffered from tic douloureux. He died 11 June 1906 in Blue Mountain, Mississippi, and was buried with Pocahontas.

The four children of Ranson Edwin Whitten and Pochontas Medora Rogers were:

Eleanor Kee Whitten
Joseph Earle Whitten
Silas Reagan Whitten
Frank Alma Whitten

The child of Ranson Edwin Whitten and Sarah "Sally" Moran Whitten was:

Alfred Tennison Whitten

FIFTH GENERATION
Children of Joseph John Whitten and Masina Deborah Adams

3. **Mary Eleanor Whitten** was born 17 November 1842 in Gowensville, South Carolina, and on 10 March 1868 in Ripley, Tippah, Mississippi, married Dr. Adrian Brown Caruth. During his last years her father lived with them and died in her home. Dr. Caruth assisted in the medical training of her brother, Dr. Frank Adams Whitten. Mary Eleanor died on 7 December 1885 in Tippah County, and was buried in the Ripley Cemetery.

Their three children were:

Albert Bedell Caruth
Rebecca Whitten Caruth
Thomas Richard "Dick" Caruth

3. **Harriett Earle Whitten** was born 15 December 1844 in Gowensville, died 30 October 1902 in Ripley, Mississippi, and was buried there.

3. **Baylis Earle Whitten** was born 31 December 1846 in Gowensville and died 23 May 1865 from wounds suffered while fighting for the Confederacy.

3. **Walter Wood Whitten** was born 25 April 1849 in Gowensville. He died 15 June 1861 in Ripley, and was

buried there.

3. **Dr. Frank Adams Whitten** was born 26 July 1851 in Ripley, and married his first cousin, Mary Dora "Molly" Whitten, on 27 April 1877 in Jonesborough. A daughter of Dr. Alfred Washington Whitten and Elliott Ann Ray, she was born 6 June 1855 in Jonesborough. Frank Adams died 23 July 1903 in Poplar Springs, Union, Mississippi, and was buried there in the same "lost cemetery," as was his aunt Rebecca. Mary Dora died 3 January 1941 in the same place but was buried in Bethel Methodist Cemetery nearby. A resident of Poplar Springs who "helped lay Mrs. Whitten out for burial" told this author that the roads were so muddy from recent rains that the Poplar Springs Cemetery could not be reached, so she might be buried with her husband. In the spring of 1995 I was very close to this old cemetery, but, assaulted by bugs, kudzu, poison ivy, and an abiding fear of snakes, I failed to reach it. The dense forests of Mississippi have swallowed it up. A younger, bolder researcher might still meet with success, especially if the attempt were made in winter.

We learn much about our Whittens from her extensive correspondence. Examples include:

Frank Adams professed Christ and joined the Poplar Springs Baptist Church in 1882 after having "a hope" for seventeen years. Receiving his medical license on 29 May 1882, he practiced in Poplar Springs for twenty-two years. His training was received from Drs. W. D. Carter and Adrian Caruth, husband of his sister, Mary Eleanor.

Their seven children were:

> Nathaniel Carter Whitten
> Mesina Elliot Whitten
> Frank Adams Whitten Jr.
> Alfred Washington Whitten
> Walter Wood Whitten
> William Holcomb Whitten
> Langston Agnew Whitten

Children of Joseph John Whitten and Mary Jane White
All born in Ripley, Mississippi

3. **Dr. William Andrew Whitten** was born 25 December 1854, and on 8 December 1887 married May Ellen Tate, who was born on 1 May 1862. Dr. Whitten was licensed to practice medicine on 29 April 1882. His office was in Orizaba; home, in Keownville, Mississippi. He died 15 June 1924; she, in 1948.

Their four children were:

> Harriet Beulah Whitten
> Harvey Earle Whitten
> William Homer Whitten
> Cora Mae Whitten

3. **Narcissa Amarylis Whitten** was born 8 May 1856, and on 8 December 1897 married Richard Allison Cox, who was born 30 January 1849. They died in Ripley: she, in 1946; he, 30 October 1917. Both were buried in the Ripley Cemetery.

3. **Elliot Kee Whitten** was born 27 February 1858, and on 1 September 1886 married James Newton Belote, who was born on 22 December 1859. Elliot Kee died 24 May 1892 in Ripley, and was buried in the cemetery there. He died 7 March 1917.

Their two children were:

> Mary Ellen Belote
> Thomas Earle Belote

3. **John Dayton Whitten** was born 30 March 1860, died 2 April 1905, and was buried in the Ripley Cemetery. He never married.

3. **Hester Virginia Whitten** was born 7 April 1862, died 11 February 1903, and was buried in the Ripley Cemetery. She did not marry.

Child of Joseph John Whitten and Maggie Davis Doyle

3. **Maggie Medora Whitten** was born 19 January 1873 in Ripley, and on 14 December 1892 in Tippah County married Mark McKinney Lowry, who was born 12 October 1868 in Benton County, Mississippi. Maggie Medora died 20 February 1955 in Ripley, and was buried there. Mark McKinney died 18 May 1959 in Benton County, and was buried in Ashland, Mississippi.

Their five children were:

> Ruth Lowry

Mark Nathaniel Lowry
Margaret Davis Lowry
William Whitten Lowry
Paul Raymond Lowry

Children of Nathan Alexander Lankford and Harriet Earle Whitten

3. **Rebecca Eugenia Lankford** was born 11 June 1846, and married Dr. T. J. Allen, who was born in 1846. She died in October 1910; he, in 1923.

3. **William Henry Lankford** was born 18 October 1847, and on 4 September 1872 married Mollie F. Gatewood. After her death he married Sarah Katherine Lettie Gatewood. He died in 1929. William Henry fought with the 11th Mississippi Cavalry, surrendered at Selma, Alabama, and moved to Sherman, Texas, in 1869.

The child of William Henry Lankford and Molly F. Gatewood was:

Henry Oswald Lankford

The three children of William Henry Lankford and Sarah Katherine Lettie Gatewood were:

William Henry Lankford Jr.
John Gunby Lankford
Ann Consuelo Lankford

3. **Anna C. Lankford** was born 14 April 1849, and on 25 January 1875 married James Sample, born 26 January 1853. She died 26 September 1883.

Their five children were:

Mollie Juanita Sample
Maurine Earle Sample
Fannie Lula Lynn Sample
Jesse Dwight Sample
Dora Eugenia Sample

3. **Thomas Earle Lankford** was born 8 January 1851, and on 6 February 1870 married Mary Adaline Frierson, who was born in Maury County, Tennessee, on 30 April 1848. He died 15 October 1887; she, 26 October 1931.

Their child was:

Mary Earle Lankford

3. **Charles Alexander Lankford** was born 29 June 1852, and on 11 February 1881 married Mary Rosanna Alexander, who died in 1933. Charles Alexander died on 11 March 1915.

Their three children were:

Ethel Pearl Lankford
Milton Alexander Lankford
Florence Kee Lankford

3. **Sallie Florence Lankford** was born 29 June 1852, and on 22 October 1876 married James William Lee, who was born 7 June 1844 and died 1 March 1916.

Their six children were:

William Ivon Lee
James Lankford Lee
John Charles Lee
Robert Earle Lee
Idanita Lee
Bertral Lee

3. **Mary Kee Lankford** was born 22 September 1855, and on 26 February 1879 married Thomas Marion Dilworth, born in 1832. They died in Waco, Texas: Mary Kee, 24 March 1924; Thomas Marion, 25 March 1932. They were buried there in Oakwood Cemetery.

Their three children were:

Thomas Gordon Dilworth
Anna Lee Dilworth
Marion Adair Dilworth

3. **Dr. John Silas Lankford** was born 27 October 1858, and on 25 July 1882 married Orienna Belle Gatewood, who was born 6 July 1860. She died 30 November 1932 in San Antonio, Texas.

Their four children were:

Lettie O'Barr Lankford

Earle Miller Lankford

Eugenia Franklin Lankford

Anna Lutie Lankford

3. **James Dwight Lankford** was born 2 October 1861, and on 6 November 1923 died, probably in Indian Territory, Oklahoma, where he owned a lumber business.

Children of Dr. Alfred Washington Whitten and Elliott Ann Ray
Born in Jonesborough, Tippah, Mississippi

3. **Mary Dora "Molly" Whitten** was born 7 June 1855, and on 27 April 1877, in Tippah County, Mississippi, married Dr. Frank Adams Whitten, her first cousin, son of Joseph John Whitten and Mesina Deborah Adams. He was born 26 July 1851 in Ripley. Mary Dora died 3 January 1941; Frank Adams, 23 July 1903, in Poplar Springs, Union, Mississippi, where they lived. He was buried in the Poplar Springs Cemetery, she in nearby Union Presbyterian Cemetery.

Their children are listed under Dr. Frank Adams Whitten.

3. **Sarah "Sallie" Kee Whitten** was born 14 November 1856, and died in July 1936 at the home of her sister, Martha Earle "Mattie" Flynn, in Olive Branch, Mississippi.

3. **John Graves Whitten** was born 9 December 1858, and on 6 December 1885 married Sallie Griffin Worsham, who was on born 21 August 1865. She died 3 September 1894 in Burgess, Lafayette, Mississippi, where she was buried in Clear Creek Cemetery. On 6 January of the following year he married Annie Frances Eaves, who was born on 30 January 1874. John Graves died 14 April 1934 in Memphis.

The four children of John Graves Whitten and Sallie Griffin Worsham were:

Artelia Clara Whitten

Alfred Washington Whitten

Benjamin Franklin Whitten

Willie Griffin Whitten

The eight children of John Graves Whitten and Anne Frances Eaves were:

Leonard Griffin Whitten

Della Kee Whitten

Edward Earle Whitten

Pearl Gladys Whitten

Hubert Fulton Whitten

John Graves Whitten Jr.

Bertha Alene Whitten

Woodrow Wilson Whitten

3. **Silas Ray Whitten** was born 10 August 1860, and on 29 November 1882 in Oxford married Ruth Sawyer Burt, daughter of Isaac Hunter Burt and Sarah Margaret Carothers. She was born 9 November 1859 in Clear Creek, Lafayette, Mississippi. He built large insurance businesses in Mississippi and South Carolina. Silas Ray died 4 February 1940; Ruth Sawyer, 24 October 1937 in Jackson, Hinds, Mississippi, where they (*my grandparents*) are buried together in Lakewood Memorial Cemetery.

Their eight children were:

Lucille Burt Whitten

Paulene Earle Whitten

Lottie Helon Whitten

Leslie Hunter Whitten

Sherod Roscoe Whitten

Ruth Christine Whitten

May Isom Whitten

Margaret Elliott Whitten

3. **Hosea Ransom Whitten** was born 10 April 1862, and married Sarah Agnes Durham on 17 March 1892 in Tippah County. She was born on 18 March 1871 in Blue Mountain, Mississippi. He died 10 July 1944 in Olive Branch, Desoto, Mississippi; she, later, while living with her daughter Paula in Texas. They were buried in the Olive Branch Cemetery. He was a teacher and president of Normal College, Pocahontas, Tennessee, and Burgess Institute in Lafayette County, Mississippi.

Their three children were:

Mary Elliott Whitten

Paula Laeta Whitten

William Douglas Whitten

3. **Rev. Bedford Forrest Whitten** was born 20 April 1864, and on 17 January 1886 married Flora Lee Bennett, who was born 4 November 1866 in Tippah County. They died in Coldwater, Tate, Mississippi: Bedford Forrest, 26 May 1943; Flora Lee, 14 May 1951. Both are buried in Memphis Memorial Park. Named after Civil War Gen. Nathan Bedford Forrest, who lived for a time near the Whittens in Tippah County, Reverend Whitten was a Baptist preacher, licensed in 1894.

Their seven children were:

Leon Theodore Whitten
Lester Calhoun Whitten
Lacy Roger Whitten
Laura Laeta Whitten
Lorimer Steadman Whitten
Loren Darnell Whitten
Lou Anna Whitten

3. **Martha Earle "Mattie" Whitten** was born 22 March 1866, and on 12 January 1904, at her parents home married George Lewis Flinn, who was born on 9 August 1858. They died in Olive Branch, DeSoto, Mississippi: she, in 1957; George Lewis, 23 February 1922; and were buried there. Her marriage was a double ceremony with sister Maude Elliott.

3. **Joseph Brooks Whitten** was born 11 August 1868, and on 20 November 1906 in Tate County, Mississippi, married Aubra Burford, who was born on 7 November 1879. Joseph Brooks died 14 April 1937 in Memphis; Aubra, 12 July 1959 in Searcy, Arkansas. They were buried in Memorial Park, Memphis.

Their seven children were:

Joseph Burford Whitten
Corinne Whitten
Aubrey DeWitt Whitten
Woodrow Carlton Whitten
Howard Brooks Whitten
Lourelia Whitten
Marie Whitten

3. **Jesse June Whitten** was born 13 June 1871, and on 29 January 1896 married Ora B. Anderson, who was born 28 June 1873 in Selmer, Hardeman, Tennessee. She died 26 March 1918 and was buried in Henry Cemetery, Corinth, Mississippi. They lived in Iuka, Tishamingo, Mississippi. On 5 June 1919 he married Mrs. Maggie Allen Harris, who was born on 13 May 1874. She died 9 March 1943 and was buried in Iuka with her first husband. Jesse June died on 11 January 1949 in Iuka, and was buried with Ora B.

The three children of Jesse June Whitten and Ora B. Anderson were:

Irene Whitten
Logan Alfred Whitten
Jesse Julian Whitten

3. **Maude Elliott Whitten** was born 12 January 1875, and on 12 January 1904 in her parents home in Tippah County married Frank Hudson Bradley, who was born 20 August 1879 in Gonzales, Texas. They died in Memphis: she, 16 January 1918; he, 7 December 1948, and were buried there.

Their five children were:

Elliott Elizabeth Bradley
Louise Elverta Bradley
Frank Herman Bradley
Naomi Bradley
Ed Farmer Bradley

Child of Elias Holcombe and Narcissa Amaryllis Whitten

3. **Isabell Tominson "Bell" Holcombe** was born 15 July 1843 in Greenville District, South Carolina. She died 29 August 1848 at the home of her uncle, Col. A. W. Holcombe, in Old Pickensville, Pickens District, South Carolina, and was buried in the Pickensville Cemetery.

Children of Silas Reagan "Pluck" Whitten Jr. and Frances Medora "Duck" Ray
Born in Jonesborough, Tippah, Mississippi

3. **Carrie Isabel Whitten** was born 30 August 1856, and on 30 November 1884 in Tippah County married Mark Pierce Richardson, who was born on 15 August 1854. They died in Tippah County: she, 7 September 1905; he, 23 February 1947, and were buried in Union Cemetery.

Their four children were:

Etta Berry Richardson

Willie Gertrude Richardson

Alabama Lee Richardson

Mark Lowrey Richardson

3. **Effie Berry Whitten** was born 29 July 1858, and married on 10 December 1895 in Jonesborough, John Caswell Perkins, who was born 20 July 1840. They died in Jonesborough: she, 6 November 1942; he, 12 February 1928; and were buried in Union Cemetery.

Their child was:

Estilla Perkins

3. **William Pendleton Whitten** was born 30 April 1860, died 15 May 1881 in Jonesborough, and was buried in the Garrett Cemetery near his home. The author visited that cemetery in 1995. It is in deep woods, soon to be overgrown and lost.

3. **Ranson Hosea Whitten** was born 21 January 1862, died 6 May 1888 in Jonesborough, and was also buried in the Garrett Cemetery. He was ill during most of his life.

Children of Ranson Edwin Whitten and Pochontas Medora Rogers

3. **Eleanor Kee Whitten** was born 20 January 1867 in Ripley, where, on 2 October 1887 she married Thomas Counseille Rucker, who was born 22 July 1861. They died in Ripley: she, 20 May 1933; he, in 1935, where they are buried.

Their five children were:

Emmaline Medora Rucker

Rupert Clyde Rucker

Joe Rogers Rucker

Ernest Rucker

Evelyn Kee Rucker

3. **Joseph Earle Whitten** was born 15 May 1868 in Ripley, and on 29 December 1898 married Lula Mae Tate, who was born on 22 May 1876. They lived for many years in Cullman, Alabama, where he died on 27 October 1943 and is buried. She died on 16 April 1950 in Jackson, Tennessee, at the home of her daughter and was buried with her husband. Joseph Earle began his career in 1894 as an engineer working at the Tennessee Coal, Iron, and Railroad Company mines in Pratt City, Alabama, which used prison labor. In Cullman he worked as a jeweler and optometrist.

Their child was:

Hazel Marie Whitten

3. **Silas Reagan Whitten** was born 6 September 1872 in Ripley, where he died on 3 October 1921 and was buried.

Our Whittens and the Panola/Tallahatchie County, Mississippi, lines have long thought themselves to be branches of the same tree, although evidence proving this has yet to be found. In an early edition of *Whittens and Allied Families*, there appears a report of a visit, in 1904, by a Silas Reagan Whitten with descendants of Lindsey and Berry Whitten during which the relationship was discovered and later forgotten. During the festivities surrounding the marriage of his daughter to the son of my first cousin, Rep. Jamie Whitten of the Tallahatchie County Whittens also spoke of it. Only this descendant of John Whitten bearing the name Silas Reagan was alive in 1904. Is it possible that he went to his death with this vital piece of the Whitten puzzle? I think not. A second version, told to me by a Tallahatchie County Whitten, claimed the meeting occurred later, and involved Silas Ray, my grandfather; and the congressman, who for a time lived within an hour's drive of one another while Jamie was a rising politician and Silas Ray an life insurance salesman. That they met is possible; discovering the link is highly improbable. Neither showed much interest in Whitten family lore nor possessed sufficient data with which to solve this mystery. Its solution lies generations before Charles and Nancy Smith Whitten.

3. **Frank Alma Whitten** was born 27 December 1875 in Ripley, and on 1 October 1896 in Tippah County married Charles Edward Tate, brother of Lula Mae Tate, the wife of Frank Alma's brother Joseph Earle Whitten. Charles Edward was born 26 May 1857. He died in Jackson, Tennessee, on 14 January 1930; she, in Memphis in 1955. *Letters to Rebecca* contains a letter to Aunt Rebecca written by Joseph Earle Whitten in which he was bitterly critical of sister Frank Alma. Evidence supplied by his grandson indicates the rift was repaired, and the siblings were close throughout the rest of their lives.

Their two children were:

Charles Edward Tate Jr.

William Irvin Tate

Child of Ranson Edwin Whitten and Sarah "Sally" Moran

3. **Alfred Tennyson Whitten** was born 1 March 1884 in Ripley, and on 1 March 1917 married Margaret Josephine Halsell, who was born on 25 March 1882 in Chickasaw County, Mississippi. They died in Jackson, Mississippi: he, 22 August 1959; she, 8 December 1963, where they were buried in Lakewood Memorial Cemetery. The couple lived in Jackson, where he was a prominent educator and assembled extensive Whitten family records. Like his father, Alfred Tennyson suffered with tic douloureux. Whitten Junior High School in Jackson bears his name.

Their child was:

Dr. Joseph Nathaniel Whitten

SIXTH GENERATION

Children of Dr. Adrian Brown Caruth and Mary Eleanor Whitten

4. **Albert Bedell Caruth** married Daisy Pope on 12 October 1905.

4. **Rebecca Whitten Caruth** was born 11 June 1877, and married Harvey Nichol.

Their two children were:

Doris Nichol

Merrill Nichol

4. **Thomas Richard "Dicka" Caruth** married Lena Boyd, who was born 16 April 1891.

Their child was:

Thomas Richard Caruth Jr.

Children of Dr. Frank Adams Whitten and Mary Dora "Molly" Whitten

4. **Nathaniel Carter Whitten** was born 14 June 1878 in Tippah County, and on 28 September 1898 in Cotton Plant, Tippah, Mississippi, married Myrtle Anna Wiseman, who was born on 1 February 1877 in New Albany, Mississippi. They died in New Albany: he, 21 December 1945; she, 7 November 1949, and were buried there.

Their seven children were:

Mamie Lorene Whitten

William Carey Whitten

Bonner Frank Whitten

Martha Azlee Whitten

Vera Vermelle Whitten

Mirian Elinor Whitten

Nathaniel Murry Whitten

4. **Mesina Elliot Whitten** was born 12 March 1881 in Poplar Springs, Pontotoc, Mississippi, and on 16 January 1902 married Varda Smith, who was born 12 May 1872, also in Poplar Springs. They died and are buried in New Albany: she, 27 October 1967; he, 1 June 1959.

Their three children were:

Frank Smith

Lola Ivy Smith

Lora V. Smith

4. **Frank Adams Whitten Jr.** was born 21 June 1882 in Poplar Springs, where he died on 8 May 1956. He was buried with his mother in Bethel Methodist Cemetery, Union County, Mississippi.

4. **Alfred Washington Whitten** was born 26 February 1885 in Poplar Springs, and died 19 July 1887 from burns suffered when he fell into his mother's wash kettle.

4. **Walter Wood Whitten** was born 21 September 1887 in Poplar Springs, and on 10 November 1912 married Martha Gordon Eason, who was born on 30 June 1886 in Byhalia, Marshall, Mississippi. She died 25 November 1946 in Macon, Mississippi, where they lived. Walter Wood then married, in Macon, Mary Lillian Peters Ogden, born in Mashulaville, Noxubee, Mississippi. He died 2 September 1973 in a nursing home in Columbus, Mississippi, and was buried in Byhalia. Walter Wood's aunt, Rebecca Berry Whitten, left him her collection of letters. After his death his widow Mary Lillian gave them to Murry Whitten, who loaned them to me for inclusion in *Letters to Rebecca*. She was living in Macon in 1993.

4. **William Holcomb Whitten** was born 21 August 1889 in Poplar Springs, died 27 April 1893, and was buried there.

4. **Langston Agnew Whitten** was born 3 December 1890 in Poplar Springs, and on 12 November 1912 married

Jesse May Potter, who was born on 20 August 1893 in Coldwater, Tate, Mississippi. They died in Tupelo: he, 25 June 1980; she, 21 September 1973. They were buried in the Endville Baptist Cemetery, Pontotoc County.

Their nine children were:

> Wood Agnew Whitten
> William Langston Whitten
> Joe Brooks Whitten
> Jessie June Whitten
> Mary Elliott Whitten
> Florence Lee Whitten
> Linda Ruth Whitten
> Doris Ann Whitten
> Dora Mae Whitten

Children of Dr. William Andrew Whitten and May Ellen Tate

4. **Harriet Beulah Whitten** was born 4 October 1888, and on 14 November 1916 married Carl Sidney Hines, who was born 8 March 1889 and died in 1932. Their two sons operated a country store in Keonville, Mississippi.

Their four children were:

> Mary Laura Hines
> Thelma Elaine Hines
> Joseph Steen Hines
> Chester Olen Hines

4. **Harvey Earle Whitten** was born 12 March 1890 and on 11 July 1920 married Lessie May Byers, who was born on 17 September 1900.

Their five children were:

> William Tate Whitten
> Harvey Earle Whitten Jr.
> Walter Andrew Whitten
> Climmie Twanda Whitten
> Allen Kendrick Whitten

4. **William Homer Whitten** was born 9 October 1892, and on 25 July 1915 married Emily Inez Wade, who was born 13 October 1898.

Their four children were:

> Birdie May Whitten
> Adriane Clive Whitten
> Mary Louise Whitten
> Homer Wade Whitten

4. **Cora Mae Whitten** was born 4 September 1896. She and her sister, Harriet Hines, wrote to Alfred Tennyson Whitten and described her family. It was dated 7 February 1957. At that time she was unmarried and living at her father's old home in Keonville, Mississippi.

Children of James Newton Belote and Elliot Kee Whitten

4. **Mary Ellen Belote** was born 24 August 1888, and on 5 June 1906 married William Mitchell Haley, who was born 21 March 1883.

4. **Thomas Earle Belote** was born 24 April 1890, and on 20 October 1919 married Annie McDaniel, who was born on 5 January 1902.

Their two children were:

> Earle Newton Belote
> Louise Holmes Belote

Children of Mark McKinney Lowry and Maggie Medora Whitten
Born in Ripley, Tippah, Mississippi

4. **Ruth Lowry** was born 7 May 1895, and on 27 August 1919 married Homer Martin, who was born on 28 November 1892. Ruth died 23 December 1959 in Memphis, where she was buried in the Mount Vernon Cemetery.

Their three children were:

> James Lowry Martin

Roy Rudolph Martin
Sarah Louise Martin
4. **Mark Nathaniel Lowry** was born 10 January 1899, and on 4 November 1923 married Vivian Strickland, who was born 23 June 1901. She died in 1936 and was buried in Wiers Chapel Cemetery in Tippah County. Following her death he married Madge Y., born in 1908. They died in Ripley: he, in 1965; she, in 1987; and lie together in the Ripley Cemetery.
The child of Mark Nathaniel Lowry and Vivian Strickland was:
Betty W. Lowry
4. **Margaret Davis Lowry** was born 18 April 1904, and on 18 June 1943 married Roderick B. McGill. In 1970 they were living in West Point, Mississippi.
4. **William Whitten Lowry** was born 6 November 1906.
4. **Paul Raymond Lowry** was born 29 January 1917, and on 20 June 1941 married Myra Belle Myers, who was born on 25 June 1916. They died in Ripley she, 30 August 1979; he, 27 April 1992. They were buried in the Ripley Cemetery.

Child of William Henry Lankford and Molly F. Gatewood
4. **Henry Oswald Lankford** was born and died 5 November 1878.

Children of William Henry Lankford and Sarah Katherine Lettie Gatewood
4. **William Henry Lankford Jr.** was born 18 April 1889 and died 26 February 1929.
4. **John Gunby Lankford**, who was born 10 June 1892 and died 15 July 1916.
4. **Ann Consuelo Lankford** was born 23 March 1895, and married Dr. John E. Neador, who was born in 1890.

Children of James Sample and Anna C. Lankford
4. **Mollie Juanita Sample** was born 3 April 1875, and in 1891 married Rev. D. M. Yarbrough.
4. **Maurine Earle Sample** was born 26 August 1877, and in 1911 married J. T. Jackson, who died in 1922.
4. **Fannie Lula Lynn Sample** was born 24 December 1878, married Charles Mauldin on 4 February 1899, and died 29 November 1929.
4. **Jesse Dwight Sample** was born 28 February 1881, and married on 23 January 1905 Margaret Rosanna Kimmons, who was born 16 February 1883.
Their six children were:
James Dwight Sample
Anna Margaret Sample
Lulyn Dorothy Sample
Jeanne Sample
Josephine Sample
Dwight Edward Sample
4. **Dora Eugenia Sample** was born 7 December 1882, and in 1916 married J. T. Davis.

Child of Thomas Earle Lankford and Mary Adaline Frierson
4. **Mary Earle Lankford** was born 2 March 1886, and married on 3 August 1914 Thomas Jefferson Avera, who was born in 1879.

Children of Charles Alexander Lankford and Mary Rosanna Alexander
4. **Ethel Pearl Lankford** was born 3 October 1881, and on 14 July 1901 married James Henry Coffield, who was born on 15 August 1882 and died 25 December 1926. Ethyl Pearl died 14 July 1915.
4. **Milton Alexander Lankford** was born 1 November 1882, and on 20 November 1912 married Elizabeth Jean Gillespie, who was born on 29 July 1888. They lived in Dallas, Texas in 1909.
4. **Florence Kee Lankford** was born 12 May 1884, married on 16 June 1909 Joseph Murrow McBride who, was born 19 July 1880, and died 16 June 1905.
Their three children were:
Florence Lankford McBride
Charles William McBride
Joseph Murrow McBride Jr.

Children of James William Lee and Sallie Florence Lankford

4. **William Ivon Lee** was born 26 July 1877, and on 9 June 1906 married Ella Byrd Bell, who was born in 1877. Their child was:

William Ivon Lee Jr.

4. **James Lankford Lee** was born 29 July 1879.

4. **John Charles Lee** was born and died on 31 May 1881.

4. **Robert Earle Lee** was born 15 April 1889 and died 5 February 1911.

4. **Idanita Lee** was born 21 June 1896, and married Huber Charles Serodina on 12 March 1926. He was born 22 June 1883.

4. **Bertral Lee**

Children of Thomas Marion Dilworth and Mary Kee Lankford

4. **Thomas Gordon Dilworth** was born 5 January 1880 in Sharp, Milan, Texas and married Gara Katherine Wheelock, who was born on 10 April 1882 in Ft. Wayne, Indiana. His second wife was Margaret Love Scott, who was born on 2 December 1889. They died in Waco: she in September 1963; he, 18 November 1944; and were buried in Oakwood Cemetery there.

The two children of Thomas Gordon Dilworth and Gara Katharine Wheelock were:

Thomas Gordon Dilworth II

Katherine Earle Dilworth

The two children of Thomas Gordon Dilworth and Margaret Scott were:

Celia Kee Dilworth

Margaret Scott Dilworth

4. **Anna Lee Dilworth** was born 26 November 1886, and married on 29 July 1917 Richard Clyde Johnson. On 7 June 1924 she married Elmer Curt Hake, died 9 April 1960, and was buried in Oakwood Cemetery.

The child of Richard Clyde Johnson and Anna Lee Dilworth was:

Marianne Dilworth Johnson

4. **Marion Adair Dilworth** was born 14 July 1897, and married on 10 June 1917 Henri S. Lucenay. She died 17 January 1977.

Their child was:

Theodore Lucenay

Children of Dr. John Silas Lankford and Orienna Belle Gatewood

4. **Lettie O'Barr Lankford** was born 6 June 1883, and on 3 June 1903 married Willoughby M. Crebau, who was born 2 April 1860 and died on 12 June 1923.

Their two children were:

Lettie Belle Crebau

Olive Gene Crebau

4. **Earle Miller Lankford** was born 29 October 1884, and on 30 July 1909 married Annie Louise Hoffman, who was born on 24 February 1888. Earle Miller died on 19 April 1918; Annie Louise, in 1914.

Their child was:

Earle Louise Lankford

4. **Eugenia Franklin Lankford** was born 22 February 1886, and on 7 July 1921 married Theodore Marchant Lawrence, who was born on 3 March 1889.

Their child was:

Virginia Belle Lawrence

4. **Anna Lutie Lankford** was born 17 July 1888, and on 12 June 1913 married Frank Pershing Hopwood, who was born on 30 November 1885 and died 21 July 1919. She lived at the home of her father in San Antonio, Texas, in 1993.

Their child was:

Frank Pershing Hopwood Jr.

Children of John Graves Whitten and Sallie Griffin Worsham

4. **Artelia Clara Whitten** was born 28 October 1886, and on 1 February 1916 married William Felix Cooper, who was born 19 June 1877.

Their child was:

William Felix Cooper Jr.

4. **Alfred Washington Whitten** was born on 8 December 1888 and died 28 April 1940.

4. **Benjamin Franklin Whitten** was born 7 January 1891 in Tippah, and on 13 June 1919 married Ora Mae Phillips, who was born on 16 February 1890 in Mississippi. Benjamin Franklin died 1 September 1971; Ora Mae, 30 May 1967 in Memphis, where they were buried in Memorial Park. He had inherited the Bible of Silas Reagan Whitten and later gave it to cousin Aubrey DeWitt Whitten. Benjamin Franklin was a real estate developer, active in East Memphis. Whitten Avenue bears his name. Their only child was born and died on 10 February 1939 in Memphis. It was buried in Memorial Park.

4. **Willie Griffin Whitten** was born 2 July 1893, died 3 October 1894, and was buried in Clear Creek Cemetery, Burgess, Mississippi.

Children of John Graves Whitten and Annie Frances Eaves

4. **Leonard Griffin Whitten** was born 23 October 1895, and on 3 May 1920 married Lois Diana Peters, who was born on 3 May 1899.

Their three children were:

Warren Norman Whitten

Leonard Griffin Whitten Jr.

Donald Homer Whitten

4. **Della Kee Whitten** was born 12 June 1897, and on 11 April 1919 married Thomas Edward Williams, who was born on 8 December 1892.

Their four children were:

Thomas Edward Williams Jr.

Frances Elizabeth Williams

Della Lucille Williams

Martha Ruth Williams

4. **Edward Earle Whitten** was born 7 June 1899, and married on 10 June 1917 Hattie Donna Crews, who was born on 17 June 1899.

Their four children were:

Edward Earle Whitten Jr.

Dorothy Louise Whitten

James Robert Whitten

Donna Alice Ruby Whitten

4. **Pearl Gladys Whitten** was born 2 September 1901, and married on 21 March 1922 William David Crews, who was born on 14 August 1888.

Their two children were:

Juanita Lucille Crews

William David Crews Jr.

4. **Hubert Fulton Whitten** was born 28 January 1904, and married on 16 September 1930 Bennie Forest Graves, who was born 19 August 1904.

Their child was:

Hubert Fulton Whitten Jr.

4. **John Graves Whitten Jr.** was born 15 May 1908, and married on 16 September 1930 Dorothy Iola Jordan, who was born 12 January 1910.

4. **Bertha Alene Whitten** was born 27 April 1910, and married on 30 July 1926 William Hutchins Roberts, born 8 September 1904.

Their child was:

Jeanette Alene Roberts

4. **Woodrow Wilson Whitten** was born 16 February 1913 and died 17 February 1913.

Children of Silas Ray Whitten and Ruth Sawyer Burt

4. **Lucille Burt Whitten** was born 4 October 1883 in Blue Mountain, Tippah, Mississippi, where she married on 5 February 1906 Winfield Quin Sharp, who was born 30 April 1881 in McComb, Mississippi. She died in Jackson, Mississippi, 19 March 1973; he, 21 July 1938 in Washington, D.C. They are buried in Lakewood Memorial Cemetery. Lucille Whitten Sharp was a well-known Mississippi artist.

Their child was:

Dorothy Sharp

4. **Pauline Earle Whitten** was born 8 October 1885 in Jonesborough, and married on 10 September 1914 Gilbert

Cameron Cunningham, who was born 19 November 1886 in Guelph, Ontario, Canada. She died 20 June 1969 in Frederickton, New Brunswick, Canada; he, in 1947 while traveling through Camden, New Jersey. Both were buried in Forest Hill Cemetery, Frederickton, New Brunswick, Canada.

Their five children were:

Gilbert Cameron Cunningham Jr.

David Hunter Cunningham

Ruth Catherine Cunningham

Paulene Whitten Cunningham

Margaret Helen Cunningham

4. **Lottie Helon "Nanny" Whitten** was born 18 May 1887 in Clear Creek, Lafayette, Mississippi, and married on 22 April 1910 in Jackson, Mississippi, Dr. Walter McDonald Merritt, who was born on 25 October 1882 in Black Hawk, Carroll, Mississippi. She died 15 January 1958 in Cleveland, Bolivar, Mississippi; he, 1 February 1948 in Memphis, Tennessee. They were buried in Lakewood Memorial Cemetery in Jackson, Mississippi.

Their two children were:

Walter McDonald Merritt Jr.

Dr. Charles Wesley Merritt

4. **Leslie Hunter Whitten** was born 26 April 1889 in Clear Creek, Lafayette, Mississippi, and married on 23 December 1926 Linnora Harvey, who was born on 16 November 1896 in West Blocton, Alabama. They died in Washington, D.C.: he, 26 October 1959; she, in 1990; and are buried in Arlington National Cemetery.

Their three children were:

Leslie Hunter Whitten Jr.

Frank Harvey Whitten

Stanley Burt Whitten

4. **Sherod Roscoe "S. R." Whitten** was born 29 December 1890 in Alesville, Lafayette, Mississippi, and on 20 May 1916 married Marie Burr, who was born 8 March 1894 in St. Louis, Missouri. He died in 1947 in Los Angeles, California; she, 16 July 1988 in Jackson, Mississippi. They are buried in Oak Hill Cemetery, Kirkwood, Missouri.

Their child was:

Sherod Ray "Sonny" Whitten

4. **Ruth Christine "Aunt Sister" Whitten** was born 25 December 1894 in Burgess, Lafayette, Mississippi, and married on 13 October 1920 Carl Gustav Levring, who was born 28 October 1893 in Copenhagen, Denmark. She died 21 February 1965 in Jackson, Mississippi, and was buried in Lakewood Memorial Cemetery. He died 13 October 1925 in Columbia, South Carolina, and was buried there.

Their child was:

Jane Duncan Levring

4. **May Isom Whitten**, mother of the author, was born 17 February 1897 in Oxford, Lafayette, Mississippi, and on 15 December 1918 at the home of her parents on Carlisle Street in Jackson, Mississippi, married William Black Moore, who was born 25 July 1895 in Oakland, Yalobusha, Mississippi. She died in Jackson 14 July 1982. He died 4 April 1984 in Kilmarnock, Virginia, having recently moved there to live with his son and daughter-in-law. They were buried in Lakewood Memorial Cemetery in Jackson, Mississippi.

Their child was:

William Black Moore Jr.

4. **Margaret Elliott Whitten** was born 7 June 1900 in Coffeevillee, Yalobusha, Mississippi, and on 13 February 1929 in Columbia, South Carolina, married William Merritt Quattlebaum, who was born there on 9 December 1897. William B. Moore Jr. served as ring bearer, Jane Duncan Levring as flower girl. They divorced shortly after marriage. She lived in Columbia, died 20 July 1983 in Raleigh, North Carolina, and was buried in Westminster Cemetery, Guilford County, North Carolina.

Children of Hosea Ransom Whitten and Sarah Agnes Durham

4. **Mary Elliott Whitten** was born 13 October 1896, died 16 January 1901, and was buried in Blue Mountain, Mississippi.

4. **Paula Laeta Whitten** was born 6 October 1903 in Blue Mountain. She lived in Dallas in 1980, and died there.

4. **William Douglas Whitten** was born 13 April 1911 in Stonewall, Oklahoma, and on 21 April 1930 in Tate County, Mississippi, married Alice Elizabeth Booth, who was born on 28 November 1913. After her death he married Marguerite Odell, who was born 29 April 1911.

The child of William Douglas Whitten and Alice Elizabeth Booth was:

114

Lora Laeta Whitten
The child of William Douglas Whitten and Marguerite Odell was:
Patricia Odell Whitten

Children of Rev. Bedford Forrest Whitten and Flora Lee Bennett

4. **Leon Theodore Whitten** was born 21 January 1886, and on 11 December 1907 married Alena Victoria Byrnes, who was born on 11 December 1889. They lived in Memphis. Leon Theodore died 2 March 1970 and was buried in Memorial Park, Memphis.

Their three children were:
Leon Theodore Whitten Jr.
Neil Durwood Whitten
Jean Marsalee Whitten

4. **Lester Calhoun Whitten** was born 12 February 1888, and married Richie Bridges. He died 27 July 1933 and was buried in Forest Hill Cemetery, Memphis.

4. **Lacy Roger Whitten** was born 16 January 1890, and on 13 August 1918 married Marie Louise Collins, who was born 22 February 1898. They lived in San Antonio, Texas.

Their two children were:
Maxine Whitten
Lacy Roger Whitten Jr.

4. **Laura Laeta Earle Whitten** was born 27 February 1892, and on 30 December 1920 married Wyatt Wolf Lipscomb, who was born on 16 September 1886. They lived in Albany, Texas.

Their two children were:
Wyatt Whitten Lipscomb
Millie Jean Lipscomb

4. **Lorimer Steadman Whitten** was born on 13 April 1894 and lived in Coldwater, Mississippi.

4. **Loren Darnell Whitten** was born 17 June 1895, and on 19 August 1922 married Helen Bower, who was born on 13 October 1900. They lived in New York City.

Their two children were:
George Bedford Whitten
Ward Bonner Whitten

4. **Lou Anna Whitten** was born 22 February 1902, and on 9 June 1925 in Memphis married United States Marshall Ticer Young, who was born on 25 June 1898 in Ripley, Tippah, Mississippi. He died in 1982 and was buried in St. Peters Cemetery, Oxford, Mississippi. She was living in Oxford in 1991 and was blind.

Their two children were:
Lester Whitten Young
Loren Ticer Young

Children of Joseph Brooks and Aubra Burford Whitten

4. **Joseph Burford Whitten** was born 7 April 1908 in Memphis, and on 23 September 1933 married Estelle Meacham. She died on 9 February 1938 in Memphis. On 11 April 1940 he married Maggie Lee Bell, who was born on 9 December 1912 in Memphis, where he died on 5 September 1986. He was buried with Estelle in Memorial Park. Maggie Lee was living in Memphis in 1992.

The child of Joseph Burford Whitten and Estelle Meacham was:
Wanda Lee Whitten
The child of Joseph Burford Whitten and Maggie Lee Bell was:
Beverly Ann Whitten

4. **Corinne Whitten** was born 28 September 1910 in Memphis, and on 19 December 1936 married William Leslie Burke, who was born 24 July 1909 in Jacksonville, Illinois. He died 18 December 1991 in Searcy, Arkansas. They lived in Syracuse, New York.

Their child was:
Leslie Carlton Burke

4. **Aubrey DeWitt Whitten** was born 19 January 1913 in Memphis, and married Iona Jernigan. They divorced, and he married Alice Adams on 6 April 1947 in Memphis. She was born 10 September 1916 in Paducah, Kentucky. DeWitt Whitten has the family Bible of Silas Reagan Whitten, which was given to him by Benjamin Franklin Whitten. DeWitt and Alice lived in Memphis in 1998.

The four children of Aubrey Dewitt Whitten and Alice Adams were:
>Alice Marie Whitten
>Rev. Aubrey DeWitt Whitten Jr.
>Mary Anne Whitten
>Benjamin Joseph Whitten

4. Woodrow Carlton Whitten, Ph.D., was born 3 January 1915 in Memphis, and married Elwanda Kniffin, who was born on 30 July 1921 in McLean, Oklahoma. He died on 24 December 1988 in California.
>Their three children were:
>Janna Lynette Whitten
>Gayla Marie Whitten
>Merri Lynn Whitten

4. Howard Brooks Whitten was born 6 January 1917 in Camden, Tennessee, and on 9 October 1938 in Memphis married Robbie Estelle Smothers, who was born on 21 October 1918. Howard Brooks died 27 January 1989 in Memphis and was buried in Memorial Park.
>Their two children were:
>Joseph Brooks Whitten
>William DeWitt Whitten

4. Lourelia Whitten was born 6 February 1920 in Memphis, and married 23 January 1942 Dewey Lee Word, born 18 February 1917 in Rison, Arkansas. They lived in Buffalo, New York.
>Their two children were:
>James Lee Word
>Kay Marie Word

4. Marie Whitten was born 11 April 1922 in Memphis, died 30 April 1932 there, and was buried in Memorial Park.

Children of Jesse June Whitten and Ora B. Anderson

4. Irene Whitten was born 18 November 1896, and married on 24 June 1917 Harry Earl Munday, who was born on 12 October 1891. Irene died 7 December 1958 and was buried in Henry Cemetery, Corinth.
>Their child was:
>Baronson Elizabeth Munday

4. Logan Alfred Whitten was born 16 February 1901, and married on 12 February 1922 Thelma Thorne, who was born 8 December 1900 in Iuka. He died 2 January 1987 and was buried in Oak Grove Cemetery, Iuka. She was living in Iuka 2 in March 1991. The couple lived most of their married life in Memphis.
>Their two children were:
>Margaret Elizabeth Whitten
>Jane Whitten

4. Jesse Julian Whitten was born 12 June 1904, and on 2 April 1925 married Louise Knight, who was born on 25 January 1906. He died in 1936 and was buried in Henry Cemetery, Corinth.

Children of Frank Hudson Bradley and Maude Elliott Whitten

4. Elliott Elizabeth Bradley was born 18 October 1904 in Chalybeate, Tippah, Mississippi, and died 22 June 1919.

4. Louise Elverta Bradley was born 19 December 1905 in Chalybeate.

4. Frank Herman Bradley was born 12 January 1909 in Olive Branch, Mississippi, and married on 22 December 1946. The name of his wife is not known.

4. Naomi Bradley was born 14 February 1911, and married on 17 October 1933 Hamilton Karch. On 25 August 1946 she married Lawrence Crudup.

4. Ed Farmer Bradley was born 14 February 1911, and on 2 July 1931 married Lina Mae Davis, who was born 23 May 1907.

Children of Mark Pierce Richardson and Carrie Isabel Whitten
All born and died in Tippah County, Mississippi

4. Etta Berry Richardson was born 25 September 1885, died 24 April 1911, and was buried in Union Cemetery.

4. Willie Gertrude Richardson was born 12 December 1887, died 21 December 1973, and was buried in Union Cemetery.

116

4. **Alabama Lee Richardson** was born 8 February 1889, died 22 February 1921, and was buried in Union Cemetery.

4. **Mark Lowrey Richardson** was born 29 January 1891, and married 27 December 1930 Alline Bennett, born 17 September 1905. He died 2 November 1976 and was buried in Union Cemetery.

Child of John Caswell Perkins and Effie Berry Whitten

4. **Estilla Perkins** was born 22 August 1900 in Tippah County, died 13 October 1900 there, and was buried in Union Cemetery.

Children of Thomas Counsielle Rucker and Eleanor Kee Whitten

4. **Emmaline Medora Rucker** was born 1 August 1888, and married on 19 December 1909 James Clifton Wall, who was born on 20 December 1889.

Their two children were:
> William Clifton Wall
> Jenny Laura Wall

4. **Rupert Clyde Rucker** was born 21 August 1891 in Tippah, and married Willie Leaty Spencer, who was born 8 September 1894 in Mississippi. They died in Tippah: he, 19 February 1940; she, 17 September 1935, and were buried in Ripley Cemetery.

Their seven children were:
> Troy Ellis Rucker
> Clyde Lafayette Rucker
> Lloyd Jackson Rucker
> Jesse Rogers Rucker
> Rufus Lee Rucker
> William Harrell Rucker
> Carol Jefferson Rucker

4. **Joe Rogers Rucker** was born 14 September 1893 in Ripley, where he died on 28 February 1968, and was buried in Ripley Cemetery.

4. **Ernest Rucker** was born 5 June 1896 in Tippah, and married on 4 June 1919 in Ripley Garnier Gill, who was born on 26 August 1895. He died 9 July 1965 in Tippah, and was buried in the Ripley Cemetery.

Their four children were:
> Sarah Lou Rucker
> Ernestine Rucker
> Mary Elaine Rucker
> Eleanor Maxine Rucker

4. **Evelyn Kee Rucker** was born on 24 May 1899, and married a Mr. Harris.

Child of Joseph Earle Whitten and Lula Mae Tate

4. **Hazel Marie Whitten** was born 22 February 1904 in Birmingham, Alabama, and married on 21 July 1927, in Hernando, Mississippi, Vance Cyril Roy, who was born in Memphis 13 December 1902 and died 16 March 1956. She died 7 December 1987 in Albany, Georgia, in the home of her son.

Their child was:
> Dr. Vance Cyril Roy Jr.

Children of Charles Edward and Frank Alma Whitten Tate

4. **Charles Edward Tate Jr.** was born 27 June 1897, and married on 3 March 1920 Rebecca Rose Love, who was born 18 April 1899.

Their child was:
> Jane Love Tate

4. **William Irvin Tate** was born 9 June 1899, and married on 15 September 1927 Dorothy Louise Joeckal, who was born 23 November 1900.

Child of Alfred Tennyson Whitten and Margaret Josephine Halsell

4. **Joseph Nathaniel Whitten** was born 30 November 1917 in Jackson, Mississippi. He received the degree of Ph.D. in education from New York University, and served for many years as librarian and instructor in library science in

several institutions, including Cooper Union College and Columbia University in New York City. He retired as professor emeritus at Palmer School of Library and Information Science, Long Island University, and moved to Madison, Mississippi, where he died 25 October 1996. Dr. Whitten was buried with his parents in Lakewood Memorial Park, Hinds County, Mississippi.

SEVENTH GENERATION

Children of Harvey Nichol and Rebecca Whitten Caruth

5. **Doris Nichol** was born 20 September 1906, and married 5 February 1932 a Mr. Logan.

5. **Merrill Nichol**, born 18 January 1908.

Child of Thomas Richard Caruth and Lena Boyd

5. **Thomas Richard Caruth Jr.**, born 12 October 1928.

Children of Nathaniel Carter Whitten and Myrtle Anna Wiseman

5. **Mamie Lorene Whitten** was born 18 September 1900 in Poplar Springs, and married 10 June 1924 in New Albany, Otis Springfield Murff, born 23 March 1900 in Greenwood Springs, Monroe, Mississippi. They died in Tupelo, Lee, Mississippi: she, 28 January 1985; he, 17 October 1980. They were buried in Glenwood Cemetery there.

> Their two children were:
> > Otis Springfield Murff Jr.
> > Patricia Lynn Murff

5. **William Carey Whitten** was born 18 January 1902 in Poplar Springs, and married 30 September 1927 in New Albany, Lucille Wilbanks, born 14 July 1904, there. He died 1 October 1954 in New Albany, Mississippi, and was buried there. Lucille died 25 August 1985 in Grenada, Mississippi, and was buried in that place.

> Their two children were:
> > John Wilbanks Whitten
> > William Benjamin Whitten

5. **Bonner Frank Whitten** was born 6 January 1904 in Poplar Springs, and married 10 August 1938 in New Albany, Dortha Estell Kirkland, who was born 6 November 1910 in Manlius, Ilinois. They lived in Corinth, Mississippi, where Bonner Frank died 12 April 1981. He was buried in New Albany.

> Their two children were:
> > Evelyn Kay Whitten
> > Bonna Fay Whitten

5. **Martha Azlee Whitten** was born 8 August 1906 in Poplar Springs, and married 19 April 1928 in New Albany, William Martin Henderson Jr., born 28 February 1906 in New Albany. They lived in Memphis.

> Their two children were:
> > Martha Ann Henderson
> > Ruby Elizabeth Henderson

5. **Vera Vermelle Whitten** was born 24 January 1908 in Poplar Springs, and married 24 August 1934 in New Albany, Jesse Dawson Mullen, born 27 July 1896 in Grenada, Mississippi. She died 7 June 1988 in Huntsville, Alabama; he, 5 September 1964 in Starkville, Mississippi, where they were buried.

> Their two children were:
> > Jacqueline Whitten Mullen
> > Nancy Jane Mullen

5. **Miriam Elinor Whitten** was born 19 June 1914 in New Albany, and married in 1938, there, Francis Marion Brewer, born in 1913 in Whistler, Alabama. They died in Clarksdale, Mississippi: she, 13 September 1982; he, 28 November 1985. They are buried in Clarksdale.

5. **Nathaniel Murry Whitten** was born 14 September 1917 in New Albany, and married 3 January 1960 in Holly Springs, Mississippi, Miriam Bonner Lesley, born 25 October 1923 in New Albany. Murry retired from a career with the United States Army Engineers and has a precious collection of Whitten family letters, which he graciously allowed me to transcribe and publish in *Letters to Rebecca*. Those letters are steeped in Whitten lore and tradition.

> Their two children were:
> > Leslie Ann Whitten
> > Nathaniel Craig Whitten

Children of Varda Smith and Mesina Elliot Whitten

Born in New Albany, Mississippi

5. **Frank Smith** was born and died 28 November 1902, and was buried in New Albany.

5. **Lola Ivy Smith** was born 19 June 1904, and married 26 June 1930, William Morris Ford, born 16 January 1908 in Patterson, Illinois.

Their child was:

David Morris Ford

5. **Lora V. Smith** was born 12 September 1908, and married Horace Turner.

Children of Langston Agnew Whitten and Jessie May Potter
Born in Poplar Springs, Mississippi

5. **Wood Agnew Whitten** was born 11 August 1915, and married 1 February 1942 in Pontotoc County, Annie Mary Tatum, who was born 6 January 1911. Wood Agnew died 6 April 1951 in Tupelo, and was buried in Bethel Methodist Cemetery, Union County. Annie Mary died 26 May 1976 in Pontotoc, and was buried with her husband.

Their four children were:

Bonnie Jo Whitten
Helen Lucille Whitten
Jerry Neal Whitten
Glenn Allen Whitten

5. **William Langston Whitten** was born 28 July 1917, and married 2 November 1942 in Macon, Georgia, Montine Taylor, born 25 November 1920 in Milan, Talfair, Georgia.

Their three children were:

William Robert Whitten
Kenneth Walter Whitten
Debora Ann Whitten

5. **Joe Brooks Whitten** was born 28 July 1919, and married 10 February 1951 in Dorsey, Mississippi, Johnnie Eugenia McKinney, born 5 February 1926 in Verona, Mississippi. He died 30 January 1986 in Tupelo, and was buried in Endville Baptist Cemetery, Pontotoc County, Mississippi.

Their four children were:

Joe Paul Whitten
Joe Phillip Whitten
Betty Jean Whitten
Rebecca Joyce Whitten

5. **Jessie June Whitten** was born 4 January 1921, and married 17 April 1941 in Pontotoc, Mildred Pauline Darwin, born 9 July 1919 in Prentis, Mississippi. Jessie June died 12 February 1974 in Locust Hill, Pontotoc County, and was buried there.

Their three children were:

Taylor June Whitten
Vivian Dale Whitten
George Langston Whitten

5. **Mary Elliott Whitten** was born 5 June 1923, and married 9 January 1943, Roy DeWitt Holcomb, born 12 December 1919 in Longview, Pontotoc, Mississippi. On 17 May 1971 she married Wilber Alex Bolt, born 14 July in Shaniko, Oregon.

The five children of Roy DeWitt Holcomb and Mary Elliott Whitten were:

Robert Charles Holcomb
Marilyn Holcomb
Donald Ray Holcomb
Jimmy Adams Holcomb
Thomas Wayne Holcomb

5. **Florence Lee Whitten**, born 13 March 1925.

5. **Linda Ruth Whitten** was born 4 April 1927, and married 1 March 1947 in Macedonia, Lee, Mississippi, William Henry Vinson, born 27 July 1926 in Belden, Lee, Mississippi.

Their three children were:

Judy Dianne Vinson
Freddy Ray Vinson
Susan Ray Vinson

5. **Doris Ann Whitten** was born 24 May 1929, and married 22 January 1949 in Tupelo, Ralph Haggard Gillespie, born 13 October 1927 in Pampa, Gray, Texas.

Their five children were:

Patricia Yvonne Gillespie
Jeffry Whitten Gillespie
Margaret Rose Gillespie
Nancy Ann Gillespie
Karen Louise Gillespie

5. **Dora Mae Whitten** was born 6 August 1931, and married 30 June 1967 in Locust Hill, Thomas Allen Rice, born 16 September 1926 in Baldwyn, Lee, Mississippi. She supplied the data on Langston Agnew Whitten and his descendants.

Children of Carl Sidney Hines and Harriet Beulah Whitten
Born in New Albany, Mississippi

5. **Mary Laura Hines** was born 25 February 1918 and died after 1958 in Mississippi.
5. **Thelma Elaine Hines** was born 20 August 1921 and died after 1958.
5. **Joseph Steen Hines**, born 11 April 1926.
5. **Chester Olen Hines**, born 18 May 1928.

Children of Harvey Earle Whitten and Lessie May Byers

5. **William Tate Whitten** was born on 14 May 1921 in Union County, Mississippi, and died there on 14 June 1973.
5. **Harvey Earle Whitten Jr.**, born 15 April 1924.
5. **Walter Andrew Whitten**, born 18 October 1928.
5. **Climmie Twanda Whitten**, born 18 September 1930.

Children of William Homer Whitten and Emily Inez Wade

5. **Birdie May Whitten**, born 19 January 1917.
5. **Adriane Clive Whitten**, born 19 January 1917.
5. **Mary Louise Whitten**, born 7 February 1920.
5. **Homer Wade Whitten**, born 17 January 1922.

Children of Thomas Earle Belote and Annie McDaniel

5. **Earle Newton Belote**, born 6 December 1921.
5. **Louise Holmes Belote**, born 25 October 1925.

Children of Homer Martin and Ruth Lowry

5. **James Lowry Martin**, born 7 May 1920.
5. **Roy Rudolph Martin** was born 14 June 1921. He married Wilma in 1941.
5. **Sarah Louise Martin**, born 20 January 1923.

Child of Mark Nathaniel Lowry and Vivian Strickland

5. **Betty W. Lowry**, born 10 April 1928.

Children of Jesse Dwight Sample and Margaret Rosanna Kimmons

5. **James Dwight Sample**, born 1 July 1906. He married Pauline McCullough 21 June 1928.
5. **Anna Margaret Sample**, born 9 March 1909.
5. **Lulyn Dorothy Sample**, born 26 April 1913.
5. **Jeanne Sample**, born 12 June 1921.
5. **Josephine Sample**, twin of Jeanne, was born 12 June 1921.
5. **Dwight Edward Sample**, born 19 December 1929.

Children of Joseph Murrow McBride and Florence Kee Lankford

5. **Florence Lankford McBride** was born 30 July 1910, and married Ray Sears Poole on 16 November 1930. He was born 27 August 1895.

5. **Charles William McBride**, born 15 July 1912.
5. **Joseph Murrow McBride Jr.**, born 10 December 1913.

Child of William Ivon Lee and Ella Byrd Bell
5. **William Ivon Lee Jr.**, born 13 November 1910.

Children of Thomas Gordon Dilworth and Gara Katharine Wheelock
Born in Waco, Texas
5. **Thomas Gordon Dilworth II** was born on 18 May 1903 in Waco, Texas, married Evelyn Elsie Jay on 8 October 1927, and died in 1963.

Their two children were:
Thomas Gordon Dilworth III
Kathryn Earle Dilworth

5. **Katherine Earle Dilworth** was born on 22 October 1905, married Meredith Hemphill 1 February 1928, and died 12 February 1990 in Baton Rouge, Louisiana. He was born 5 March 1902 and died on 4 May 1969.

Their four children were:
Jean Earl Hemphill
Shirley Kee Hemphill
Meredith Hemphill Jr.
Kent Wheelock Hemphill

Children of Thomas Gordon Dilworth and Margaret Love Scott
Born in Waco, Texas
5. **Celia Kee Dilworth** was born 1 March 1917, married Edward Briggs Morgan on 7 June 1941, and died 11 February 1994 in Houston. He was born 19 December 1915 in Waco and died in Georgetown, Texas, on 11 September 1983.

Their four children were:
Susan Scott Morgan
Nancy Lee Morgan
Betsy Jane Morgan
Mary Lou Morgan

5. **Margaret Scott Dilworth** was born 3 June 1918, married William Tyre Cooper III on 1 May 1918 in Waco, and died on 30 July 1966 in Houston. He was born 1 May 1918 in Waco and died 10 January 1987 in San Antonio. She was buried in Oakwood Cemetery in Waco.

Their three children were:
Margaret Ann Cooper
William Tyre Cooper IV
Cathy Cooper

Child of Richard Clyde Johnson and Anna Lee Dilworth
5. **Marianne Dilworth Johnson** was born 3 June 1918, married Robert Culmore Berkeley on 12 March 1959, and died in February 1999. He died 22 March 1977. They were buried in Waco's Oakwood Cemetery.

Child of Henri S. Lucenay and Marian Adair Dilworth
5. **Theodore Lucenay**, born 18 January 1925.

Children of Willoughby M. Crebau and Lettie O'Barr Lankford
5. **Lettie Belle Crebau** was born 15 June 1904, and married on 20 September 1924 Cecil V. Dix, who was born 4 June 1896.

Their two children were:
Dorothy Ann Dix
John Lankford Dix

5. **Olive Gene Crebau** was born 3 February 1907, and married 29 March 1927 Rex J. Elmore, born 12 July 1904.
Their child was:
Rex Lankford Elmore

Child of Earle Miller Lankford and Annie Louise Hoffman

5. **Earle Louise Lankford** was born 13 September 1920, and married 18 April 1930 Paul Cedric Wenger, born 8 July 1918.

Their child was:

Paul Cedric Wenger Jr.

Child of Theodore Marchant Lawrence and Eugenia Franklin Lankford

5. **Virginia Belle Lawrence**, born 19 May 1924.

Child of Frank Pershing Hopwood and Anna Lutie Lankford

5. **Frank Pershing Hopwood Jr.**, born 17 April 1916.

Child of William Felix Cooper and Artelia Clara Whitten

5. **William Felix Cooper Jr.**, born 3 June 1921.

Children of Leonard Griffin Whitten and Lois Diana Peters

5. **Warren Norman Whitten**, born 26 July 1922.
5. **Leonard Griffin Whitten Jr.**, born 18 February 1929.
5. **Donald Homer Whitten**, born 4 October 1931.

Children of Thomas Edward Williams and Della Kee Whitten

5. **Thomas Edward Williams Jr.**, born 19 February 1920.
5. **Frances Elizabeth Williams**, born 25 June 1921.
5. **Della Lucille Williams**, born 12 May 1926.
5. **Martha Ruth Williams**, born 24 March 1928.

Children of Edward Earle Whitten and Hattie Donna Crews

5. **Edward Earle Whitten Jr.**, born 15 September 1920.
5. **Dorothy Louise Whitten**, born 23 April 1923.
5. **James Robert Whitten**, born 12 December 1927.
5. **Donna Alice Ruby Whitten**, born 9 March 1930.

Children of William David Crews and Pearl Gladys Whitten

5. **Juanita Lucille Crews**, born 10 November 1923.
5. **William David Crews Jr.**, born 10 November 1923.

Child of Hubert Fulton Whitten Jr. and Bennie Forest Graves

5. **Hubert Fulton Whitten Jr.**, born 28 June 1929.

Child of William Hutchins Roberts and Bertha Alene Whitten

5. **Jeanette Alene Roberts**, born 6 December 1927.

Child of Winfield Quin Sharp and Lucille Burt Whitten

5. **Dorothy Sharp** was born 5 December 1907 in Jackson, and married 14 September 1930, there, George Austin Wilson, who was born 22 December 1903. Both died in Jackson and are buried in Lakewood Memorial Cemetery: she, 15 July 1951; he, 29 January 1935. Dorothy was a well-known interior decorator in Jackson, Mississippi.

Their child was:

Dorothy Jane Wilson

Children of Gilbert Cameron Cunningham and Paulene Earle Whitten

5. **Gilbert Cameron Cunningham Jr.** was born 15 September 1915 in Burlington, Vermont, and married Margaret Faye Hartt, who was born in Frederickton, New Brunswick, Canada. Gilbert Jr. died 1 July 1962 in Toronto, and was buried in Forest Hill Cemetery, Frederickton. She died in New Brunswick before Gilbert Jr.

Their two children were:

James Cameron Cunningham
Katherine Ann Cunningham

5. **David Hunter Cunningham** was born 14 July 1917 in New Brunswick, Canada, and married Thelma Tibble. Their two children were:

> Robert Edwin Cunningham
> David Scott Cunningham

5. **Ruth Catherine Cunningham** was born 23 March 1919 in Frederickton, New Brunswick, Canada, where she died in 1992.

5. **Pauline Whitten Cunningham** was born 6 September 1921 in Marysville, New Brunswick. She died in 2012 in Fredericktown, New Brunswick, Canada.

5. **Margaret Helen Cunningham** was born 4 October 1926 on Heron Island in Canada, and married J. Patric Marceau, who was born 17 March 1921 in Canada. She died 29 April 2004 in Great Falls, New Brunswick, Canada. Their eleven children, several adopted, were:

> Patricia Anne Marceau
> Debra Jean Marie Marceau
> Jean Paul Etienne Marceau
> Julien Pierre Joseph Marceau
> Juliette Elida Marie Marceau
> Joseph Michael Sylvair Marceau
> Daniel Joseph Marceau
> Louis Joseph Gabriel Marceau
> Diane Marie Marceau
> Louis Medgar Silas Marceau
> Sylvia Marie Yolanda Marceau

Children of Dr. Walter McDonald Merritt and Lottie Helon Whitten

5. **Walter McDonald Merritt Jr.** was born 3 October 1912 in Jackson, Mississippi, and married 24 November 1935 in Okeene, Blaine, Oklahoma, Dorris Christine Luder, born 6 June 1914, there. Walter died 30 October 1979 in Ft. Worth, Texas; Dorris, 2 February 1981 in McAllen, Hidalgo, Texas. They were buried in Cleveland, Mississippi. Walter became vice president of Home Life Insurance Company in New York before turning to farming and operating large cotton farms in Mexico, South Texas, and Boliver County, Mississippi. He was active is state politics, ran for the Mississippi Senate, and for some years before his death served as industrial development officer for Washington County, Mississippi. Their two children were:

> Kristin Merritt
> Dr. Walter McDonald Merritt III

5. **Dr. Charles Wesley Merritt** was born 24 November 1922 in Boyle, Mississippi, and married 19 July 1947 in Clarksdale, Coahoma, Mississippi, Mary Martha Presley, born 2 November 1922 in Tutwiler, Tallahatchie, Mississippi. Mary Martha died on 15 May 1994 in Beckley, West Virginia. She served in the West Virginia House of Delegates, on the State Board of Education, as State Workers Compensation commissioner from January 1985 to November 1987, as West Virginia regent of the DAR, and as state president of Colonial Dames. "Bootsy" was a scratch golfer and talented baseball player. Called up by the New York Yankees, he opted for medical school and the WWII navy, becoming a prominent physician for whom a wing of the Columbia Raleigh General Hospital in Beckley, West Virginia, is named. He died on 24 February in Atlanta, Georgia, and was buried with Mary Martha in Clarksdale, Mississippi. Their three children were:

> Presley McDonald Merritt
> Charles Wesley Merritt Jr.
> Ann Whitten Merritt

Children of Leslie Hunter Whitten and Linnora Hunter

5. **Leslie Hunter Whitten Jr.** was born 21 February 1928 in Jacksonville, Florida, and married 11 November 1951 in Paris, France, Phyllis Webber, born 6 August 1928 in Heidelberg Township, Pennsylvania. He was an investigative reporter with Jack Anderson and has become a well-known author and poet. They lived in Silver Spring, Maryland, in 2004. Their three children were:

> Leslie Hunter Whitten III
> Andrew Cassius Whitten
> Daniel Lee Whitten

5. **Frank Harvey Whitten** was born 5 June 1930 in Jacksonville, Florida.

5. **Stanley Burt Whitten** was born 2 February 1935 in Washington, D.C., and married 29 June 1962 in Lynchburg, Virginia, Rose Marie McNerney, born 13 July 1931 in Norton, Virginia. He died on 13 November 2011 in Madison, WI.
Their four children were:
>Cosmas Anne Whitten
>Stanley Burt Whitten Jr.
>Mary Catherine Whitten
>Lewis Edward Whitten

Child of Sherod Roscoe Whitten and Marie Burr

5. **Sherod Ray Whitten** was born 9 September 1919 in Jackson, Mississippi, and married 25 August 1946, Mary Ritchey. They were divorced. He died 27 October 1986 in Jackson, and was buried in Lakewood Memorial Cemetery.
Their two children, both adopted, were:
>Stephen R. Whitten
>Thomas G. Whitten

Child of Carl Gustav Levring and Ruth Christine Whitten

5. **Jane Duncan Levring** was born 11 March 1925 in Jackson, and married 25 August 1946 in Hendersonville, North Carolina, Paul Bowman Stam, Ph.D., born 9 April 1924 in Patterson, New Jersey. He died in 1990 in Greensboro, North Carolina, and was buried in Arlington Memorial Cemetery. In 2004 she married Dr. Jack Minor, a medical missionary who was born 27 March 1919 and died 18 January 2011.
Their four children were:
>Karen Jane Stam
>Paul Bowman "Skip" Stam Jr.
>Carl Levring "Chip" Stam
>William Whitten Stam

Child of William Black Moore and May Isom Whitten

5. **William Black Moore Jr.** was born 18 September 1924 in Jackson, Mississippi, and married 14 September 1946 in Greenwood, LeFlore, Mississippi, Lillian Fredonia Wells, born 27 October 1925 there. He was vice president and general manager of Reynolds Metals Company's Architectural and Building Products Division. Retiring in 1980 to Virginia's Northern Neck, he wrote this book and *Letters to Rebecca*, also about Whittens and related families, cofounded the Rappahannock Foundation, and served as its president for ten years. Lillian's grandfather was federal judge and governor of Mississippi, Andrew Houston Longino.
Their three children were:
>Kathryn Ramsey Moore
>William Black Moore III
>Bethany Ann Moore

Child of William Douglas Whitten and Alice Elizabeth Booth
5. **Lora Laete Whitten**, born 8 October 1932.

Child of William Douglas Whitten and Marguerite Odell
5. **Patricia Odell Whitten**, born 24 October 1938.

Children of Leon Theodore Whitten and Alena Victoria Byrnes
Born in Memphis, Tennessee
5. **Leon Theodore Whitten Jr.** was born 10 June 1911, and married Florence Williams.
5. **Neil Durwood Whitten**, born 7 June 1914.
5. **Jean Marsalee Whitten** was born 27 October 1925, and married in June 1947 in Memphis, where both children were born.

Children of Lacy Roger Whitten and Marie Louise Collins

5. **Maxine Whitten**, born 14 February 1921.
5. **Lacy Roger Whitten Jr.**, born 17 April 1924.

Children of Wyatt Wolf Lipscombe and Laura Laeta Earle Whitten
5. **Wyatt Whitten Lipscomb**, born 25 June 1927.
5. **Millie Jean Lipscomb**, born 1 April 1929.

Children of Loren Darnell Whitten and Helen Bower
5. **George Bedford Whitten**, born 19 June 1924.
5. **Ward Bower Whitten**, born 21 November 1927.

Children of Ticer Young and Lou Anna Whitten
Born in Ripley, Mississippi
5. **Lester Whitten Young** was born 29 June 1926, and married 22 July 1950, in Oxford, Mississippi, Elizabeth Caldwell, born in 1931, there. Lester, twin of Loren, was living in Oxford in 1991.
Their three children were:
Nancy Lynn Young
Marsha Lee Young
David Lester Young
5. **Loren Ticer Young** was born 29 June 1926, and married Patricia Brown. He died 24 September 1980, and was buried in St. Peters Cemetery in Oxford.
Their three children were:
Leslie Glen Young
Debra Brown Young
Lucinda Baron Young

Child of Joseph Burford Whitten and Estelle Meacham
5. **Wanda Lee Whitten**, born and died 9 February 1938.

Child of Joseph Burford Whitten and Maggie Lee Bell
5. **Beverly Ann Whitten** was born 8 May 1945 in Memphis, and married 1969, there, George Elmo Holley, born 20 April 1942.
Their child was:
George Alan Holley

Child of William Leslie Burke and Corinne Whitten
5. **Leslie Carlton Burke** was born 30 November 1941 in Memphis, and married 29 December 1960 in California, DeeVonne Clark, born 6 February 1941.
Their four children were:
Carlton Clark Burke
Steven Dean Burke
Deborah Lynne Burke
Sarah Lorinne Burke

Children of Aubrey DeWitt Whitten and Alice Adams
Born in Memphis, Tennessee
5. **Alice Marie Whitten** was born 27 October 1948, and married 6 November 1982, there, John Joseph Dudas, who was born 12 June 1947 in Chicago, Illinois.
Their two children were:
Anne Marie Dudas
Andrew Adams Dudas
5. **Rev. Aubrey DeWitt Whitten Jr.** was born 2 January 1950, and married 11 September 1976 in Louisville, Kentucky, Jane Proctor, who was born 8 September 1952. In 1995 he was pastor of Mount Arayat Baptist Church of Stafford, Virginia.
Their two children were:

Jane Allison Whitten
Julianne Marielle Whitten

5. **Mary Anne Whitten** was born 7 June 1953, and married 12 July 1981 in Memphis, Harry Lee Poe, who was born 16 November 1950 in South Carolina. They are distant cousins, both being descendants of Col. John Earle, of Earle's Fort, North Carolina. Mary Ann is a great-great-granddaughter of Eleanor Kee Earle, Colonel John's daughter by his second wife, Rebecca Berry Wood; Harry; a great-great-great-great-grandson of Colonel John and his first wife, Thomasine Prince.

This reunion of Earles and Whittens is one of those fascinating discoveries that make family research fun. I lived in Greenville, South Carolina, for four years, during which my parents' closest friends were Harry Poe's grandparents, Harry and Julia May Poe. My mother and Mrs. Poe remained in contact throughout the remainder of their lives without, I feel certain, knowing they were related.

Their two children were:
Rebecca Poe
Mary Ellen Poe

5. **Benjamin Joseph Whitten** was born 11 February 1955, and married 12 March 1983 in Memphis, Cardelia Capehart, born 23 April 1953 in Arkansas.

Their three children were:
Aubra Cardelia Whitten
Patience Stone Whitten
Worth Benjamin Whitten

Children of Dr. Woodrow Carlton Whitten and Elwanda Kniffin

5. **Janna Lynette Whitten** was born 4 December 1947, and married Richard Edward Tasker, who was born 16 July 1952 in New York.

Their two children were:
Terra Sage Tasker
Raya Laurel Tasker

5. **Gayla Marie Whitten** was born 25 July 1949, and married Michael Blood. She later married Eric Parish, born 24 May 1950 in Dallas, Texas.

The child of Michael Blood and Gayla Marie Whitten was:
Annabelle Lee Blood
The two children of Eric Parish and Gayla Marie Whitten were:
Andrew Terlain Parish
Amanda Parish

5. **Merri Lynn Whitten** was born 19 May 1956, and married Charles Stein, born 15 April 1955 in Place, New York.

Their child was:
Grace Jasmine Stein

Children of Howard Brooks Whitten and Robbie Estelle Smothers

5. **Joseph Brooks Whitten** was born 25 June 1941, and married 26 April 1971, there, Carol Teresa Boyles, born 7 July 1949.

Their two children were:
Laurie Leigh Whitten
Joseph Brooks Whitten Jr.

5. **William DeWitt Whitten** was born 22 August 1945, and married 14 February 1970 Susan Smith. He died 20 December 1990 in Memphis and was buried in Memorial Park.

Their child was:
Christopher Mark Whitten

Children of Dewey Lee Word and Lourelia Whitten

5. **James Lee Word** was born 21 November 1946 in Memphis, and married 21 August 1982, Lenora Rivoire, born 28 May 1949.

Their two children were:
Sarah Jean Word

Daniel Paul Word
5. **Kay Marie Word** was born 27 December 1948 in Memphis, and married 27 September 1980, there, Kenneth Eugene Mills, born 24 April 1946.
Their two children were:
Rebecca Kay Mills
Jennifer Marie Mills

Child of Harry Earl Munday and Irene Whitten
5. **Baronson Elizabeth Munday** was born 5 May 1918, and married Gen. Claude F. Clayton. They lived in Tupelo, Lee, Mississippi, and had three children.

Children of Logan Alfred Whitten and Thelma Thorne
5. **Margaret Elizabeth Whitten** was born 7 September 1922 in Iuka, and married 5 October 1942 in Memphis, Capt. Robert L. Cardenas, born in San Diego, California. They were divorced and later, in Iuka, she married Benjamin Franklin McRae, born 24 January 1915 there. He died 13 September 1990 and was buried in Oak Grove Cemetery, Iuka.
5. **Jane Whitten** was born 24 September 1924 in Corinth, and married 3 March 1944 in Chicago, Richard Alexander Mcree III, who was born in Iuka. In 1991 he was president of an Iuka Bank.
Their two children were:
Michael Alexander Mcree
Marsha Mcree

Children of James Clifton Wall and Emmaline Medora Rucker
5. **William Clifton Wall**, born 21 June 1911, died in 1955.
5. **Jenny Laura Wall**, born 27 June 1912, died in 1959.

Children of Rupert Clyde Rucker and Willie Leaty Spencer
5. **Troy Ellis Rucker**, born 4 June 1913.
5. **Clyde Lafayette Rucker**, born 10 August 1914.
5. **Lloyd Jackson Rucker**, born 10 August 1916.
5. **Jesse Rogers Rucker**, born 4 June 1918.
5. **Rufus Lee Rucker**, born 8 August 1924.
5. **William Harrell Rucker**, born 7 November 1926.
5. **Carol Jefferson Rucker**, born 3 June 1928.

Children of Ernest Rucker and Garnier Gill
5. **Sarah Lou Rucker**, born 26 January 1921.
5. **Ernestine Rucker**, born 30 April 1923.
5. **Mary Elaine Rucker**, born 8 November 1925.
5. **Eleanor Maxine Rucker**, born 4 April 1928.

Child of Vance Cyril Roy and Hazel Marie Whitten
5. **Dr. Vance Cyril Roy Jr.** was born in Jackson, Tennessee, 23 February 1939, and on 14 June 1960 married Charlotte Ann Hughes, born 6 June 1941. He became a neurosurgeon. They divorced, and on 23 March 1981 in Huntsville, Alabama, he married Cynthia Ann Burt, who was born 25 January 1958 at Elgin Air Force Base, Florida. Now retired, they live in Switzerland. *While exchanging family records with Dr. Roy, I was pleased to learn that his family had enjoyed a close relationship with his grandfather's sister, Frank Alma Whitten Tate. In 1894 Joseph Earle wrote his Aunt Rebecca implying that he had no further use for sister Frank Alma. The rift appeared to be a permanent one. Obviously, it was not.*
The two children of Vance C. Roy and Charlotte Ann Hughes were:
Vanessa Lyn Roy
Adam Hughes Roy

Child of Charles Edward Tate Jr. and Rebecca Rose Love
5. **Jane Love Tate**, born 22 February 1922.

EIGHTH GENERATION

127

Children of Otis Springfield Murff and Mamie Lorene Whitten

6. **Otis Springfield Murff Jr.** was born 27 June 1926 in Tupelo, and married 19 January 1952 in Aiken, South Carolina, Betty Moody, born 30 June 1929.

Their three children were:
Cathy Lynn Murff
Miriam Elizabeth Murff
Clarence Mitchell Murff

6. **Patricia Lynn Murff** was born 9 August 1931 in Tupelo, and married Jack Cooley on 30 July 1951 in Baldwyn, Mississippi. He who was born 17 March 1932 in Tupelo, died 3 June 1989, and was buried there.

Their three children were:
Lucinda Jane Cooley
Jeffrey King Cooley
William Marshall Cooley

Children of William Carey Whitten and Lucille Wilbanks

6. **John Wilbanks Whitten** was born 21 December 1931 in New Albany. He lived in Durham, North Carolina in 1992.

6. **William Benjamin Whitten** was born 3 September 1929 in New Albany, and married 5 January 1955 in Baltimore, Maryland, Jane Peebles, born 10 July 1929 in Norfolk, Virginia. In 1992 they lived in Chadds Ford, Pennsylvania.

Their three children were:
Nathaniel Carter Whitten II
William Benjamin Whitten Jr.
Victoria Lucian Whitten

Children of Bonner Frank Whitten and Dortha Estell Kirkland

6. **Evelyn Kay Whitten** was born 30 December 1939 in New Albany, Mississippi, and married 8 June 1961 in Corinth, Frank Burkitt, who was born there. On 13 October 1984 she married Douglas Jenkins in Pascagoula, Mississippi.

The child of Frank Burkitt and Evelyn Kay Whitten was:
Lee Anne Burkett

6. **Rev. Bonna Fay Whitten** was born 17 December 1943 in New Albany, and married 27 December 1970 in Corinth, Richard Frank Stovall, born 5 November 1947 in Atlanta. They lived in Atlanta.

Children of William Martin Henderson Jr. and Martha Azlee Whitten

6. **Martha Ann Henderson** was born 23 July 1930 in Memphis, and married 28 July 1952 there, John Thomas McCallen, born in February 1929 in that city. She died 17 September 1979 in Memphis, and was buried in Forest Hill Cemetery.

Their four children were:
Kay McCallen
Martha Laurie McCallen
Mary Elizabeth McCallen
William Thomas McCallen

6. **Ruby Elizabeth Henderson** was born 8 September 1939 in Memphis, and married 15 September 1962, in Memphis, Howard Marvin Graham, born 7 September 1939. He died 10 June 1974 in Memphis.

Their three children were:
Kathryn Martin Graham
Howard Marvin Graham Jr.
Martha Ann Graham

Children of Jesse Dawson Mullen and Vera Vermelle Whitten

6. **Jacqueline Whitten Mullen** was born 29 February 1940 in Starkville, Mississippi, and married 24 March 1963 William Raymond Reynolds.

Their three children were:
Jacqueline Rhea Reynolds
William Jack Reynolds

William Raymond Reynolds Jr.

6. **Nancy Jane Mullen** was born 9 October 1945 in Starkville. Before 1962 she married a Mr. Coleman, and on 5 March 1966, in Starkville, married Clifton Eugene Cartledge.

The child of Mr. Coleman and Nancy Jane Mullen was:
    Michael Scott Colemen

The three children of Clifton Eugene Cartledge and Nancy Jane Mullen were:
    Melanie Beth Cartledge
    Jacquelene Kay Cartledge
    Kevin Bradley Cartledge

Children of Nathaniel Murry Whitten and Miriam Bonner Lesley

6. **Lesley Ann Whitten** was born 16 September 1961 in Memphis, and married 6 August 1988 in Starkville, James Robert Morton, born 22 June 1962 in Jackson, Mississippi.

6. **Nathaniel Craig Whitten** was born 4 December 1963 in Memphis, and married 11 August 1990 in Flat Rock, North Carolina, Cecile Boyd Young, born 24 November 1966 in Savannah, Georgia.

Child of William Morris Ford and Lola Ivy Smith

6. **David Morris Ford** was born 5 January 1937 in Kansas City, Missouri, and married 2 September 1958 in Nederland, Texas, Linda Gayle Lester.

Their child was:
    David Scott Ford

Children of Wood Agnew Whitten and Annie Mary Tatum

6. **Bonnie Jo Whitten** was born 4 June 1943 in Pontotoc, and died the same day.

6. **Helen Lucille Whitten** was born 15 September 1944 in Pontotoc, and married 11 July 1964, Thomas Arthur Mize Jr., born 6 August 1945 in Baldwyn, Lee, Mississippi.

Their child was:
    Barry Thomas Mize

6. **Jerry Neal Whitten** was born 6 May 1946 in Pontotoc, and married 24 September 1965 in Union County, Sandra Rakestraw, born in 1948 in Arkansas. After her death in Mississippi, he married 2 February 1973 in Pontotoc, Jane Tutor, born 6 May 1948, there. A third wife, whom he married 18 May 1984 in Pontotoc, was Myra Jean Prather, born 19 October 1947 in New Albany.

The child of Jerry Neal Whitten and Sandra Rakestraw was:
    Geana Carol Whitten

The child of Jerry Neal Whitten and Jane Tutor was:
    Jeffry Langston Whitten

The child of Jerry Neal Whitten and Myra Jean Prather was:
    Kamesha Danielle Whitten

6. **Glen Allen Whitten** was born 9 August 1950 in Pontotoc, and married 20 October 1973 in Banks, Arkansas, Susan Gay Forrest, who was born 2 May 1958 in Warren, Bradley, Arkansas. He died 15 February 1987 in Little Rock and was buried in Warren, Arkansas.

Their two children were:
    Ronaldo Whitten
    Susan Amanda Whitten

Children of William Langston Whitten and Montine Taylor

6. **William Robert Whitten** was born 17 October 1943 in Alma, Bacon, Georgia, and married 5 October 1986 in Round, Lake, Illinois, Carol Margaret Gifford, born 28 December 1946 in Chicago. He married a second time in Waukegan, Illinois, Sandy LaBelle, born, there, 12 December 1940.

The two children of William Robert Whitten and Carol Margaret Gifford were:
    Julie Michele Whitten
    Nicole Lynn Whitten

6. **Kenneth Walter Whitten** was born 21 February 1946 in Tupelo, and married 28 June 1969 in Round, Lake, Illinois, Maureen Margaret Foster, born 20 December 1947 in Chicago.

Their three children were:

> Kelly Marie Whitten
> Carrie Lynn Whitten
> Eric Matthew Whitten

6. **Debora Ann Whitten** was born 20 August 1956 in Waukegan, and died 17 February 1977.

Children of Joe Brooks Whitten and Johnnie Eugenia McKinney

6. **Joe Paul Whitten** was born and died in Tupelo, Mississippi, 4 October 1953, and was buried in Endville Baptist Cemetery.

6. **Joe Phillip Whitten** was born 25 May 1955, and married 23 November 1978 in Endville, Betty Lou Lyons Sibley, born 25 May 1943 in Richmond, Mississippi. She died in that state.

> Their five children were:
> Valarie Renate Whitten
> Venetta Viola Whitten
> Veronica Constance Whitten
> Victoria Brook Whitten
> Joanna Vashti Whitten

6. **Betty Jean Whitten** was born 3 July 1957, and married 30 May 1980 in Endville, Ralph Douglass Womack, born 20 June 1951 in San Antonio, Texas. They had a child who was born and died in 1986.

6. **Rebecca Joyce Whitten** was born 28 September 1959, and married 12 October 1985 in Endville, John Richard Jackson, born 28 September 1951.

> Their two children were:
> Anna Clara Jackson
> Brooks Harrison Jackson

Children of Jesse Whitten and Mildred Paulene Darwin

6. **Taylor June Whitten** was born 17 December 1942, and married 24 March 1967 in Dorsey, Mississippi, Peggy Ann Gurley, born 2 March 1945 in Mississippi.

> Their child was:
> Chadwick Taylor Whitten

6. **Vivian Dale Whitten** was born 20 August 1944, and married 24 April 1964 in Locust Hill, William Vance Mayo, born 14 March 1940 in New Albany. The entire family was killed in a car-train wreck 30 December 1965 in Sherman, Union, Mississippi. They were buried in Locust Hill.

> Their child was:
> William Whitten Mayo

6. **George Langston Whitten** was born 22 November 1946, and married 15 September 1967 in Union County, Brenda Gregory, born 22 November 1947 in New Albany. On September 14 1985 he married DeWayne Rasco.

> The three children of George and Brenda Whitten were:
> Cary Langston Whitten
> Mark Kevin Whitten
> Bridget Dawn Whitten

Children of Roy DeWitt Holcomb and Mary Elliott Whitten

6. **Robert Charles Holcomb** was born 21 October 1943 in Pontotoc, and married 24 February 1968 in Waukegan, Illinois, Sherry Lynn Kreusher, born 30 July 1948 there.

> Their four children were:
> Robert Charles Holcomb Jr.
> Shannon Lee Holcomb
> Dana Andrew Holcomb
> Jodie Marie Holcomb

6. **Marilyn Holcomb** was born 14 June 1945 in Tupelo, and married 10 October 1964, Raymond Edward Dohr, born 26 July 1943 in Merrill, Wisconsin.

> Their child was:
> Linda Carol Dohr

6. **Donald Ray Holcomb** was born 24 January 1947 in Tupelo, and married 24 February 1978, Dorothy Mary Cole, born in Peoria, Illinois.

Their child was:
Meghan Holcomb
6. **Jimmy Adams Holcomb** was born 24 January 1948 in Tupelo, and married 25 September 1971, Linda Kravanger, born 24 February 1951 in Milwaukee.
Their two children were:
Julie Ann Holcomb
Tracy Marie Holcomb
6. **Thomas Wayne Holcomb** was born 25 January 1956 in Waukegan, and died 20 December 1986.

Children of William Henry Vinson and Linda Ruth Whitten
Born in Jackson, Tennessee
6. **Judy Dianne Vinson** was born 22 December 1947, and married 28 April 1973, there, David Hay Rice, born 4 July 1944 in Crockett, Tennessee.
Their two children were:
Melody Dianne Rice
Christopher David Rice
6. **Freddy Ray Vinson** was born 2 October 1950, and married 17 November 1974, there, Jane Arthur Haynes, born 16 June 1949 in Jackson.
Their two children were:
James William Vinson
Jill Ray Vinson
6. **Susan Ray Vinson** was born 24 September 1951, and married 7 December 1975, Donald Gene Cupples, born 1 May 1950 in Henderson, McNairy, Tennessee
Their two children were:
Linda Jane Cupples
William Benjamin Cupples

Children of Ralph Haggard Gillespie and
Born in Tupelo, Mississippi
6. **Patricia Yvonne Gillespie** was born 11 March 1951, and married 15 December 1972 in Karo, Pontotoc County, Timothy DeLane Holcomb, born 17 September 1951 in Pontotoc.
Their three children were:
Jenifer Clair Holcomb
Jacob Loy Holcomb
Julie Erin Holcomb
6. **Jeffry Whitten Gillespie** was born 26 March 1953, and married 16 October 1982, in Tupelo, Elizabeth Elaine Harper, born 14 September 1958 in Birmingham.
Their child was:
Whitten Harper Gillespie
6. **Margaret Rose Gillespie** was born 30 August 1958, and married 10 October 1981 in Sherman, Pontotoc, Mississippi, Frank Magers Anderson, born 29 October 1957 in Okolona, Chickasaw, Mississippi.
Their three children were:
Anna Rose Anderson
Frank Magers Anderson Jr.
Samuel Gillespie Anderson
6. **Nancy Ann Gillespie** was born 9 February 1960, and married 31 August 1984 in Sherman, Lawrence Mitchell Brazeal, born 13 December 1957 in Baldwyn, Lee County, Mississippi.
Their two children were:
Kayla Marie Brazeal
Haley Elizabeth Brazeal
6. **Karen Louise Gillespie** was born 14 October 1962, and married Charles George Capps, born 12 November 1958 in Pensacola, Florida.
Their two children were:
Charles Ross Capps
Kacey Morgan Capps

Children of Thomas Gordon Dilworth II and Evelyn Elsie Jay
6. **Kathryn Earle Dilworth** was born in September 1922, and married Meredith Hemphill.
Their three children were:
    Jean Earle Hemphill
    Shirley Kee Hemphill
    Meredith Hemphill Jr.
6. **Thomas Gordon Dilworth III**, born 17 July 1928 in Texas.

Children of Meredith Hemphill and Katherine Earle Dilworth
6. **Jean Earle Hemphill** was born 25 March 1929, and on 6 September 1952 married George Willard Pugh, who was born on 17 August 1925.
Their four children were:
    William Whitmel Pugh
    George Willard Pugh Jr.
    David Nichols Pugh
    James Hemphill Pugh
6. **Shirley Kee Hemphill** was born on 22 September 1930, and married Harlan Robinson Jessup on 24 November 1956. He was born on 28 February 1933.
Their four children were:
    James Harlan Jessup
    Jennifer Hemphill Jessup
    Benjamin Kent Jessup
    Susan Jean Jessup
6. **Meredith Hemphill Jr.** was born on 12 October 1931, and married Mary Beverly Bell, born 29 December 1933.
Their four children were:
    Mary Katherine Hemphill
    Meredith Scott Hemphill
    Geoffery Guy Hemphill
    Mark Alexander Hemphill
6. **Kent Wheelock Hemphill** was born 29 June 1934, and married Suzanne Daversa on 8 March 1958. She was born 9 August 1935.
Their three children were:
    Katherine Ann Hemphill
    Judith Hemphill
    Kent Wheelock Hemphill Jr.

Children of Edward Briggs Morgan and Celia Kee Dilworth
6. **Susan Scott Morgan** was born 4 May 1943 on Farragut Naval Base in Idaho, and died 5 January 1971 in Shawnee Mission, Kansas.
6. Nancy Lee Morgan was born 11 September 1948 in Dallas, and married Phil David Wedemeyer on 7 August 1971. He was born in Huntsville, Texas, on 2 June 1949.
Their three children were:
    John Phillip Wedermeyer
    Stephen Edward Wedemeyer
    David Charles Wedermeyer
6. **Betsy Jane Morgan** was born in Dallas on 22 April 1950, and married Dean William Baesel on 5 August 1972. Dean was born in Dayton, Ohio, on 2 May 1950. On 29 September 1989 she married Paul Garvin, who was born on 21 September 1956.
The two children of Dean William and Betsy Jane were:
    Christopher Morgan Baesel
    Kelly Lee Baesel
6. **Mary Lou Morgan** was born 19 June 1951 in Dallas, and on 11 October 1980 married Gregory Wayne Yarborough, who was born on 6 August 1954.

Their child was:

    Jason Wayne Yarborough

Children of William Tyre Cooper III and Margaret Scott Dilworth
Born in Waco, Texas

6. **Margaret Ann Cooper** was born on 15 May 1941, and married Robbie Don Godwin on 19 August 1960. He was born in Levelland, Texas, on 24 July 1939.

Their two children were:

    John Scott Godwin

    Brian Frank Godwin

6. **William Tyre Cooper IV** was born on 17 June 1943, and married Betty Jane Wyke on 15 January 1967. Betty Jane was born on 15 January 1943.

Their two children were:

    Misty Jeanine Cooper

    Danielle Louise Cooper

6. **Cathy Cooper** was born 20 December 1951, and married Phil Jordan in 1976. He was born on 26 August 1941.

Children of Cecil V. Dix and Lettie Belle Crebau

6. **Dorothy Ann Dix**, born 16 October 1925.

6. **John Lankford Dix**, born 2 February 1929.

Child of Rex J. Elmore and Olive Gene Crebau

6. **Rex Lankford Elmore**, born 31 August 1929.

Child of Paul Cedric Wenger and Earle Louise Lankford

6. **Paul Cedric Wenger Jr.**, born 10 October 1932.

Child of George Austin Wilson and Dorothy Sharp

6. **Dorothy Jane Wilson** was born 3 April 1933 in Jackson, Mississippi, and married 19 June 1954 in Setauket, Long Island, New York, Burtis Albert Lauber, born 2 August 1933 in Oceanside, New York. After marriage they lived on Long Island and moved to Antrim, New Hampshire, in 1998 and presently live in Sarasota, Florida. Jane is a talented artist and photographer.

Their two children were:

    Pamela Jane Lauber

    Steven Burtis Lauber

Children of Gilbert Cameron Cunningham Jr. and Margaret Faye Hartt

6. **James Cameron Cunningham** was born on 12 April 1954, and married Gail. They divorced, and he married Dawn.

The child of James and Gail was:

    James Tyler Cunningham

6. **Katherine Ann Cunningham** was born on 24 December 1946, and married Paul Reid.

Their child was:

    Andrea Reid

Children of David Hunter Cunningham and Thelma Tibble
Born in Toronto, Canada

6. **Robert Edward Cunningham** was born on 9 December 1949.

6. **David Scott Cunningham** was born in 1967.

Children of Joseph Patrice Marceau and Margaret Helen Cunningham
Born in Canada

6. **Patricia Anne Marceau** was born on 20 February 1956 in Baie Triniti, Quebec, and married Michael Burzynski on 21 June 1980. He was born in Hertford, England, on 20 February 1954.

6. Debra Jean Marie Marceau was born 4 December 1956 in New Brunswick, and married Hugh McLaughlin,

whom she divorced before marrying Ken Craig.

The three children of Ken and Debra Jean were:

Hugh John McLaughlin Craig

Cleo Sauree Deanne Craig

Melanie Jean Marie Craig

6. **Jean Paul Etienne Marceau** was born on 9 January 1960 in New Brunswick, and married Chantal.

Their two children were:

Justin Patrice Albert Marceau

Sophie Deaine Marceau

6. **Julien Pierre Joseph Marceau** was born on 15 October 1961 in Grand Falls, New Brunswick, and married Aubrey Judith Meyer. They were divorced. She was born in Seattle, Washington, on 25 June 1967.

6. **Juliette Elida Marie Marceau** was born on 4 January 1963 in New Brunswick, and married Robert McLeod.

6. **Joseph Michael Sylvair Marceau** was born 5 April 1964, and died on 12 April 1964.

6. **Daniel Joseph Marceau** was born 27 January 1965 in New Brunswick, and married Lorraine.

Their child was:

Liam Daniel Marceau

6. **Louis Joseph Gabriel Marceau**, born 7 February 1967 in New Brunswick.

6. **Diane Marie Marceau** was born 29 June 1968 in New Brunswick, and married Rino Leveque.

Their two children were:

Nicholas Nelson Leveque

Helen Margaret Leveque

6. **Louis Medgar Silas Marceau**, born 7 December 1969 in New Brunswick.

6. **Sylvie Marie Yolanda Marceau**, born 10 July 1971 in New Brunswick.

Children of Walter McDonald Merritt Jr. and Doris Christine Luder

6. **Kristin Merritt** was born 28 August 1939 in Boyle, Bolivar, Mississippi, and married 27 November 1959 in Cleveland, John Robert Germany Jr., who was born 17 September 1932 in Greenville, Washington, Mississippi. She died in Conroe, Texas, 25 February 1997, and was buried in Houston.

Their three children were:

Kristina Lynne Germany

John Robert Germany III

Lucie Hope Germany

6. **Dr. Walter McDonald Merritt III** was born 7 February 1942 in Greenwood, LeFlore, Mississippi, and married 26 July 1966 in Charleston, Tallahatchie, Mississippi, Beverly Rebecca Whitten, daughter of the late Rep. Jamie and Rebecca Whitten of Washington, D.C., who was born 14 January 1946 in Charleston. Several members of both these Whitten family branches claim a relationship, but no proof has, as yet, been found. Walter and Beverly divorced, and in Fort Worth on 22 January 1983, he married Nancy Elizabeth Thompson, who was born 30 March 1943. Dr. and Mrs. Merritt lived in Ft. Worth, Texas, in 1997.

The two children of Walter Merritt III and Beverly Rebecca Whitten were:

Walter McDonald Merritt IV

Lisa Whitten Merritt

Children of Dr. Charles Wesley Merritt and Mary Martha Presley

6. **Presley McDonald Merritt** was born 13 April 1949 in Mobile, Alabama, and married 4 August 1973 in Beckley, West Virginia, Dr. Joel Morris Wagoner, who was born 19 February 1949 in Greensboro, North Carolina. Presley held various positions with the Colonial Dames and DAR, and was elected president general of the DAR in 2004. On her watch the priceless NSDAR genealogical records were digitized and made available to researchers.

Their three children were:

Joel Merritt Wagoner

. Andrew Johnston Wagoner

Mary Elizabeth Davis Wagoner

6. **Charles Wesley Merritt Jr.** was born 29 November 1952 in Beckley, West Virginia, and married Alice Christine McCulloch Smith in Beckley on 23 July 1977. She was born in Beckley 25 April 1950, the daughter of former West Virginia Governor Hulett Carlson Smith and Mary Alice Tieche.

Their three children were:

Christine Carlson Merritt
Charles Wesley Merritt III
Martha Larkin Alexander Merritt

6. **Ann Whitten Merritt** was born 2 April 1954 in Beckley, West Virginia, where, in 1979, she married Dr. Thomas Jarrett, an orthodontist. They divorced, and on 4 May 1984, Anne married Thomas Earl DuPree Jr., born 14 May 1952 in Bainbridge, Georgia. He was chairman and CEO of Apple South Company, of Madison, Georgia. They, too, are divorced.

The child of Thomas Earle and Ann was:
Thomas Earle DuPree III

Children of Leslie Hunter Whitten Jr. and Phyllis Webber

6. **Leslie Hunter Whitten III** was born 1 March 1953 in Munich, Germany. He married Esther Riggs 9 September 1983 in Carroll County, Maryland. She was born 3 November 1949 in Martinsburg, West Virginia.

6. **Andrew Cassius Whitten** was born 15 January 1956 in New York, and married Carla Wardenburg 25 May 1986 in South Lake Tahoe, California. She was born 5 November 1956 in Madison, Wisconsin.

Their three children were:
Olivia Linnore Whitten
Siera Isabelle Whitten
Elena Hunter Whitten

6. **Daniel Lee Whitten**, born 15 February 1965 in Washington, D.C.

Children of Stanley Burt Whitten and Rose Marie McNerney

6. **Cosmas Anne Whitten** was born 24 April 1964, and married Thomas Edward Skaife in Northbrook, Illinois, 5 August 1989. He was born 3 August 1963 in Madison, Wisconsin, where they lived in 1995.

Their two children were:
Edward Francis Skaife
Samuel Thomas Skaife

6. **Stanley Burt Whitten Jr.**, born 21 May 1965 in Washington, D.C.

6. **Mary Catherine Whitten**, twin of Lewis Edward, was born 26 September 1966 in Silver Spring, Maryland.

6. **Lewis Edward Whitten** was born 26 September 1966 in Silver Spring. In 1995 he was dealing blackjack in Las Vegas.

Children of Sherod Ray Whitten and Mary Ritchey

6. **Stephen R. Whitten**
6. **Thomas G. Whitten**

Child of Paul Bowman Stam and Jane Duncan Levring

6. **Karen Jane Stam** was born 15 March 1948 in Princeton, New Jersey, and married Dr. Carter Brooks Jennings Jr. They were divorced. She was living in Salt Lake City in 2004 serving as a public defender.

Children of Paul Bowman Stam and Jane Duncan Levring

6. **Paul Bowman "Skip" Stam Jr.** was born 5 September 1950 in Princeton, and married 19 May 1973 in Raleigh, North Carolina, Dorothy Electa Mills, born 20 September 1948, there. They live in Apex, where he practices law. First elected to the state's General Assembly in 1988, Skip has served as both minority and majority leader and is credited with the successful effort, in 2012, to amend the state's constitution to recognize marriages only between a man and woman.

Their two children were:
Nathaniel Edward Stam
Jane Ariel Stam

6. **Carl Levring "Chip" Stam** was born 10 March 1953 in Danville, Virginia, and married 9 August 1975, Doris Ann Perry, born 29 December 1954 in Greensboro, Guilford, North Carolina. They are both musicians. For many years he directed the choruses at Notre Dame University. By 2004 they had moved to Louisville, Kentucky, where he served as professor of music and preaching at The Southern Baptist Seminary. He died 1 May 2011 in Louisville after a long fight with cancer, and is buried in the Cave Hill Cemetery there.

Their three children were:
Carl Michael Stam

Timothy Martin Stam

Christine Stam

6. **William Whitten Stam** was born 10 April 1957 in Greensboro, and married 9 June 1979 Nancy Lynn Fordham, who was born 9 August 1957 in Chapel Hill, North Carolina.

Their two children were:

Eric Emery Stam

Kevin Fordham Stam

Children of William Black Moore Jr. and Lillian Fredonia Wells

Born in Louisville, Kentucky

6. **Kathryn Ramsey Moore** was born 24 September 1948, and married 22 August 1970 in Richmond, Virginia, John Mark Dannels, born 27 August 1948 in Cleveland, Ohio. They were divorced in 1995. In 1998 she was living in Indianapolis, where she was director of development for the Indianapolis Civic Theater.

Their two children were:

Karen Wells Dannels

Mark Emerson Dannels

6. **William Black Moore III** was born 16 October 1952, and married 23 October 1983 in Gladwyn, Pennsylvania, Mary Shufford Davis, daughter of John William Sutphin and Sarah Nelson Dawson Davis, who was born 10 February 1953. In 1998 they lived in Manakin-Sabot, Virginia. They divorced in 2008.

Their two children, born in Phoenixville, Pennsylvania, were:

Sarah Latham Moore

Kathryn "Kate" Longino Moore

6. **Bethany Ann Moore** was born 18 October 1956, and married 11 September 1982 in Kilmarnock, Northumberland, Virginia, Dr. John Dwight Richmond, born 20 March 1948 in Beckley, Raleigh, West Virginia. In 1998 they were living in Dalton, Georgia, where he practiced medicine. They are divorced.

Their two children were:

Andrew "Andy" Wells Richmond

John McQuilken "Mac" Richmond

Children of Lester Whitten Young and Elizabeth Caldwell

6. **Nancy Lynn Young**, born 2 July 1951 in Oxford, Mississippi.

6. **Marsha Lee Young**, born 3 November 1953 in Oxford.

6. **David Lester Young**, born 6 March 1957 in Oxford.

Children of Loren Ticer Young and Patricia Brown

6. **Leslie Glenn Young**

6. **Debra Brown Young**

6. **Lucinda Baron Young**

Child of George Elmo Holley and Beverly Ann Whitten

6. **George Alan Holley**, born 25 November 1969 in Memphis.

Children of Leslie Carlton Burke and DeeVonne Clark

6. **Carlton Clark Burke** was born 12 January 1963, and married 22 June 1991 Celia Kay Davis, born 23 December 1961.

6. **Stephen Dean Burke** was born 16 May 1964, and married 7 April 1984 Vielka Rosa Gilkes, born 22 June 1961.

Their two children were:

Crystal Lynne Burke

Tiffany Lynne Burke

6. **Deborah Lynne Burke** was born 27 September 1965, and married 27 June 1987 Kevin Scott Bay, born 27 November 1965.

Their child was:

Ethan Luke Bay

6. **Sarah Lorinne Burke**, born 19 July 1969.

Children of John Joseph Dudas and Alice Marie Whitten

6. **Anne Marie Dudas**, born 4 August 1984 in Memphis.
6. **Andrew Adams Dudas**, born 7 June 1986 in Memphis.

Children of Rev. Aubrey DeWitt Whitten Jr. and Jane Procter
6. **Jane Allison Whitten**, born 9 March 1981 in Louisville, Kentucky.
6. **Julianne Marielle Whitten** was born 29 November 1984 in Louisville.

Children of Harry Lee Poe and Mary Ann Whitten
6. **Rebecca Poe** was born 24 May 1987 in Louisville, Kentucky.
6. **Mary Ellen Poe** was born 4 October 1990 in Louisville.

Children of Benjamin Joseph Whitten and Cardelia Capehart
Born in Memphis, Tennessee
6. **Aubra Cardelia Whitten**, born 22 October 1987.
6. **Patience Stone Whitten**, born 6 June 1989.
6. **Worth Benjamin Whitten**, born 27 July 1992.

Children of Richard Edward Tasker and Janna Lynette Whitten
6. **Terra Sage Tasker**, born 15 August 1985 in Denver.
6. **Raya Laurel Tasker**, born 9 April 1989 in Denver.

Child of Michael Blood and Gala Marie Whitten
6. **Annabelle Lee Blood**, born 25 June 1969 in Tucson, Arizona.

Children of Eric Parish and Gayla Marie Whitten
6. **Andrew Terlain Parish**, born 11 November 1984 in San Diego, California.
6. **Amanda Parish**, born 15 August 1992 in San Diego.

Child of Charles Stein and Merri Lynn Whitten
6. **Grace Jasmine Stein**, born 4 November 1990 in Boulder, Colorado.

Children of Joseph Brooks Whitten and Carol Teresa Boyles
6. **Laurie Leigh Whitten**, born 31 July 1973 in Memphis.
6. **Joseph Brooks Whitten Jr.**, born 2 April 1976 in Memphis.

Child of William DeWitt Whitten and Susan Smith
6. **Christopher Mark Whitten**, born 21 September 1974 in Memphis.

Children of James Lee Word and Lenora Rivoire
6. **Sarah Jean Word**, born 31 December 1984.
6. **Daniel Paul Word**, born 18 February 1986.

Children of Kenneth Eugene Mills and Kay Marie Word
6. **Rebecca Kay Mills**, born 11 October 1983.
6. **Jennifer Marie Mills**, born 14 October 1988.

Children of Richard Alexander Mcree and Jane Whitten
6. **Michael Alexander Mcree**, born 8 August 1950.
6. **Marsha Mcree** was born in 1947, and married a Mr. Ross.

Children of Dr. Vance Cyril Roy Jr. and Charlotte Ann Hughes
6. **Vanessa Lyn Roy** was born 26 January 1966, and on 25 November 1990 married Richard Deane Morse Jr., born 26 December 1965. They lived in Florence, Alabama, in 1996.
Their child was:
Peter Deane Morse III

6. **Adam Hughes Roy** was born 31 October 1967.

NINTH GENERATION
Children of Otis Springfield Murff Jr. and Betty Moody

7. **Cathy Lynn Murff** was born 5 November 1952 in Augusta, Georgia, and married 15 September 1984 in Lexington, South Carolina, Steve Lyman.

7. **Miriam Elizabeth Murff** was born 16 September 1953 in Augusta, Georgia, and married 31 July 1977 in Rock Hill, South Carolina, John Apperson. In Concord, North Carolina, she married Henry Durkin 20 October 1984.

The child of John Apperson and Miriam Elizabeth Murff was:

Elizabeth Ingles Apperson

The child of Henry Durkin and Miriam Elizabeth Murff was:

Jeffrey Michael Durkin

7. **Clarence Michael Murff**, born 5 November 1958 in Mobile, Alabama.

Children of Jack Cooley and Patricia Lynn Murff

7. **Lucinda Jane Cooley** was born 1 August 1952 at Scott AFB, Illinois, and married 16 January 1968 in Eutaw, Alabama, George Holcomb. She married Russell Allen Maxey 17 March 1982 in Florida; then, in Cordover, Tennessee, married Barry Mack Cooper.

The two children of George Holcomb and Lucinda Jane Cooley were:

Mary Shannon Holcomb

Stephanie Leigh Holcomb

The child of Russell Allen Maxey and Lucinda Jane Cooley was:

Russell Allen Maxey Jr.

7. **Jeffrey King Cooley** was born 29 September 1957 in Tupelo, Mississippi, and married 16 August 1990 in Atlanta, Frances Darlene Hunnicutt.

Their child was:

Abigail Julia Cooley

7. **William Marshall Cooley** was born 22 November 1966 in Tupelo, and married 1 September 1990, there, Candace Camille Skelton.

Children of William Benjamin Whitten and Jane Peebles
Born in West Chester, Pennsylvania

7. **Nathaniel Carter Whitten II** was born 18 August 1960, and married 20 April 1990 in Brooklyn, New York, Kathleen May O'Neill.

7. **William Benjamin Whitten Jr.**, born 11 November 1964.

7. **Victoria Lucian Whitten**, born 7 September 1968.

Child of Frank Burkett and Evelyn Kay Whitten

7. **Lee Anne Burkitt**, born 3 February 1962 in Corinth, Mississippi.

Children of John Thomas McCallen and Martha Ann Henderson

7. **Kay McCallen** was born 23 April 1953 in Norfolk, Virginia, and married in 1990 in Memphis, Robert Bruce Cain.

Their child was:

Robert Neil Cain

7. **Martha Laurie McCallen** was born 26 February 1955 in Norfolk, Virginia, and married 29 July 1978 in Memphis, Gregory Bainer.

Their two children were:

Whitney Ann Bainer

Madeline Jane Bainer

7. **Mary Elizabeth McCallen** was born 6 July 1956 in Memphis, and married 1 July 1978, there, Michael Ray Spurlock.

Their three children were:

Stephanie Ann Spurlock

Michael Ray Spurlock Jr.

Elizabeth Mai Spurlock

7. **William Thomas McCallen** was born 19 July 1960 in Memphis, and married 25 June 1983, there, Janice Gyetvay, born 14 February 1961 in Washington, D.C.
Their child was:
John Thomas McCallen II

Children of Howard Marvin Graham and Ruby Elizabeth Henderson
Born in Memphis
7. **Kathryn Martin Graham**, born 8 October 1963.
7. **Howard Marvin Graham Jr.**, born 18 April 1967.
7. **Martha Ann Graham** was born 14 June 1968, and married 20 June 1992 in Memphis, Jerry Chadwick Mask, born 17 June 1970 in Jackson, Mississippi.

Children of William Raymond Reynolds and Jacquelene Whitten Mullen
7. **Jacqueline Rhea Reynolds**, born 17 December 1963 in Starkville, Mississippi.
7. **William Jack Reynolds**, born 3 January 1968 in Huntsville, Alabama.
7. **William Raymond Reynolds Jr.**, born 8 March 1972 in Huntsville.

Child of Mr. Coleman and Nancy Jane Mullen
7. **Michael Scott Coleman**, born 22 October 1962 in Starkville, Mississippi.

Children of Clifton Eugene Cartledge and Nancy Jane Mullen
7. **Melanie Beth Cartledge**, born 13 October 1966 in Huntsville, Alabama.
7. **Jacqueline Kay Cartledge**, born 15 December 1968 in Huntsville.
7. **Kevin Bradley Cartledge**, born 13 November 1971 in Conover, North Carolina.

Child of David Morris Ford and Linda Gayle Lester
7. **David Scott Ford**, born 11 December 1959 in Waco, Texas.

Child of Thomas Arthur Mize Jr. and Helen Lucille Whitten
7. **Barry Thomas Mize** was born 5 January 1968 in Memphis, and married 15 November 1986 in Southaven, Desoto, Mississippi, Linda Leava Betterton, born 15 April 1967 in Memphis.
Their two children were:
Ashley Marie Mize
Tori Ann Mize

Child of Jerry Neal Whitten and Sandra Rakestraw
7. **Geana Carol Whitten**, born 24 August 1966 in Pontotoc, Mississippi.

Child of Jerry Neal Whitten and Jane Tutor
7. **Jeffry Langston Whitten**, born 7 September 1973 in Pontotoc.

Child of Jerry Neal Whitten and Myra Jean Prather
7. **Kamesha Danielle Whitten**, born 23 October 1985 in Tupelo.

Children of Glenn Allen Whitten and Susan Gay Forrest
7. **Ronaldo Whitten** was born 12 February 1962 in Birkenfield, Germany, and married 2 December 1988 in Mango, Florida, Christine Pedrosa.
Their child was:
Christopher Whitten
7. **Susan Amanda Whitten**, born 16 February 1986 in Tupelo, Mississippi.

Children of William Robert Whitten and Carol Margaret Gifford
7. **Julie Michele Whitten**, born 11 November 1966 in Waukegan, Illinois.
7. **Nicole Lynn Whitten** was born 8 September 1970 in Tupelo, Mississippi, and married 17 September 1988 in

Mundelein, Illinois, James John Pickens, born 21 June 1969 in Japan.

Their child was:

James Joshua Pickens

Children of Kenneth Walter Whitten and Maureen Margaret Foster

7. **Kelly Marie Whitten**, born 1 September 1971 in Waukegan, Illinois.

7. **Carrie Lynn Whitten**, born 14 October 1974 in Waukegan.

7. **Eric Matthew Whitten**, born 25 August 1981 in Burlington, Racine, Wisconsin.

Children of Joe Phillip Whitten and Betty Lou Lyons Sibley

7. **Valarie Renate Whitten**, born 3 March 1962 in Phoenix, Arizona.

7. **Venetta Viola Whitten**, born 19 March 1963 in Phoenix.

7. **Veronica Constance Whitten**, born 14 March 1966 in Pensacola, Florida.

7. **Victoria Brooke Whitten**, born 7 September 1981 in Tupelo, Mississippi.

7. **Joanna Vashti Whitten**, born 10 June 1986 in Tupelo.

Children of John Richard Jackson and Rebecca Joyce Whitten

7. **Anna Clara Jackson**, born 2 June 1988 in Jackson, Mississippi.

7. **Brooks Harrison Jackson**, born 25 February 1992 in Jackson.

Child of Taylor June Whitten and Peggy Ann Gurley

7. **Chadwick Taylor Whitten**, born 20 December 1971 in Tupelo, Mississippi.

Child of William Vance Mayo and Vivian Dale Whitten

7. **William Whitten Mayo**, who was born 24 January 1965 in New Albany, Mississippi, was killed with his parents.

Children of George Langston Whitten and Brenda Gregory

7. **Cary Langston Whitten**, born 7 April 1968 in Tupelo, Mississippi.

7. **Mark Kevin Whitten**, born 16 August 1972 in Tupelo.

7. **Bridget Dawn Whitten**, born 1 August 1973 in Tupelo.

Children of Robert Charles Holcomb and Sherry Lynn Kreusher
Born in Waukegan, Illinois

7. **Robert Charles Holcomb Jr.**, born 9 August 1968.

7. **Shannon Lee Holcomb**, born 19 July 1969.

7. **Dana Andrew Holcomb**, born 23 February 1972.

7. **Jodie Marie Holcomb**, born 1 April 1974.

Child of Raymond Edward Dohr and Marilyn Holcomb

7. **Linda Carol Dohr** was born 20 February 1967 in Waukegan, and married 15 October 1988, there, James Persman, born 10 June 1967, also in Waukegan.

Child of Donald Ray Holcomb and Dorothy Mary Cole

7. **Meghan Holcomb**, born 15 February 1980 in Libertyville, Lake, Illinois.

Children of Jimmy Adams Holcomb and Linda Kravanger
Born in Waukegan, Illinois

7. **Julie Ann Holcomb**, born 30 June 1972.

7. **Tracy Marie Holcomb**, born 25 November 1974.

Children of David Hay Rice and Judy Dianne Vinson

7. **Melody Dianne Rice**, born 27 May 1974 in Memphis.

7. **Christopher David Rice**, born 10 May 1987 in Memphis.

Children of Freddy Ray Vinson and Jane Arthur Haynes

7. **James William Vinson**, born 21 April 1977 in Jackson, Tennessee.

7. **Jill Ray Vinson**, born 15 March 1981 in Jackson.

Children of Donald Gene Cupples and Susan Ray Vinson

7. **Lydia Jane Cupples**, born 3 June 1986 in Memphis.

7. **William Benjamin Cupples**, born 3 August 1987 in Memphis.

Children of Timothy DeLane Holcomb and Patricia Yvonne Gillespie

7. **Jenifer Clair Holcomb**, born 28 December 1973 in Tupelo, Mississippi.

7. **Jacob Loy Holcomb**, born 10 August 1979 in New Albany.

7. **Julie Erin Holcomb**, born 28 February 1983 in New Albany.

Child of Jeffry Whitten Gillespie and Elizabeth Elaine Harper

7. **Whitten Harper Gillespie**, born 17 November 1984 in Tupelo.

Children of Frank Magers Anderson and Margaret Rose Gillespie
Born in Tupelo, Mississippi

7. **Anna Rose Anderson**, born 5 January 1984.

7. **Frank Magers Anderson Jr.**, born 29 September 1985.

7. **Samuel Gillespie Anderson**, born 23 December 1987.

Children of Lawrence Mitchell Brazeal and Nancy Ann Gillespie
Born in Tupelo, Mississippi

7. **Kayla Marie Brazeal**, born 19 August 1986

7. **Haley Elizabeth Brazeal**, born 6 June 1988.

Children of Charles George Capps and Karen Louise Gillespie

7. **Charles Ross Capps**, born 5 March 1988 in San Antonio, Texas.

7. **Kacey Morgan Capps**, born 2 November 1989 in Colorado Springs, Colorado.

Children of Meredith Hemphill and Kathryn Earle Dilworth

7. **Jean Earle Hemphill**

7. **Shirley Kee Hemphill**

7. **Meredith Hemphill Jr.**

Children of George Willard Pugh and Jean Earle Hemphill

7. **William Whitmel Hill Pugh** was born 25 March 1954, and married Beth Elaine Smith on 12 March 1983. She was born 7 January 1954.

Their three children were:
  Brendon Kelly Pugh
  Bryan Clayton Pugh
  Katherine Elaine Pugh

7. **George Willard Pugh Jr.** was born on 6 September 1956, and married on 14 December 1986 Janelle Ann Nacarri, who was born on 30 April 1956.

Their two children were:
  George Willard Pugh III
  Meredith Caitlin Pugh

7. **David Nichols Pugh** was born 17 June 1958, and on 25 May 1986 married Cynthia Lynn Simpson, born on 10 December 1958.

7. **James Hemphill Pugh**, born 6 September 1966

Children of Harlan Robinson Jessup and Shirley Kee Hemphill

7. **James Harlan Jessup**, born 7 July 1958

7. **Jennifer Hemphill Jessup** was born 1 September 1960, and married Neil Vincent Kelly on 24 December 1990. He was born 1 September 1949.

Their two children were:
    Malaika Anne Kelly
    Linnea Jeanette Kelly
7. **Benjamin Kent Jessup** was born on 29 June 1963, and married Kimberly Kay Schultz on 6 August 1994. She was born 7 January 1962.
7. **Susan Jean Jessup** was born 13 August 1965, and married James Michael Caldwell on 22 September 1991. He was born on 23 September 1955.

Children of Meredith Hemphill Jr. and Mary Beverly Bell
7. **Mary Katherine Hemphill**, born 14 June 1963, married Andrew William Markley 19 August 1991.
Their child was:
    Sarah Katherine Markley
7. **Meredith Scott Hemphill,** born on 5 June 1963, married Kris Elaine Harrison on 10 August 1991.
Their three children were:
    Kevin Meredith Hemphill
    Brian Robert Hemphill
    Rachel Ann Hemphill
7. **Geoffery Guy Hemphill**, born on 16 February 1967, married Tracy Pierce Tucker on 18 July 1992.
Their child was:
    James Dilworth Hemphill
7. **Mark Alexander Hemphill**, born 3 November 1970

Children of Kent Wheelock Hemphill and Suzanne Daversa
7. **Katherine Anne Hemphill**, born 6 January 1959, married Alan Sharp 27 December 1989.
7 **Judith Hemphill**, born 28 October 1962, married Timothy M. Galusha 9 October 1992.
Their child was:
    Erin Emily Galusha
7. **Kent Wheelock Hemphill Jr.**, born 21 November 1966, married Toni Lynne Smith 9 September 1995.

Children of Phil David Wedermeyer and Nancy Lee Morgan
Born in Houston, Texas
7. **John Phillip Wedermeyer**, born 16 September 1977.
7. **Stephen Edward Wedermeyer**, born 12 November 1979.
7. **David Charles Wedemeyer**, born 3 September 1981.

Children of Dean William Baesel and Betsy Jane Morgan
7. **Christopher Morgan Baesel**, born 23 January 1979.
7. **Kelly Lee Baesel**, born 23 July 1981

Child of Gregory Wayne Yarborough and Mary Lou Morgan
7. **Jason Wayne Yarborough**, born 24 April 1994 in Houston.

Children of Robbie Don Godwin and Margaret Ann Cooper
7. **John Scott Godwin** was born 14 November 1962 at Ft. Knox, Kentucky, and married Jennifer Curington on 13 June 1987. She was born 22 November 1965 in Houston.
Their two children were:
    Jessica Mauree Godwin
    Mary Aline Godwin
7. **Brian Frank Godwin** was born on 5 March 1967 in Houston, and on 2 March 1990 married Rony Klein, who was born 30 November 1966.
Their two children were:
    Joshua Tyree Godwin
    Eileen Godwin

Children of William Tyre Cooper IV and Betty Jane Wyke

7. **Misty Jeanine Cooper**, born 17 November 1975.
7. **Danielle Louise Cooper**, born 24 May 1995.

Children of Burtis Albert Lauber and Dorothy Jane Wilson
7. **Pamela Jane Lauber** was born 27 March 1956 in Augsburg, West Germany, and married 29 December 1976, Stephen Robert Kok, born 29 October 1956 in Setauket, New York.
  Their two children were:
     Stephen Randall Kok
     Lisa Jane Kok
7. **Steven Burtis Lauber** was born 8 January 1958 in Mineola, New York, and married Victoria Taylor Simpson on 14 February 1988 in Bradford, Massachusetts. She was born 14 May 1965 in Hinsdale, Illinois.
  Their three children were:
     Michael Burtis Lauber
     Jessica Taylor Lauber
     Jacob Steven Lauber

Child of James Cameron Cunningham and Gail
7. **James Tyler Cunningham**, born in Canada on 29 September 1964.

Child of Paul Reid and Katherine Ann Cunningham
7. **Andrea Reid**

Children of Ken Craig and Debra Jean Marie Marceau
Born in New Brunswick, Canada
7. **Hugh John McLaughlin Craig**, born 8 October 1975, married Crystal McCourt.
7. **Cleo Sauree Deanne Craig**, born 5 October 1978.
7. **Melanie Jean Marie Craig**, born 3 June 1980.

Child of Julien Pierre Joseph Marceau and Audrey Judith Meyer
7. **André Julien Marceau**, born 9 December 1992 in Frederickton, New Brunswick.

Child of Daniel Joseph Marceau and Lorraine
7. **Liam Daniel Marceau**, born 16 August 1998.

Children of Rino Leveque and Diane Marie Marceau
Born in Canada
7. **Nicholas Nelson Levegue**, born 11 August 1994.
7. **Helen Margaret Leveque**, born 31 October 1998.

Children of John Robert Germany Jr. and Kristin Merritt
Born in Greenville, Mississippi
7. **Kristina Lynne Germany** was born 16 August 1960, and married Sean Patrick Argabright on 22 October 1987 in Grand Junction, Colorado. They lived in Spring, Texas, in 1996.
7. **John Robert Germany III** was born 27 November 1961, and married 16 May 1992 in Montgomery, Texas, Laura Ann Beam. They have since divorced.
7. **Lucie Hope Germany**, born 11 April 1965.

Children of Walter McDonald Merritt III and Beverly Rebecca Whitten
7. **Walter McDonald Merritt IV**, born 15 November 1967 in Jackson, Mississippi.
7. **Lisa Whitten Merritt**, born 12 January 1970 in La Jolla, California.

Children of Joel Morris Wagoner and Presley McDonald Merritt
7. **Joel Merritt Wagoner**, born 17 January 1976 in Decatur, Georgia.
7. **Andrew Johnston Wagoner**, born 30 October 1978 in Beckley, West Virginia.
7. **Mary Elizabeth Davis Wagoner**, born 20 October 1981 in Beckley, West Virginia.

Children of Charles Wesley Merritt Jr. and Alice Christine McCulloch Smith
7. **Christine Carlson Merritt**, born 23 August 1982 in Houston, Texas.
7. **Charles Wesley Merritt III**, born 10 February 1984 in Atlanta, Georgia.
7. **Martha Larkin Alexander Merritt**, born 21 January 1989 in Atlanta.

Child of Thomas Earle DuPree Jr. and Ann Whitten Merritt
7. **Thomas Earl DuPree III**, born 6 February 1985 in Greenville, South Carolina.

Children of Andrew Cassius Whitten and Carla Wardenburg
Born in Scottsdale, Arizona
7. **Olivia Linnore Whitten**, born 19 November 1992.
7. **Siera Isabelle Whitten**, born 19 August 1994.
7. **Elena Hunter Whitten**, born 27 February 1997.

Children of Thomas Edward Skaife and Cosmas Anne Whitten
7. **Edward Francis Skaife**, born in 1992 in Madison, Wisconsin.
7. **Samuel Thomas Skaife**, born in 1995 in Madison.

Children of Paul Bowman Stam Jr. and Dorothy Electa Mills
7. **Nathaniel Edward Stam**, born 17 January 1977 in Durham, North Carolina.
7. **Jane Ariel Stam**, born 13 March 1980 in Raleigh, North Carolina.

Children of Carl Levring Stam and Doris Ann Perry
7. **Carl Michael Stam**, born 1 March 1979.
7. **Timothy Martin Stam**, born 24 November 1980.
7. **Christine Stam** was born 9 January 1988 in South Bend, Indiana.

Children of William Whitten Stam and Nancy Lynn Fordham
7. **Eric Emery Stam**, born 21 January 1988 in Raleigh.
7. **Kevin Fordham Stam**, born 14 February 1991 in Durham.

Children of John Mark Dannels and Kathryn Ramsey Moore
7. **Karen Wells Dannels**, born 17 June 1973 in St. Louis, Missouri, and married Damon DiSantes 10 August 1996 in Indianapolis, Indiana. They lived in west Chicago in 2004.
Their two children were:
 Andrew William Desantis
 Kyle Anthony Desantis
7. **Mark Emerson Dannels**, born 6 December 1978 in Richmond, Virginia.

Children of William Black Moore III and Mary Shufford Davis
7. **Sarah Latham Moore**, born 23 October 1985 in Phoenixville, Pennsylvania.
7. **Kathryn "Kate" Longino Moore**, born 12 December 1989 in Phoenixville.

Children of Dr. John Dwight Richmond and Bethany Ann Moore
7. **Andrew "Andy" Wells Richmond**, born 22 October 1985 in Dalton, Georgia.
7. **John McQuilken "Mac" Richmond** was born 4 October 1989 in Dalton.

Children of Stephen Dean Burke and Vielka Rosa Gilkes
7. **Crystal Lynne Burke**, born 16 May 1992.
7. **Tiffany Lynne Burke**, born 16 May 1992.

Child of Keven Scott Bay and Deborah Lynne Burke
7. **Ethan Luke Bay**, born 5 February 1992.
Child of Richard Dean Morse Jr. and Vanessa Lyn Roy

144

7. **Peter Deane Morse**, born 8 May 1996.

TENTH GENERATION

Child of John Apperson and Miriam Elizabeth Murff
8. **Elizabeth Ingles Apperson**, born 19 March 1979 in Charlotte, North Carolina.

Child of Henry Durkin and Miriam Elizabeth Murff
8. **Jeffrey Michael Durkin**, born 2 July 1987 in Charlotte.

Children of George Holcomb and Lucinda Jane Cooley
8. **Mary Shannon Holcomb**, born 19 August 1968 in Tupelo, Mississippi.
8. **Stephanie Leigh Holcomb**, born 15 October 1971 in Tupelo.

Child of Russell Allen Maxie and Lucinda Jane Cooley
8. **Russell Allen Maxey Jr.**, born 7 January 1984 in Tupelo.

Child of Jeffrey King Cooley and Frances Darlene Hunnicutt
8. **Abigail Julia Cooley**, born 28 July 1991 in Atlanta.

Child of Robert Bruce Cain and Kay McCallen
8. **Robert Neil Cain**, born 13 January 1991 in Memphis.

Children of Gregory Bainer and Martha Laurie McCallen
8. **Whitney Ann Bainer**, born 9 April 1985 in Memphis.
8. **Madeline Jane Bainer**, born 23 February 1990 in Memphis.

Children of Michael Ray Spurlock and Mary Elizabeth McCallem
Born in Memphis, Tennessee
8. **Stephanie Ann Spurlock**, born 19 December 1982.
8. **Michael Ray Spurlock Jr.**, born 3 October 1984.
8. **Elizabeth Mai Spurlock**, born 17 July 1987.

Child of William Thomas McCallen and Janice Gyetvay
8. **John Thomas McCallen II**, born 4 March 1988 in Memphis.

Children of Barry Thomas Mize and Linda Leava Betterton
8. **Ashley Marie Mize**, born 18 March 1988 in Memphis.
8. **Tori Ann Mize**, born 1 December 1990 in Southaven, Mississippi.

Child of Ronaldo Whitten and Christine Pedrosa
8. **Christopher Whitten**, born October 1990 in Alexandria, Louisiana.

Child of James John Pickens and Nicole Lynn Whitten
8. **James Joshua Pickens**, born 4 April 1989 in Waukegan.

Children of William Whitnel Hill Pugh and Helen Elaine Smith
8. **Brendan Kelly Pugh**, born 24 October 1980.
8. **Bryan Clayton Pugh**, born 28 October 1984.
8. **Katherine Elaine Pugh**, born 31 January 1987.

Children of George Willard Pugh Jr. and Janelle Ann Nacarri
8. **George Willard Pugh III**, born 6 September 1956.
8. **Meredith Caitlin Pugh**, born 4 January 1989.

Children of Neil Vincent Kelly and Jennifer Hemphill Jessup

8. **Malaika Anne Kelly**, born 15 August 1993.
8. **Linnea Jeanette Kelly**, born 10 July 1997.

Child of Andrew William Markley and Mary Katherine Hemphill
8. **Sarah Katherine Markley**, born 2 September 1994.

Children of Meredith Scott Hemphill and Kris Elaine Harrison
8. **Kevin Meredith Hemphill**, born 5 June 1993.
8. **Brian Robert Hemphill**, born 6 March 1996.
8. **Rachel Ann Hemphill**, born 6 March 1996.

Child of Geoffrey Guy Hemphill and Tracy Pierce Tucker
8. **James Dilworth Hemphill**

Child of Timothy M. Galusha and Judith Hemphill
8. **Erin Emily Galusha**, born 29 November 1995.

Children of John Scott Godwin and Jennifer Curington
8. **Jessica Mauree Godwin**, born 21 November 1990 in Houston.
8. **Mary Aline Godwin**, born 8 December 1993 in Orlando, Florida.

Children of Brian Frank Godwin and Romy Klein
Born in Austin, Texas
8. **Joshua Tyree Godwin**, born 31 March 1994.
8. **Eileen Godwin**, born 21 December 1995.

Children of Stephen Robert Kok and Pamela Jane Lauber
8. **Stephen Randall Kok**, born 1 April 1985 in Concord, New Hampshire.
8. **Lisa Jane Kok**, born 30 March 1989 in Concord.

Children of Steven Burtis Lauber and Victoria Taylor Simpson
Born in Beverly, Massachusetts
8. **Michael Burtis Lauber**, born 11 September 1988.
8. **Jessica Taylor Lauber**, born 16 January 1990.
8. **Jacob Steven Lauber**, born 1 July 1994.

Children of Damon Desantis and Karen Wells Dannels
Born in Chicago
8. **Andrew William Desantis**, born 23 September 2002.
8. **Drew Anthony Desantis**, born 26 July 2007.

THIRD GENERATION
ALFRED WHITTEN

1. **Alfred Whitten**, sixth child of John and Mary Reagan Whitten, was born 8 June 1797 in Greenville District, South Carolina, and married 4 October 1825 in Rutherford County, North Carolina, Caroline Matilda Prince, born in 1809 in Greenville District. She died from scarlet fever 15 November 1833 in Gowensville, South Carolina.

On 5 September 1834 in South Carolina, he married Bridget Graham, born about 1801 in that state. She may have been a daughter of John Graham from Greenville District, who became a prominent early settler of Fayette County, Tennessee. Some researchers believe John Graham's wife was a sister of Alfred's father, John Whitten. After marriage, Alfred and Bridget moved to Fayette County, where she died 10 September 1841. While residing in that county, Alfred's father and mother died, and he was named executor of John Whitten's will, being bonded with David Jernigan and John Graham as security.

On 25 April 1842 he married, in Fayette County, Mrs. Nancy Ann Lewis Malone, born 25 June 1821 in Davidson County, Tennessee. She may have been a daughter of Hulda Reding and William C. Lewis. Hulda's niece, a younger Hulda Reding, later married John Whitten Barrett, son of Alfred's sister Elizabeth. By 1845 Alfred had joined the Cumberland

146

Presbyterians, attending their General Assembly in Cincinnati in 1847. During the same period he served as justice of the peace in Fayette County.

In September 1849 Alfred wrote from Mt. Comfort, Tennessee, to Mr. William L. Gilliam of Montgomery County, Texas, stating he had sold his land and was preparing to move to that state. He asked that Gilliam and a "John" make certain preparations for the move. In *Letters to Rebecca*, where the full text of this letter appears, "John" was erroneously identified as John Whitten Barrett. He was, instead, John Baker Reding, in whose collection of letters and documents the letter was found. He was Nancy Ann's uncle, who had made a Fayette to Montgomery move earlier. In November of that year the Alfred Whitten family left Fayette County, traveling by water "without wagon or horse" to Montgomery County, Texas, settling a few years later in nearby Madison County. He became a respected member of the community, was elected sheriff in 1862, serving until August 1864. In 1869 Alfred was appointed to fill the unexpired term of Sheriff J. W. McKinzie.

Alfred and Nancy died in Madison County, Texas: he, 9 June 1884; she, 12 May 1898. They were buried in Park Cemetery. Many of their descendants continue to reside in the area.

The two children of Alfred Whitten and Caroline Matilda Prince were:
      Rebecca Ann M. Whitten
      Mary Jane Whitten
The four children of Alfred Whitten and Bridget Graham were:
      Sarah Eleanor Whitten
      John D. G. Whitten
      James Frank Whitten
      Martha Whitten
The eight children of Alfred Whitten and Nancy Ann Malone were:
      Harriett Louise Whitten
      Alice Anderson Whitten
      Helen Josephine Whitten
      Ervin Dunaway Whitten
      Eugene Grimes Whitten
      Hulda Eugenia Whitten
      Alfred W. Whitten
      Robert Lee Whitten

FOURTH GENERATION
Children of Alfred Whitten and Caroline Matilda Prince

2. **Rebecca Ann M. Whitten** was born 7 February 1829 in Greenville District, South Carolina, and married 13 August 1844 in Fayette County, Tennessee, Sam Louis Deshough, born about 1819 in North Carolina.
      Their two children were:
          William Deshough
          Martha Deshough

2. **Mary Jane Whitten** was born 18 June 1832 in Greenville District, and married 12 November 1846 in Fayette, Edward Americus Anderson, born 1 February 1820 in Sumner, Tennessee. He was a cabinetmaker, poet, musician, master mechanic, and inventor. They first settled in old Danville, Texas; then, moved to Willis. After the death of Mary Jane about 1862 in Montgomery County, he married Lucy Ann Hulon 24 July 1863, and they had eleven children. He died 1 December 1896 in Willis, Montgomery, Texas, and was buried there.

Children of Alfred Whitten and Bridget Graham

2. **Sarah Eleanor Whitten** was born 20 May 1835 in Fayette, and married about 1857 in Montgomery County, Texas, M. A. McCrory, born in 1834 in Tennessee. He was captured 11 January 1863 at Ft. Hindman, Arkansas, while serving with the 24th Regiment, Texas Cavalry, CSA, deserted the Confederacy in May 1863, and pledged allegiance to the U.S. Government at Camp Butler, Illinois. The family left Texas after that time.
      Their two children were:
          M. E. McCrory
          S. McCrory

2. **John D. G. Whitten** was born 27 October 1836 in Fayette County, Tennessee, and married 7 March 1861 in Montgomery County, Texas, Antoinett Folk, born 13 July 1844 there. During the Civil War he served under Capt. S. D. Wooldridge in Company B, 24th Regular Texas Cavalry, CSA. About 1870 the family moved to Brazos County, Texas,

returning to Madison County about 1885. John D. G. died 20 October 1894 in Madison, and was buried in Elwood Cemetery. She returned to Brazos and died there 13 September 1923.

Their ten children were:

> Melissa Ann Whitten
> Mary Jane Whitten
> Alford Francis Whitten
> William Walter Whitten
> Harriett Irene Whitten
> Alice Edna Whitten
> Nettie D. Whitten
> Emma Landusky Whitten
> Pearl Whitten
> John South Whitten

2. **James Frank Whitten** was born in 1838 in Fayette County, Tennessee. Letters written by his cousin Harriet Earle Whitten Lankford in 1846 tell of his visit with her family in Pontotoc County, Mississippi. He moved to Texas in 1849 with his father and died, probably before 1860.

2. **Martha Whitten** was born in 1840 in Fayette County, Tennessee, and moved to Texas in 1849 with her father. She, too, probably died in Montgomery County prior to 1860.

Children of Alfred Whitten and Nancy Ann Lewis Malone

2. **Harriett Louise Whitten** was born 22 August 1843 in Fayette County, Tennessee, and married 15 November 1866 in Madison County, Texas, Augustus James Morgan, born 29 May 1839 in Alabama. They died and are buried in Madison: she, 14 November 1930; he, 6 April 1894.

Their eight children were:

> Minnie J. Morgan
> Annie E. Morgan
> Lucy Irene Morgan
> Thomas Carroll Morgan
> Oran Morgan
> Lewis Irving Morgan
> Benton Houston Morgan
> Banton Austin Morgan

2. **Alice Anderson Whitten** was born 10 December 1845 in Fayette, Tennessee, and married 14 March 1866 in Madison County, Texas, David Edward Roten, who was born 1 May 1834 and died 10 September 1917. She died 10 November 1937. They lived near Rusk, Texas. Rotens still reside in that part of the state.

Their eight children were:

> Howard Macon Roten
> Edward Whitten Roten
> Harriett Alice Roten
> Ruba Lee Roten
> William Marvin Roten
> Irvin Tabor Roten
> Benny Oran Roten
> Annie Barnett Roten

2. **Helen Josephine Whitten** was born 28 December 1848 in Fayette County, Tennessee, and married James A. Stewart Jr. She later married a Mr. Hanson, and died in 1904. At birth she was named Helen Pulleam and later renamed Helen Josephine.

The four children of James A. Stewart and Helen Josephine Whitten were:

> Dan Stewart Jr.
> Norman Stewart
> Jim Stewart
> Mary Helen Stewart

2. **Ervin Dunaway Whitten** was born 27 December 1851 and died 20 December 1855 in Madison County, Texas.

2. **Eugene Grimes Whitten**, born in 1855 in Madison County.

2. **Hulda Eugenia Whitten** was born 25 January 1855 in Madison, married Sheriff Columbus Warren Crabb there

on 7 January 1872, and died 11 January 1944. He was born in May 1826 and died 9 March 1917.

Their seven children were:

Hanan P. Crabb

Columbus Warren Crabb Jr.

Jesse Ila Crabb

Ava Lee Crabb

Ludie Ann Crabb

Sam Aaron Crabb

Minnie Ray Crabb

2. **Alfred W. Whitten** was born 19 March 1858 in Madison County, where, on 19 February 1879, he married Martha E. Park, who was born 1 April 1863. Martha died 21 September 1887 in Madison County and was buried in Park Cemetery. Shortly thereafter, Alfred got into some sort of trouble. A posse went after him, and he was never heard from again.

Their four children were:

Leven H. Whitten

Berry W. Whitten

Mada Olivia Whitten

Ruth Whitten

2. **Robert Lee Whitten** was born 23 July 1861 in Madison, where he married, on 25 July 1892, Cordia D. Savell, who was born 19 October 1868. They died in 1902 in Madison County: he, 21 March; she, 16 April, and were buried in Park Cemetery.

Their three children were:

Sam Whitten

Edd Whitten

Abb Whitten

FIFTH GENERATION
Children of Sam Louis Deshough and Rebecca Ann Whitten

3. **William Deshough** was born and died about 1846 in Fayette.

3. **Martha Deshough**, born about 1848 in Fayette.

Children of M. A. McCrory and Sarah Eleanor Whitten

3. **M. E. McCrory**, female, born in Texas in 1858.

3. **Sarah McCrory**, born in Texas in 1859.

Children of John D. G. Whitten and Antonett Folk

3. **Melissa Ann Whitten** was born 26 March 1862 in Montgomery County, and married 19 February 1884 in Brazos County, Joe F. Crenshaw. They lived in Madison County, moving back to Brazos by 1896. She died 6 April 1940 and is buried in Wesson Cemetery, Brazos County. He died shortly before. Some report her name as Malyja.

Their seven children were:

Ruby Edith Crenshaw

Roland Franklin Crenshaw

Mary E. Crenshaw

Etna May Crenshaw

Arthur Wayne Crenshaw

Erma D. Crenshaw

Jessie Lee Crenshaw

3. **Mary Jane Whitten** was born 23 April 1866, died 1 December 1886, and was buried in Elwood Cemetery, Madison, Texas.

3. **Alford Francis Whitten** was born 20 July 1868, died 20 November 1894, and is buried in Elwood Cemetery.

3. **William Walter Whitten** was born 9 August 1870, died 23 August 1870, and is buried in Wickson Cemetery, Brazos County.

3. **Harriett Irene Whitten** was born 9 November 1871, married Henry Allphine 17 December 1891 in Madison County, died 30 March 1893, and is buried in Elwood Cemetery.

Their child was:

Hatti Pearl Allphine

3. **Alice Edna Whitten** was born 19 May 1874, died 27 February 1882, and was buried in Wesson Cemetery, Brazos County.

3. **Nettie D. Whitten** was born 4 December 1876, and married Augustus Lee Moody 7 February 1915 in Wheelock, Brazos, Texas. He was born in Arkansas 26 January 1878 and died 26 June 1955 in Houston. Nettie died 28 May 1953 in Bryan, and is buried in Wickson Cemetery, Brazos County, Texas.

Their three children were:
- Aubrey Lee Moody
- Ruby Ethel Moody
- Charles Oran Moody

3. **Emma Landuskey Whitten** was born 26 March 1879 in Brazos County, and married John Lummus 13 December 1899 in Madison County. He was born 7 December 1880. Emma died 31 December 1912 and is buried in Wickson Cemetery, Brazos County. Todeykey has been reported by others as her middle name.

Their three children were:
- Ernest Ray Lummus
- John Harrison Lummus
- Clara Lummus

3. **Pearl Whitten** was born 2 August 1881, died 20 September 1882, and was buried in Wesson Cemetery, Brazos County.

3. **John South "Johnnie" Whitten** was born 4 October 1885 in Madison County, Texas, and married Myrtle Freeman, who was born 15 December 1895. He died 13 July 1962 in Bryan, Texas, where he is buried. Like many Whittens, "Johnnie" loved to sing.

Children of Augustus James Morgan and Harriett Louise Whitten

3. **Minnie J. Morgan** was born in 1867 in Madison County Texas, died in 1873, and was buried there.

3. **Annie E. Morgan** was born 18 June 1870 in Madison, died 5 August 1872, and was buried there.

3. **Lucy Irene Morgan** was born 21 March 1873 in Madison and died in Oklahoma 30 December 1952. She married Elihu Sidney Venable, who was born 21 February 1880 and died 23 October 1957.

Their five children were:
- Mary Louise Venable
- Maxine Venable
- Tom Helsey Venable
- Pauline Venable
- Aline Venable

3. **Thomas Carroll Morgan** was born 31 January 1876 in Texas, died 10 December 1958 in Madison, and was buried there. He married Dora Melvina Park, who was born 26 September 1881 and died 26 March 1961.

Their seven children were:
- Eula Morgan
- Euna Morgan
- Tama Lee Morgan
- Gussie Morgan
- T. J. Morgan
- Ola Morgan
- Edna Earle Morgan

3. **Oran Morgan** was born in 1878, died in 1888, and was buried in Madison County, Texas.

3. **Lewis Irving Morgan** was born in 1880 in Texas, died 4 July 1954, and married Lola Bledsoe. She was born 7 September 1893 and died in 1929.

Their six children were:
- Norman G. Morgan
- Nova Jessie Morgan
- Lucy Geraldine Morgan
- Edith Cavell Morgan
- Gus Morgan
- Joseph Lewis Morgan

3. **Benton Houston Morgan**, twin of Banton, was born 10 November 1885 in Madison, and married Mary Crabb,

who was born 19 February 1890 and died 4 February 1972. He died 24 July 1963, and was buried in Madison County.

Their two children were:

Benton Houston Morgan Jr.

Virgil Northrup Morgan

3. **Banton Austin Morgan**, twin of Benton, was born 10 November 1885 in Madison, married Loulan Venable, and died 24 July 1969.

Their child was:

Peggy Morgan

Children of David Edward Roten and Alice Anderson Whitten

3. **Howard Macon Roten** was born 11 April 1868 in Texas, and married 28 February 1894 in Cherokee County, Martha Ellen Evans, born in 1874. They died in Montgomery County: he, 29 July 1940; she in 1964. They were buried in Oakwood Cemetery.

Their seven children were:

Ruby Lee Roten

Anella Roten

Clara Roten

Ernest Roten

Leola Roten

Nena Roten

Elsie Roten

3. **Edward Whitten Roten** was born 30 June 1871 in Texas, and married, 19 December 1895, May J. Laughter in Cherokee County. He then married Lucy Odom. Edward Whitten died 27 February 1949 in Hardin, Texas, and was buried in Resthaven Cemetery.

The two children of Edward Whitten Roten and May J. Laughter were:

Bertie L. Roten

Edward Roten

The four children of Edward Whitten Roten and Lucy Odom were:

Neil Roten

Luray Roten

Pleasant Roten

Oran Roten

3. **Harriett Alice Roten** was born 10 December 1873 in Texas, and married 14 September 1892, in Cherokee County, Charles Albert Vining, twin of George Albert Vining, who married her sister Ruba Lee. On 22 June 1904 in Cherokee County, she married John Raper, who was born in 1861 and died in 1939.

The three children of Charles Albert Vining and Harriett Alice Roten were:

Lucy Vining

Agnes Vining

Charles Macon Vining

The two children of John Raper and Harriett Alice Roten were:

Edward Raper

John Raper Jr.

3. **Ruba Lee Roten** was born 26 April 1876 in Midway, Madison, Texas, and married 28 February 1894 in Cherokee, George Albert Vining, twin of Charles Albert. On 1 July 1908 in Palestine, Texas, she married E. Lee Ross, died 23 April 1966 in Rusk, and was buried in Cedar Hill Cemetery.

The two children of George Albert Vining and Ruba Lee Roten were:

William Macon Vining

Fitzhugh Vining

3. **William Marvin Roten** was born 9 October 1878 in Texas, and married in 1910, Callie Woodward, born in 1889. She died in Cherokee County in 1930, and William Marvin married, the following year, Alta Mae Sherman. He died 18 November 1970, and was buried with Callie in Cedar Hill Cemetery, Cherokee County, Texas.

The three children of William Marvin Roten and Callie Woodward were:

Walter Roten

David Roten

Marvinal Roten

The child of William Marvin Roten and Alta Mae Sherman was:
Travis Roten

3. **Irvin Tabor Roten** was born 4 January 1881 in Iola, Grimes, Texas, and married 30 September 1903 in Rusk, Jessie McDowell, born 17 July 1885. They died in Corpus Christi, Texas: she, 9 October 1956; he, 12 September 1966; where they were buried in Memory Gardens.

Their five children were:
Wallace Wesley Roten
James Whitten Roten
Lucy Victoria Roten
Helen Louise Roten
Jo Bess Roten

3. **Benny Oran Roten** was born 25 November 1883 and died 19 August 1885 in Texas.

3. **Annie Barnett Roten** was born 14 February 1886 in Madison County, Texas, and married 5 January 1910 in Cherokee County, Claude L. Barley, born in 1883. He died in 1914, and she married 26 December 1917 Arthur McIver, in Cherokee. Annie died 7 December 1972, and was buried in Cedar Hill Cemetery.

The two children of Claude L. Barley and Annie Barnett Roten were:
Thomas Luther Barley
Pauline Ross Barley

The child of Arthur McIver and Annie Barnett Roten was:
George David McIver

Children of James A. Stewart and Helen Josephine Whitten

3. **Dan Stewart Jr.**
3. **Norman Stewart**
3. **Jim Stewart**
3. **Mary Helen Stewart** was born 12 January 1870, and married James William Park, who was born in 1868 and died 30 June 1931. She died 17 February 1956.

Their three children were:
Thomas Henry Park
William Hiram Park
Helen Beatrice Park

Children of Sheriff Columbus Warren Crabb and Hulda Eugenia Whitten

3. **Hanan P. Crabb** was born 19 April 1873, and married Mary Etta Womble, born in 1885. He died 19 April 1956.

Their two children were:
Emma Ray Crabb
Hanan P. Crabb Jr.

3. **Columbus Warren Crabb Jr.** was born in March 1877, and married Hallye Park, who was born in 1879 and died in 1955. He died in 1958.

3. **Jessie Ila Crabb** was born in 1878, married John Womble, and died in 1974.

3. **Ava Lee Crabb** was born 11 September 1881 and died 17 July 1965. She married Horace Carter, who was born 13 February 1882 and died 27 December 1964.

Their two children were:
Paulene Carter
Rachel Grace Carter

3. **Ludie Ann Crabb** was born in November 1884 and died 17 November 1956. She married Tom C. Farris, who was born 28 September 1878 and died 29 July 1932.

Their three children were:
Lamar Farris
Olin Farris
Helen Farris

3. **Sam Aaron Crabb,** who was born in December 1888, married Callie Bell Smith and Ruby Johnson, and died in May 1974.

The child of Sam Aaron Crabb and Callie Bell Smith was:

Ruth Crabb

3. **Minnie Ray Crabb** was born in April 1893, and married Bruno Earl Sloan, who was born in 1890 and died in 1916.

Their child was:

Hope Natalie Sloan

Children of Alfred W. Whitten Jr. and Martha E. Park

3. **Leven H. Whitten** was born 3 May 1881 in Madisonville, Texas, and married 14 December 1903 in Madison County, Fannie Carter, born 7 March 1884. They died there: he, 10 April 1959; she, 11 January 1968; and were buried in Park Cemetery.

Their six children were:

Arthur Whitten
Hazel Whitten
Lois Whitten
Opal Whitten
Harriet Louise Whitten
Levin H. Whitten Jr.

3. **Berry W. Whitten** was born 5 November 1882 in Madisonville, and married 8 May 1905, there, Ellen Floyd, born 5 August 1885. They died in Madison County, Texas: he, 1 October 1951; she, 25 December 1970. They were buried in Park Cemetery.

3. **Mada Olivia Whitten** was born in April 1884 in Madison, married William LeRoy McGaughey, who was born 13 December 1878 and died 21 December 1914. After his death she married Henry Culbreth, who was born in 1886 and died in 1953. Mada died in 1968.

The four children of William McGaughey and Mada Olivia Whitten were:

Eska Lamar McGaughey
Leven B. McGaughey
Will Ernest McGaughey
Alfred McGaughey

The child of Henry Culbreth and Mada Olivia Whitten was:

Dorothy Mae Culbreth

3. **Ruth Whitten** was born in April 1886, married 23 November 1905 Harry Landers, and died in 1974. She lived her entire life in Madison County, Texas.

Their child was:

Oveleta Landers

Children of Robert Lee Whitten and Cordia D. Savell

3. **Sam Whitten** was born 16 September 1894 in Madison, and married Ruby Farris, born 12 February 1895. He died 13 May 1980; she, 5 May 1981.

Their three children were:

Melba Whitten
Harold Whitten
Faye Whitten

3. **Edd Whitten** was born 4 March 1896 in Madison County, and married Emily C. Brownlee, who was born 25 December 1896. He died 25 March 1968 in Madison, and was buried in Park Cemetery. Emily died after 1973 in Texas.

Their three children were:

LaRue Whitten
Robert Whitten
Edward Whitten

3. **Abb Whitten** was born 31 January 1898 in Madison County, married Pauline Wakeland, and died in Texas in 1979.

SIXTH GENERATION
Children of Joe F. Crenshaw and Melissa Ann Whitten

4. **Ruby Edith Crenshaw** was born 7 December 1884, died 17 June 1886, and was buried in Wesson Cemetery, Brazos County.

4. **Roland Franklin Crenshaw** was born 2 August 1887, and married Lillian Elliott. He died 20 March 1966, and was buried at Alexander, near Tabor, Texas.

The child of Roland Franklin Crenshaw and Lillian Elliott was:

Roland Franklin Crenshaw Jr.

4. **Mary E. Crenshaw** was born 13 July 1891 and died 31 October the same year. She was buried in Elwood Cemetery, Madison County, Texas.

4. **Etna May Crenshaw** was born 12 February 1893, and married John Archie Robinson 11 September 1911. He was born 1 June 1891.

Their two children were:

Harriet Louise Robinson

Archie Wayne Robinson

4. **Arthur Wayne Crenshaw** was born 15 October 1895, died 3 July 1896, and was buried in Wesson Cemetery, Brazos County.

4. **Erma D. Crenshaw** was born 13 August 1900, died before 1974, and was buried in Wesson Cemetery.

4. **Jessie Lee Crenshaw** was born 12 July 1903, and married Rufus P. Batten, born 10 January 1897.

Their nine children were:

Doris Batten

Dorothy Batten

Ruth Batten

Carleton Lee Batten

Mary Batten

Jean Batten

Hazel Batten

Catherine Batten

Ronnie Batten

Child of Henry Allphine and Harriett Irene Whitten

4. **Hatti Pearl Allphine** was born 16 January 1893, married Walter G. Lindsay, and was living in Bryan, Texas, in 1974.

Children of Augustus Lee Moody and Nettie Whitten

4. **Aubrey Lee Moody** was born 2 January 1916 in Bryan, Texas, and married Faye Epperson. He died 29 August 1976 in Brigham, Box Elder, Utah.

4. **Ruby Ethel Moody** was born 8 December 1912, married J. J. Pitts, and was living in Leveland, Texas, in 1974.

4. **Charles Oran Moody**, born 6 August 1922.

Children of John Lummus and Emma Landuskey Whitten

4. **Ernest Ray Lummus**, born 20 December 1900.

4. **John Harrison Lummus** was born 23 August 1904 and died before 1974.

4. **Clara Lummus** was born 22 December 1910 and died in Houston in 1972.

Children of Elihu Sidney Venable and Lucy Irene Morgan

4. **Mary Louise Venable**, who was born 24 January 1909, and married Stearns H. Gardiner.

4. **Maxine Venable**, who was born 9 October 1910, and married Melvin Ray Gundy.

4. **Tom Helsey Venable**, who was born 9 March 1913, and married Mrs. Florence Elaine Richey Morrell.

4. **Pauline Venable**, who was born 9 March 1913, married Arnold Robert Benedict, and died before 1975.

4. **Aline Venable**, who was born 9 March and died 22 June 1913.

Children of Thomas Carroll Morgan and Dora Melvina Park

4. **Eula Morgan**, twin of Euna, was born 20 September 1901, and married Ercel C. Kelton, born 6 December 1893. He died 27 September 1975; she, 15 August 1993. They were buried in Park Cemetery.

Their six children were:

Melva Ann Kelton

Borden Carroll Kelton

Crystal Kelton

Fred Kelton
Ercel Morgan Kelton
Harriett Cavelle Kelton
4. **Euna Morgan**, twin of Eula, was born 20 September 1901, and married Frank R. Kelton, born 29 March 1895. His brother, Ercel, married Eula. Euna died 21 April 1983, and was buried in Park Cemetery.
Their three children were:
Mary Frank Kelton
Curtis Carroll Kelton
Paula Kay Kelton
4. **Tama Lee Morgan** was born 16 September 1903, and married William Harris, born 16 May 1900 and died 21 March 1961. She died 21 March 1994, and is buried in Park Cemetery.
Their child was:
Billy Gene Harris
4. **Gussie Morgan**, who helped compile these records, was born 31 December 1905, and married William Earl Hopkins, born 6 January 1902. He died in Madison County 22 December 1989, and is buried in Park Cemetery.
Their two children were:
Suzanne Hopkins
William Park Hopkins
4. **T. J. Morgan** was born 10 June 1910 and died 30 August 1930.
4. **Ola Morgan** was born 3 December 1917, and married Delmer Quincy Bowman.
Their two children were:
Linda Jane Bowman
Elizabeth Ann Bowman
4. **Edna Earle Morgan** was born 21 February 1921 and died 11 July 1935.

Children of Lewis Irving Morgan and Lola Bledsoe
4. **Norman G. Morgan** was born in 1912, married Berta Baines, and died before 1975.
Their child was:
Ken Morgan
4. **Nova Jessie Morgan** was born 20 March 1914, and married Hugh Branch McGaughey, born 2 August 1909.
Their three children were:
Ruby Kathryn McGaughey
Lola Ruth McGaughey
Anita Geraldine McGaughey
4. **Lucy Geraldine Morgan** was born 17 January 1916, and married William Ray McAlister, born 13 August 1916.
Their two children were:
William Ray McAlister Jr.
Robert Otis McAlister
4. **Edith Cavell Morgan** was born 16 May 1918, and married Thomas Carl Blackshear, born 16 October 1913.
4. **Gus Morgan** was born 25 February 1920, and married Thyra Howard, born 18 March 1922. He died 10 November 1983.
Their three children were:
Toni Kay Morgan
Randall Howard Morgan
Mark Anthony Morgan
4. **Joseph Lewis Morgan** was born 19 April 1927, and married Gloria Gay Daniel, born 1 March 1932.
Their two children were:
Terry Jo Morgan
Daniel Lewis Morgan

Children of Benton Houston Morgan and Mary Crabb
4. **Benton Houston Morgan Jr.**, born in 1917.
4. **Virgil Northrup Morgan** was born 19 December 1925 and died 1 May 1927.
Child of Banton Austin Morgan and Loulan Venable

4. Peggy Morgan, who married Wallace Osborne.
Their two children were:
  Carroll Osborne
  Clark Osborne

Children of Howard Macon Roten and Martha Ellen Evans

4. Ruby Lee Roten was born 30 September 1895 in Harris County, Texas, and married 2 November 1912 in Montgomery County, J. C. Jackson.

4. Anella Roten was born 15 August 1897 in Harris County, and married 23 December 1923 in Montgomery County, Texas, Lud Tucker.

4. Clara Roten was born 2 November 1900 in Montgomery, and married 22 April 1923, there, Pete Boles.

4. Ernest Roten was born in 1903 in Montgomery where, on 12 June 1927, he married Coda Burke, and died in 1977.

4. Leola Roten was born 22 March 1905 in Montgomery, and married 6 June 1925, there, James Metts.

4. Nena Roten was born 23 December 1909 in Montgomery, married 9 April 1927, there, Joseph McDonald, who died 18 June 1933. She was buried in Oakwood Cemetery.

4. Elsie Roten was born 30 March 1914 in Montgomery, and married 26 July 1931, there, Wilmot Limroth Everett. Elsie was buried in Oakwood Cemetery. They had three children.

Children of Edward Whitten Roten and May J. Laughter

4. Bertie L. Roten, born in November 1896 in Madison County.
4. Edward Roten, born in June 1899.

Children of Edward Whitten Roten and Lucy Odom

4. Neil Roten, born in 1899 in Madison County, Texas.
4. Luray Roten, born in 1902 in Texas.
4. Pleasant Roten, born 6 January 1904 in Cherokee County, Texas.
4. Oran Roten, born 7 January 1906 in Cherokee.

Children of Charles Albert Vining and Harriett Alice Roten

4. Lucy Vining was born 1894 in Texas, and married 1 July 1914 in Cherokee County, Paul Guinn.
4. Agnes Vining, born in 1896 in Texas.
4. Charles Macon Vining, born in 1898 in Texas.

Children of John Raper and Harriett Alice Roten

4. Edward Raper
4. John Raper Jr.

Children of George Albert Vining and Ruba Lee Roten

4. William Macon Vining was born 20 January 1896 in Cherokee County, and married 28 January 1944 Eddie Bea Roark. They had two children.

4. Fitzhugh Vining was born 29 March 1898 in Cherokee, died 21 August 1902, there, and was buried in Cedar Hill Cemetery.

Children of William Marvin Roten and Callie Woodward

4. Walter Roten
4. David Roten
4. Marvinal Roten, who married Floyd Manes.

Child of William Marvin Roten and Alta Mae Sherman

4. Travis Roten

Children of Irvin Tabor Roten and Jessie McDowell

4. Wallace Wesley Roten was born 16 November 1904 in Rusk, and married 27 June 1926 in Jacksonville, Cherokee, Texas, Nellie Grace Wilson. They lived in Winnie, Texas, in 1990.

156

Their three children were:

    Loyce Marie Roten

    Shirley Ann Roten

    Robert Wallace Roten

4. **James Whitten Roten**, who was born 4 May 1910 in Rusk, was living in Benson, Arizona, in 1990.

4. **Lucy Victoria Roten** was born 3 November 1913 in Rusk, and married 2 July 1938 in Sinton, Nueces, Texas, Emmitt Harlan Duty, who died 30 June 1963 in Calhoun, Texas. She was living in Corpus Christi in 1990.

Their three children were:

    Victoria Sue Duty

    Edward Booth Duty

    James Wallace Duty

4. **Helen Louise Roten** was born 26 November 1919 in Rusk, and married 28 March 1943 in San Antonio, Benjamin Fenton. She lived in Houston in 1990.

Their two children were:

    Joan Barbara Fenton

    Frances Margaret Fenton

4. **Jo Bess Roten** was born 7 October 1924 in Jacksonville, Cherokee, Texas, and married 9 November 1941, there, William L. Casey. She lived in Marble Falls, Texas, in 1990.

Their two children were:

    Linda Jo Casey

    Jefferson Roten Casey

Children of Claude L. Barley and Annie Barnett Roten

4. **Thomas Luther Barley** was born 21 September 1910 in Cherokee County, and married Beatrice Carlton there 30 December 1939.

4. **Pauline Ross Barley** was born 7 December 1912 in Cherokee County, and married James Salmon there 21 March 1931. Later she married J. R. Disharoon.

Child of Arthur McIver and Annie Barnett Roten

4. **George David McIver**, who married Edna Schrank.

Children of James William Park and Mary Helen Stewart

4. **Thomas Henry Park** was born 11 July 1891, and married Annie Lemons, who died in 1920. Later he married Ruth Frances True, who was born 8 May 1890 and died 23 June 1971. Thomas Henry died 16 June 1970.

4. **William Hiram Park** was born 13 October 1894, married Daisy Cook, and died 15 August 1958.

Their child was:

    Billy Gordon Park

4. **Helen Beatrice Park** was born 13 January 1896, and married Edward Ellsworth Reed, born 20 August 1901. She died 16 September 1940.

Their three children were:

    Kathleen Helen Reed

    Mary Maxine Reed

    James Edward Reed

Children of Hanan P. Crabb and Mary Etta Womble

4. **Emma Ray Crabb**, who married R. P. Lanier.

4. **Hanan P. Crabb Jr.**

Children of Horace Carter and Ava Lee Crabb

4. **Paulene Carter**, who married a Mr. Foster.

4. **Rachel Grace Carter**, who married a Mr. Avet.

Children of Tom C. Farris and Ludie Ann Crabb

4. **Lamar Farris**, who married Louise Whitley and died before 1995.

4. **Olin Farris**, who married Rosalyn Byers.

William B. Moore Jr.

4. **Helen Farris**, who married Joe Tinkle.
Their two children were:
    Tommy Jo Tinkle
    Dawn Tinkle
4. **Ruth Crabb**, who married Walter Anthony.

Child of Bruno Earl Sloan and Minnie Ray Crabb
4. **Hope Natalie Sloan** was born 23 April 1914, and married Dr. M. D. Hanson.
Their child was:
    Joseph Warren Hanson

Children of Leven H. Whitten and Fannie Carter
4. **Arthur Whitten** was born 2 November 1904, married Gladys Norwood, and died 6 June 1967.
Their child was:
    Katika Whitten
4. **Hazel Whitten** was born 17 September 1905 and died later that year.
4. **Lois Whitten** was born 18 September 1908, and married Hamp Rigby. Later she married Oscar Sowers and died 3 May 1980.
The child of Hamp Rigby and Lois Whitten was:
    Billy Rigby
4. **Opal Whitten** was born 12 January 1912, married Henry Carter, and died 21 January 1938.
4. **Harriet Louise Whitten** was born 31 August 1914, married George A. Staples, and died 2 April 1943.
Their two children were:
    George A. Staples Jr.
    Leven Staples
4. **Leven H. Whitten Jr.** was born 21 December 1917, and married Mozelle Manning.
Their three children were:
    Gary Whitten
    Donna Kaye Whitten
    Karen Lynn Whitten

Children of Willliam LeRoy McGaughey and Mada Olivia Whitten
4. **Eska Lamar McGaughey**, born 2 August 1907 in Madison County.
4. **Leven B. McGaughey**
4. **Will Ernest McGaughey**
4. **Alfred McGaughey**

Child of Henry Culbreth and Mada Alevia Whitten
4. **Dorothy Mae Culbreth**

Child of Harry Landers and Ruth Whitten
4. **Oveleta Landers**

Children of Sam Whitten and Ruby Farris
4. **Melba Whitten** was born 16 October 1916, and married R. V. Bowman.
4. **Harold Whitten** was born 25 October 1925, and married Beatrice Rhodes.
4. **Faye Whitten** was born 28 October 1928, and married J. L. Bradley.

Children of Edd Whitten and Emily C. Brownlee
4. **LaRue Whitten**, who married Douglas Robertson.
4. **Robert Whitten**
4. **Edward Whitten**

SEVENTH GENERATION
Child of Roland Franklin Crenshaw and Lillian Elliott

5. **Roland Franklin Crenshaw Jr.** was born 1 September 1922, and married Catherine Menahan. They had three daughters.

Children of John Archie Robinson and Eta May Crenshaw

5. **Harriett Louise Robinson** was born 27 August 1918, and married first a Mr. Lindley; then, 10 August 1962, Charles H. Moore.

5. **Archie Wayne Robinson**, born 27 April 1923.

Children of Rufus P. Batten and Jessie Lee Crenshaw

5. **Doris Batten**, born 2 October 1923.

5. **Dorothy Batten**, born 9 February 1925.

5. **Ruth Batten**, born 2 December 1926.

5. **Carleton Lee Batten**, born 19 November 1928.

5. **Mary Batten**, born 28 April 1931.

5. **Jean Batten**, born 13 January 1933.

5. **Hazel Batten**, born 28 April 1935.

5. **Catherine Batten**, born 16 September 1937.

5. **Ronnie Batten**, born 10 July 1944.

Children of Ercel C. Kelton and Eula Morgan

5. **Melva Ann Kelton**, born 26 November 1929.

5. **Bordon Carroll Kelton**, who was born 22 February 1930, and married Ruby Day, born 10 April 1929.

5. **Crystal Kelton** was born 22 February 1932, and married Marvin Spillers.

5. **Fred Kelton** was born 29 September 1934, and married Shirley Ann Charlton, born 4 November 1937.

5. **Ercel Morgan Kelton** was born 6 November 1938, and married Amy Horn, born 6 November 1940.

5. **Harriett Cavelle Kelton** was born in 1945, and married Ben Johnson.

Children of Frank R. Kelton and Euna Morgan

5. **Mary Frank Kelton** was born 16 April 1930, and married Ivan Blume.

5. **Curtis Carroll Kelton** was born 21 August 1932, and married Carolyn Bice.

5. **Paula Kay Kelton** was born 10 April 1934, and married Larry Byrd.

Child of William Harris and Tama Lee Morgan

5. **Billy Gene Harris**, born 4 May 1928.

Children of William Earl Hopkins and Gussie Morgan

5. **Suzanne Hopkins** was born 15 January 1941, and married Thomas Warren Mueke.
Their two children were:
> Thomas Warren Mueke Jr.
> Karen Sue Mueke

5. **William Park Hopkins** was born 4 February 1945, and married Mrs. Nancy Moorehead Mayes. On 26 July 1986, in Madisonville, he married Paula Tucker.
The child of William Park Hopkins and Nancy Moorehead Mayes was:
> Melyn Suzanne Mays Hopkins

Children of Delmer Quincy Bowman and Ola Morgan

5. **Linda Jane Bowman** was born 17 July 1942, and married Barton B. Gilman. In 1995 she married Robert Walker.
The two children of Barton B. Gilman and Linda Jane Bowman were:
> Mark Thomas Gilman
> Douglas Brockmeier Gilman

5. **Elizabeth Ann Bowman** was born 12 July 1947, and married Michael A. Andrews.
Their two children were:
> Caroline Andrews
> Emily Andrews

Child of Norman G. Morgan and Berta Baines

159

5. Ken Morgan

Children of Hugh Branch McGaughey and Nova Jessie Moran
5. **Ruby Kathryn McGaughey** was born 17 October 1932, and married Sylvestor Byrd, born 26 January 1933.
5. **Lola Ruth McGaughey** was born 15 July 1934, and married Doyle Wesley Wyatt, born 8 November 1938.
5. **Anita Geraldine McGaughey** was born 6 January 1936, and married Gene Dale Wyatt, born 8 December 1932.

Children of William Ray McAlister and Lucy Geraldine Morgan
5. **William Ray McAlister Jr.**, who was born 5 September 1941 and died 10 May 1949.
5. **Robert Otis McAlister**, who was born 7 October 1944, and married Linda Eggleston, born 1 September 1949.

Children of Gus Morgan and Thyra Howard
5. **Toni Kay Morgan** was born 1 September 1943, and married John Hardy.
5. **Randall Howard Morgan** was born 13 January 1945, and married Monty Withers.
5. **Mark Anthony Morgan** was born 17 September 1951, and married Melanie Wells.

Children of Joseph Lewis Morgan and Gloria Gay Daniel
5. **Terry Jo Morgan**, born 13 July 1956.
5. **Daniel Lewis Morgan**, born 6 December 1960.

Children of Wallace Osborne and Peggy Morgan
5. **Carroll Osborne**
5. **Clark Osborne**
5. **Loyce Marie Roten** was born 3 March 1929 in Troup, Smith, Texas, and married 12 September 1948 in Texas City, Eugene Ernest LaCombe. In Dickinson, Texas, 21 March 1975 she married William Henry Sampson, and 24 September 1982 married John E. Dunker. Loyce Marie died 17 August 1988 in San Antonio.
The two children of Eugene Ernest LaCombe and Loyce Marie Roten were:
    David Eugene LaCombe
    James Robert LaCombe
5. **Shirley Ann Roten** was born 6 December 1930 in Jacksonville, Cherokee, Texas, and married 20 August 1948 in Texas City, Roland Edmond Guidry. They lived in Winnie, Texas, in 1990.
Their three children were:
    Dana Ann Guidry
    Ava Danielle Guidry
    Paula Suzanne Guidry

Children of Wallace Wesley Roten and Nellie Grace Wilson
5. **Robert Wallace Roten** was born 1 June 1934 in Jacksonville, Texas, and married 19 August 1955 in Texas City, Carole Lynne Rousculp. They lived in Houston in 1990.
Their four children were:
    Karen Leigh Roten
    Patricia Dianne Roten
    Laura Ann Roten
    Patrick Robert Roten

Children of Emmitt Harlan Duty and Lucy Victoria Roten
5. **Victoria Sue Duty** was born 19 July 1939 in Wharton, Texas, and married 4 February 1964 in Corpus Christi, Michael Edward Cassidy.
Their two children were:
    Kenneth Sean Cassidy
    Bryon Patrick Cassidy
5. **Edward Booth Duty**, born 26 November 1945 in Corpus Christi.
5. **James Wallace Duty** was born 15 June 1948 in Corpus Christi, where on 2 May 1969 he married Kathryn Jane Little.
Their three children were:

James Jason Duty
John Jeffrey Duty
Michael Harlan Duty

Children of Benjamin Fenton and Helen Louise Roten
5. **Joan Barbara Fenton**, born 17 October 1946 in Corpus Christi.
5. **Frances Margaret Fenton** was born 23 June 1950 in Corpus Christi, and married 21 January 1971, there, John Lytton.

Children of William L. Casey and Jo Bess Roten
5. **Linda Jo Casey** was born 17 April 1947 in Corpus Christi, and married 10 September 1956 in San Antonio, Lawrence Leslie Garcia.
   Their two children were:
      William Frederick Garcia
      Casey Marie Garcia
5. **Jefferson Roten Casey** was born 21 May 1951 in Corpus Christi, and married 24 August 1974 in San Antonio, Bettie Ann Massey.
   Their child was:
      Ryan Kendrick Casey

Child of William Hiram Park and Daisy Cook
5. **Billy Gordon Park** was born 12 July 1931, and married Patsy J. Reeves, born 26 July 1933.
Their four children were:
      Laura Sue Park
      David Gordon Park
      Sarah Ellen Park
      Amy Jo Park

Children of Edward Ellsworth Reed and Helen Beatrice Park
5. **Kathleen Helen Reed** was born 18 June 1927, and married Lorn John Laney, born 12 March 1904.
Their two children were:
      Sandra Kay Laney
      Leesa Lou Laney
5. **Mary Maxine Reed** was born 22 June 1929, and married Luthur Miles Zimmerman.
Their two children were:
      Marilyn Gwen Zimmerman
      Joan Zimmerman
5. **James Edward Reed** was born 24 June 1931, and married Louise Watson.
Their two children were:
      Mary Kathryn Reed
      Patti Gayle Reed

Children of Joe Tinkle and Helen Farris
5. **Tommy Jo Tinkle**, who married Joe Manning.
5. **Dawn Tinkle**

Child of Dr. M. D. Hanson and Hope Natalie Sloan
5. **Joseph Warren Hanson**

Child of Arthur Whitten and Gladys Norwood
5. **Katika Whitten**, born 18 December 1938.

Child of Hamp Rigby and Lois Whitten
5. **Billy Rigby**, born 19 April 1930.
      Children of George A. Staples and Harriet Louise Whitten

5. **George A. Staples Jr.**, born 7 March 1940.
5. **Leven Staples**, born 11 September 1942.

Children of Levin H. Whitten Jr. and Mozelle Manning
5. **Gary Whitten**, born 16 September 1951.
5. **Donna Kaye Whitten**, who was born 12 June and died 21 July 1953.
5. **Karen Lynn Whitten**, who was born the 18th and died 24 September 1954.

EIGHTH GENERATION
Children of Thomas Warren Mueke and Suzanne Hopkins
6. **Thomas Warren Mueke Jr.**, born 20 August 1963.
6. **Karen Sue Mueke**, born 13 September 1965.

Child of William Park Hopkins and Nancy Moorehead Nayes
6. **Melyn Suzanne Mays Hopkins**, born 10 September 1963.

Children of Barton B. Gilman and Linda Jane Bowman
6. **Mark Thomas Gilman**, born in 1965.
6. **Douglas Brockmeier Gilman**, born in 1967.

Children of Michael A. Andrews and Elizabeth Ann Bowman
6. **Caroline Andrews**, born 17 January 1978.
6. **Emily Andrews**, born 6 July 1980.

Children of Eugene Ernest LaCombe and Loyce Marie Roten
6. **David Eugene LaCombe** was born 12 October 1950 in Texas, and married 7 June 1975 in Port Arthur, Patricia Lynne Holton.
6. **James Robert LaCombe** was born 22 September 1951 in Texas, and married 24 March 1974 in Deer Park, Texas, Twyla Shae Gantenbein. On 13 April 1988 in Houston, he married Helena Galindo LeSavege.

Children of Roland Edmond Guidry and Shirley Ann Roten
6. **Dana Ann Guidry** was born 18 February 1949 in Port Arthur, and married 3 June 1967, Milton Douglas Eckles. In 1990 they lived in Huntsville, Texas.
  Their two children were:
    Troy Eckles
    Julie Eckles
6. **Ava Danielle Guidry** was born 24 August 1950 in Galveston, and married 2 August 1969 in Port Arthur, Paul Byron Clubb.
  Their child was:
    John Wesley Clubb
6. **Paula Suzanne Guidry** was born 24 August 1954 in Texas, and married 8 July 1972 Lexie Leon Hopson. In May 1989 in Port Neches, Texas, she married James West.

Children of Robert Wallace Roten and Carole Lynne Rousculp
6. **Karen Leigh Roten** was born 9 May 1957 in Texas City, and married 13 August 1983 in Houston, George Zachary Crawford. They lived in Sugarland, Texas, in 1990.
  Their child was:
    Zachary Robert Crawford
6. **Patricia Dianne Roten** was born 8 April 1959 in Texas City, and married 17 April 1982 in Chesterfield, Missouri, James Edward Hammelman. They lived in Houston in 1990.
  Their two children were:
    Lauren Elizabeth Hammelman
    James Robert Hammelman
6. **Laura Ann Roten** was born 13 January 1962 in Texas City. In 1990 she lived in Houston.
6. **Patrick Robert Roten** was born 21 November 1963 in Texas City, and lived in Austin in 1990. He compiled

most of this Roten family record.

Children of Michael Edward Cassidy and Victoria Sue Duty
6. **Kenneth Sean Cassidy** was born 16 October 1971 in Corpus Christi and died in 1990.
6. **Byron Patrick Cassidy** was born 21 April 1973 in Corpus Christi.

Children of James Wallace Duty and Kathryn Jane Little
6. **James Jason Duty** was born 21 April 1973 in Corpus Christi.
6. **John Jeffrey Duty** was born 23 August 1975 in Rockwall, Texas.
6. **Michael Harlan Duty** was born 5 July 1981 in Houston.

Children of Lawrence Leslie Garcia and Linda Jo Casey
6. **William Frederick Garcia** was born 13 May 1973 in San Antonio.
6. **Casey Marie Garcia** was born 17 March 1976 in Houston.

Child of Jefferson Roten Casey and Bettie Ann Massey
6. **Ryan Kendrick Casey** was born 1 April 1984 in Houston.

Children of Billy Gordon Park and Patsy J. Reeves
6. **Laura Sue Park**, born 17 July 1955.
6. **David Gordon Park**, born 10 October 1958.
6. **Sarah Ellen Park**, born 13 April 1962.
6. **Amy Jo Park**, born 20 May 1966.

Children of Lorn John Laney and Kathleen Helen Reed
6. **Sandra Kay Laney** was born 12 November 1952, and married Larry Ray McGraw, born 9 October 1952.
6. **Leesa Lou Laney**, born 25 May 1956.

Children of Luthur Miles Zimmerman and Mary Maxine Reed
6. **Marilyn Gwen Zimmerman** was born 8 April 1952, and married Ronnie Joe Palmer.
6. **Joan Zimmerman** was born in August 1953.

Children of James Edward Reed and Louise Watson
6. **Mary Kathryn Reed** was born 12 October 1952, and married Donald Hice.
6. **Patti Gayle Reed** was born in March 1954, and married Donald Guttierrez.

NINTH GENERATION
Children of Milton Douglas Eckles and Dana Ann Guidry
7. **Troy Eckles**, born 8 August 1971
7. **Julie Eckles**, born 20 June 1975.

Child of Paul Byron Clubb and Ava Danielle Guidry
7. **John Wesley Clubb** was born 14 September 1970 in Beaumont, Texas.

Child of George Zachary Crawford and Karen Leigh Roten
7. **Zachary Robert Crawford** was born 22 February 1989 in Houston.

Children of James Edward Hammelman and Patricia Dianne Roten
7. **Lauren Elizabeth Hammelman** was born 15 September 1986 in Houston.
7. **James Robert Hammelman** was born 23 August 1990 in Houston.

THIRD GENERATION
ISAAC SMITH WHITTEN
1. **Dr. Isaac Smith Whitten**, seventh child of John Whitten and Mary Reagan, was born 23 July 1800 in Greenville District, South Carolina, and married 22 November 1827 in Abbeville, South Carolina, Martha Jackson, born 5

November 1805, there. She died 5 October 1831, and was buried in the Patrick Calhoun family cemetery in Abbeville District. Patrick was a pioneer South Carolinian and father of John C. Calhoun. I have visited this lovely site and cannot help but wonder at her presence among some twenty members of the Calhoun family, its only other occupants. Either she was a Calhoun, or she and/or Dr. Whitten were dear friends of this illustrious family. Isaac Smith later married Martha F. Meriwether, a wealthy widow, born about 1806 in South Carolina. Neither marriage produced children. He died after 1862.

The Whitten home, near Sparta and within two miles of Mt. Zion, Georgia, was called Mound Farm. Located in the Shoulderborne area along Whitten Creek, it was said to be the largest ever built in Hancock County, Georgia, and was beautifully furnished. He had about seventy slaves, forty of whom were field hands, the rest children and house servants. With Martha Merriwether, he owned a plantation in Arkansas. In the Montgomery County, Virginia, Deed Book Q, page 424, is recorded the sale of an interest in the White Sulfur Springs Company to I. S. Whitten of Hancock County, Georgia.

Isaac Smith tried to remain in touch with his brothers and sisters, visiting their homes in South Carolina, and that of brother James in Georgia. He often invited relatives to visit him. Some accepted his invitations; among them was Narcissa Amaryllis Holcombe, daughter of brother Silas Reagan, who wrote several letters while there. Children of his cousin, Alvin Earle Whitten, of Wharton County, Texas, visited him at least once. His sister Mariam seems to have been a favorite. They corresponded regularly over the years. The stepdaughter of Dr. Whitten, who, like her mother, was named Martha Meriwether, kept in touch with the Whittens. She wrote, visited, and is mentioned in a number of family letters.

Dr. Isaac Smith Whitten seemed to disappear after 1862, when he took a mortgage on twenty slaves as security for two promissory notes from a David W. Lewis. His lovely home no longer stands. As Mound Farm was between Atlanta and the sea, it was easy to speculate that it was burned by General Sherman's marauding soldiers and that the Whittens were either killed or had fled. William C. Whitten Jr., coauthor of *Whittens and Allied Families*, has reason to believe the house survived the Union Army. When visiting Sparta, Georgia, in about 1980, he met an elderly man who spoke of remembering the house, which he said burned in 1935. In a letter written by niece Narcissa Amaryllis Holcombe, who was a guest in Dr. Whitten's home in 1851, she tells of his desire to visit Cuba and later to settle on his plantation in Arkansas. Researchers speculated that to avoid Union soldiers bent upon his destruction, he took his family to one of these places, where he died and was buried.

Fortunately, Felice Dissmeyer, descendant of James Whitten and diligent Whitten researcher, rediscovered the good doctor by locating, in the Hancock County courthouse, this information:

Dr. Whitten died on 8 July 1866 in his Hancock County home and was buried there. Later his remains were moved to nearby Eatonton, Georgia. He was among the agrarian reformers who led Hancock County to prosperity. He raised fine livestock and had a racecourse on his property.

Isaac Smith Whitten lived his adult life in a different social stratum from that of his brothers and sisters. He was a wealthy southern plantation owner with all the trappings thereof. That he began to practice medicine in Abbeville, home of so many South Carolina first families, and married two women from among them must have played a strong role in shaping the course of his life.

THIRD GENERATION
MARIAM WHITTEN

1. **Mariam Whitten**, eighth child of John and Mary Reagan Whitten, was born 16 September 1802 in Greenville District, South Carolina, and there married about 1825 David Mc. Davis, who was born 10 April 1800, died 21 February 1862 in Mississippi, and was buried in Zion Presbyterian Cemetery, Pontotoc County. The Davis family's South Carolina home was on land adjoining that of Mariam's father, Silas Reagan Whitten. David and Mariam moved from South Carolina to Mississippi in about 1840 and lived near Palmetto in a section of Pontotoc County that became Lee County. Five years later, her newlywed niece, Harriet Earle Whitten, and husband, Nathan Alexander Lankford, journeyed from Gowensville, South Carolina, to Pontotoc County, and settled nearby. Following David's death in 1862, Mariam moved to Montgomery County, Texas, and lived near her brother Alfred until her death 13 July 1887.

Their eight children were:
Isaac Alvin Davis
James Addison Davis
Nancy Ellen Davis
Mary Elizabeth Davis
Martha Caroline Davis
Harriet Whitten Davis
Joseph Alexander Davis
Josephine Rebecca Davis

FOURTH GENERATION

164

Children of David Mc. Davis and Mariam Whitten

2. **Isaac Alvin Davis** was born 10 February and died 12 August 1826 in Greenville District, South Carolina.

2. **James Addison Davis** was born 25 September 1827 in Greenville District, and married 11 August 1854 in Mississippi, Elizabeth C. Miller, born 6 June 1830 in Alabama. She died 14 April 1867 in Pontotoc County, Mississippi, and was buried in Zion Presbyterian Cemetery. Remaining in Mississippi, James Addison then married Olive, who was born 3 October 1850, and died 23 March 1884 in Palmetto, Lee, Mississippi, where she is buried. He moved to Texas after her death, died 3 August 1897 in Reagor Springs, and was buried in the Boren cemetery there.

The four children of James A. Davis and Elizabeth C. Miller were:

> John Alexander Davis
> Nancy M. Davis
> James Alvin Davis
> Thomas Davis

The child of James A. Davis and Olive was:

> David Oliver Davis

2. **Nancy Ellen Davis** was born 11 December 1829 in Greenville District, South Carolina, and married 18 October 1854 in Mississippi, S. Finis Handley, born in 1828 in Alabama. Nancy Ellen died 18 July 1878 in Lee County, Mississippi, and was buried in Tupelo.

Their child was:

> Robert D. Handley

2. **Mary Elizabeth Davis** was born 8 January 1833 in Greenville District, and married 1 February 1855 in Mississippi, Bunyan B. Barmore.

2. **Martha Caroline Davis** was born about 1835 in Greenville District, and married Hosea H. Porter, born in 1830 in South Carolina. He was a dentist, and died before 1900.

Their two children were:

> Mariam D. Porter
> Laura Porter

2. **Harriet Whitten Davis** was born 18 October 1838 in Greenville District, South Carolina, died 27 October 1866 in Pontotoc County, Mississippi, and was buried in Zion Presbyterian Cemetery.

2. **Joseph Alexander Davis** was born 16 January 1843 in Pontotoc County, died 11 December 1849, there, and was buried in Zion Presbyterian Cemetery. He was the twin of Josephine Rebecca.

2. **Josephine Rebecca Davis** was born 16 January 1843 in Pontotoc, and there on 14 December 1879 married W. M. Cunningham, born 8 July 1827. She died in Brownwood, Brown, Texas; he, before 1900, also in that state.

Their three children were:

> William J. Cunningham
> David E. Cunningham
> George C. Cunningham

FIFTH GENERATION

Children of James Addison Davis and Elizabeth C. Miller

3. **John Alexander Davis** was born about 1855 in Pontotoc, Mississippi, and married Mrs. Pally, a widow with two sons. He later married an Indian woman in Oklahoma, where John Alexander died in 1940.

3. **Nancy M. Davis** was born about 1858 in Pontotoc County, and married Tom Dupree, an engineer on a Mexican railroad. They lived near Laredo, Texas, where Nancy M. died during childbirth.

3. **James Alvin Davis** was born 25 March 1861 in Pontotoc, and married 19 November 1885 in Tupelo, Mississippi, Georgia Earl Helms, born 15 November 1862 in Saltillo, Mississippi. They died in Texas; James Alvin, 25 February 1947 in Waxahachie; Georgia Earl, 3 January 1936 in Reagor Springs. They lie together in Myrtle Cemetery, Ennis, Texas.

Their two children were:

> Addison Dupree Davis
> Jewell Celeste Davis

3. **Thomas Davis** was born about 1864 in Lee County, Mississippi, and married Florence Cunningham. He was buried in Boren Cemetery, Reagor Springs, Texas.

Their three children were:

> Stanley Davis
> Elizabeth Davis

William B. Moore Jr.

Lucille Davis

Child of James Addison Davis and Olive
3. **David Oliver Davis** was born in Mississippi, married Ruth, and died about 1965 in Texas. He married several times.

The three children of David Oliver and Ruth Davis were:
Ava Ruth Davis
Bernice Davis
Olive Davis

Child of S. Finis Handley and Nancy Ellen Davis
3. **Robert D. Handley**, born about 1858 in Cherry Creek, Pontotoc County, Mississippi.

Children of Hosea H. Porter and Martha Caroline Davis
3. **Mariam D. Porter**, born about 1859 in Harrisburg, Lee, Mississippi.
3. **Laura Porter**, born about 1880 in Brownwood, Texas.

Children of W. M. Cunningham and Josephine Rebecca Davis
Born in Mississippi
3. **William J. Cunningham**
3. **David E. Cunningham**
3. **George C. Cunningham**

SIXTH GENERATION
Children of James Alvin Davis and Georgia Earl Helms
4. **Addison Dupree Davis** was born 1 July 1891 in Tupelo, Mississippi, and married 5 September 1922 in Waxahachie, Texas, Mary Ethel Sharp, born 6 February 1897 in Boyce, Texas. He died 13 June 1958 in Waxahachie; she, 16 June 1983 in Beaumont. They are buried in Myrtle Cemetery, Ennis, Texas.

Their three children were:
Mary Jean Davis
Addison Dupree Davis Jr.
Bobby Graham Davis
4. **Jewel Celeste Davis**, born 7 September 1897 in Ellis County, Texas.

Children of Thomas Davis and Florence Cunningham
4. **Stanley Davis**
4. **Elizabeth Davis**
4. **Lucille Davis** was born in 1891, and married Bert Odom. She died in 1981 and was buried in Waxahachie, Texas.

Their three children were:
Geraldine Odom
Glenn Odom
Peggy Odom

Children of David Oliver Davis and Ruth
4. **Ava Ruth Davis**
4. **Bernice Davis**
4. **Olive Davis**, twin of Bernice.

SEVENTH GENERATION
Children of Addison DuPree Davis and Mary Ethel Sharp
Born in Waxahachie, Texas
5. **Mary Jean Davis** was born 23 November 1923. In 1994 she lived in Beaumont, Texas, and supplied much of this Davis family information.
5. **Addison Dupree Davis Jr.** was born 29 August 1926, and married in September 1951, Marianna Johnson, born

19 June 1931 in Iowa.
>Their two children were:
>>Susan Leigh Davis
>>Cathy Davis

5. **Bobbie Graham Davis** was born 8 September 1930, and married 25 January 1955, Joyce Walker.
>Their three children were:
>>Robert Scott Davis
>>Mary Lynne Davis
>>Linda Gail Davis

Children of Bert Odom and Lucille Davis

5. **Geraldine Odom**
5. **Glenn Odom**
5. **Peggy Odom**

EIGHTH GENERATION

Children of Addison DuPree Davis Jr. and Marianna Johnson

6. **Susan Leigh Davis**, born 29 March 1954.
6. **Cathy Davis**, born 7 October 1956.

Children of Bobby Graham Davis and Joyce Walker

6. **Robert Scott Davis**, born 19 April 1957.
6. **Mary Lynne Davis**, born 24 December 1958.
6. **Linda Gail Davis**, born 9 January 1963.

THIRD GENERATION

RANSON WHITTEN

1. **Ranson Whitten**, ninth child of John and Mary Reagan Whitten, was born 1 November 1805 in Greenville, District, South Carolina, and married 27 February 1838 in Hall County, Georgia, Elizabeth Sullivan, born 3 October 1814 in South Carolina. She died 17 August 1857 in Ripley, Tippah, Mississippi, and was buried in Ross Chapel Cemetery in that county. After her death, he married, on 16 December 1862 in Ripley, Susan Elizabeth Morgan, born 2 November 1831 in Tennessee. She died 24 July 1899 at the home of her daughter, Kate Whitten Spencer, in Benton County, Mississippi, where she was buried in Old Antioch Cemetery. Susan Elizabeth had been married to a J. J. Morgan and had a total of seven children, five living at her death. Ranson died after the 1880 census and before 1887, when tax rolls of Tippah County showed his land owned by Elizabeth Whitten. It is probable that he is buried in the Ross Chapel Cemetery with his first wife. The site is almost lost to the forests and is in a poor state of repair, with many broken and unreadable stones.

Ranson moved to Hall County, Georgia, with his parents, before 1830. His first child was born in Cherokee County, Alabama, where his Uncle Charles Whitten Jr. lived. From Cherokee, Ranson moved to Fayette County, Tennessee, where his sister Elizabeth had settled in 1827. They were soon joined by the families of sister Nancy, brother Alfred, and their parents, John and Mary Reagan Whitten. In the summer of 1856, Ranson moved his family to Tippah County, Mississippi, and lived with his brother, Silas Reagan Whitten, until he married a second time. With his new wife he acquired property in the Shady Grove community and made his home in that location.

The seven children of Ranson Whitten and Elizabeth Sullivan were:
>Edwin Whitten
>Harriet M. Whitten
>Lewis Irvine Whitten
>James Lawson Whitten
>M. Fidelia Whitten
>Sarah Elizabeth Whitten
>William R. Whitten

The five children of Ranson Whitten and Susan Elizabeth Morgan were:
>Rev. Henry Lee Whitten
>Sam Whitten
>Kate Whitten
>Laura L. "Tish" Whitten

William B. Moore Jr.

Albert Whitten

FOURTH GENERATION
Children of Ranson Whittten and Elizabeth Sullivan

2. **Edwin Whitten** was born in 1835 in Cherokee County, Alabama.

2. **Harriet M. Whitten** was born in 1838 in Fayette County, Tennessee, and married, in Mississippi, Luther White, born about 1825 in South Carolina. He died 21 January 1867 in Tippah County, and she married, in Tippah, 16 October 1868, Willis John Moran, son of Henry and Sarah Young Moran, who was born during 1806 in Halifax, North Carolina. Willis John died in 1888 in Canaan, Benton, Mississippi, where he was buried in the Moran family Cemetery. Willis John's first wife was Martha Portis. The Moran cemetery, sadly, has been bulldozed and destroyed. Harriet M. died in 1901 in Benton County, and was buried with her second husband.

It is of interest to note that both the children of Harriet and Luther White were listed as living with Harriet's sister, M. Fidelia, in the 1870 Tippah County, census.

The two children of Luther White and Harriet M. Whitten were:
> M. E. White
> William E. White

The three children of Willis John Moran and Harriett M. Whitten were:
> Hatty Moran
> Thomas P. Moran
> Effie Moran

2. **Lewis Irvine Whitten** was born in 1842 in Fayette, County, Tennessee.

2. **James Lawson Whitten** was born about 1846 in Fayette County, and married 26 January 1869 in Tippah, F. Bowdon E., born about 1848 in Mississippi. They both died in an accident in Florida in January 1907 and were buried in Benton County, Mississippi.

Their three children were:
> R. Whitten
> Carry Whitten
> J. J. Whitten

2. **M. Fidelia Whitten** was born in August 1848 in Fayette, Tennessee. She was listed as living with sister Harriet M. White in the 1860 Tippah County census.

2. **Sarah Elizabeth Whitten** was born about 1851 in Fayette, and died after 1860.

2. **William R. Whitten** was born about 1855 in Tippah County, and married Jane Delton 10 December 1881 in Marshall County, Mississippi.

Children of Ranson Whitten and Susan Elizabeth Morgan

2. **Rev. Henry Lee Whitten** was born in October 1863 in Shady Grove, Tippah, Mississippi, and married 17 November 1885, there, Sarah Frances Hobson, born in October 1866. Henry Lee died in 1939; Sarah Frances, in 1949. They are buried in Ashland Cemetery, Benton County, Mississippi.

Henry Lee was a hard-shell Baptist preacher. They lived in Jackson for seventeen years while he served in the Mississippi legislature.

Their eighteen children were:
> Luther M. Whitten
> Ethyl W. Whitten
> Henry E. Whitten
> Willie Frankie Whitten
> Lemuel Lawson Whitten
> Albert Ray Whitten
> Allie P. Whitten
> Arthur Whitten
> Alfred L. Whitten
> Ellis H. Whitten
> Elizabeth Whitten
> Mary H. Whitten
> Howard Lee Whitten
> Carl Grady Whitten

168

Unnamed son Whitten
Rev. Milton Clay Whitten
Henrietta Whitten
Hugh Collins Whitten

2. **Sam Whitten**, born about 1866 in Tippah County, Mississippi.

2. **Kate Whitten** was born about 1868 in Tippah, and there married W. A. C. Spencer on 28 January 1892. They lived in adjacent Benton County.

2. **Laura L. (Tish) Whitten** was born about 1869 in Tippah, County and married 23 December 1884 there, William C. Graves, born in 1862. He died 8 November 1941 in Holly Springs, Mississippi, and was buried in Shady Grove.

2. **Albert Whitten** was born 6 June 1873 in Tippah, and married Ida S. Barber, born 17 November 1870 in Tippah County. She died 14 February 1898 in Tippah, and was buried in Ross Chapel Cemetery. After Ida's death he married Nora Barber, probably Ida's sister. She was born in Mount Pleasant, Mississippi. They died in Memphis: Albert, 19 February 1948; Nora, in 1961. They were buried in Memorial Park.

The two children of Albert Whitten and Ida S. Barber were:
Bama Whitten
Effie Whitten

The five children of Albert Whitten and Nora Barber were:
Elton B. Whitten
Hermie Lee Whitten
Elizabeth Whitten
Albert Whitten Jr.
Henry A. Whitten

FIFTH GENERATION

Children of Luther White and Harriett M. Whitten

3. **M. E. White**, born about 1858 in Tippah County, Mississippi.

3. **William E. White** was born in 1860 in Tippah and died before 1932.

Children of Willis John Moran and Harriet M. Whitten

3. **Hatty Moran** was born about 1869 in Benton County, and married a Mr. Gates. In 1932 she was living with her daughter, Belle, in Bartlett, Tennessee.

Their child was:
Belle Gates

3. **Thomas P. Moran** was born about 1872 in Benton County, Mississippi, and died before 1932.

3. **Effie Moran** was born about 1874 in Benton, and died before 1932.

Children of James Lawson Whitten and F. Bowden E.
Born in Benton County, Mississippi

3. **R. Whitten**, born about 1871.

3. **Carry Whitten**, born about 1874.

3. **J. J. Whitten** was born about 1878, and married 14 January 1904 in Kemper County, Mississippi, Allie White, who was born there. She died 12 December 1906 in Mississippi.

Children of Rev. Henry Lee Whitten and Sarah Frances Hobson

3. **Luther M. Whitten** was born in December 1886 in Tippah County, died 27 April 1974 in Memphis, and was buried in Memorial Park.

3. **Ethyl W. Whitten**, born in February 1888 in Tippah.

3. **Henry E. Whitten** was born in March 1889 in Tippah, and married Ira. He died in March 1909 in Jackson, Mississippi, and was buried in Shady Grove.

3. **Willie Frankie Whitten** was born 13 March 1890 in Tippah, died 7 October 1904, and was buried in Shady Grove Cemetery.

3. **Lemuel Lawson Whitten** was born 2 March 1891 in Tippah, died 17 September the same year, and was buried in Shady Grove.

3. **Albert Ray Whitten** was born 26 April 1892 in Tippah, died 14 September of that year, and was buried in Shady Grove.

3. **Allie P. Whitten** was born in December 1893 in Tippah, and died before 1995 in Benton County. She married W. Simon Childers, who was living in a nursing home in Ashland, Benton, Mississippi, in 1995.

Their four children were:

Simon Earl Childers
James W. Childers
Frank Childers
Margaret Childers

3. **Arthur Whitten**, born in September 1894 in Tippah.

3. **Alfred L. Whitten** was born 26 April 1895 in Tippah, died 9 March 1918, and was buried in Shady Grove. His death was caused by pneumonia contracted in a Louisiana army camp.

3. **Ellis H. Whitten** was born about 1897 in Benton County, and married Nettie Mae Hand. He died before 1967 in Raymond, Hinds, Mississippi. She then married Rev. Milton Clay Whitten, brother of Ellis H.

The child of Ellis H. Whitten and Nettie Mae Hand was:

Wanda Dale Whitten

3. **Elizabeth Whitten** was born in January 1898 in Tippah, and lived in New York City.

3. **Mary H. Whitten** was born in February 1899 in Tippah, died in 1909, and was buried in Shady Grove Cemetery.

3. **Howard Lee Whitten** was born in 1901 in Benton. He lived in Memphis in 1992.

3. **Carl Grady Whitten** was born 19 April 1903 in Tippah, died 17 January 1904 there, and was buried in Shady Grove.

3. **An unnamed son Whitten** was born and died 19 April 1903 in Tippah, and was buried in Shady Grove.

3. **Rev. Milton Clay Whitten** was born in 1905 in Hinds County, Mississippi, and married in 1926 in Ashland, Mallie Viola Bright, born in 1904. She died in 1958 in DeSoto County, Mississippi, and was buried in Hernando. After her death Milton Clay married Nettie Mae Hand, widow of his brother, Reverend Ellis H. Whitten, died in 1967 in Jackson, and was buried with Mallie Viola.

He attended Mississippi College and the Southern Baptist Theological Seminary. His churches included: Elk Creek and Bloomfield, in Kentucky; and Hernando, Eudora, Oak Grove, Senatobia, Looxahoma, Grays Creek, Byhalia, Raymond, and Terry, in Mississippi.

The five children of Rev. Milton Clay Whitten and Mallie Viola Bright were:

Milton Clay Whitten Jr.
Robert Bailey Whitten
Edward Lee Whitten
Shirley Ann Whitten
James Allen Whitten

3. **Henrietta Whitten** was born and died 4 March 1909 in Jackson, and was buried in Shady Grove.

3. **Hugh Collins Whitten** was born 16 February 1910 in Jackson, and married Ruby. He died 3 October 1971 in Jackson, and was buried in Lakewood Memorial Cemetery. They lived on the Gulf Coast of Mississippi.

Children of Albert Whitten and Ida S. Barber

3. **Bama Whitten** was born in December 1892 in Tippah, and married Reuben W. Spencer. They died in Memphis: Reuben, 6 February 1985; Bama, 25 January 1992. They were buried in Memorial Park.

3. **Effie Whitten** was born 4 July 1896 in Tippah, and married 14 July 1921 in Ripley, Vibrait L. Street, born there 30 October 1887. They died in Memphis: Effie, 9 October 1976; Vibrait, 23 March 1966; and are buried together in the Ripley Cemetery.

Their four children were:

John Whitten Street
Vernon Street
Anita Street
Robert Street

Children of Albert Whitten and Nora Barber

3. **Elton B. Whitten** was born in 1907 in Tippah County, Mississippi, and married Ethel Duckworth. He died in 1989 in Winston Salem, North Carolina, and was buried there.

Their child was:

Betty Jo Whitten

3. **Hermie Lee Whitten** was born in 1909 in Tippah, died in 1989 in Memphis, and was buried in Memorial Park.

3. **Elizabeth Whitten**, who was born in 1911 in Tippah, was living in Memphis in January 1992.

3. **Albert Whitten Jr.** was born in 1913 in Tippah, and married Lucille Kane. They were living in Memphis in 1992.

Their two children were:

    William Albert Whitten

    James Thomas Whitten

3. **Henry A. Whitten** was born in Tippah County, Mississippi, and married Betty C. In January of 1992 they were living in Memphis.

Their child was:

    Wanda Whitten

SIXTH GENERATION
Child of Mr. Gates and Hatty Moran

4. **Belle Gates**, who lived in Bartlett, Tennessee.

Children of W. Simon Childers and Allie P. Whitten

4. **Simon Earl Childers**, who died before 1995.

4. **James W. Childers**, who lived in Birmingham in 1995.

4. **Frank Childers**, who lived in Greenville, Mississippi in 1995.

4. **Margaret Childers**, who lived in Texas in 1995.

Child of Ellis H. Whitten and Nettie Mae Hand

4. **Wanda Dale Whitten**

Children of Rev. Milton Clay Whitten and Mallie Viola Bright

4. **Milton Clay Whitten Jr.** was born in 1927 in Clinton, Hinds, Mississippi, and married in 1946 in Hernando, Mississippi, Lucile Overton Lamar who was born, there, in 1928. He supplied information on descendants of Rev. H. L. Whitten. Milton Clay Jr. died in Hernando in 1994, and is buried there.

Their two children, born in Memphis, were:

    Thomas Edward Whitten

    David Milton Whitten

4. **Robert Bailey Whitten** was born in 1928 in Terry, Hinds, Mississippi, and married in 1950 in Eudora, Mississippi, Vera Ann Pounders, who was born in 1930 in Eudora. Robert Bailey was named in honor of Mississippi's Governor Bailey.

Their two children were:

    Robert Bailey Whitten Jr.

    Amy Dale Whitten

4. **Edward Lee Whitten** was born in 1932 in Jackson, and married in 1952 in Hernando, Frances Ann Yates, born there in 1934.

Their child was:

    Edward Lee Whitten Jr.

4. **Shirley Ann Whitten** was born in 1934 in Louisville, Kentucky, and married in 1952 in Hernando, Edward Taylor Wilkinson, born in 1932 in Hughes, Arkansas. He died in 1989 in Memphis, and was buried in Hernando. She and her brother Milton Clay Whitten Jr. supplied much of this information on the family of Rev. Henry Lee Whitten.

Their five children were:

    Patricia Ann Wilkinson

    Edward Taylor Wilkinson Jr.

    Sherlene Wilkinson

    Charles Clay Wilkinson

    Mark Russell Wilkinson

4. **James Allen Whitten** was born in 1935 in Memphis, and married in 1955 in Marks, Mississippi, Jeanette Bryant, born in 1936 in Hernando.

Their two children were:

    James Allen Whitten Jr.

Kenneth Bright Whitten

Children of Vibrait L. Street and Effie Whitten

4. **John Whitten Street** was born 15 April 1925 in Ripley, and married 16 September 1953 in Tupelo, Lee, Mississippi, Hazel Franklin. In 1992 he supplied, from his home in Tupelo, information on the descendants of Effie Whitten.

Their two children were:
> John Franklin Street
> Sarah Elizabeth Street

4. **Vernon Street** was born 28 July 1928 in Ripley, and married 22 October in Baldwyn, Mississippi, Mavis Miller. They lived in Corinth, Mississippi, in 1992.

Their two children were:
> Ronnie Street
> Russell Street

4. **Anita Street** was born 15 April 1932 in Ripley, and married in Houston, Texas, James G. Horton. In 1992 they lived in Glen Ellyn, Illinois.

Their three children were:
> David Horton
> Joe Horton
> James Horton

4. **Robert Street** was born 25 April 1939 and married Mary Rogers. In 1992 they lived in Arlington, Tennessee.

Their three children were:
> Vick Street
> Robin Street
> Shannon Street

Child of Elton B. Whitten and Ethel Duckworth

4. **Betty Jo Whitten**, who married a Mr. May.

Their two children were:
> Michael Richard May
> Gordon May

Children of Albert Whitten Jr. and Lucille Kane

4. **William Albert Whitten**

His two children were:
> Andrew Whitten
> Daniel Whitten

4. **James Thomas Whitten**, who died in 1990.

Child of Henry A. Whitten and Betty C.

4. **Wanda Whitten**

SEVENTH GENERATION

Children of Milton Clay Whitten Jr. and Lucile Overton

5. **Thomas Edward Whitten** was born in 1948, and married in 1972 in Stratford, Connecticut, Pamela Ann Refkofsky.

Their two children were:
> Thomas Edward Whitten II
> Alexandra Marie Whitten

5. **David Milton Whitten** was born in 1951, and married in 1977 in Hernando, Christy McElroy, who was born there. In 1991 he married, in Hernando, Patricia Smith, who was born in 1949 in Memphis.

The child of David Milton Whitten and Christy McElroy was:
> Anna Elizabeth Whitten

Children of Robert Bailey Whitten and Vera Ann Pounders

5. **Robert Bailey Whitten Jr.** was born in 1960 in Memphis, and married in 1989 in Dallas, Julie Mims, born in 1964 in Longview, Texas.

5. **Amy Dale Whitten** was born in 1953 in Memphis. In 1992 she was counsel to the Mississippi Supreme Court.

Child of Edward Lee Whitten and Frances Ann Yates

5. **Edward Lee Whitten Jr.** was born in 1953 in Jackson, and married in 1986 in Hawaii, Elizabeth Bailey, born in 1961 in Desoto County, Mississippi.

Their two children were:

Edward Lee Whitten III

Nicholas Boone Whitten

Children of Edward Taylor Wilkinson and Shirley Ann Whitten

5. **Patricia Ann Wilkinson** was born in 1953 in Fairbanks, Alaska, and married in 1975 in Memphis, Robert D. Holdford, who was born in 1952, there. In 1981, also in Memphis, she married Daniel Eugene Autry, born, there, in 1953.

The child of Robert D. Holdford and Patricia Ann Whitten was:

David Jarrod Holdford

The child of Daniel Eugene Autry and Patricia Ann Wilkinson was:

Dustin Eugene Autry

5. **Edward Taylor Wilkinson Jr.** was born in 1955 in Memphis, and married in 1982 there, Donna Jean Mullish, born in 1959 in Lake Charles, Louisiana.

Their two children were:

Allison Marie Wilkinson

Alysia Jenet Wilkinson

5. **Sherlene Wilkinson** was born in 1956 in Memphis, and married in 1977, there, Leslie Allen Grant, born in 1956 in Hernando. In 1981 in Memphis, she married Mark Anderson Printup, born in 1956, there.

The child of Leslie Allen Grant and Sherlene Wilkinson was:

Leslie Allen Grant II

The two children of Mark Printup and Sherlene Wilkinson were:

Mario Anderson Printup

Vince Ray Printup

5. **Charles Clay Wilkinson** was born in 1959 in Memphis, and married in 1984 in Jackson, Tennessee, Elizabeth Ann Seaman, born in 1953 there.

5. **Mark Russell Wilkinson**, born in 1961 in Memphis.

Children of James Allen Whitten and Jeanette Bryant

5. **James Allen Whitten Jr.** was born in 1956 in Memphis, and married Peggy Stovall.

Their child was:

Jimmy Bryan Whitten

5. **Kenneth Bright Whitten** was born in 1965 in Memphis, died in 1968 there, and was buried in Hernando, Mississippi.

Children of John Whitten Street and Hazel Franklin

5. **John Franklin Street**, who died in 1981.

5. **Sarah Elizabeth Street**, who lived in Oxford, Mississippi, in 1992.

Children of Vernon Street and Mavis Miller

5. **Ronnie Street**, who lived in Corinth, Mississippi, in 1992.

5. **Russell Street**, who lived in Birmingham, Alabama, in 1992.

Children of James G. Horton and Anita Street

5. **David Horton**

5. **Joe Horton**

5. **James Horton**

Children of Robert Street and Mary Rogers

5. **Vick Street**, who lived in Memphis, in 1992.
5. **Robin Street**
5. **Shannon Street**

Children of Mr. May and Betty Jo Whitten

5. **Michael Richard May**
5. **Gordon May**

Children of William Albert Whitten

5. **Andrew Whitten**
5. **Daniel Whitten**

EIGHTH GENERATION
Children of Thomas Edward Whitten and Pamela Refkofsky
Born in Jackson, Mississippi
6. **Thomas Edward Whitten II**, born in 1986.
6. **Alexandra Marie Whitten**, born in 1988.

Child of David Milton Whitten and Christi McElroy
6. **Anna Elizabeth Whitten**, born in 1977 in Paducah, Kentucky.

Children of Edward Lee Whitten Jr. and Elizabeth Bailey
6. **Edward Lee Whitten III**, born in 1987 in Memphis.
6. **Nicholas Boone Whitten**, born in 1991 in Southaven, Mississippi.

Child of Robert D. Holdford and Patricia Ann Wilkinson
6. **David Jarrod Holdford**, born in 1978 in Memphis.

Child of Daniel Eugene Autry and Patricia Ann Wilkinson
6. **Dustin Eugene Autry**, born in 1982 in Memphis.

Children of Edward Taylor Wilkinson Jr. and Donna Mullish
Born in Memphis, Tennessee
6. **Allison Marie Wilkinson**, born in 1982.
6. **Alysia Jenet Wilkinson**, born in 1985.

Child of Leslie Allen Grant and Sherlene Wilkinson
6. **Leslie Allen Grant II**, who was born in 1979 in Memphis, was later adopted by Sherline's second husband and his name changed to Printup.

Children of Mark Printup and Sherlene Wilkinson
6. **Mario Anderson Printup**, born in 1982 in Memphis.
6. **Vince Ray Printup**, born in 1987 in Memphis.

Child of James Allen Whitten Jr. and Peggy Stovall
6. **Jimmy Bryan Whitten**, born in 1979 in Memphis.

Book III
DESCENDANTS OF CHARLES WHITTEN JR.

In 1984, when Virginia Wood Alexander and William C. Whitten Jr. published the second edition of the book *Whittens and Allied Families*, very little was known about Charles Whitten Jr. and his family. Researchers knew him as the youngest son of Charles Whitten and Nancy Smith, who had married Millicent Reagan, sister of Mary, the wife of his brother John. That he followed his parents from Virginia to upper South Carolina, had a fairly large family, and lived in Greenville and Pendleton Districts of South Carolina, settling finally in Cherokee County, Alabama, had been documented. Few of his children were known, and nothing of his third generations had come to light.

Today information of genealogical and historical value concerning this family abounds. Much of it is contained in letters: some saved by his great-niece Rebecca Berry Whitten and published in *Letters to Rebecca*; some written and collected by John E. Holt; and others written by Penny Holsomback McNair. Help has come from numerous descendants of Charles Jr. and Millicent, including the outstanding research of Laura Barnwell of Marietta, Georgia.

This is what we know today: Born 18 January 1769 in Virginia, Charles Whitten Jr. settled first in Greenville District, South Carolina, buying land near his father on Beaverdam Creek, which flows into the Tiger (*current spelling*) River. Both he and Millicent Reagan, his first wife, who was born about 1769 in Stafford County, Virginia, and whom he married about 1788 at her home in Rockingham County, North Carolina, joined the Tygar (*old spelling*) River Baptist Church in 1803. In 1807, they requested letters of transfer, and the following year sold their Greenville District land.

The North Carolina Genealogical Society Journal for November 1978, page 261, shows them living in Buncombe County, North Carolina, in 1807. It is probable that they moved from Greenville District to that place with cousins Eliakim and Anna Reagan Hamlin, who were known to have made a similar move in 1805. Before 1810, they transferred to Pendleton District, South Carolina, buying land across the river from present-day Clemson in 1812. Charles Jr. appears, with a growing family, in Pendleton in censuses of 1810 and 1820, and in 1830 in Pickens District, which was carved out of Pendleton in 1826. The family was recorded in Cherokee County, Alabama, in both 1840 and 1850.

Census records, an obituary printed by the *Pendleton Messenger* in 1827 stating that Mrs. Charles Whitten died on October 27 of that year, and the omission of Millicent's name from her father's 1821 will combine to confuse researchers attempting to establish the date of Millicent's death and the subsequent marital status of Charles Jr.

The oldest female listed in the 1820 census was younger than forty-five; Millicent was fifty-one. In 1830 the oldest female was under thirty. Millicent either died before 1820 or was sensitive about her age. The will leads one to believe she died before 1820. Charles Jr. may have taken a second wife before 1820, she died in 1827, and the *Messenger* printed the news. The Pickens District census of 1830 shows the family with a male and female born after 1820 and other females, ages ten to fifteen and twenty to thirty in the household. The younger children could be those of a second wife, and she the older female. That assumption ignores the 1827 obituary. In 1825 Albert, the firstborn of Charles Jr. and Millicent, was killed, leaving a young wife and daughter, Mary Ann Whitten, who was a minor in 1825. They may well have been the ten to fifteen and twenty to thirty females in 1830. The young male and female also could have been grandchildren. Charles and Millicent had several by 1830. Later enumerations in Cherokee County, Alabama, shed no light on this mystery. No trace of any children of a second marriage has been found in South Carolina or Alabama. Several grandchildren are known to mesh with the 1830 census claims. It is possible that the *Pendleton Messenger* obituary recorded the death of the mother of Charles Jr., who was known to be living with him in his Greenville District home. Because Mrs. Charles Whitten Sr. is not to be found in the two prior censuses, this seems unlikely.

In 1840 and 1850 Charles Jr. was in Cherokee County, Alabama, near Leesburg. Both he and daughter Mariah S. were granted land in Section 3 of Township 10, Range 8, East. Charles Jr. received the SE1/4 of NE1/4 1 October 1844, the NE1/4 of SW1/4 13 October 1845, and the SW1/4 of NE1/4 11 August 1848, a total of 120 acres. Mariah S. obtained the NW1/4 of SE1/4 13 October 1845, 40 acres. Her letter appearing in *Letters to Rebecca* tells that Charles Jr. was eighty-one years of age in 1850. As he did not appear in the next census, we can assume he died prior to 1860.

That Dudley J. Whitten died in New Orleans in 1859 from yellow fever while on a trip to Alabama to settle his father's estate further supports this theory. Dudley's father, Alvin Earle Whitten, lived in South Carolina, Georgia, Mississippi, and Texas, never in Alabama. The most obvious source of assets in that state would have been a legacy from his father.

The destruction by fire of the Cherokee County Courthouse in May 1882 makes a full accounting of the Charles

Whitten Jr. family difficult.

Alexander and Whitten in *Whittens and Allied Families*, 2nd ed., speculate that Zachariah, William, and Albert may have been among the children of Charles Jr.; Zachariah due to the close proximity of the Charles Whitten home in Pickens District to that of Zachariah's wife, Margaret Whitten; Albert, who was thrown from a horse and killed in Pendleton, and whose executor was Charles Jr. and William S. Whitten, who bought land in Pendleton in 1830 and was listed in 1850 and later censuses, close to Charles Jr., in Cherokee County, Alabama.

But old letters identify four children with certainty. On 5 October 1849 daughter Mariah S. wrote to cousin Silas Reagan and gave the birth date of her father, Charles Whitten Jr. Eliza Whitten, daughter of Rev. James Whitten, wrote on 12 October 1851 to Ranson E. Whitten, and mentioned cousin Alvin Earle in Texas. He can be connected to Charles Jr. by elimination. These letters are contained in *Letters to Rebecca*. Another letter written in the early 1900s from Cameron, Texas, probably by Talitha Emily Bell, daughter of Rev. Arphax Whitten, son of Rev. James, to a relative, possibly Anne Ard in Stewart County, Georgia, mentions, as relatives, two descendants of Alvin Earle: Mrs. Lee Blanchard and Julia Foster. Her letter opines that the Whittens from Mississippi and Texas were "very proud and aristocratic." This letter appears in the chapter on Whittens in Texas. Writing, in 1863, from camp near Chattanooga, Ranson E. tells his father of meeting, in Marietta, Georgia, Nancy Thomason, Charles Jr.'s daughter, and learning of her brothers: John, somewhere in Mississippi; and Silas Reagan (b. 1815).

Later research produced proof that William S. was a son of Charles Jr., and that the John of Ranson E. Whitten's letter was John R. Alvin Earle, known to be a son; William S. and John R. paid taxes for each other for several years in Carnesville, Franklin, Georgia, where Alvin Earle lived at the time and is quite close to the South Carolina home of their father. That the children of William S., after his death, sold the Cherokee, Alabama, land originally granted to Charles Jr. and his daughter Mariah S. adds weight to the conclusion that William S. was Charles Jr's. son, who passed along land inherited from his fathers and sister to his children.

The following are excerpts from letters written during 1991 and 1992 by a Charles Jr. descendant, Penny Holsomback McNair of Meridian, Mississippi, to Arthur Reagan, William C. Whitten Jr., and me. In them she told what she knew of the life of her great-grandfather, Silas Reagan Whitten (b. 1815), and his family:

I am delighted to find someone with knowledge of my Whittens. I never heard my father mention him (*Silas Reagan Whitten, b. 1815*), as he died soon after they went to Texas. Of course Papa (*George Everett Holsomback*) was a grandson and Silas and Martha had teenagers. I am sending you our family information.

In 1873 the Whittens and their daughter Mary Amelia and her two small children, one being my father, left Louisville, Winston, Mississippi, and went to Texas where Silas died. They were accompanied by lots of cousins, uncles, and aunts.

What they did not know was that Silas and Martha's son Charles Everett Whitten was alive and well. He had left Mississippi when he was 17 years old and lived to be 95 or 96 and died in Houston, Texas after he had again met with my father in the 1940s. Charles had led quite a life as a prospector for gold in Mexico, a Texas Ranger, and many other things. He was bright, remarkably intelligent, with a startling memory. Charles Everett called my brother in Houston and asked to speak to George Holsomback. My brother said it was he. Uncle Charlie asked how old he was and George said 35. Uncle Charlie said "No, the boy I'm looking for would be about 75." That was my father. Papa met him and still was not sure this was Mother's twin brother. He coyly asked if Uncle Charlie remembered the old dog they had in Mississippi 70 years before. Uncle Charlie said, "You mean old dog Blue? Fine dog."

Silas had lost a leg, I'm told. My oldest sister said he lost a leg in the War between the States. I don't believe this as he would have been near 50. (*Silas did not serve in the CSA.*) I was in Crippled Children's Hospital in Memphis in 1932 or 1933 and met a child there named Pearl Whitten from Clarksdale, Mississippi. She had one leg that had never grown, a baby's leg really, and her middle finger was missing. They removed the leg and sewed the hand down to meet the other fingers. When I told my father about her, he said, "She is kin to you." Whether he recognized the name, or a genetic fault I don't know.

If you want my sisters and brothers and their children let me know. I am the youngest and last. I am a generation nearer my Silas (*b. 1815*) than Mr. Moore is to his. My father was 53 when I was born and my mother 42. They wanted a puppy. I was the 10th also.

Penny

Many descendants of Charles Jr. and Millicent—Nancy H., Silas Reagan, William S., and Alvin Earle—are known, some still living. None from a possible second marriage have, as yet, been identified.

Six proved and two possible children of Charles Whitten Jr. and Millicent Reagan were:

Albert Whitten (possible)
Nancy Hollan Whitten
Alvin Earle Whitten
John R. Whitten
Mariah S. Whitten
Zachariah Whitten (possible)
William S. Whitten
Silas Reagan Whitten

What is known about these makes up the following pages.

THIRD GENERATION
ALBERT WHITTEN

1. **Albert Whitten**, possibly the first child of Charles Whitten Jr., was born about 1795 in Greenville District, South Carolina, and married Margaret. He was killed when thrown from a horse in 1825 in Anderson, South Carolina. Charles Whitten Jr. was the executor of his will, and Margaret a buyer at his estate sale.

Their child was:
Martha Ann Whitten

FOURTH GENERATION
Child of Albert Whitten and Margaret

2. **Martha Ann Whitten** was born in South Carolina after 1807. She was a minor in 1825.

THIRD GENERATION
NANCY HOLLAN WHITTEN

1. **Nancy Hollan Whitten**, second child of Charles Whitten Jr., was born 7 May 1799 in Greenville District, South Carolina, and married James Thomason there on 29 September 1817. They lived in Anderson District, South Carolina, first in Honea Path and later in the county seat. Family tradition holds that Thomason was born in England 6 June 1796, came to the United States as a small boy, and was raised in Spartanburg, South Carolina. His parents died aboard ship during the crossing, and he was bound out. Mistreated, he ran away. At sixteen years of age he volunteered and served as a private under Colonel Brannon during the War of 1812, being stationed at Charleston, South Carolina. Their daughter, Sarah M. Neese, in the 1890 Cobb County, Georgia, census, confirms her father's English birth. The family moved to Marietta in 1855, where James died 10 January 1863. Nancy died 22 May 1878 in Floyd County, Georgia, at the home of their son. In September 1863, according to a letter written by her cousin Ranson Edwin Whitten after passing through Marietta on his way to the battle of Chicamauga, she was living there with daughter, Sarah M. Neese, and teenage son. Nancy and James are buried in Citizens Cemetery, Marietta.

Their four children were:
Harriet Permelia Thomason
Sarah M. Thomason
Mary Ann Thomason
James Judson Jepthia? Thomason

Several Cobb County censuses report that Nancy could neither read nor write. All her known brothers could. So could her sister Mariah H., whose well-written letter is contained in *Letters to Rebecca*. I have wondered how this could be. The following letter, generously shared with me by John E. Holt, her descendant, casts doubt on the enumerators' claim that she was illiterate, although it does not provide positive proof to the contrary. It was addressed to their daughter's husband and signed "Nancy and James Thomason."

James and Nancy Thomason to Alfred and Sarah M. Neese—Anderson Court House, South Carolina, to Lebanon, Cobb, Georgia, 3 July 1854

Dear Children,
I sit down to drop you a few lines for the purpose of scolding a little that I have had no account from you since I sent your box and no note whether you ever received it or not. I took it to Elberton, Georgia (*Elbert County*) on the 23rd of May and Griffin took it to Lexington (*near Athens in Oglethorpe County, Georgia*) the 24th, and he says he put it on the cars on the 25th. Have never heard if it came safe to hand or not, or whether you wanted any

more sent the same way. We have been looking for a letter every mail but in vain. I have concluded you will be here soon as crops will soon be laid by and you don't write. I have thought perhaps you would meet me at Elberton for every trip for some time but don't see you.

We have some sickness here, diarie (diarrhea). Mary (*daughter, Mary Ann*) has been very sick but is better. Mr. J. R. Smith's wife is dead and old Parson Fant is to be buried this evening at four. Old Mrs. Reed is very low and Eliza Rice's wife is no hopes for her living. She is given up by her friends. She has the consumption. We were at Honea Path this morning a week passed. Holt's family (*of daughter, Harriet P.*) were well as common. We have had as hot weather as is common and dry for some two weeks past till last Saturday. We had a heavy rain and wind and perhaps as hard thunder as has ever been in one storm. Mcully had a Negro boy coming from mill and a tree fell on his mule and wagon killing the mule and breaking the wagon to pieces and never hurt the boy.

I must conclude for my time is short and my hand cramps so bad I can't write. Write as soon as you get this whether you are coming soon or not so we may hear from you. Always looking at every line you get as the last as death is certain and life very uncertain so farewell till we meet again either personal or by letter in time or eternity.

James and Nancy Thomason

This letter sounds so much like the several hundred written by various Whittens and included in *Letters to Rebecca* that I am inclined to believe Nancy wrote it.

Children of James Thomason and Nancy Whitten

2. **Harriett Permelia Thomason** was born in Anderson District, South Carolina, on 3 August 1824, where she married Alfred Holt 21 March 1844. He was born 7 June 1814 near Greenville, Green, Tennessee. They lived in Honea Path, Anderson, South Carolina, until about 1864, when, trying to escape Sherman's Army marching north from Savannah, they moved to Lexington, Oglethorpe, Georgia, and, in August 1866, reached Lane County, Oregon, where they lived with Holt's brothers Jimmie and Sammie until their home in nearby Harrisburg was ready for them. They settled finally in Rebel Flat, near Colfax, Washington, where both died and are buried: he, 29 August 1875; she, 4 April 1878.

Their nine children were:

> Julia Ann Holt.
> Frances Adella Holt
> William Whitten Holt
> James Barrett Holt
> Dyonisius Melville Holt
> Tallulah Tecoa Holt
> Sarah Eugenia Holt
> Minnie Lee Holt
> Walter Alfred Holt

The following, written by Harriet Permelia to sister Sarah M. Neese, describe her trip to Oregon and early impressions of life in its Willamette Valley, western terminus of the famous Oregon trail. The family sailed from Savannah, Georgia, to New York City; boarded a second steamer bound for Aspinwall in the part of Colombia that is now Panama; there they debarked and crossed the isthmus by rail. Having reached the Pacific they boarded a third ship and sailed to San Francisco, where a fourth vessel waited to take them to Portland, Oregon, near the mouth of the Columbia River, and yet another carried them to Salem on the Willamette River. The final leg of the journey to Linn County was by wagon. The entire trip consumed about forty days. By 1865 this route had become that of choice for those hardy souls migrating from America's East to its West Coast. It became obsolete when transcontinental rail service was opened a few years later. The letters that follow are contained in the files of John E. Holt of Gresham, Oregon. They shed light on life in Georgia immediately after the Civil War, the journey to Oregon, and life in the Willamette Valley during their first few years of residence.

Harriett Permelia Thomason Holt to Sarah M. Thomason Neese—Lane County, Oregon, to Marietta, Georgia, 22 November 1866

My dear sister,

You will be surprised to hear from me as it has been some time since I wrote to you and I fear that my letter will prove very uninteresting to you as my stock of news at this time is very limited but I suppose that you are like I am, glad to hear anything from you. All of the family are well with the exception of Jane (*sister-in-law*).

She has been down some two months. It is an attack of the Dyspepsia.

So far we are all pleased with Oregon. It is now the 22nd day of November and not one day of cold weather, not one bit of ice. The climate is much colder there than here. There is considerable rain here during the winter months but the summer is so very pleasant, no rain at all. The grasses on the prairie are as green here now as it is ever in May so you may judge for yourself that we have warm winters. The farmers never feed their cattle unless a snow falls and covers up the grass so long that the cattle get on starvation and it looks like stock ought to be fed. There is so much here to feed stock on you have no idea how much hay, oats, and the like that Jimmie and Sammie (*brothers-in-law*) have that they made this season. They make more on their cattle than they do at farming but they are going to farming more now. They have bought a large farm since we came. They paid three thousand dollars for it. It is splendid farming land. It joins this body of land which is quite extensive.

You wished to know what Mr. Neese could do here. Well, Sallie, I would not be the means of you coming here for nothing in the world for fear you would not like the country as some do that have come here but you know that nothing would please me so well as to meet you on the shores of Oregon.

I am well satisfied that Mr. Neese could do well here at anything that he might wish to follow. As to farming it is very profitable. The best of land can be bought for ten dollars and from thirty to forty bushels of wheat and oats made on it and everything else in proportion except corn. There is none made here. That will suit you as well as it does my family and as to stock raising, this is very profitable. Those that stock raise for a living live up in the hills and mountains so the cattle can graze on the hill grass. Sheep is very profitable stock as they increase so fast. But if you wish to live in a town you can do so and make a good living too. All of the merchants soon get rich here. If you was a carpenter you could fare well or a brick mason. There is a man here that offers a ranch part bottom part hill lands for sale. He has been stock raising. It is some two miles from here. There is no danger but that you could do well here and get a home as soon as you get here.

You will have to go through many hard places before you get here but you will not have so many children as I did to bring through but I will assure you that a sea voyage is not pleasant but it would do well enough if you was not frightened to death all the time for fear of a storm at sea which must be awful. You must start with a brave heart like I did. You know I am quite brave. Do not be afraid of a little freight and leave all your things behind like I did. Be sure and bring all the bedding that you will ever want as there is no feathers here for less that one dollar a pound and no cotton pad quilts. All dry goods are very high here.

The beauty of the country is the money being gold and no thieving Negroes round you. You would be surprised to think that soon you would get accustomed to doing without Negroes. It is all right with us now. The good of it is that all have to do their own work. There is no one smuffing at you here because you are doing your own washing and other work.

The people of Oregon are very easy to get acquainted with. All seem very sociable and a great deal better enlightened than you think for the country is filled up with emigrants from the western states. I suppose that you think as I did that Indians as thick here as the Negroes there but you are quite out of it for there is none here. They are all east of the Cascade range. All of the principle towns are on the Willamette River. Boats run up it as far as Eugene City in the winter. That is twelve miles above us. We are still living with Jimmie and Sammie but expect to move to ourselves this winter. Jimmie has a carpenter working and refitting up the house now. It is about a mile and a half from here. It is a good house when done. You ought to see Jim (*son*) and Mr. Holt (*husband*) plowing. You would not know Jim if you was to see him. He has growed. Jimmie and Sammie has given the boys as fine a pair of matched horses as you ever saw. You have no idea how much they do for us. All the children growing fast except Nishy (*son, Dyonisius*). He is runty yet. Write often and tell everything you know.

Yours, H. P. Holt

P.S. Tell us about the Crawford Keys affair as we are very anxious to hear all about it and all other news that you can think of.

(*What follows is in different handwriting, probably that of one of the children.*) Aunt Sallie, bring plants and flowers and all kinds of trees. I think they will live across. Bring all kinds of garden and flower seed. When you send, pepper seeds in every letter that you send.

Anna Myrtle Grimes Calef (*daughter of Frances Adella Holt*) to Nancy Harriet Holt (*daughter of Walter Alfred Holt*), written in about 1939.

Dear Harriett and all,
Was so glad to receive your good letter. Those letters meant so much to me that I took a chance on having them copied hoping someone else would care too. I have been much pleased with the response they have called out. I

certainly have no objections to your using them as you will. They are about your family and so are yours to honor in any way you can. I am sending a few pages I have written for you if they help any. Aunt Gena (*Sarah Eugenia Holt*) says she could talk some of these things but can't write them. Yes, Mahlon (*her husband*) did get the letters from your father (*Walter Alfred Holt*); thanks.

Incidents Mama (*Frances Adella Holt*) has told us:

A letter from Aunt Gena says that it was at Honea Path that Grandfather (*Alfred Holt*) sold out and took all the money in Confederate money in spite of all of Grandmother's (*Harriet Parmelia Thomason*) pleas that he take at least part of it in U. S. coin. I think the letter he wrote to his niece makes his faith in the South very clear. It was in Lexington, Georgia in the first old mansion of the first Governor, Oglethorpe, that the incident occurred of their having to feed the northern soldiers, returning home. When the large company of soldiers arrived and demanded food for them and their horses, Grandfather protested as they had so little themselves. The Captain said his men were yet obeying his commands though they had been discharged and they needn't. He hoped he could keep them orderly and so he must obtain food for them. Grandfather gave the Masonic distress sign and the Captain happened to be a Mason. He at once announced that he would station a guard around the house and around the kitchen which, as the custom, was away from the house. There the Negro mammies had fled in terror. They were at last quieted and cooked the food. It was after these men had left next morning that my mother helped to pick up and shell the few grains of corn from the ears that the horses had fed on. It was this old colonial home that Uncle Jim Holt remembered and wrote of once and had his life printed in a Colfax (*Washington*) paper.

I think you know that 3 days before Sherman marched into and took Atlanta, the Holt family with three other families had hastily put as many belongings as possible into a freight car and they and their possessions were taken to Lexington, Georgia. So many refugees had come into Lexington that they couldn't get a house in town so went 3 miles out in the country and rented the Oglethorpe home. The slaves were rented with it.

It was here they removed the boards from the ceiling of the porch and hid what valuables as they had. Here also Grandfather locked Aunt Julia in an upstairs bedroom; she, in her hotheaded way, might insult the Yankees and bring more trouble to them. Her letters constantly showed her open rebellion against the North, and who knows if she had not been a second Scarlet of *Gone with the Wind* if she hadn't had a wise father and mother to hold her in check.

The following letters were written by Julia Ann and Frances Adella Holt, daughters of Harriet Parmelia Thomason and Alfred Holt, to their Aunt Sallie (*Sarah M. Thomason*) and her husband, Alfred Neese, who lived near Marietta, Georgia.

Lexington, Georgia, 29 October 1865
Dear Uncle and Aunt,

I will now try and answer your letter of recent date. This leaves us all very well with the exception of Ma. Her arm is some better but she has very little use of it. Has something like neuralgia. Minnie (*sister, Minnie Lee*) has been sick with dysentery but is better now. I have so much news to write that I do not know where to commence. One thing is Berna Boggs and Sergeant McDaniel, one of the Yanks, were married on the 17th and on the 20th he took her to the depot and told her to go to Augusta. The whole command went off that day and we heard nothing more from her until this morning and that was that when McDaniel arrived in Augusta at six in the evening he could not find Berna until twelve that night and then he found her in a saloon. So much for marrying a strange Yankee. Her folks were bitterly opposed to it but who can pity her. We have a new set of Yanks. They behave well considering they are Yanks. While I am on the Yankee subject I will tell you about my letter a few nights ago. Pa says, Julia, here is a letter for you and when I broke it open it claimed to be from a Yankee raking me for treating the Yanks so contemptible. He said that he guessed that would be the means of making me take the oath (of loyalty to the United States) but I am happy to tell you I have not taken the oath yet and I do not know how Pa got the letter without me taking the oath. But one thing I do know and that is that I have not taken it and as they are all so bad off about it I don't intend to take it until compelled to. I am sorry to hear that the girls and widows are keeping company with the hateful Yanks.

Well, Aunt Sally, I have woven 25 yards of cloth and that's something. Let me tell you that Adella and I have bought us a caliker dress, Adella a new hoop. We gave 25 cents a yard for our dresses and $2.00 for Adella's hoops. Adella says that it cannot be described. Adella says if you had seen her going to church today with her new hoop and dress on you would have thought that she was a balloon.

I heard from Honea Path. My old sweetheart married, James A. Wright and Miss Pawl Robinson. Three cheers for them. I will close. Write soon and give all the news. All join in love to you both.

Julia Holt

During and immediately thereafter the Civil War, Southerners were required to pledge loyalty to the Union in order to receive mail through the U.S. Postal Service; thus her quandary concerning the letter and her need to restate her loyalty to the Confederacy.

Lexington, Georgia, 7 December 1865
Dear Uncle and Aunt,
    Your communication of recent date has been duly received and the contents thereof carefully perused but I fear that I shall fail to interest you in answer as I am perfectly without news of any description but you know what kind of a stupor Lexington can get in so you could not get a thimble full of news if you was to scrape the town over.
    Today is quite a public day in Lexington. It is sale day and then the freedmen by some means got it circulated that there was going to be speaking here today to tell them what they must do next year and I think there is about 2000 in town. The Militia organizes here today. I wish that they would turn loose on the freedmen and make them skeedadle home. Tis said that Mr. Liddle overheard some Negroes say that they were going to rise last Friday night and kill all the whites. You may imagine what an excitement it caused among our most quiet and sensible citizens.
    Mr. Boggs has received a letter from Burna. She writes very flattering letters, says she is dreadfully well pleased. I am very sorry to hear of the girls and widows doing so up there but they can do as they please but I have my first Yank to speak to yet.
    You wish to know when I was coming to Marietta. That will be impossible for me to tell you as I do not know myself. I would like very much to spend Christmas there but it will be impossible for me to do it. I think that you might visit us Christmas and tell us all the news. I forgot to tell you that all was well.
                              Write soon and often,
                              Julia

Dear Uncle and Aunt,
    I will now attempt to answer your epistle of recent date although my moments are very important as we are very much hurried at work for we are at the very important point of quilt peasing and you know that my time is very precious.
    Aunt Sally if I was with you this evening I doubt not but what I can tell you is a great deal of news but as it is I fear that it will be but a small stock that I will communicate. Well, one thing I believe that we have not told is that old Mrs. Gilmer has broken up housekeeping and gone to Virginia. She sold everything she had.
    There was a great deal of excitement in Lexington yesterday. The freedmen from the surrounding country came in to hear some speaking. They came with their expectations very high but I think they had them lowered for Col. Mathew and Col. Hardeman spoke to them and they were not very well pleased as they both told them to go home and to go to work.
    Aunt Sally, you spoke of a great deal of robbery going on up there. We had some of that here the other night. Some person broke into Mr. Young's shop and stole a great deal of jewelry, mostly watches.
    Aunt Sally, if you have any winter up there I will try to come up to see some for we have none here. There is but few days that we need fire but I think that it is a great blessing especially of Sundays for people have so many new dresses to wear that it makes a great many sick if they have to wear a cloak to hide them. I never saw people so crazy for finery in my life. Write soon and tell us all the news.
Goodbye,
Adella

Lexington, Georgia, 6 January 1866
Dear Uncle and Aunt,
    I have concluded this beautiful evening to answer your letter of recent date which was gladly received for it had been so long since I had heard from you that I had concluded that you had the smallpox or something else worse.
    Aunt Sally, I will begin with the greatest news first, that is that it has cleared off. It is no stranger than true that it is clear and has been for 2 days for the first time in 4 weeks. We made good use of it today and went to preaching at the Baptist. Mr. Jennings is our pastor for another year. Dr. Robertson is the Presbyterian pastor for

another year.

Aunt Sally, Christmas has come and gone and the whites are still alive. No Negro rising yet. There were a great many of our citizens very much surprised to think that they are alive. There were a great many families in Lexington that never went to bed at all the whole of Christmas week. As for me, I never lost a moments sleep.

Aunt Sally, Gina (*sister, Sarah Eugenia*) says to tell you that she has learned to spell and count a hundred and is going to start to school Monday and wear her new cloak and dress and bonnet. She and Lula and Mishy (*sister Tallulah Tecoa and brother Dyonisius*) start to Mr. Moss Monday. Gena and Lula say to tell you what Santa Clause gave them. it was a nice doll apiece, a bottle of cologne each, and a nice lot of confectioneries.

Uncle Neese, you need not boast too much over your tight for I guess that I am up with you for if ever one person was tight off eggnog I was Christmas morning and New Years morning I was tight right they say but it appears to me I was tight wrong.
Goodbye, write soon
Della
Della was eighteen during this holiday.

Dear Uncle and Aunt,

As Della has got the advantage of me this time and written first, of course you will expect no news from me. Christmas has passed and oh. how dull. The Negroes did not even rise to give us a little excitement. The people of Athens had quite a lively time up there Christmas week. There was a show there and the Yanks commenced robbing the people and that started a row. A Yank insulted a lady and her son took it up and the Yank knocked him over. There was a Negro standing by that formerly belonged to the lady so he pitched in and gave the Yank a good thrashing. The Yank went to his headquarters and got his crowd and when he got back to the scene of operation the citizens had armed themselves and had their officers. When the Yanks came up they pitched in a regular battle. There was some 15 or 16 wounded on both sides but no one was killed. The Rebs drove the Yanks out of town and into their houses. The case was duly investigated and the Yankee commander justified the citizens. I say three cheers for that Negro, don't you?

I saw Bill Norton's wife at church yesterday. I think that she is a real home spun girl. I think that she will be the talk for a month among the girls of Lexington, jealous you know. Minnie is as fat and sweet as ever. She had a very bad rising under her arm last week but she stood it like a little Job. Write soon and often.
All is well,
Julia

Lexington, Georgia, 2 May 1866
Dear Uncle and Aunt,

Doubtless you will be greatly surprised to see another letter coming from me, but when you read it you will not be astonished at me for writing immediately, for Pa received a letter from his brothers in Oregon this evening. You know that we have been writing to you for some time that Pa was going to move there this fall for he was not able to go now but this letter contains the news that they are to send a check on the Bank of New York which will reach us next week. The check is for $1000 which is to pay Pa's and family and Aunt Jane's (*father's sister*) expenses to that state and of course he will accept and start as soon as he can in the course of 1 or 2 months.

Aunt Sally, I hasten to write expressly that you and Uncle Neese may make your arrangements to come and see us before we leave, if you will not consent to go with us. Oh, Aunt Sally, do please come down, you and Uncle Neese, before we go, for you know it is impossible for us to ever see each other again on earth if you do not come down, and I do know your chance is so good to come.

Of course, I do not know we will start that soon but the check will, if not delayed, be here next week and you know that next month will be a good time to travel and that the summer months will be dangerous on the waters. I will write again soon. Write as soon as you get this and let us know.
Yours affectionately,
Adella

Dear Uncle and Aunt,

Della has informed you of the great theme that is agitating all our minds tonight. Aunt Sally and Uncle Neese, if I could tell you how I feel tonight I would do it but it is impossible. Della has informed you that Pa has decided to go to Oregon soon.

I have but one great object in view in writing to you tonight which is to plead with you to come and see us one more time before we leave for it is impossible for us to come to see you and I do know you can come here. Oh, how glad I would be if you would go with us. I will be so lonely to go without anyone but the family. Aunt Jane will go with us, I suppose. Aunt Sally, Ma says for me to plead in her name that Uncle and you visit us soon as it will be the last time that we will ever get to see each other on this earth. I know that we will have to encounter many hardships and dangers before we ever reach that foreign shore and in those dangers we may perish. We are in our Creator's hands everywhere, the same on the broad ocean that we are around our peaceful firesides and you know this country has no charms to hold anyone here, much less us who have no home to claim and will have to hunt some place this fall and why not there. Aunt Sally, write soon and often. I will write to you soon again and tell you more about it than I can tonight. Again I ask you to come to see us.

My love to all, write soon

Julia

Lexington, Georgia, 13 May 1866

Dear Uncle and Aunt,

I will try this beautiful Sabbath evening to answer your very kind and interesting letters that we received on Friday evening also one that we received yesterday evening which I assure you was gladly received and read with pleasure but it grieves me greatly to learn that you take our departure so hard as it will be useless. Dear Uncle and Aunt, you know not the many sighs and tears it cost us to part with you for you know that our affection for you both is great, the more so as we have no other relatives that have ever treated us so kind as you have. It really seems as though fate has had a great deal to do with us in this great move of ours for as soon as the war ended so the Uncles could write we received a letter from them urging us to come to that country at once. Before they could get an answer to that letter here came another letter informing us that a check would be here the next week calling for $1000 in gold on the Bank of New York, and sure enough, it came, and you both know we have no ties to hold us to this country any longer with the exception of you which I admit is very great but we cannot always be together. You know as well as I do that there is no chance whatever for us to make a living here. It is all that Pa can do to get bread for us to eat. He has planted cotton this year as have all other persons but there is very bad prospects for cotton and I do not see how we are to get along at all, and then we have no home here and never can have one. Pa and Ma wish to move to some new country before their children begin to leave them and why not go to Oregon where we have friends that have offered to help us as long as they can and where we can stand a better chance to help ourselves. You both know that this country will soon be in a deplorable condition. I know that Pa and Ma are both very old (*52 and 42*) and very probably will not live many years but the country is perfectly healthy and I hope that if they were taken that Providence will provide for us children. All of us feel it is a duty to go. I do not wish you to think we are all in a glee to go for the sake of the journey for I assure you that is what we dread worst of all other things.

I know that we will meet with many hardships before we reach that foreign shore if we ever do. We are in our Creator's hands the same on the deep that we are around our peaceful firesides and in Him will we trust to carry us safe over. I know it is useless to ask you to go with us but if you would go I would go with a cheerful heart.

Aunt Sally, you know how we appreciate your and Uncle Neese's kind offer but you know at the same time that Pa and Ma never would have consented to part with either of us. You know it is our duty to try and help take care of the small children, which duty I hope we have fulfilled so far and hope to do more in the future if needed, so I ask you to please cheer up by the time we get there and let us spend our last hours as pleasant as possible and just think how glad we will be to get letters from each other and what a great pleasure we will take in answering them. You telling about the speeches delivered in Congress by the freedmen about equal rights and me telling you about my nice ride on a buffalo hunting cattle. I do worse than carry geese to water and in a few years will have you coming out there to help us eat fruit and cheese and a great many other things to tedious to mention.

Yours.

Julia

Have all our friends there to see us as we would like to see all of them. Write soon and often and pick up a brave heart and be ready to go with us.

Dear Uncle and Aunt,

I, this lonely Sabbath evening, have concluded to answer your more than welcome letter that I have just received and you may guess how glad I was for it had been some time since we heard from you. But I would much rather be with you this evening as to interest you by writing as we have no news here except Oregon, Oregon. I know how much that subject has grieved you but I do not censure you for taking it hard for it caused me many hours heavy heart. We cannot always be together but we are going farther apart than I would like.

You know that it is very hard for a man ever to take a start in this old country with as large a family as Pa has. It would change the matter if we had any home but that we have not and I think that it is best for us to go to a new country and try to start with the country as it rises. Aunt Sally, you say that it would change the subject if we had husbands to go with us. That is about half that I am going for, for don't you know how hard I have been trying to get one these many years. So I am going out there and try my best to deceive some man. Aunt Sally, I know that you will say that I am delighted and excited with the go but you are badly mistaken. If we could get there without going I would be very glad indeed but I think it is right for us to brave our hardships and make the attempt for the uncles have promised to do more for us than we can ever do for ourselves in this old country. If they do so much to get us there, as they have, they certainly will not drop us entirely when they get us there. If we ever intend going now is the proper time. But enough on the subject. I will finish telling you all when we get there on our way.

Ma and Jim (*brother James Barrett*) have gone to Honea Path after Aunt Jane. They will be back some time the last of next week. The sale will be the 22nd. We expect to leave here the 24th and get to your house that night at 9, so you may have the big pot in the little one. We expect to go to New York and take the steamer to San Francisco and from there to Portland in Oregon where uncles are to met us with teams. The distance from there is 120 miles. We are to telegraph when we are in San Francisco.

Colonel Mathews and Miss Mary made their first appearance in Lexington today. They started to Alabama the day they were married after his little girl. They returned yesterday.

Write soon,

Della

Lexington, Georgia, 22 May 1866

Dear Uncle and Aunt,

I snatch a few moments to write to you and let you know that we will start today by way of Savannah. If we have done wrong in going this way and not by Marietta you will forgive us for we could go for $300 cheaper and you know that we will need a great deal of money. You have no idea how bad we hate to go and leave you and never see you again but we will write as often on the way as possible.

The sale came off on Tuesday. The things sold very well considering money being so scarce. Aunt Sally, please excuse my short note for you know not my feelings this morning. All of the family are well. I will write you from Savannah and from New York if we ever reach there. Tell all our friends goodbye for us. All the family join in love to you both. I will close as we have a great deal of company. If you never hear from us again you may know that we perished in some way what we thought to be our duty.

Your affectionate niece,

Julia Holt

The journey begins. It costs less to travel from Georgia by steamer than by train.

Savannah, Georgia, Pulaski House, 25 May 1866

Dear Uncle and Aunt,

As we are laying over here I will make use of the opportunity to drop you a few lines which will inform you of our whereabouts. We left home yesterday morning and arrived here this morning at 7 o'clock. We are waiting for the vessel to start. It will leave tomorrow at 3 in the evening. Pa has already procured tickets. The fare is $20 each to New York. We will sail on the San Salvador. It is said to be a very safe one, the best on the line.

Aunt Sally, I know that you and Uncle Neese will be disappointed about our not coming that way but this route was much the quickest and a great deal the cheapest and it stands us in hand to be as saving as possible and more than that. I think that it the best for it would have been very hard for us to part. The day that we would have spent together would have been a very disagreeable one for it would have been spent in tears. I think that it would be almost impossible for me to have parted with you both face to face and as it is we can hardly realize that we have parted and that for life unless you move there this fall as I hope you will do. I think that there is fully 100 that has promised Pa to move there this fall.

Aunt Sally, Ma says that she has just gone down to the wharf and been all through the vessel that we go in. She is very much delighted with it. You will please excuse haste and we will write to you every chance and we will keep you posted. Aunt Sally, I want you to write in about 2 weeks and address Harrisburg, Linn County, Oregon. We are all well and have stood the trip so far fine. We will get to New York Tuesday evening next.

Yours truly, farewell,

184

Della

Off the coast of Virginia on board the San Salvador, 28 May 1866.
Dear Uncle and Aunt,

I have nothing to do this evening and am well again to sit up so I will try and pass away a few hours in writing to you. Hours it will take for the old ship rocks so I can scarcely make a letter at all. We went on board the San Salvador at nine in the morning of the 26th and put to sea at half past three the same evening. I suppose you will expect me to give you an idea or two on traveling by sea and how I like it. I enjoyed the ride to the ocean extremely well, the distance of 20 miles (*Savannah to the mouth of the Savannah River*). We all, I mean all the passengers, remained on deck to see the last land that we could. We had not been on the ocean more than 30 minutes when the last one of our family ran down to our berths, the sickest people you ever saw, and not our family alone, but all the passengers. Out of 200 passengers I think fully 150 were on the sick list in less than one hour. We were dreadful sick and throwing up two nights and one day, so much so that not one was able to wait on another. Lula remained sick the longest and Pa the shortest and was the last to take sick. Della was the first on the sick list. I have eaten only one meal. Pa, Jim, and Jane can eat but the rest cannot. I think it is all over with now for all appear pretty well this evening. We will get to New York tomorrow evening.

We have had very calm and clear weather. The sea has been very smooth. I would like to travel be sea so much if the old vessel did not rock so bad. You have no idea how pretty it is to sit on deck of an evening and see other vessels pass us and see the different kinds of fish plunging and dashing through the blue waves. Some of them are half as large as the vessel. The water is much bluer than the sky.

We get splendid fare but that makes me mad for I cannot eat it. We have everything that you could think of that is good and about 12 of the nicest waiters you ever saw to wait on us. The vessel is very clean and finely furnished. I like the Captain very much. His name is Atkins. Our fare from Savannah to New York is $140. We will have to lay over in New York a day or two. I will finish this letter there if we be so fortunate as to reach there.

Well, it is so. We have reached New York. You have no idea how thankful I am to reach here. Dear Uncle and Aunt, I wish I could describe to you the beautiful scenery that I have witnessed already as we came up New York Bay. I know that we have seen fully 2000 vessels lying around in the different harbors and the beautiful towns on the sea coast is more than I can describe.

This evening was foggy and raining or we could have witnessed a good deal more. We met up with two very kind gentlemen who took great pains in showing us every place of interest. As yet I have not had the chance of displaying my rebel sentiments but if you hear of a rebel speech delivered in front of the National Hotel you may just know that I was the speaker

We are all very well this morning. I think that traveling will agree with us. Ma is perfectly well, has a splendid appetite for all she can get to eat. So has all the family. I only weighed 95 pounds when we left home but I expect to weigh 193 when I get through.

New York is nothing new to me. I would not give one hour at sea for one year in a dusty old city, but I tell you that it is quite cold up here in the old Yankee states. I have not seen a Negro up here yet and hope we will never see another one. We have Irish girls and boys to wait on us and cannot understand one word they say.

Pa has just procured tickets to San Francisco. We will sail on the Arizona, the Pacific mail steamship, a safe vessel. We will leave on the first of June. Will write to you as soon as I can and give you a bill of fare; also a way bill so you may follow on after us if Providence will only take us safe through. All is well and ready to start. My love to all friends. All join in love to you all,
Yours,
Julia

On board the Arizona off the Isle of Cuba, 5 June 1866
Dear Uncle and Aunt,

I will try and be as good as my word and write every opportunity even if what I write never reaches you. My letter will fail to interest you this time. We went on board the Arizona on the first of the present month and sailed at half past twelve on the same date. We found the vessel to be a very good one but the accommodations are not near as good as on the San Salvador coming over from Savannah. We took second cabins. The fare was $180 a piece and first cabin was $300. There are 900 on board and mostly in second cabins. We get plenty to eat. The place we have to sleep in is very warm down in this hot climate but we have not suffered from heat as I expected we would. There is always a cool breeze going. We spend the most of our time on deck and would find it very pleasant if the old boat didn't rock so bad. We had very calm seas for the first day but since that the sea has been very rough, so much so that I cannot sleep at night. Lulu has been sick all the time. Pa and Minnie have not been sick at all on board this vessel. It is well that someone can wait on the rest of us.

There are a great many on board going to Oregon, some to the same county that we are. I think that there are about 500 children on board and such yelling at times as you never heard. But the poor things, I don't blame them. I would cry when I am sick if it would do any good. Some ladies on board do cry but it does no good that I can see. If a storm comes I will do my crying then.

We passed the vessel, New York, yesterday on its way from Aspenwall (*on the East coast of the Isthmus of Panama, then a part of Colombia*) to New York. She had a great many passengers on board. We will reach Aspenwall on Saturday morning and cross the Isthmus that day and get on board the Golden City which is to take us to San Francisco. There we take another vessel at that place for Portland in Oregon and there to be met by Uncles to go 120 miles overland, a right smart journey of itself.

All the family are getting along splendid so far. There is no sickness on board except sea sickness. Providence has taken care of us so far and to Him we look for further protection. I forgot to say in the right place that we have to cross the Isthmus by railroad. It will take 12 hours to cross. I expect that we will find it very warm there but it will be a great relief to get on land once more. But I fear we will be sick again. You have no idea how bad it is to be sick and no remedy. When you hear people speaking of preventatives and cures for sea sickness just tell them that I say that there is no such thing but to lie still and throw up just as long as there is anything in you and after there is none.

June 6

Well another night has passed and we are all alive and well but we had a very rough sea last night and it is very rough now. The waves ran over the hurricane deck this morning the height of 20 feet.

June 7

We came very near having a storm last night. Neither Pa, Ma, or I slept any last night but everybody seems jovial this morning as we think it is the last day on this vessel. It is the rainy season down here. It is a beautiful sight to see it rain a calm rain. The sea is very calm this evening. We will reach Aspinwall tonight at 10. With that good news I will have to close my letter. It will take 15 days to reach San Francisco and three days to Portland. We will sail on the Golden City to San Francisco. All the family are perfectly well and join in love to you both. I hope that you will have the pleasure of hearing from me again. Love to all my friends.

Yours,

Julia

I will give you the distance run by our vessel from 12 one day until 12 the next. You will see that we gained all the time.

June 1 253 mi.
June 2 235 mi.
June 3 248 mi.
June 4 247 mi.
June 5 250 mi.
June 6 281 mi.
June 7 291 mi.

The trip across the isthmus from the Gulf of Mexico to the Pacific Ocean was via the Panamanian Railroad. Opened in 1855 to accommodate the flood of Easterners surging west in order to find riches in California's newly discovered gold fields, this line helped shorten the ocean voyage between the two major oceans by thousands of miles and many days.

West Point, Linn Count.y, Oregon, 31 August 1866

Dear Uncle and Aunt,

I hasten this afternoon to write to you as I have three of your letters unanswered. You know how any person in a new country has a great many things to attract their attention, and more than that, we have been very busy. It is a busy time of the year here. The farmers are trying to take care of their grain. I have no news that will interest you as we have no Negroes or Yanks to write about. We all live very quiet and happy. This has been a very good crop year. Wheat yields from 45 to 50 bushels to the acre and oats 75 to the acre. No corn raised. Wheat is $0.50 a bushel and oats $0.25. The farmers raise our old fashioned English garden pea for the hogs. I have seen a 25 acre field in garden peas and the hay, you have no idea how much the ground does yield. Uncle Sammy and

Jimmy (*father's brothers*) have saved more hay this season than they will use for years but they can get $25.00 a ton for it in the winter. They have such good grazing ground that their cattle need no feed in the dead of winter unless a heavy snow falls. The cattle not merely live here but are as fat as they can be.

Pa and family are still living at Uncle Jimmie and Sammy's and expect to remain there during the winter. Pa's trade is very good here. Della is off teaching school. She comes home every Friday evening. She likes teaching but I assure you we have fine times laughing over the green scholars and their green ways. I am all alone staying at Uncle Ben's (*father's married brother*). I do wish you could see Uncle Ben. He is one of the best men you ever did see, so kind and good. Well, suffice it to say he in every act reminds me of Uncle Neese. Both Uncle and Aunt (*Savannah*) say I have to be an old maid and live with them the rest of their days. You know that it will never take much to persuade me to be an old maid. I have not forgotten that old sweetheart that I left behind. You must take good care of him but I fear you will never see him as he lives a long distance from you. You must bring him with you when you come if you can find him. You will know him for he is the best looking soldier that General Lee had in his army.

I am sorry to hear such a bad account of the conditions of the country especially the crops. I fear that a great many of the widows and their children are going to suffer. It takes so much to keep the Negroes in their laziness that the poor whites will stand a bad chance. Thank goodness we have no Negroes or Yanks. You have no idea how pleasant it is to be without any Negroes. You are not afraid every day that you will have everything stolen. Ma makes $12 a week churning. The men do the milking. Jim and Nish can milk as good as Ma can.

I will look for you next summer. The fall and winter on the Pacific coast are too stormy. Start in May or June. No person can ask for a better trip than we had. It cost us about $1500 to come; $20 to Savannah, $20 to New York, $180 to San Francisco, $15 to Portland, $5 to Salem and then the wagon the rest of the way. I see that the fare is greatly reduced since we came over.

Now Uncle and Aunt, I will not persuade you to take the long and tedious journey that we have just made. You will have to make up your minds to undergo a great many hardships and a great many pleasures. You know that nothing would half-way please us so well as to meet you here on the Pacific shores. Still I will not persuade you to come for fear of some accident and then I should always feel myself to blame but I assure you that this is a splendid country. All of Pa's family are in fine health. You ought to see Minnie and Gina. How fat and sassy they are. They are dreadfully petted by Uncle Jinnie and Sammy. So are all the children. They have given Jim and Nish a fine horse apiece worth $200 apiece. They are a large span of blacks. You ought to see me in my new riding habit and see me get on one of Uncle Ben's carriage horses. Bring Salem over. I can beat you riding. I think that I will run a race down at the fair this fall.

I received a letter from Almeda. No news. Almeda is a good girl but very unfortunate. Write soon and tell all the news. Give my love and respects to all my friends. The family join in love to you. Ma says be sure and write often. Tell Uncle Neese to write.
Yours affectionately,
Julia Holt

Della is at school. She gets $25 a month in gold. I can get a school next spring close to home.

The Holts have been in Oregon only one month. So much has happened so quickly.

Lane County, Oregon, 28 October 1866
Dear Uncle and Aunt,

I have been waiting some time to receive a letter from you before writing, but as I have one letter on hand, I suppose I had better answer it and not be waiting for another one. You must not look for anything interesting in this letter. There has been so much going and coming is the reason that I have not written to you long ago. Uncle Ben, Aunt Savannah, Pa, Nish, and Mr. Wilkins all went to the state fair at Salem. Aunt Savannah left me to keep house. Della would come home of a night and stay with me but you may guess that I did not lack for company as the young ladies would come and stay all night and bring their brothers so you may suppose that we did not spend much lonesome time. There was a protracted meeting (*revival*) going on five miles distant and we would get on our horses and back of a night. Yes, Uncle Neese, I can ride any horse as far as I want and as fast. Don't you suppose that I will soon be an Oregonian? I do love to ride horseback.

You ought to see my sweetheart that I have to go with me. He lives about a mile distant. When I go he is always on hand. All the girls of Oregon marry by the time they are fifteen and the boys eighteen and in about a year they are parted. There is a law that will not give anyone a license until they are of age but the young people are too smart for them. They run away and go three miles out to sea and there is no law there and all those that run away are parted in a short time but enough on that subject.

Well, Aunt Sally, we have been here over three months and we all like Oregon as well as ever. All have the best of health. The push of work is over now, grain is all brought in, rails and wood all hauled in. There is a great deal of rain here in the winter and the farmers all prepare for it. Some sow their wheat in the fall but the most in the spring. The wild geese and cranes take it up when it is sowed in the fall. You have no idea how much grain there is in Oregon. Just think of feeding hogs on wheat. The country is overflowing with everything that could make anyone happy and contented. The fall rains cause the grass to come up and grow as well as it does in the spring so the cattle can graze in the winter as well as summer.

Uncle Jimmie and Sammie make more off their cattle than they do on their farm. They are hauling in squashes now. They have squashes that are all one man can do to carry. They are like pumpkins only a great deal larger and are not hollow. They make excellent feed for the hogs during the winter (*citrons?*).

Well, to tell you the truth, I believe this is one of the bountifullist countries you ever heard of. You must be sure and come next spring that is if you are willing to risk the dangers of a sea voyage. Aunt Sally, be sure and send some pepper seed in every letter you send all winter so Ma can have some to sow in the spring. When you come bring all kinds of seeds and bring limbs of all kinds of flowers and the seed also. You wanted prairie flower seed. They were all gone before you wrote and bring all kinds of mechanics with you, especially carpenters. They can get $4.00 a day in gold all the season. Write soon and often. Tell me all the news.
My love to all,
Julia

Della's school will be out in three weeks. Don't you suppose she will be glad. When you come bring all woolen goods especially Uncle Neese's clothes as there is no cotton clothes worn by men. You can buy them cheaper there than you can here. In your next let us know if you are coming and when and where.

Harrisburg, Oregon, 20 March 1867, Wednesday evening
My Dear Uncle and Aunt,

As I have not got anything else to do I have concluded to spend an hour or two writing to you. I know that you think that you will get considerable quantity of news if I am going to write an hour or two but you are mistaken for it will take that long to think of anything to write. I have written everything that I can think of. I have described the valley until I know you can lay of a night with your eyes shut and see Oregon in all of its beauty so I think I had better stop for fear that you will become disgusted with my description of it. The next thing is to tell you all is well and getting pretty accustomed to our new home. I wish that you could see what a pretty little home we have got away out here in the Western State. You think like I did that there is not anything out here but little log huts, but you are quite out of it. You will see for yourself some day I hope.

I guess that I must tell you about the crop. Well it is all in (*planted*) but I cannot tell you how many different kinds of grain or how many acres in each kind as all that I have to do is jump up soon, very soon, each morning and help get breakfast so they can get to work soon but they have it all in and are now putting in a new plank fence round the lot here. There is no gardening done here until in April as the springs are cool and backward but vegetation grows very fast when it once gets started. We are needing rain here now as the grass is drying up and the stock of all kinds is beginning to get poor. I think that we will have a good fruit year as the spring is so very backward that the fruit trees are not beginning to show the least sign of blooming yet. I fear that it will be too late to dry much fruit except in dry houses and dried fruit brings a good price here in the spring. Everything brings a better price than wheat.

There is so much grain raised here that it cannot bear a good price but the wild geese and ducks look to me like they will take all the grain that is sowed. There are geese that go in gangs of thousands and thousands. The farmers have to put up scarecrows to keep them from devouring the grain entirely. They leave here in April and do not come back until in the fall.

Well, if you knew how hard it was for me to fill up this paper you would excuse me if I stopped right here. I do not know what else to say as Ma has not yet any young chickens, not even a setting hen, and I have told you about the crop so I have gin out. Della has yet the other side to fill up. Don't you pity her if her stock of news is as near out as mine. Aunt Jane is considerable better, thinks she will soon be up. Be sure and write often and tell us all the news. We are glad to hear anything. My paper is full and I am glad. So are you.
Julia Holt

Dear Uncle and Aunt,

As Julia has handled the big end of nothing to such a good advantage of course you will not look for me to do as much with the little end of it and it will not surprise you if my end is very dull for Julia has taken all the news to complete hers. But I think I ought to write a very interesting letter as this is the first one that I have written from my new home and new it is to me as it has been only a few days since I got home as I had to stay my first week with my new Aunt (*Uncle Sammy's new wife*) and initiate her with housekeeping in her new home. But now I am home and expect to stay here and enjoy the comforts of home as it is only a few days that I will get to be at home. I expect to begin school the first day of April unless it sets in very bad weather and I hope it will not for I am anxious to begin early so that I will get through early in the fall. I will take up a six month school this summer. I get the same that I did last summer. That is $25 per month. It is a very good house that I have to teach in. It is only a mile and a half from here so I will get to go from home this year. That is the good part for I thought it would certainly kill me sometimes last summer to go the rounds with the scholars but as fortune had it I survived all difficulties and came safe through.

Aunt Sally, you may consider this an April fool or anything you please as it is very near April, but I did not think of writing one when I sat down here for I have several ones to write and if they are all as hard as this one I am sure that some person will have to go without any and that will be a great pity for I have found out who wrote all my Valentines and I am sure that I am going to try to pay a few of them back in April Fools.

Friday morning. Well, the last hour has arrived that I have to finish this interesting epistle in and still no news but it will have to be closed as Nishey is ready to go to the office if he does not freeze up for it has cleared up and it is as cold this morning as the coasts of Greenland and it has the appearance of staying cold and clear for a century. Every person is anxious to see it rain as the grass is almost frozen out and the cattle are getting poor. The grass is very backward, much more so that usual. It is an uncommon cold spring. It has been the coldest winter that any person ever saw on the Pacific Coast but it is not any colder that any winter that you have in Georgia.

Write soon and tell us all of the news for if you move in the spring you cannot more than answer this before starting.
Farewell for this time,
Della Holt

Lane County, Oregon, 22 October 1867
My Dear Uncle and Aunt,

I know that you think that I am dead or gone off to some foreign land but in both you would be mistaken. But I am alive and right here at home. So it will be useless for me to make excuses of any kind but I will promise that I will do better in the future. All the family are well except Gena (*sister, Sarah Eugenia*). The is the perfect Job in the way of sores but she is better now. She has more patience than the rest of the family. Ma is getting along very well, so is her big boy (*new brother, Walter Alfred, born 28 September 1867*) and you may guess that she is proud of it.

Fall has set in but we are having a beautiful fall, no rain but heavy frosts and cold nights and mornings. The farmers are having a splendid time to take care of what they have made. There was not as much made this year as last but it is the same to the farmer as the prices for everything is so much better that it makes up for the quantity. Wheat is selling at 75 cents and everything else in proportion. Pa has 20 hogs up feeding now. Hogs in Oregon are mostly fattened on squashes and chopped wheat and oats. Pa will have about a thousand pounds to sell. As we have everything else to eat here we never think to eat meat. Now is a busy time gathering in fruit for the winter. Pa has built us a new apple house and he is filling it well with all kinds of apples and he has gone this afternoon after grapes to put up for winter.

Oh Uncle Neese, I do wish that you were here. I know you would enjoy the winters so much. When the rain sets in we are like a parcel of hogs. We are housed up but I will assure you that we are ample prepared in the way of eatables and it is well that we have something to pass off the time but the thought of staying at home all winter nearly takes my life but I ought to be satisfied for I know I have done as much going as anybody. I never have enjoyed a summer as I have this summer.

Jimmie is going to school three miles off. He rides there. In the winter is all the time that boys get to go to school as they are so busy in the summer they cannot go. Della is speaking of going to school in Harrisburg as she expects to teach school again this summer.

Both of the fairs have come off and not much at that, not half as good as last year. We did not attend either. There has been so much horse racing done at them that there is not much satisfaction in going. Ma says send over a name for her boy as she has named out. You would not know Minnie (*sister, Minnie Lee*) if you saw her. She has grown so much. So has Jimmie (*brother, James Barrett*). He is as tall as Pa. Nish and Lula (*brother Dyonisius Melville and sister Tallulah Tecoa*) has grown some but not near as much as the other two. Della and I

189

only grow in beauty but you know there is not much room for improvement in that line. We have received both of your photographs and thankful for them. Do write often and long letters. I will try and do better hereafter,

Yours,

Julia

Lane County, Oregon, 1 March 1868

My Dear Uncle and Aunt,

As I have two of your letters on hand that are unanswered and nothing particular to do I will spend a few leisurely moments in writing to you this morning, not that I have anything in the way of news. If you were acquainted with the people in the neighborhood I could tell you of a great many marriages and deaths that would interest you as there have been over twenty weddings in this neighborhood in the last four months. You spoke of some news from Lexington that I had not heard of. I had heard that Almeda Stephens was going to marry but not to a yank and then Mrs. Fisher wrote to Adella that his name was Ben Bigby so we know he was the same Ben Bigby that used to be around Honea Path. You will remember how no account he was. I am sorry for Almeda. She had better be dead.

As Della has told you about our cold winter and long snow I will not say anything about it as it is all over with now but not the effects as we have all had the worst colds but are better now. Della has quit going to school. She has been at home two weeks. She stayed with me last night to help me quilt. I am quilting my basket quilt now and find it quite a job to quilt alone as you know that is something new to me but I suppose that I will soon get used to it.

Della received a letter from cousin Davy a few weeks ago. Uncle Harvey and family and William Patterson and family had just started to Arkansas. Uncle Harvey's oldest son, John, was married the day before he started. They left Mississippi on account of sickness and I fear that he will fare worse in Arkansas but you know he is of a roving disposition and will never be satisfied, go where he will.

What do you think about coming to Oregon? If you are coming this spring you had better begin to know it. I know that you would like the summers but do not know that you would be willing to stand the rainy winters for the sake of the summer but I wish you were here if I knew that you would be as satisfied as I am.

Aunt Sally, as to having my cake and credit by not telling you beforehand and giving you an invitation to our wedding I will tell you the reason. I would have liked to have had you there but was afraid you would not accept the invitation so I would have felt sold. If you wish or intend to be on hand at my next party you had better be on the road now or you might be late again and thereby miss either of the parties. Write often and long letters.

Yours,

W. M. and J. A. Mansfield

Julia Ann married William Mansfield on 24 November 1867 and was expecting her first child, Laura, who was born 5 November 1868.

Lane County, Oregon, 2 June 1868

My dear Uncle and Aunt,

I expect you think it is time I was answering some of your letters and I know it is. I have been very busy for the last while. You come to Oregon and have the company I have and see if you are not busy most of the time. Billie and I have not eaten a dozen meals by ourselves since we were married. Sometimes I wish we lived 100 miles from anyone but instead we live on the main road that runs up and down the river and you have no idea the company we have. The prospects for crops was never better than this spring. It is a wet spring and that is the kind to suit here. There is as much grain sowed as last year. We will have awful heavy harvests. I do dread to see the time come, Aunt Sally, you don't know what work is. You come out and help me this harvest and see.

I am keeping batch this week. Billie started to Portland last Thursday morning after a thresher. He will be gone eight or nine days. I don't see how I am going to stand it for it is the first time he has ever left me. But I know there is money in it so I will try to do the best that I can. He pays $800 for the thresher but it will pay for itself the first year. He has a reaper now so between the two he will be gone from home most of the time. Uncle Ben has gone after a header. That is a kind of reaper that takes off the head without binding it and it is carried straight to the thresher.

Nishy is staying with me this week. Pa and Ma and Minnie went to Harrisburg last week and had their photos taken. Della and I are going down Saturday and if they are done we will send you one of each. Saturday is all the idle time she has. She has a splendid school and is well liked for a teacher and you know that she likes

children so well. Pa is shearing sheep this week. He gets five pounds from a sheep and has a hundred and thirty sheep. Give my love to all.
Yours,
Julia A. Mansfield

Dear Uncle and Aunt,

I am back again in my old room at the same occupation as last summer. I was sure that I would never teach another school but I changed my mind. My school was out on the third of this month but I only got one week of rest. They have employed me for another quarter. I have become such a miser that I suppose I shall teach as long as I can make one dollar and seventy cents in gold. Last quarter I went home every Friday night but they will be too busy harvesting to come for me every week now. All the neighbors work together harvesting. They will have to work hard to cut the grain this year as there is the greatest prospects for good crops this year.

In your last letter you spoke of Grandma (*Nancy Whitten Thomason*) being sick. Ma wants me to ask how she is and who cares for her. Jimmy is growing better looking that Nish but Minnie is going to knock the shine off of the rest of us for she is almost a beauty. She is as smart a child as I ever saw but woe for the temper as she has plenty of that for one dozen children her size. Time to take up school.
Della

2. **Sarah M. Thomason** was born 2 September 1827 in Anderson County, South Carolina, and was married before 1850 there. In 1863, Ranson E. Whitten's letter has her living with her mother in Marietta, Georgia, with her husband away fighting for the Confederacy. Several censuses show Sarah M. married to Alfred M. Neese, born in North Carolina 29 September 1826. His estate included three lots in Marietta, which he purchased from the estate of Sarah's mother. They died in Marietta: he, 9 December 1893; she, 1 March 1915; and are buried in Citizen's Cemetery, Marietta, Cobb, Georgia.
Their child was:
Harriett Neese
2. **Mary Ann Thomason** was born 21 November 1829, and married, in Anderson County, South Carolina, a Mr. Moor. Nothing further is as yet known of this family.
2. **James Judson Jepthia? Thomason** was born 4 October 1846 in Anderson County, South Carolina, and was identified as living with his mother in Ranson Edwin Whitten's 1863 letter. The name Jepthia was attached to him in early records but ceases to appear later. He became a printer, and on 2 April 1870, in Floyd County, Georgia, married Omazelia Britt, who was born about 1854 in Alabama. The couple moved to Desoto Township, near Rome, Floyd, Georgia, shortly after the marriage. Several children were born there. The Floyd County home was sold 28 October 1880, and the family moved to Atlanta. James Judson was the administrator of his mother's estate and alive in 1907 when his sister wrote her will. He and Omazelia appear in the Atlanta, Georgia, censuses in 1900, 1910, and 1920. In 1930 they were not listed and probably were dead.
Their seven children were:
James Thomason
John Thomason
Ettie Thomason
Allen or Albin Thomason
Bernice Thomason
Otto Clyde Thomason
Walter H. Thomason

FIFTH GENERATION
Children of Alfred Holt and Harriet Permelia Thomason
3. **Julia Ann Holt** was born 14 September 1845 in Honea Path, South Carolina, and, on 24 November 1869, in Harrisburg, Oregon, married William Mansfield, who was born 10 September 1840 and died 18 June 1873 in Harrisburg. On 18 May 1876 she married W. W. Beach and died 24 January 1885 in Colfax, where she is buried.
The child of William Mansfield and Julia Ann Holt was:
Luna Mansfield
The child of W. W. Beach and Julia Ann Holt was:
Lola Beach
3. **Frances Adella Holt**, another of our letter writers, was born 6 December 1847 in Honea Path, South Carolina, and married John William Grimes, who was born 17 February 1843 in Harrisburg, Oregon, 27 October 1870. They died

there: he, 24 October 1912; she, 26 October 1928. She was buried at Harrisburg. The Cobb County, Georgia, census of 1860 shows her living with her beloved Aunt Sally in Marietta.

Their five children were:

Henry Loring Grimes
Ollie Adella Grimes
William Alfred Randal Grimes
Anna Myrtle Grimes
Zola Ena Grimes

3. **William Whitten Holt** was born 7 October 1849 in Honea Path, where he died 22 October 1850 and was buried.

3. **James Barrett Holt**, born 21 September 1851 in Honea Path, and married Henrietta Tabor 28 November 1875 in Linn County, where she was born 3 August 1853. Both died in Pullman, Washington, 25 July 1930.

Their three children were:

Cleo Holt
Eva Holt
Harold Holt

3. **Dyonisius Mellville Holt** was born 15 November 1854 in Honea Path, and in Colfax, Washington, on 23 February 1879, married Nancy Smith, who was born in 1862 in Lane County, Oregon. He died 9 April 1928 in Oregon City, Oregon; she, 15 October 1935 in Olympia, Washington.

Their five children were:

Della Holt
Creed Holt
Helen Holt
Zeena Holt
Walter A. Holt

3. **Tallulah Tecoa Holt** was born 20 January 1857 in Honea Path, and married William Hamilton 24 December 1872 in Colfax, Washington. He was born 25 October 1850 in Salem, Oregon. They died in Colfax: she, 13 January 1882, where she is buried; he, 31 October 1925.

Their four children were:

Ortis Hamilton
Norma Hamilton
Boyd Hamilton
Earl Hamilton

3. **Sarah Eugenia Holt** was born 23 September 1860 in Honea Path, and married Horeb Marmian Boone 13 July 1879 in Colfax. He was born 1 January 1858 in Eola, Polk, Oregon. They died in Dayton, Washington, where she is buried: he, 6 June 1936; she, 15 March 1946.

Their five children were:

William Wirt Boone
Myrtle Minnie Boone
Eola Lexa Boone
Holt Horeb Boone
Ralph Reece Boone

3. **Minnie Lee Holt** was born 21 December 1864 in Lexington, Georgia, and married John Muir, born in 1852. They died in Seattle, where she was buried: he, 21 August 1920; she, 8 November 1943.

3. **Walter Alfred Holt** was born 28 September 1867 in Harrisburg, Oregon, and married Agnes Leah Burden Earhart, who was born 2 February 1782 in Salem, on 19 February 1896 in Portland, where they both died: she, 30 September 1920; he, 4 August 1936. She was buried there.

Their three children were:

Alfred Preston Holt
Nancy Harriet Holt
Agnes Elizabeth Holt

Child of Alfred M. Neese and Sarah M. Thomason

3. **Harriett Neese** was born 27 February 1862, died 23 May 1963, and was buried in Citizen's Cemetery, Marietta, Cobb, Georgia.

Children of James Judson Jeptha? Thomason and Omazeliah Britt

3. **James Thomason**, born about 1871 in Desoto Township, Floyd, Georgia.

3. **John Thomason**, born about 1874 in Desoto Township.

3. **Ettie Thomason**, born about 1876 in Desoto Township.

3. **Allen (or Albin) Thomason**, born about 1879 in Desoto Township.

3. **Bernice Thomason** was born in April 1884 in Atlanta where, in 1904, she married Hoke T. McCollum, who was born in 1883 in Georgia.

Their four children were:

Huel J. McCollum
Emma I. McCollum
James J. McCollum
Hoke T. McCollum Jr.

3. **Otto Clyde Thomason**, born in July 1889 in Atlanta.

3. **Walter H. Thomason**, born in January 1892 in Atlanta.

SIXTH GENERATION
Child of William Mansfield and Julia Ann Holt

4. **Luna Mansfield** was born 3 October 1868 in Harrisburg, Oregon, and died 18 December 1897 in Colfax, Washington.

Child of W. W. Beach and Julia Ann Holt

4. **Lola Beach** was born 19 February 1877 in Harrisburg. On 1 March 1898 in Colfax she married George Schuler, born in April 1870. They died in Colfax: she, 6 June 1905; he, in 1926.

Their child was:

Ruth Schuler

Children of John William Grimes and Frances Adella Holt
Born in Linn County, Oregon

4. **Henry Loring Grimes** was born 22 January 1872. On 30 June 1908 he married Amelia Sorenson, born in 1880 in Springfield, Oregon. They died in Harrisburg: he, 14 June 1937; she, 13 June 1965.

Their six children were:

Lloyd Grimes
Edgar Grimes
Zena Grimes
Randall Grimes
John Grimes
Elmer Grimes

4. **Ollie Adella Grimes** was born 27 May 1873 and died 10 February 1928 in Harrisburg.

4. **William Alfred Randal Grimes** was born 27 August 1874 in Linn County, and on 19 September 1903 married Bessie Lusby in Harrisburg. She was born 14 November 1882. He died 22 May 1946 in Eugene.

Their two children were:

Alfred Holt Grimes
Lyle Clark Grimes

4. **Anna Myrtle Grimes** was born 9 October 1876, and married Mahlon Calef 11 September 1902 in Harrisburg. He was born 27 January 1877 in Portland, where both died: she, 24 August 1965; he, 20 February 1963.

Their three children were:

Gladys Calef
Lucie Calef
Elizabeth Calef

4. **Zola Ena Grimes** was born 12 July 1878 in Linn County, Oregon, and married Bernard Sorenson 6 June 1907. She died in Harrisburg on 8 October 1959.

Their three children were:

Edward Sorenson
Rozal Sorenson

Neta Della Sorenson

Children of James Barrett Holt and Henrietta Tabor

4. **Cleo Holt** was born 11 December 1876 in Pullman, Washington, where she married Walter Ray Bloor 25 July 1904. They died in Colorado Springs: he, 16 January 1966; she, 26 December 1973. Walter was born 3 July 1877 in Ingersall, Canada.

Their three children were:

Norma Bloor

John Bloor

Robert John Bloor

4. **Eva Holt** was born in February 1881 and died in 1890 in Whitman, Washington.

4. **Harold Holt** was born 4 October 1892 in Wawawai, Washington, married Helen Lawrence in Junction City, Kansas, on 28 November 1920, and died 18 January 1969 in San Antonio, Texas.

Children of Dyonisius Melville Holt and Nancy Smith

4. **Della Holt** was born 23 November 1879 in Whitman and died 29 October 1957 in San Mateo, California. On 30 April 1905 in Astoria, Oregon, she married Eldon Claude Turnbow, who was born 11 November 1882 in Oregon and died 14 July 1977 in Oakdale, California.

Their four children were:

Eugene Creed Turnbow

Lois Zena Turnbow

Kenneth Turnbow

William Robert Turnbow

4. **Creed Holt** was born 11 July 1881 in Whitman, and married Sarah Baily 29 October 1907 in Spokane, Washington. Sarah was born 23 August 1882 in Humboldt, Nebraska, and died in March 1963.

Their two children were:

Harriet Baily Holt

Raymond Creed Holt

4. **Helen Holt** was born 28 August 1884 in Whitman and died 21 October 1918 in Olympia. In Pullman, Washington, she married Lyle Ormsbee 9 November 1909. He was born 28 July 1888 in Waitsburg, Washington, and died 21 March 1949 in Olympia.

Their child was:

Nancy Ormsbee

4. **Zeena Holt** was born 8 February 1888 in Whitman, married James Davis 19 February 1910 in Colfax, Washington, and died 21 August 1918 in Pullman.

Their three children were:

James Davis

Walter Wood Davis

Duane Davis

4. **Walter A. Holt** was born 6 September 1891 in Pullman, and died 21 January 1972 in Pendleton, Oregon. He married Blanche Clements 23 December 1916 in Walla Walla, Washington. She was born 10 January 1896 in Richland, Washington, and died 5 January 1988 in Pendleton.

Their three children were:

Betty Holt

Walter Holt

Bruce Holt

Children of William Hamilton and Tallulah Tecoa Holt

4. **Ortis Hamilton** was born 22 September 1873 in Whitman, Washington, and married Mary Savage, who was born in 1874.

4. **Norma Hamilton** was born 25 March 1876 in Whitman and died 23 November 1945 in Colfax. She married Albert Stuht 3 August 1897. He was born 10 August 1871 and died 15 December 1945.

Their three children were:

Ernest Stuht

Albert Stuht

William Boyd Stuht
    4. **Boyd Hamilton** was born 22 October 1878 in Colfax and married Alta May Browne 20 September 1900 in Spokane, Washington. She was born in 1881.
    4. **Earl Hamilton**, born in 1880 and died in 1883 in Colfax, Washington.

Children of Horeb Marmian Boone and Sarah Eugenia Holt

    4. **William Wirt Boone** was born 20 October 1880 in Colfax and died 11 October 1958 in Corte Madera, California. On 11 November 1903 in Palouse, Washington, he married Myrtle Turnbow, who was born there 22 September 1880 and died in Centralia, Washington, 20 February 1979.
    Their four children were:
        Gwendolyn Eugenia Boone
        Horeb Max Boone
        John Eldridge Boone
        Janice May Boone
    4. **Myrtle Minnie Boone** was born 27 August 1882 in Colfax and died 27 July 1957 in Los Angeles. She married Fred Archer Pratt in Palouse in 1905. He was born in 1880 and died 9 November 1957.
    4. **Eola Lexa Boone** was born 27 February 1885 in Colfax and died 15 November 1946 in Glendale, California. In 1905 she married Roy Patton in Palouse. He was born in 1880 and died 9 November 1957.
    Their child was:
        Marion Helen Patton
    4. **Holt Horeb Boone** was born 25 November 1888 in Colfax and died 20 May 1972 in Dayton, Washington. On 31 May 1916 in Sedro Wooley, Washington, he married Ella Sophia Thompson, who was born 26 December 1892 and died in Tacoma, Washington, 13 February 1974.
    Their four children were:
        William Holt Boone
        Bernice Alma Boone
        Doris Louise Boone
        Diane Muriel Boone
    4. **Ralph Reece Boone** was born 19 January 1893 in Palouse and on 29 August 1918 in Dayton, Ohio, married Neva Marie MacGregor, who was born 22 April 1896 in Hooper, Whitman, Washington. They died in Glendale, California: he, 5 February 1968; she, 1 December 1978.
    Their three children were:
        Betty Jean Boone
        Patricia Ann Boone
        Stanley D. Boone

Children of Walter Alfred Holt and Agnes Leah Burden Earhart
Born in Portland, Oregon

    4. **Alfred Preston Holt** was born 20 June 1898 and died 21 September 1959 in Portland, where he was buried. He married Laurentia Marie Olbrich 8 October 1924 in Palo Alto, California. She was born 9 May 1899 in Lincoln, Nebraska, and died 24 April 1952 in Portland.
    Their three children were:
        Walter Wesley Holt
        James Preston Holt
        John Earhart Holt
    4. **Nancy Harriet Holt** was born 18 June 1900 and died 18 March 1994 in Vancouver, Washington. In Portland on 25 June 1923 she married Robert Goulding Kendall, born 15 October 1898.
    Their three children were:
        Nancy Catherine Kendall
        Sally Ann Kendall
        Robert Goulding Kendall
    4. **Agnes Elizabeth Holt** was born 11 August 1911 and died 14 April 1970 in Portland.

Children of Hoke T. McCollum and Bernice R. Thomason
Born in Atlanta, Fulton, Georgia

5. **Huel J. McCollum**, born about 1905.
5. **Emma I. McCollum**, born about 1908.
5. **James J. McCollum**, born in August 1909.
5. **Hoke T. McCollum Jr.**, born about 1912.

SEVENTH GENERATION
Child of George Schuler and Lola Beach
5. **Ruth Schuler** was born 12 October 1904 in Colfax, Washington, where she died 2 July the following year.

Children of Henry Loring Grimes and Amelia Sorenson
Born in Harrisburg, Oregon
5. **Lloyd Grimes** was born 1 August 1909 and died 20 September 1988 in Milledgeville, Georgia. In Kent, Washington, he married Ida Helen Reese on 11 September 1935. She was born 14 June 1935 in Oak Grove, Oregon.
Their four children were:
Rodney Lee Grimes
Carolyn Kay Grimes
Mary Leanne Grimes
Lloyd Harold Grimes
5. **Edgar Grimes** was born 1 December 1910, and married Marian Shelmau 20 June 1940. She was born 28 March 1911 in Asotin, Washington.
Their five children were:
Mahlon Henry Grimes
Edna May Grimes
Lee Allen Grimes
Roy Edgar Grimes
Bruce Bell Grimes
5. **Zena Grimes** was born 6 September 1912 in Harrisburg and in Kelso, Washington, married William Moura 6 July 1934. He was born 1 November 1908 in Durkee, Oregon, and died in Bend, Oregon, 2 November 1957.
5. **Randall Grimes** was born 5 March 1914 in Harrisburg, and there, on 13 April 1947, married Johnnie Joyce Atteberg, born 12 April 1929 in Borden County, Texas. He died in Harrisburg 5 December 1968.
Their seven children were:
William Edward Grimes
Glenda Joyce Grimes
Robert Randall Grimes
Donald Frank Grimes
Dena Marie Grimes
David John Grimes
Cindy Christine Grimes
5. **John Grimes** was born 9 December 1915, and married Helen June Murphy 24 September 1938 in Portland. She was born in Harrisburg on 24 June 1917.
Their three children were:
Jocile Norene Grimes
Michael Clinton Grimes
Steven Patrick Grimes
5. **Elmer Grimes** was born 16 August 1918 and died 18 November 1982 in Eugene, Oregon. He married Emily Cramer in Harrisburg 25 December 1939. Emily was born 26 October 1917 in Harrisburg and died in Eugene 18 November 1982.
Their five children were:
Richard Grimes
James Grimes
Eileen Grimes
Steven Grimes
Betty Grimes

Children of William Grimes and Bessie Lusby
Born in Harrisburg, Oregon

5. **Alfred Holt Grimes** was born 18 June 1904 and died in 1960 at Cottage Grove, Oregon. On 16 June 1934 in Burns, Oregon, he married Myrtle Hubbell.

Their child was:

Richard Grimes

5. **Lyle Clark Grimes** was born 21 February 1980 and married Gwen Lamson 15 June 1935 in Eugene. She was born in Artesian, South Dakota, on 9 December.

Their two children were:

William Ralph Grimes

Darby Clark Grimes

Children of Mahlon Calef and Anna Myrtle Grimes

5. **Gladys Calef** was born 19 April 1906 in Palouse, Washington, and married Albert Hanson 26 October 1929.

5. **Lucie Calef** was born 2 August 1907 in Palouse, and in Portland on 2 August 1932, married James Walp, born 24 July 1905 in Coalinga, California. They died in Portland: she, 23 August 1982; he, 5 August 1988.

Their two children were:

Ronald Walp

James Calef Walp

5. **Elizabeth Calef** was born 12 June 1915 in Portland, where she married Mansfield Howells 14 August 1939. He was born there 22 October 1914.

Their three children were:

Laura Howells

Richard Howells

Robert Howells

Children of Bernard Sorenson and Zola Ena Grimes
Born in Harrisburg, Oregon

5. **Edward Sorenson** was born 9 October 1908, and on 30 May 1929 married Agnes Forbs, who was born 13 March 1906 and died in Canyon City, Oregon. 22 May 1980.

5. **Rozal Sorenson** was born 20 January 1910 and died 24 August 1981. On 30 April 1935 he married Dorothy.

5. **Neta Della Sorenson** was born 21 January 1913 and died 3 April that same year.

Children of Walter Ray Bloor and Cleo Holt

5. **Norma Bloor** was born 25 March 1905 in Pullman, and married Arthur Roosevelt Bowles 10 August 1935 in Canandaigua, New York. He was born 4 February 1906 in Brooklyn, New York, and died in Indianapolis, Indiana, in September 1941.

Their two children were:

Nancy Norma Bowles

Carol Cynthia Bowles

5. **John Bloor** was born 25 March 1905 in Pullman and died in 1907 in Ingersoll, Canada.

5. **Robert John Bloor** was born 25 March 1916 in Boston, Massachusetts, and married Martha Ann Emmel 9 May 1942 in Chicago. She was born 14 December 1915 in St. Louis and died 8 July 1987 in Pueblo, Colorado.

Their three children were:

John Holt Bloor

Thomas Lewis Bloor

Andrew Walter Bloor

Children of Eldon Claude Turnbow and Della Holt

5. **Eugene Creed Turnbow** was born 7 February 1907 in Kennewick, Washington, and died 30 September 1986 in Oakdale, California. In 1928 he married Mildred Heisterkamp in Palo Alto, California.

5. **Louis Zena Turnbow** was born 29 September 1909 in Kennewick, and married Harry Kalender.

5. **Kenneth Turnbow** was born 18 June 1911 in Pullman, and married Margaret Woods in May 1938 in Santa Rosa, California.

Their two children were:

Melvin Kenneth Turnbow

Carol Jean Turnbow

5. **William Robert Turnbow** was born 8 February 1914 in Courtney Station, Oregon, and died 23 November 1981 in San Francisco, where he married Dorothy Buchan 15 April 1939. She was born in Merced, California, 11 November 1919.

Their three children were:
> William R. Turnbow
> Judith Jeanne Turnbow
> Dorothy Jean Turnbow

Children of Creed Holt and Sarah Baily

5. **Harriet Baily Holt** was born 22 March 1910 in Hanford, Washington, and married Willard Lee in 1929.
Their two children were:
> Sarah Holt Lee
> George Raymond Lee

5. **Raymond Creed Holt** was born 5 February 1913, and married Betty Hamlink in Los Angeles.
Their two children were:
> Michael Barrett Holt
> Richard Power Holt

Child of Lyle Ormsbee and Helen Holt

5. **Nancy Ormsbee** was born 6 December 1914 in Walla Walla, Washington, and died 16 April 1989 in Virginia Beach, Virginia. She married Horace Simmons in Norfolk, Virginia, 21 July 1934.

Their child was:
> Martha Jean Simmons

Children of James Davis and Zeena Holt

5. **James Davis**, born in 1911.
5. **Walter Wood Davis**
5. **Duane Davis**

Children of Walter A. Holt and Blanche Clements

5. **Betty Holt** was born 30 April 1918 in Okanogan, Washington, and married Jay Graybeal 27 January 1942 in Pendleton, Oregon. Jay was born 22 January 1917 in Pendleton, Oregon.

Their four children were:
> Gary Holt Graybeal
> Nancy Graybeal
> Mark Finley Graybeal
> Maryl Graybeal

5. **Walter Holt**, born 26 July 1920 in Winthrop, Washington.
5. **Bruce Holt** was born 28 May 1923 in Oregon City and died in Pendleton 1 June 1991. He married Katherine Healy.

Their child was:
> Patti Jean Holt

Children of Albert Stuht and Norma Hamilton
Born in Colfax, Washington

5. **Ernest Stuht**, born 2 August 1898 and died in 1901.
5. **William Boyd Stuht**, born 23 January 1906 and died in 1968.
5. **Albert Stuht**, born in 1908 and died 15 February 1924.

Children of William Wirt Boone and Myrtle Turnbow

5. **Gwendolyn Eugenia Boone** was born 4 April 1906 in Palouse, and married Jack Frame.
Their child was:
> Robert Bruce Frame

5. **Horeb Max Boone** was born 1 April 1908 in Palouse, and married Iris Shinkowsky 20 July 1932.
Their child was:

Roberta Boone
5. **John Eldredge Boone** was born 14 January 1910 in Hanford, Washington, and died 13 July 1931 in Dayton, Washington.

5. **Janice May Boone** was born 15 December 1914 in Kennewick, Washington, and died 21 January 1969 in Pendleton, Oregon. She married John Jay Hoffman 28 July 1984.

Their two children were:
Jack Jay Hoffman
Ronald B. Hoffman

Child of Roy Patton and Eola Lexa Boone
5. **Marian Helen Patton** was born 23 October 1913 and died 23 April 1932.

Children of Holt Horeb Boone and Ella Sophia Thompson
5. **William Holt Boone** was born 18 April 1917 in Okanogan, Washington, and married Patricia Kemp in February 1941.

5. **Bernice Alma Boone** was born 9 June 1919 in Walla Walla, Washington, and married Gordon Lish 4 October 1941.

Their child was:
Shelly Marie Lish

5. **Doris Louise Boone** was born 4 September 1922 in Dayton, Washington, and died 24 March 1971. She married Robert Votendahl.

5. **Diane Muriel Boone** was born 8 December 1934 in Dayton, and married Douglas Allen Fogle 20 October 1956.

Their three children were:
Sheryl Fogle
Marcia Fogle
Michael Allen Fogle

Children of Ralph Reece Boone and Neva Marie MacGregor
5. **Betty Jean Boone** was born 13 June 1922 in Los Angeles, and married Edwin Lamson Peatross 26 June 1947 in Glendale, California. He was born 3 May 1915 in Phoenix, Arizona.

Their three children were:
Christine Susan Peatross
Scott Lamson Peatross
Bradley Boone Peatross

5. **Patricia Ann Boone** was born 29 March 1926 in Glendale, California, and married Charles Keith Railsback 21 May 1949 there. He was born 3 February 1923 in Vinton, Iowa.

Their two children were:
Stanley Keith Railsback
Brian Evan Railsback

5. **Stanley D. Boone** was born 8 January 1931 in Glendale, and married Kay Lynn Krechel 14 September 1963 in Los Angeles. She was born 23 November 1932.

Their child was:
Bonnie Erica Boone

Children of Alfred Preston Holt and Laurentia Marie Olbrich
Born in Portland, Oregon
5. **Walter Wesley Holt** was born 9 February 1928, died 25 October 1975 in Sao Paulo, Brazil, and was buried in San Francisco. He married Grace Woodworth 27 June 1964 in San Francisco. She was born 16 July 1935 in Atascadero, California.

Their child was:
Philip Preston Holt

5. **James Preston Holt** was born 14 October 1929, and married Anita Anderson 5 May 1962 in Mt. Vernon, Washington. She was born 25 October 1932 in Prescott, Wisconsin.

Their two children were:
Richard Preston Holt

Laura Katharine Holt

5. John Earhart Holt was born 14 October 1929 and married Tomo Hamamura 2 March 1958 in Ft. Pierce, Washington. She was born 2 January 1926 in Portland and died 18 December 1992 there, where she was buried.

Their two children were:

John Joseph Holt

George Frederick Holt

Children of Robert Goulding Kendall and Nancy Harriet Holt

5. Nancy Catherine Kendall was born 12 March 1926 in Portland, Oregon, and married George Francis 27 December 1947 there. He was born 3 May 1926 in San Mateo, California.

Their three children were:

Katherine Conant Francis

Linda Kendall Francis

Steven Samuel Francis

5. Sally Ann Kendall was born 12 August 1927 in Portland, and married John Cudlipp, Mr. O'Grady, and Mr. Hipp.

The child of John Cudlipp and Sally Ann Kendall was:

Theresa Lee Cudlipp

The two children of Mr. O'Grady and Sally Ann Kendall were:

Peggy Ann O'Grady

Timothy Kendall O'Grady

The two children of Mr. Hipp and Sally Ann Kendall were:

David Leonard Hipp

Daniel Lawrence Hipp

5. Robert Goulding Kendall was born 9 October 1931 in Manila, Phillipine Islands, and married Joanne Schulenberg 16 September 1961 in Seattle. She was born in Hillsboro, Oregon, 3 April 1934.

Their two children were:

Leslie Nancy Kendall

Kristin Edna Kendall

EIGHTH GENERATION

Children of Lloyd Grimes and Ida Helen Reese

6. Rodney Lee Grimes was born 18 November 1936 in Redding, California, and died 13 December that year in Harrisburg.

6. Carolyn Kay Grimes was born 8 February 1941 in Eugene, Oregon, and on 15 December 1962 married Carroll Neff in Atlanta, Georgia.

6. Mary Leanne Grimes was born 13 June 1943 in Macon, Georgia, and married Douglas Grimes in Atlanta on 29 December 1961.

Their four children were:

Vici Christena Grimes

Tracy Travis Grimes

Leanne Kaye Grimes

Lenore Lynn Grimes

6. Lloyd Harold Grimes was born 7 July 1947 in Sandersville, Georgia, and died in Cambodia 25 September 1970. On 30 November 1968 in East Point, Georgia, he married Marsha Henslee.

Their two children were:

Karen Jeanelle Grimes

Jason Adam Grimes

Children of Edgar Grimes and Marian Shelmau

Born in Corvallis, Oregon

6. Mahlon Henry Grimes was born 31 March 1941, and married Melissa Elliott in 1968.

6. Edna May Grimes was born 19 October 1942, and married Peter Robert Osborn Cheeke 27 June 1970 there.

Their four children were:

Tanya Elizabeth Cheeke

> Robert Allan Cheeke
> Ryan Pierre Cheeke
> Clark Douglas Cheeke

6. **Lee Allen Grimes** was born 23 April 1944 in Tallahassee, Florida, and married Annalee Marie Glennen.
Their two children were:
> Daniel Allen Grimes
> Jeffrey Neil Grimes

6. **Roy Edgar Grimes** was born 12 September 1946 in Corvallis, Oregon.

6. **Bruce Bell Grimes** was born 5 September 1947 in Corvallis, and married Heidi Hrung in Honolulu.
Their four children were:
> Dustin Chancellor Grimes
> Donovan Grimes
> Derrick Grimes
> Angelica Crystal Grimes

Children of Randall Grimes and Johnnie Joyce Attebug

6. **William Edward Grimes**, born 14 October 1948 in Eugene, Oregon.

6. **Glenda Joyce Grimes**, born 11 May 1950 in Eugene.

6. **Robert Randall Grimes** was born 27 April 1954 in Eugene, and in Bakersfield, California, 9 October 1982 married Melanie Norlund.
Their two children were:
> Stephen Randall Grimes
> Jennifer Michele Grimes

6. **Donald Frank Grimes** was born 11 August 1955 and died 10 February 1968 in Eugene.

6. **Dena Marie Grimes**, born 26 September 1957 in Springfield, Oregon.

6. **David John Grimes** was born 6 May 1959 in Springfield, and married Shelia Ann Dean 27 December 1980.
Their child was:
> Terra Lynn Grimes

6. **Cindy Christin Grimes**, born 25 January 1962 in Springfield.

Children of John Grimes and Helen June Murphy

6. **Jocile Norene Grimes** was born 26 January 1940 in Eugene, Oregon, and in Dallas, Oregon, on 17 September 1968 married Larry Clark Coate.
Their two children were:
> Linda Kathleen Coate
> Michelle Elizabeth Coate

6. **Michael Clinton Grimes** was born 14 April 1942 in McMinnville, Oregon, and married Joanne McEwen 23 August 1969.
Their child was:
> Angela Marie Grimes

6. **Steven Patrick Grimes** was born 13 October 1944, and married Linda Zito 29 August 1964.
Their children were:
> Brandon Patrick Grimes
> Bryan Kelly Grimes

Children of Elmer Grimes and Emily Cramer
Born in Eugene, Oregon

6. **Richard Grimes** was born 25 June 1942, and married Sandy.
Their three children were:
> Robert Grimes
> Kevin Grimes
> Sherri Grimes

6. **James Grimes** was born 15 November 1943, and married Deanna May Doane 20 May 1977 in Eugene.

6. **Eileen Grimes** was born 2 February 1945, and married John Haney 23 February 1970 in Reno, Nevada.

6. **Steven Grimes**, born 14 October 1946.

6. **Betty Grimes** was born 1 September 1948, and married Lawrence Kaluzok 17 May 1976 at Lake Tahoe, Nevada.

Child of Alfred Holt Grimes and Myrtle Hubbell
6. **Richard Grimes** was born 25 June 1942 in Tillamook, Oregon, and married Sharyl Gentry.
Their two children were:
>Megan Grimes
>Bevin Grimes

Children of Lyle Clark Grimes and Gwen Lamson
6. **William Ralph Grimes** was born 1 July 1938 in Portland, and married Diane Keim 6 December 1966.
Their three children were:
>Jenifer Grimes
>Michael Grimes
>Douglas Grimes

6. **Darby Clark Grimes** was born 20 May 1942 in Ft. Lewis, Washington, and married Richard Wyatt 6 April 1978.

Children of James Walp and Lucie Calef
6. **Ronald Walp** was born 6 November 1937 in Long Beach, California, and married Sandra Lovett, who was born in Seattle 7 May 1938.
Their two children were:
>Bradley Walp
>Jody Lynn Walp

6. **James Calef Walp** married Wilma Hanson.
Their three children were:
>Elliot Walp
>Brian Walp
>Dawn Walp

Children of Mansfield Howells and Elizabeth Calef
6. **Laura Howells** was born 23 June 1942 in Seattle and married David Myrvold.
Their child was:
>Christopher Allen Myrvold

6. **Richard Howells** was born 26 June 1945 in Portland, and married Katherine Weddle.
Their two children were:
>Lindsay Howells
>Evan Allen Howells

6. **Robert Howells** was born 17 July 1952 in Portland, and married Karen Halm, born 8 November 1955.
Their two children were:
>Nathan Robert Howells
>Rachael Elizabeth Howells

Children of Arthur Roosevelt Bowles and Norma Bloor
Born in Valhalla, New York
6. **Nancy Norma Bowles** was born 22 May 1936, and married Joseph Ellin in March 1962.
Their two children were:
>David Ellin
>Jane Ellin

6. **Carol Cynthia Bowles** was born 7 May 1938, and married Clyde Tyndall.
Their two children were:
>Timothy Parker Tyndall
>Elizabeth Tyndall

Children of Robert John Bloor and Martha Ann Emmel
6. **John Holt Bloor** was born 3 December 1944 in Staten Island, New York, and married Anita Gay Chew 1 July

1972 in San Diego, California.
> Their child was:
>> Katherine Helen Bloor

6. **Thomas Lewis Bloor** was born 4 June 1947 in Rochester, New York, and married Susan Welch 1 August 1969 in Dowagiac, Michigan.
> Their child was:
>> Alexis Susan Bloor

6. **Andrew Walter Bloor**, born 26 May 1950 in Rochester.

Children of Kenneth Turnbow and Margaret Woods
Born in Santa Rosa, California

6. **Melvin Kenneth Turnbow** was born 9 February 1941, and married Karine Bird in Miami, Florida, in March 1973.

6. **Carol Jean Turnbow** was born 23 December 1941, and married Charles Kling in 1962 in Lake Forest, Illinois.

Children of William Robert Turnbow and Dorothy Buchan
Born in San Francisco, California

6. **William R. Turnbow** was born 20 June 1940, and married Judith Aviani 22 August 1964. She was born in Oakland, California, 25 July 1943.
> Their two children were:
>> Brian Turnbow
>> Jacelyn Turnbow

6. **Judith Jeanne Turnbow**, born 7 July 1942.

6. **Dorothy Jean Turnbow**, born 11 October 1952.

Children of Willard Lee and Harriet Baily Holt

6. **Sarah Holt Lee** was born 18 August 1930 in Albemarle, North Carolina, and married William Stubblefield in Los Angeles in 1950.

6. **George Raymond Lee** was born 16 October 1931 in High Point, North Carolina, and married Marilyn Twitchell 26 November 1960 in Santa Rosa, California. She was born in Santa Cruz, California, 9 August 1931.
> Their three children were:
>> Sandra Jean Lee
>> Jeffrey Raymond Lee
>> Robert Raymond Lee

Children of Raymond Creed Holt and Betty Hamlink

6. **Michael Barrett Holt**

6. **Richard Power Holt**

Child of Horace Simmons and Nancy Ormsbee

6. **Martha Jean Simmons** was born 7 May 1936 in Norfolk, Virginia, and married Vernon Edward Stevens 21 July 1954 in Virginia Beach. He was born in Princess Anne, Virginia, 15 March 1928.
> Their three children were:
>> David Simmons Stevens
>> Nancy Lu Stevens
>> Vernon Edward Stevens

Children of Jay Graybeal and Betty Holt

6. **Gary Holt Graybeal** was born 20 January 1947 in Portland, and in Moses Lake, Washington, married Karen Duffy 15 August 1979. She was born 29 December 1952.
> Their two children were:
>> Kylee Graybeal
>> Travis Graybeal

6. **Nancy Graybeal** was born 11 October 1948 in Pendleton, and married Stuart Childs 29 December 1979 there.
> Their two children were:

Cameron Childs
Spencer Childs

6. **Mark Finley Graybeal** was born 11 September 1956 in Pendleton, where he married Connie Marie Crist 15 March 1980. She was born in Niagara Falls, New York, 20 February 1960.
Their two children were:
Jason Graybeal
Danielle Graybeal

6. **Maryl Graybeal** was born 19 September 1957 in Pendleton, where she married Barry Featherstone 6 August 1988.
Their two children were:
Alexandria Nicole Featherstone
Lauren Featherstone

Child of Bruce Holt and Katherine Healy
6. **Patti Jean Holt**

Child of Jack Frame and Gwendolyn Eugenia Boone
6. **Robert Bruce Frame**, born 19 August 1941 in Tacoma, Washington.

Child of Horeb Max Boone and Iris Shinkowsky
6. **Roberta Boone** was born 23 January 1935 in Colfax, Washington, and married a Mr. Lasata.
Their three children were:
Lisa Lasata
Eric Lasata
Keith Lasata

Children of John Jay Hoffman and Janice May Boone
6. **Jack Jay Hoffman** was born 4 May 1935 in Walla Walla, Washington, and married Gail Leach.
Their three children were:
Brad Hoffman
Brett Hoffman
David Hoffman

6. **Ronald B. Hoffman** was born 12 April 1945 in Pendleton, Oregon, and married Teresa Monahan.
Their three children were:
Heidi Hoffman
Andrea Hoffman
Nicholis Hoffman

Child of Gordon Lish and Bernice Alma Boone
6. **Shelly Marie Lish** was born 14 February 1949 in Richland, Washington, where on 27 December 1969 she married Peter Jay Sorenson, born 28 July 1947 in Bangor, Maine. She died 29 May 1985 in Houston, Texas.
Their four children were:
Holt Peder Sorenson
Sarah Vina Sorenson
Laura Khristina Sorenson
Clarissa Eliza Sorenson

Children of Douglas Allen Fogle and Diane Muriel Boone
6. **Sheryl Fogle**
6. **Marcia Fogle**
6. **Michael Allen Fogle**

Children of Edwin Lamson Peatross and Betty Jean Boone
Born in Glendale, California
6. **Christine Susan Peatross** was born 21 August 1951.

6. **Scott Lamson Peatross** was born 28 February 1954, and married Catherine Whitesell 29 October 1988.

6. **Bradley Boone Peatross** was born 29 June 1957, and married Grace Matusiewicz 13 August 1988.

Children of Charles Keith Railsback and Patricia Ann Boone
Born in Glendale, California

6. **Stanley Keith Railsback**, born 24 January 1953.

6. **Brian Evan Railsback** was born 24 September 1959, and married Sandra Lei Gary 6 August 1983 in Ventura, California, where she was born 15 December 1959.

Their two children were:
Travis Evan Railsback
Justin Gary Railsback

Child of Stanley D. Boone and Kay Lynn Krechel

6. **Bonnie Erica Boone**, born 14 October 1964 in Glendale, California.

Child of Walter Wesley Holt and Grace Woodworth

6. **Philip Preston Holt**, born 23 March 1965 in San Francisco.

Children of James Preston Holt and Anita Anderson
Born in Portland, Oregon

6. **Richard Preston Holt**, born 22 May 1963.

6. **Laura Katharine Holt** was born 18 March 1965, and married Michael James DeForge 13 May 1991 in Portland. He was born 4 January 1962.

Children of John Earhart Holt and Tomo Hahamura
Born in Sagami, Japan

6. **John Joseph Holt** was born 24 September 1960, and married Linda Church 20 June 1981 in Nyssa, Oregon, where she was born 12 October 1959.

Their four children were:
John Cristopher Holt
Lauren Mae Holt
Taryn Marie Holt
Kirsten Leigh Holt

6. **George Frederick Holt**, born 6 December 1961.

Children of George Francis and Nancy Catherine Kendall

6. **Katherine Conant Francis** was born 3 May 1950 in Portland, and married Kenneth Doctor 14 June 1971 in Santa Cruz, California.

6. **Linda Kendall Francis** was born 15 June 1952 in Eugene, Oregon, and married Stephen Carter 23 March 1973 in Roseburg, Oregon.

6. **Steven Samuel Francis** was born 29 July 1955 in Washington, D.C., and married Katie Lipscomb 16 August 1987 in South Bend, Indiana.

Child of John Cudlipp and Sally Ann Kendall

6. **Theresa Lee Cudlipp**, born 6 June 1948 in Portland, Oregon.

Children of Mr. O'Grady and Sally Ann Kendall

6. **Peggy Ann O'Grady**, born 11 January 1953 in Seattle.

6. **Timothy Kendall O'Grady**, born 2 July 1955 in Portland.

Children of Mr. Hipp and Sally Ann Kendall
Born in Portland, Oregon

6. **David Leonard Hipp**, born 19 May 1962.

6. **Daniel Lawrence Hipp**, born 6 April 1963.

William B. Moore Jr.

Children of Robert Goulding Kendall and Joanne Schulenberg
Born in Vancouver, Washington
6. **Leslie Nancy Kendall**, born 11 April 1964.
6. **Kristin Edna Kendall**, born 22 March 1967.

NINTH GENERATION
Children of Douglas Grimes and Mary Leanne Grimes
Born in Atlanta, Georgia
7. **Vicki Chrintena Grimes** was born 2 September 1963, and married Michael Saxon 16 November 1984 in Lilburn, Georgia.
7. **Tracy Travis Grimes** was born 8 March 1969.
7. **Leanne Kaye Grimes** was born 9 September 1974.
7. **Lenore Lynn Grimes** was born 9 September 1974.

Children of Lloyd Harold Grimes and Marsha Henslee
7. **Karen Jeanelle Grimes** was born 8 February 1965.
7. **Jason Adam Grimes** was born 28 July 1970 in College Park, Georgia.

Children of Peter Robert Osborne Cheeke and Edna May Grimes
Born in Corvallis, Oregon
7. **Tanya Elizabeth Cheeke**, born 22 April 1978.
7. **Robert Allan Cheeke**, born 2 March 1980.
7. **Ryan Pierre Cheeke**, born 4 May 1982.
7. **Clark Douglas Cheeke**, born 12 March 1984.

Children of Lee Allen Grimes and Annalee Marie Glennen
7. **Daniel Allen Grimes**
7. **Jeffrey Neil Grimes**

Children of Bruce Bell Grimes and Heidi Hrung
7. **Dustin Chandler Grimes**, born 3 September 1976 in Salem, Oregon.
7. **Donovan Grimes**, born 16 March 1979 in Salem, Oregon.
7. **Derrick Grimes**, born 8 April 1984 in Ketchikan, Alaska.
7. **Angelica Crystal Grimes** was born 19 February 1978 in Newport, Oregon, and died a few days later.

Children of Robert Randall Grimes and Melanie Norlund
Born in Bakersfield, California
7. **Stephen Randall Grimes**, born 17 September 1985.
7. **Jennifer Michele Grimes**, born 30 July 1987.

Child of David John Grimes and Shelia Ann Dean
7. **Terra Lynn Grimes**, born 9 January 1983 in Oregon City, Oregon.

Children of Larry Coate and Jocile Norene Grimes
7. **Linda Kathleen Coate** was born 15 October 1961 in Selma, Alabama, and married John Steven Rabb 28 July 1984.
7. **Michelle Elizabeth Coate**, born 9 February 1964 in Enid, Oklahoma.

Child of Michael Clinton Grimes and Joanne McEwen
7. **Angela Marie Grimes**, born 10 August 1973 in Portland.

Children of Steven Patrick Grimes and Linda Zito
Born in Eugene, Oregon
7. **Brandon Patrick Grimes**, born 21 October 1972.
7. **Bryan Kelly Grimes**, born 21 October 1978.

Children of Richard Grimes and Sandy
Born in Eugene, Oregon

7. **Robert Grimes**
7. **Kevin Grimes**
7. **Sherri Grimes**

Children of Richard Grimes and Sharyl Gentry

7. **Megan Grimes**
7. **Kevin Grimes**

Children of William Ralph Grimes and Diane Kein

7. **Jenifer Grimes**, born 19 January 1968.
7. **Michael Grimes**, born 7 February 1969.
7. **Douglas Grimes**, born 7 February 1969.

Children of Ronald Walp and Sandra Lovett

7. **Bradley Walp**, born 6 October 1962.
7. **Jody Lynn Walp**, born 27 April 1965.

Children of James Calef Walp and Wilma Hanson

7. **Elliot Walp**, born 23 May 1961.
7. **Brian Walp**, born 12 April 1965.
7. **Dawn Walp**, born 3 January 1967.

Child of David Myrvold and Laura Howells

7. **Christopher Allen Myrvold**, born 28 June 1973.

Children of Richard Howells and Katherine Weddle

7. **Lindsay Howells**, born 14 May 1981.
7. **Evan Allen Howells**, born 17 October 1983.

Children of Robert Howells and Karen Halm

7. **Nathan Robert Howells**, born 25 April 1986.
7. **Rachael Elizabeth Howells**, born 3 April 1988.

Children of Joseph Ellin and Nancy Norma Bowles

7. **David Ellin**, born 12 August 1965.
7. **Jane Ellin**, born 19 January 1970.

Children of Clyde Tyndall and Carol Cynthia Bowles

7. **Timothy Parker Bowles**, born 23 June 1961.
7. **Elizabeth Tyndall**, born 24 December 1974.

Child of John Holt Bloor and Anita Gay Chew

7. **Katherine Helen Bloor**, born 8 February 1981 in Buffalo, New York.

Child of Thomas Lewis Bloor and Susan Welch

7. **Alexis Susan Bloor**, born 7 June 1972 in Shelbyville, Illinois.

Children of William R. Turnbow and Judith Aviani

7. **Brian Turnbow**, born 9 November 1970 in Oakland, California.
7. **Jacelyn Turnbow**

Children of George Raymond Lee and Marilyn Twitchell

7. **Sandra Jean Lee** was born 13 March 1951 at Camp Pendleton, California, and married Keith Coultrap in

Phoenix, Arizona, on 25 July 1973.

Their four children were:

Keith Henry Coultrap

Joyce Patricia Coultrap

Raymond Craig Coultrap

William Lance Coultrap

7. **Jeffrey Raymond Lee** was born 14 July 1961 in Burbank, California, and married Katherine Wittbrout 24 September 1988 in Omaha, Nebraska.

7. **Robert Raymond Lee** married Keri Gloria Delgado 11 August 1984 in Phoenix, Arizona.

Children of Vernon Edward Stevens and Martha Jean Simmons

7. **David Simmons Stevens** was born 30 May 1957 in Virginia Beach, Virginia, and married Carrie Sisson there 21 July 1954.

Their child was:

Alex David Stevens

7. **Nancy Lu Stevens** was born 23 July 1958, and married Michael White in Virginia Beach 15 May 1977.

Their two children were:

Russ Michael White

Shelley Ann White

7. **Vernon Edward Stevens** was born 20 November 1963, and married Jane Hoover in Virginia Beach 14 February 1985.

Their child was:

Kyle Vincent Stevens

Children of Gary Holt Graybeal and Karen Duffy
Born in Pendleton, Oregon

7. **Kylee Graybeal**, born 9 June 1981.

7. **Travis Graybeal**, born 1 March 1983.

Children of Stuart Childs and Nancy Graybeal

7. **Cameron Childs**, born 21 August 1985 in Corvallis, Oregon.

7. **Spencer Childs**, born 30 December 1988 in Vancouver, Washington.

Children of Mark Findley Graybeal and Connie Marie Crist
Born in Pendleton, Oregon

7. **Jason Graybeal**, born 15 May 1981.

7. **Danielle Graybeal**, born 30 August 1982.

Children of Barry Featherstone and Meryl Graybeal

7. **Alexandria Nicole Featherstone**, born 20 February 1990 in Walnut Creek, California.

7. **Lauren Featherstone**, born 23 November 1992 in Naperville, California.

Children of Mr. Lasata and Roberta Boone

7. **Lisa Lasata**

7. **Eric Lasata**

7. **Keith Lasata**

Children of Jack Jay Hoffman and Gail Leach

7. **Brad Hoffman**

7. **Brett Hoffman**

7. **David Hoffman**

Children of Ronald B. Hoffman and Teresa Monahan

7. **Heidi Hoffman**

7. **Andrea Hoffman**

7. **Nicholas Hoffman**

Children of Peter Jay Sorenson and Shelly Marie Lish
7. **Holt Peter Sorenson**, born 29 December 1973 in Seattle, Washington.
7. **Sarah Vina Sorenson**, born 31 October 1975 in Everett, Washington.
7. **Laura Kristina Sorenson**, born 13 December 1977 in Provo, Utah
7. **Clarissa Eliza Sorenson**, born 14 November 1980 in Ohio.

Children of Brian Evan Railsback and Sandra Lei Gary
7. **Travis Evan Railsback**, born 14 June 1986 in Ventura, California.
7. **Justin Gary Railsback**, born 9 May 1988 in Athens, Ohio.

Children of John Joseph Holt and Linda Church
Born in Boise, Idaho
7. **John Christopher Holt**, born 9 August 1987.
7. **Lauren Mae Holt**, born 1 May 1990.
7. **Taryn Marie Holt**, born and died 5 April 1993.
7. **Kirsten Leigh Holt**, born 1 September 1994.

TENTH GENERATION
Children of Keith Coultrap and Sandra Jean Lee
8. **Keith Henry Coultrap**, born 2 May 1975 in Phoenix, Arizona.
8. **Joyce Patricia Coultrap**, born 14 March 1977 in Phoenix.
8. **Raymond Craig Coultrap**, born 19 October 1979 in Burbank, California.
8. **William Lance Coultrap**, born 11 December 1980 in Sierra Vista, California.

Child of David Simmons Stevens and Carrie Sisson
8. **Alex David Stevens**, born 17 October 1984 in Virginia Beach, Virginia.

Children of Michael White and Nancy Lu Stevens
Born in Virginia Beach, Virginia
8. **Russ Michael White**, born 9 June 1985.
8. **Shelley Ann White**, born 5 October 1989.

Child of Vernon Edward Stevens and Jane Hoover
8. **Kyle Vincent Stevens**, born 9 May 1988 in Norfolk, Virginia.

THIRD GENERATION
ALVIN EARLE WHITTEN
1. **Alvin Earle Whitten**, third child of Charles Whitten Jr., was born in 1803 in Greenville District, South Carolina, and married 22 February 1827 in Carnesville, Franklin, Georgia, Catharine Whiting Jones, born in 1815 there. He died 2 July 1852; she, 20 March 1851 in Wharton, Texas. Both are buried in that county. From Carnesville they moved to Holmes County, Mississippi, and, in 1847, to Matagorda County, Texas, where they settled in an area that became, in 1849, Wharton County.
Their nine children were:
    Julia F. Whitten
    Dudley J. Whitten
    Judge Terrill J. Whitten
    Maj. James Drayton Whitten
    Isaac B. Whitten
    Charles Henry Whitten
    Martha E. Whitten
    Alice C. Whitten
    William S. Whitten

FOURTH GENERATION
Children of Alvin Earle Whitten and Catharine Whiting Jones

2. **Julia F. Whitten** was born about 1828 in Carnesville, Franklin, Georgia, and married, about 1850 in Wharton, Texas, William C. C. Foster, born in Alabama. He died 16 July 1876, and was buried in Elmwood Cemetery in Memphis. She was robbed and murdered at her home near Wilson's Station, Shelby County, Tennessee 26 January 1879, and was buried with her husband. Julia F. and William C. C., with her brother and sister, visited Dr. Isaac Smith Whitten and his brother, Reverend James, in Georgia in 1851.

2. **Dudley J. Whitten** was born about 1829 in Carnesville, and died 15 July 1859 of yellow fever in New Orleans. He became infected while traveling to Alabama attempting to settle his father's estate.

2. **Judge Terrell J. Whitten** was born in 1832 in Carnesville, and married 4 August 1881, in Wharton, Texas, Sarah F. Still Callaway. She was born in 1845 in Alabama. Both died in Wharton: he, 28 March 1899; she, about 1892.

Their child was:
Fannie Eugenia Whitten

2. **Maj. James Drayton Whitten** was born 16 January 1833 in Carnesville, and married 18 April 1855 in Wharton, Corinne Levinia Thomas, who was born 10 April 1836 in Mississippi. The couple died in Wharton: he, 11 April 1878; she, 19 January 1907, and are buried in the East Avenue Cemetery there. He settled in Wharton in 1851, and served in the first Texas Assembly after the war with Mexico. James Drayton was listed as head of family in the 1880 census of Wharton County with wife, six children, and Banny Whitten born in Mississippi, age seventy. No Whitten of this line was in that state in 1810. For Banny to be a son of Charles Whitten Jr., he would have to have been born in South Carolina. Instead, he was a slave, left to James Drayton in his father's will.

Their nine children were:
Kathryn Marie "Kate" Whitten
Corinne Eahi Whitten
Dudley V. Whitten
James Dudley Dee Whitten
Corinne T. Whitten
Lula A. Whitten
William E. Whitten
Julia F. Whitten
Leona A. Whitten

2. **Isaac B. Whitten** was born in Carnesville about 1836 and died in Wharton, about 1894.

2. **Charles Henry Whitten** was born 25 April 1837 in Carnesville, and married 12 June 1865 in Montgomery, Alabama, Christiana "Anna" Turner, who was born 25 November 1845 in Rugeley Place, Lowndes, Alabama. They died in Rugeley Place, and were buried in Oakview Cemetery there: he, 16 November 1901; she, 27 September 1877. Charles was with his parents in Holmes County, Mississippi, in 1840 and Wharton, Texas, in 1850. He moved to Montgomery, Alabama, before 1860, and lived in Lowndes County from 1870 until his death. He served in Company E, 6th Alabama Infantry, CSA.

Their six children were:
Unnamed daughter
Harriet Anna Whitten
Charles Alvin Whitten
Julia Alice Whitten
Carlinne Whitten
Unnamed son

2. **Martha E. Whitten** was born about 1840 in Carnesville, and married in October 1857 in Wharton, Dr. Bushrod W. Bell, born 20 April 1820 in Alabama. Both died in Texas: Martha E., before 1894; Dr. Bell, 3 February 1883 in Ft. Bend. He was buried in Richmond, Texas.

Their three children were:
Frank W. Bell
Mattie E. Bell
Edward Dudley Bell

2. **Alice C. Whitten** was born in Lexington, Holmes, Mississippi, about 1844 and died 15 August 1870 in Memphis, where she is buried in Elmwood Cemetery.

2. **William S. Whitten** was born about 1846 in Lexington, Holmes, Mississippi, died 6 November 1917 in Caldwell, Burleson, Texas, and was buried in Wharton. The book *Texas and Texans* contains his story: William S. joined

the Army of the Confederacy in Alabama at age thirteen. He served in Company C, 35th Alabama Infantry, Prestons Brigade, Breckenridge Division, as messenger boy to Jefferson Davis in Montgomery until the Confederate capital was moved to Richmond, Virginia. He had dropped out of LaGrange Military School in Franklin, Alabama, to join. William S. fought at Vicksburg as a sharpshooter, and was captured during the battle of Iuka, Mississippi, on 19 September 1862. He was held at Corinth and Hatchie, Mississippi, and forwarded to Columbus, Kentucky. From there he was shipped on the steamer *Dacotan* to near Vicksburg, where he was exchanged 18 October 1862. On 27 April the following year William S. Whitten was discharged as a minor.

FIFTH GENERATION
Child of Judge Terrell J. Whitten and Sarah F. Still Callaway
3. **Fannie Eugenie Whitten**

Children of Maj. James Drayton Whitten and Corinne Levinia Thomas
3. **Kathryn Marie "Kate" Whitten** was born 31 May 1856 in Wharton, and married there in 1891, William A. Hansen, who was born 1 October 1864 in Denmark. Both died and are buried in Wharton, Texas: she, 8 January 1940; he, 22 April 1938. They were in Wharton in 1880; Colorado County, Texas, in 1900; and Galveston, Texas, in 1914. She entered the DAR (#130640) as descending from John Whitten, which was not the case. Kathryn Marie also was a Daughter of The Republic of Texas, (#1480), whose files contain a note from a Mr. Barnes: "your father came to Texas with my brother, E. S. Barnes, Uncle Jerry Sanders, and Willis Sanders." William A. Hansen was a pharmacist.
3. **Corinne Eahi Whitten** was born in 1857 and died before May 1866 in Wharton, Texas.
3. **Dudley V. Whitten** was born in 1860 in Wharton, and married 16 June 1886 Mattie E. Bell, daughter of Dr. Bushrod W. and Martha E. Whitten Bell, who was Dudley's aunt. Mattie was born in July 1870 in Richmond, Fort Bend, Texas. Dudley V. died before June 1900 in Wharton; Mattie E. died 15 June 1935 in Richmond, where she was buried.
   Their two children were:
   Eileen Aubrey Whitten
   Hamilton Dudley Whitten
3. **James Dudley Dee Whitten** was born 19 December 1864 in Wharton, and there married, on 7 September 1886, Alma C. Maguire, who died in August 1887 in Wharton, where she was buried. They had no children. On 30 December 1890 in Wharton, he married Minnie Irene Shannon, who was born 2 August 1870 in Texas. They died in Wharton where they are buried: he, 8 January 1936; Minnie Irene, 29 December 1943.
   The two children of James Dudley Dee Whitten and Minnie Irene Shannon were:
   Faye B. Whitten
   James Dudley Whitten Jr.
3. **Corinne T. Whitten** was born in May 1866 in Wharton, and married 2 March 1889 there, Burton Lee Blanchard, who was born in March 1863 in Georgia. She died after 1918 in Wharton; Burton Lee, about 1917 in Caldwell, Burleson, Texas. Corinne T. also joined the DAR (#78278) as descended from John Whitten. Actually, her ancestor was John's brother Charles. A letter, written about 1920 by a daughter of Rev. Arphax Whitten, contains these words: "as she never rested until she got in the DAR and was so haughty I never sought her company though I know she was a Whitten of Mississippi or Texas."
   Their child was:
   Ione Blanchard
3. **Lula A. Whitten** was born about 1869 in Wharton, Texas, and married 5 May 1886 there, Judge T. T. Adams, who was born in Mississippi. She died about 1890 in Wharton, for the Wharton County census of that year lists her children with the Hanson family in Colorado County, Texas.
   Their two children were:
   Katy Lin Adams
   John B. Adams
3. **William E. Whitten** was born about 1871 in Wharton, and there married on 26 April 1903 Ida S., who was born in 1878 in South Dakota. Both died before 1920 and were buried in Wharton County, Texas: William E., in the town of Wharton; Ida S., in El Campo. A deputy sheriff, he was alive in 1914. William E. murdered Ida S. while she was teaching school in El Campo, then, killed himself. Two of their children were present.
   Their three children were:
   Lt. Dudley E. Whitten
   Hilda Ida Mae Whitten
   Julia Corrine Whitten

3. **Julia F. Whitten** was born about 1874 in Wharton and died after 1880.

3. **Leona A. Whitten** was born about 1877 in Wharton, and married 22 December 1896 there, Robert E. Moreland, who was born in January 1871 in Alabama. He died after 1930 in Galveston, Texas. She was killed in a runaway horse accident in 1899 in Wharton. Her children were with her mother in the census of 1900.

Their four children were:

> Robert E. Lee Moreland
> Rembert B. Moreland
> Vockker Moreland
> Nancey Mae Moreland

Children of Charles Henry Whitten and Christiana "Anna" Turner

3. **An unnamed daughter** was born and died 23 February 1866 at Rugeley Place, Lowndes, Alabama, and was buried in Oakview Cemetery in Lowndesboro.

3. **Harriet Anna Whitten** was born 18 April 1867, died of typhoid fever 20 August 1888 in Rugeley Place, and was buried in Oakview Cemetery.

3. **Charles Alvin Whitten** was born 1 September 1869 at Rugeley Place, and married 4 November 1891 in Atlanta, Kitty Clyde Hearne, born 13 April 1869 in Eatonton, Putnam, Georgia. Charles Alvin was an Alabama legislator at age thirty-one. He died 16 March 1903 in Las Vegas, San Miguel, New Mexico, and was buried in Oakview Cemetery, Lowndesboro, Alabama. Kitty Clyde died 15 March 1915 in Eatonton.

Their four children were:

> Charles Alvin Whitten Jr.
> Richardson Whitten
> Clyde Hearne Whitten
> Margerite Whitten

3. **Julia Alice Whitten** was born 27 March 1872 at Rugeley Place, where, on 15 October 1895, she married David Edward Whitby, born 4 August 1873. They died in Georgiana, Butler, Alabama: Julia Alice, 29 August 1953; David Edward, 26 July 1904. After his death she married Wallace Hutchison, and was buried in Oakwood Cemetery.

The three children of David Edward Whitby and Julia Alice Whitten were:

> Thomas Whitten Whitby
> David Edward Whitby Jr.
> Julia Carlene Whitby

3. **Carlinne Whitten** was born 23 April 1875 at Rugeley Place, Alabama, and married 8 June 1898 in Columbus, Georgia, John Hubert Higgins, born 2 December 1868 in Montgomery. Carlinne died 16 April 1952 in Prattville, Alabama, and was buried in Oakview Cemetery, Lowndesboro, Alabama, with her husband, who died 14 August 1938 at Rugeley Place.

Their four children were:

> Julia Clara Higgins
> Carline Whitten Higgins
> Hulit Elizabeth Higgins
> Anna Turner Higgins

3. **An unnamed son** of Charles Henry and Christiana Whitten was born and died 20 September 1877 in Rugeley Place, Lowndes, Alabama. He was buried in Oakview Cemetery there.

Children of Dr. Bushrod W. Bell and Martha E. Whitten
Born in Texas

3. **Frank W. Bell** was born in 1859 and died 10 July 1935 in Wharton County, Texas.

3. **Mattie E. Bell** was born in July 1870 and died in Kaufman, Texas, 7 March 1935. She married her cousin Dudley V. Whitten 16 June 1886 in Wharton, Texas. Their family is described with that of Maj. James Drayton Whitten.

3. **Edward Dudley Bell** was born in 1869 and died in Gonzales, Texas, 3 March 1932.

SIXTH GENERATION
Children of Dudley V. Whitten and Mattie E. Bell

4. **Eileen Aubrey Whitten** was born in September 1887 in Wharton, died 3 April 1936 in Sugarland, Fort Bend, Texas, and was buried in Richmond County, Texas.

4. **Hamilton Dudley Whitten** was born 29 March 1890 and married 24 September 1915 in Richmond County,

212

Laura Sydney Phillips, born 3 August 1893 in Guy, Texas. He died 27 April 1930 in San Antonio, and was buried in Morton Cemetery Fort Bend County, Texas. She died 28 March 1984 in Richmond County, and was buried there.
Their child was:
Mattie Jo Whitten

Children of James Dudley Dee Whitten and Minnie Irene Shannon
4. **Faye B. Whitten** was born 5 January 1892 in Wharton, Texas, and married, after 1920, Edgar L. Moore, born 26 May 1891. Faye B. died 9 December 1951 in Wharton, Texas, and was buried there. Edgar L. died 10 October 1976 in Texas.
4. **James Dudley Dee Whitten Jr.** was born 17 July 1893 in Wharton, died of tuberculosis 14 February 1923 in Miami, Gila, Arizona, and was buried in Wharton.

Child of Burton Lee Blanchard and Corinne T. Whitten
4. **Ione Blanchard** was born in June 1889 in Alabama.

Children of Judge T. T. Adams and Lula A. Whitten
4. **Katy Lin Adams**, born in March 1887 in Wharton, married, had two sons, and lived in DeRidder, Louisiana.
4. **John B. Adams**, born in Wharton, Texas, 6 June 1891.

Children of William E. Whitten and Ida S.
4. **Lt. Dudley E. Whitten** was born in 1905 in Wharton, and married Dorothy, who was born in Dallas, Texas. He was buried in Arlington National Cemetery in Virginia.
4. **Hilda Ida Mae Whitten** was born in 1908 in Texas, and married Asa Kriegbaum. She died about 1984 in Albuquerque, New Mexico. She had received an old Whitten family Bible from sister Julia Corinne. When she died, it was sold at auction. In 1995 Asa was living in a nursing home in Albuquerque.
Their two children were:
Dr. Dudley Kriegbaum
Phillip Kriegbaum
4. **Julia Corinne Whitten**, born in 1909 in Texas, married William C. Rowlett about 1969, and died in Houston.

Children of Robert E. Moreland and Leona A. Whitten
4. **Robert E. Lee Moreland** was born in January 1898 in Wharton, died 30 January 1979 in Galveston, Texas, where he was buried in Forest Park West Cemetery.
4. **Rembert B. Moreland** was born in April 1910 in Texas, and married Marjorie Stocker. He died 5 April 1993 in Houston, and was buried in Forest Park Cemetery. Marjorie died later. They lived in Houston in 1979.
Their four children were:
Nan Moreland
Rembert Moreland Jr.
Robert Moreland
Randolph Moreland
4. **Vockker Moreland** was born in 1914 in Missouri and died before 1979.
4. **Nancey Mae Moreland** was born in 1917 in Missouri, married a Mr. Harris, and died after 1979 in Houston, Texas.

Children of Charles Alvin Whitten and Kitty Clyde Hearne
4. **Charles Alvin Whitten Jr.** was born 5 July 1893 in Eatonton, Georgia, and married 16 September 1924 in Moss Point, Mississippi, Grace Evans, who was born 19 March 1907 in Fulton, Alabama. They had two children.
4. **Richardson Whitten** was born 3 October 1894 in Eatonton, and died 18 June 1895 in Lowndesboro, Lowndes, Alabama.
4. **Clyde Hearne Whitten** was born 24 January 1897 in Eatonton, and married Frank Gordon. She later married J. B. McCart. Clyde Hearne died 7 December 1973 in Montgomery, Alabama.
4. **Margerite Whitten** died as an infant.

Children of David Edward Whitby and Julia Alice Whitten
4. **Thomas Whitten Whitby** was born 5 July 1897 in Selma, Dallas, Alabama, and married 21 May 1918 in

Glouster, Ohio, Mamie Woods. Later he married Lois Parkman, who died 14 January 1994 in Montgomery, Alabama.
The three children of Thomas Whitten Whitby and Mamie Woods were:
> William Simpson Whitby
> Alvin Turner Whitby
> Mary Alice Whitby

The two children of Thomas Whitten Whitby and Lois Parkman were:
> Thomas David Whitby
> Ethel Irene Whitby

4. **David Edward Whitby Jr.** was born 23 October 1901 in Selma, Dallas, Alabama, and married 16 June 1922 in Annapolis, Maryland, Helen Lee. He died 21 February 1983 in Georgiana, Butler, Alabama.
Their three children were:
> Edward Graham Whitby
> Wallace Whitby
> Margaret Whitby

4. **Julia Carline Whitby** was born 15 September 1904 in Lowndes, Alabama, and married 1 August 1925 in Montgomery, Max Wright. She died 12 October 1935 in Atlanta.
Their child was:
> Max Wright Jr.

Children of John Hubert Higgins and Carlene Whitten

4. **Julia Clara Higgins** was born 16 March 1899 in Montgomery, and married 11 June 1923 in Lowndesboro, Alabama, Albert Hamilton Collins, born 13 November 1894 in Fayette, Alabama. Julia Clara died 7 May 1969 in Auburn; he, 24 June 1945 in Lowndesboro. Both are buried in Oakview Cemetery, Lowndes, Alabama. After Albert Hamilton died, Julia Clara married Dr. Charles S. Isbell, who was born in Auburn.
The four children of Albert and Julia Collins were:
> Mavis Carline Collins
> Julia Claire Collins
> Elizabeth Anne Collins
> Alberta Collins

4. **Carline Whitten Higgins** was born 6 December 1900 in Montgomery, Alabama, and married 15 June 1929 there, Alfred Norman Ramage, born 29 November 1904. Carline Whitten died 28 July 1985 in Troy, Alabama, and was buried there. Alfred Norman died 27 December 1963 in Montgomery.
Their child was:
> Carline Ramage

4. **Hulit Elizabeth Higgins** was born 23 June 1903 in Montgomery, and married 23 December 1933 there, James Mallory Jenkins, born 12 February 1902 in Berney's Station, Alabama. She died 20 June 1993 in Wetumpka, Alabama; he, 1 March 1977 in Roanoke, Alabama, where both were buried.
Their two children were:
> Harriet Elizabeth Jenkins
> James Mallory Jenkins Jr.

4. **Anna Turner Higgins** was born 19 November 1907, and married 7 February 1931 in Lowndesboro, Alabama, William Benjamin Holmes, born 10 October 1892 in Montgomery. Both died in Montgomery, Alabama: she, 16 February 1988; he 6 January 1951. She was buried in Greenwood Cemetery there; he, in Oakwood.
Their two children were:
> William Benjamin Holmes Jr.
> Laura Ann Holmes

SEVENTH GENERATION
Child of Hamilton Dudley Whitten and Laura Sydney Phillips

5. **Mattie Jo Whitten** was born 27 September 1925 in Richmond County, Texas, and married in 1943, Earl William Gless, born 30 December 1921 in Louise, Texas. He died 25 October 1989 in Richmond, where he was buried.
Their three children, all born in Texas, were:
> Sydney Ann Gless
> Earl William Gless Jr.
> Terry Whitten Gless

Children of Asa Kriegbaum and Hilda Ida Mae Whitten
5. **Dr. Dudley Kriegbaum**, who lived in San Jose, California, in 1993.
5. **Phillip Kriegbaum**

Children of Rembert B. Moreland and Marjorie Stocker
5. **Nan Moreland**, who married James Liuzza.
5. **Rembert Moreland Jr.**, who married Kathleen.
5. **Robert Moreland**, who married Nancy.
5. **Randolph Moreland**

Children of Thomas Whitten and Mamie Woods
5. **William Simpson Whitby** was born 14 February 1919 in Glouster, Ohio, and married 17 June 1940 in Barberton, Ohio, Wanda Maxine Ward, born there 24 August 1925.
5. **Alvin Turner Whitby** was born 4 February 1920 in Glouster, and married 22 February 1941 in Akron, Ohio, Marian Florence Ward, sister of Wanda Maxine, born 19 February 1924 in Barberton.
5. **Mary Alice Whitby** was born 17 May 1921, and died April 1922 in Glouster, Ohio.

Children of Thomas Whitten Whitby and Lois Parkman
5. **Thomas David Whitby**, born 19 July 1933 in Montgomery, Alabama.
5. **Ethel Irene Whitby** was born 6 June 1935 in Montgomery, and married a Mr. Green.

Children of David Edward Whitby Jr. and Helen Lee
5. **Edward Graham Whitby**
5. **Wallace Whitby**
5. **Margaret Whitby**

Child of Max Wright and Carline Whitby
5. **Max Wright Jr.**, born 8 November 1929 in Georgiana, Butler, Alabama.

Children of Albert Hamilton Collins and Julia Clara Higgins
5. **Mavis Carline Collins** was born 26 May 1925 in Ramer, Alabama, and died 28 February 1937 in Lowndesboro.
5. **Julia Claire Collins** was born 27 August 1929 in Opelika, Alabama, and married 8 September 1948 in Lowndesboro, Albert James Smith Jr.
Their three children were:
    Julia Ann Smith
    Albert James Smith III
    William Collins Smith
5. **Elizabeth Anne Collins** was born 31 August 1931 in Auburn, Alabama, and there married, on 12 August 1955, Hugh Compton Williams, who was born 10 August 1931 in Nevada, Missouri. He died 13 November 1992 in Richmond, Virginia.
Their two children were:
    Collins Compton Williams
    Christianna Stearns Williams
5. **Alberta Collins** was born 13 February 1939 in Montgomery, and married 25 August 1960 in Auburn, Shelby Harold Baker, born 16 November 1937 in Opelika, Alabama.
Their two children were:
    Elizabeth Claire Baker
    Joseph Wiley Baker

Child of Alfred Norman Ramage and Carline Whitten Higgins
5. **Carline Ramage** was born 19 February 1934 in Troy, Alabama, and there married on 3 June 1961, Riley P. Green. He was born 1 June 1935 in Troy, where he died 10 August 1998.
Their three children were:
    Carline Ramage Green

Riley P. Green Jr.
Bettie Louise Green

Children of James Mallory Jenkins and Hulit Elizabeth Higgins

5. **Harriet Elizabeth Jenkins** was born 14 February 1939 in Roanoke, Alabama, and married 29 July 1961 there, Edward Dozier Landrum, who was born 6 September 1934 in Vredenburg, Alabama.

Their two children were:

Elizabeth Mallory Landrum

Floi Slater Landrum

5. **James Mallory Jenkins Jr.** was born 19 June 1942 in Roanoke, Alabama, and married 1 July 1967 in Birmingham, Virginia Lewis Holmes, born 27 September 1944 there.

Their two children were:

James Mallory Jenkins III

Mary Virginia Jenkins

Children of William Benjamin Holmes and Anna Turner Higgins

5. **William Benjamin Holmes Jr.** was born 8 January 1932 in Montgomery, and married 25 November 1955 there, Patsy Lynn Moores, born 5 March 1935 in Wetumpka, Alabama.

Their two children were:

Stephen Michael Holmes

Patrick Moores Holmes

5. **Laura Ann Holmes** was born 2 September 1940, and married 17 July 1965 in Montgomery, Alabama, James Foster Barnwell, born 22 October 1940 in Decatur, Alabama. Laura, who lived in Marietta, Georgia, in 1997, has made many important contributions to this genealogy.

Their two children were:

Laura Catherine Barnwell

Patricia Ann Barnwell

EIGHTH GENERATION
Children of Earl William Gless and Mattie Jo Whitten

6. **Sydney Ann Gless** was born 17 June 1944 in Rosenberg, where she married Richard J. Stadnicki 1 January 1966.

Their two children were:

Chad Joseph Stadnicki

Jill Laurett Stadnicki

6. **Earl William Gless Jr.** was born 17 June 1947 in Sugarland, Texas, and married 31 January 1970 Grace Ann Cordes in Rosenburg.

Their two children were:

Kelly Christopher Gless

Corey Michael Gless

6. **Terry Whitten Gless** was born 20 November 1950 in Richmond, and married 6 May 1982 in Austin, Timothy J. Dean.

Their child was:

Laura Delia Dean

Children of Albert James Smith Jr. and Julia Claire Collins

6. **Julia Ann Smith**, born 18 October 1951.

6. **Albert James Smith III**, born 8 December 1953.

6. **William Collins Smith**, born 23 November 1957.

Children of Hugh Compton Williams and Elizabeth Anne Collins

6. **Collins Compton Williams** was born 25 February 1962 in Bethesda, Maryland, and married 30 June 1984 in St. Louis, Missouri, Georgeann Hibbard, born 3 December 1961.

Their two children were:

Anne Meriwether Williams

Caroline Collins Williams

6. **Christianna Stearns Williams** was born 7 February 1964 in Bethesda, Maryland, and married 1 July 1989, Henrik Gunar Dohlman, born 9 November 1950.

Their child was:

Anders Benton Dohlman

Children of Shelby Harold Baker and Alberta Collins

6. **Elizabeth Claire Baker**, born 5 October 1962 in Hartsville, South Carolina.

6. **Joseph Wiley Baker** was born 30 May 1966 in Tifton, Georgia, and married 9 July 1988 there, Dawn Ann Pittman, born 8 January 1968 in Ithaca, New York.

Their children were:

Joseph Shelby Baker

Daughter Baker

Children of Riley P. Green and Carline Ramage

6. **Carlene Ramage Green** was born 4 August 1964 in Troy, Alabama, and married 1 August 1987 there, Judson Langley, born 1 June 1962.

Their children were:

Amanda Carlene Langley

Sally Marie Langley

6. **Riley P. Green Jr.** was born 18 January 1966 in Troy, Alabama, and married 10 November 1990 in Lake Wales, Florida, Yvonne Sweat, who was born 14 March 1967 in that state.

Their children were:

Whitten Green

Mark Green

6. **Bettie Louise Green**, born 4 November 1969 in Troy.

Children of Edward Dozier Landrum and Harriet Elizabeth Jenkins

6. **Elizabeth Mallory Landrum** was born 23 March 1966 in Wetumpka, Alabama, and married 19 June 1993 there, James Patrick Michalets.

Their child was:

Sarah Elizabeth Michalets

6. **Floi Slater Landrum**, born 30 December 1968 in Wetumpka, Alabama, and on 19 July 1997, in Montgomery, Alabama, married James Benjamin Rowlett.

Children of James Mallory Jenkins Jr. and Virginia Lewis Holmes

6. **James Mallory Jenkins III**, born 9 September 1970 in Sylacauga, Alabama.

6. **Mary Virginia Jenkins**, born 28 January 1974 in Birmingham.

Children of William Benjamin Holmes Jr. and Patsy Lynn Moores

6. **Stephen Michael Holmes**, born 5 June 1967 in Birmingham.

6. **Patrick Moores Holmes**, born 1 May 1971 in Dothan, Alabama, and married, in Montgomery, on 28 October 1995, Melissa Kay Spivey.

Their child was:

Jessica Renee Holmes

Children of James Foster Barnwell and Laura Ann Holmes

6. **Laura Catherine Barnwell** was born 29 October 1967 in Loma Linda, California, and married 21 July 1990 in Covington, Georgia, William Roger Singletary, born 22 June 1965 in Pensacola, Florida.

Their children were:

Meredith Adele Singletary

William Foster Singletary

6. **Patricia Ann Barnwell** was born 20 May 1970 in Montgomery, Alabama, and married Kenneth Lawrence Richardson in Marietta, Georgia, on 19 April 1997. He was born on 21 May 1971 in Raleigh, North Carolina.

William B. Moore Jr.

Children of Richard J. Stadnicki and Sidney Ann Gless
7. **Chad Joseph Stadnicki**, born 1 October 1971, in Richmond, Texas.
7. **Jill Laurett Stadnicki**, born 3 June 1975 in Richmond.

Children of Earle William Gless Jr. and Grace Ann Cordes
7. **Kelly Christopher Gless**, born 21 July 1973 in Houston.
7. **Corey Michael Gless**, born 20 September 1975 in Houston.

Child of Timothy J. Dean and Terry Whitten Gless
7. **Laura Delia Dean**, born 5 September 1989 in Houston, Texas.

Children of Collins Compton Williams and Georgeann Hibbard
7. **Anne Meriwether Williams**, born 16 June 1989 in Greensboro, North Carolina.
7. **Caroline Collins Williams**, born 6 November 1992 in Raleigh, North Carolina.

Child of Henrik Gunar Dohman and Christianna Stearns Williams
7. **Anders Benton Dohlman**, born 25 April 1993 in New Haven, Connecticut.

Children of Joseph Wiley Baker and Dawn Ann Pittman
7. **Joseph Shelby Baker**, born 28 May 1993 in Memphis, Tennessee.
7. **Daughter Baker**, born before 1997.

Children of Judson Langley and Carlene Ramage Green
7. **Amanda Carlene Langley**, born 19 December 1993 in Atlanta.
7. **Sally Marie Langley**, born 28 June 1998 in Atlanta.

Children of Riley P. Green Jr. and Yvonne Sweat
7. **Whitten Green**, born 2 April 1994 in Troy, Alabama.
7. **Mark Green**, born in November 1995 in Troy, Alabama.

Child of James Patrick Michalets and Elizabeth Mallory Landrum
7. **Sarah Elizabeth Michalets**, born 23 May 1998 in Asheville, North Carolina.

Child of Patrick Moores Holmes and Melissa Kay Spivey
7. **Jessica Renee Holmes**, born 24 June 1991.

Children of William R. Roger Singletary and Laura Catherine Barnwell
7. **Meredith Adele Singletary**, born 1 March 1995 in Conyers, Georgia.
7.**William Foster Singletary**, 16 January 1998 in Conyers, Georgia.

THIRD GENERATION
JOHN R. WHITTEN
1. **John R. Whitten**, fourth child of Charles Whitten Jr., was born in 1805 in Greenville District, South Carolina, and married Mary Phips 30 April 1833 in Franklin County, Georgia. She was born in Georgia in about 1812. John R. and brothers Alvin Earle and William S. paid taxes for each other in Franklin County during the years 1835–1838. John and Mary lived in Tuscaloosa County, Alabama, in 1840 with three children. The 1850 census of Choctaw County, Mississippi, shows they settled in the Greensboro community. The 1870 census lists him alone. He does not appear in 1880. She must have died before 1870, he before 1880.

Their six children were:
Ann Hasseltin Whitten
Alvin Earle Whitten
Sarah Whitten
Basil M. Whitten
Louisa Whitten

Elizabeth Whitten

FOURTH GENERATION
Children of John R. Whitten and Mary Phips

2. **Ann Hasseltin Whitten** was born about 1834 in Alabama, and married a Mr. Corbin in Choctaw County, Mississippi, about 1855. She, "a spinster," and their children were listed as living with her parents in the 1860 census.
Their children were:
Alice Corbin
Alvin Corbin

2. **Alvin Earle Whitten** was born about 1835 in Alabama. Enlisting 8 December 1861, he served as Teamster, Company D, 3rd Battalion, Mississippi Infantry, CSA. He married Frank, born about 1847 in Mississippi.
Their two children were:
John Whitten
Jesse Whitten

2. **Sarah Whitten** was born about 1838 in Alabama.

2. **Basil M. Whitten** was born about 1842 in Choctaw County, and enlisted in May 1861 in the 15th Mississippi Infantry, CSA. He was killed 5 April 1862 during the battle of Shiloh.

2. **Louisa Whitten** was born about 1844 in Choctaw County.

2. **Elizabeth Whitten** was born about 1849 in Choctaw County.

FIFTH GENERATION
Children of Mr. Corbin and Ann Hasseltin Whitten

3. **Alice Corbin**, born about 1855.
3. **Alvin Corbin**, born about 1856.

Children of Alvin Earle Whitten and Frank

3. **John Whitten**, born about 1868 in Choctaw County, Mississippi.
3. **Jesse Whitten**, born about 1873 in Choctaw.

THIRD GENERATION
MARIAH S. WHITTEN

1. **Mariah S. Whitten**, fifth child of Charles Whitten Jr., was born about 1810 in Pendleton District, South Carolina, and died after 1850 and before 1902 in Cherokee County, Alabama, where she is probably buried with her farther in an unmarked grave on the old home place.

THIRD GENERATION
ZACHARIAH WHITTEN

1. **Zachariah Whitten**, probably the sixth child of Charles Whitten Jr., was born about 1810 in Pendleton District, South Carolina, and married about 1830 in Pickens District, Margaret Whitten, who was born about 1815 there. Both died after 1870 in Abbeville, South Carolina. The reason to suspect that Zachariah was Charles Jr.'s son is that his was the only other Whitten family in the area of Pickens District, where Margaret's Whittens lived.
Their eight children were:
Malachi Burt Whitten
Margaret Whitten
Austin Whitten
Harriett Whitten
John Whitten
Baylis Whitten
A. F. Whitten
Zachariah Whitten

FOURTH GENERATION
Children of Zachariah Whitten and Margaret Whitten
Born in South Carolina

2. **Malachi Burt Whitten** was born about 1835 and married Mary Jane Burkett, born in 1841. He died in 1912;

she, in 1926.

> 2. **Margaret Whitten**, born about 1844.
> 2. **Austin Whitten**, born about 1847.
> 2. **Harriett Whitten**, born about 1848.
> 2. **John Whitten**, born about 1849.
> 2. **Baylis Whitten**, born about 1849.
> 2. **A. F. Whitten**, born about 1853.
> 2. **Zachariah Whitten Jr.**, born about 1855.

THIRD GENERATION
WILLIAM S. WHITTEN

1. **William S. Whitten**, seventh child of Charles Whitten Jr., was born about 1811 in Pendleton District, South Carolina, and married, about 1841 in Pickens District, Hariet A. Honet (or Howard. Son Jesse T. Whitten's headstone states mother is Honet. His certificate of death states Howard and was signed by his son, Erby J. Whitten), born about 1826 in North Carolina. Both died in Cherokee, Alabama, around 1900. Records of Franklin County, Georgia, show that William S. had extensive dealings there with brothers Alvin Earle and John R. during the years of 1835–1838. Shortly after 1900 his children sold all the Cherokee County, Alabama, land granted to his father, Charles Jr., and sister, Mariah S., in 1844–1845. William S., the last child left in that county, must have inherited it all. No records have been found of other land belonging to William S. and his wife, so it is easy to speculate that they lived on land belonging to his father or sister.

Their ten children were:

> Mary M. E. Whitten
> Duett Gordon Whitten
> Charles Mack Whitten
> George Whitten
> Silas L. Whitten
> William F. Whitten
> Martha Sharlotta Whitten
> Laura Permelia Whitten
> Willie Ann Whitten
> Jessie Thomas Whitten

FOURTH GENERATION
Children of William S. Whitten and Hariet A. Honet (or Howard)
Born in Cherokee County, Alabama

2. **Mary M. E. Whitten** was born 20 May 1842 in Cherokee County, Alabama, died 18 September 1905 at Bristow in that county, and is buried in Shady Grove Cemetery there. On 4 May 1880 she married William G. Brown in Dekalb County, Alabama. He was born 20 May 1842 in South Carolina, and died 24 May 1903 in Bristow. He served as private, Company C, 21st Regiment, Georgia, CSA, and was wounded at Manassas. In 1903 she sold her one-eighth interest in the land originally granted her grandfather and her aunt in Cherokee County, Alabama.

2. **Duett Gordon Whitten** was born in 1849 in Cherokee County, Alabama. In Etowah County, Alabama, he married Georgia Allen 1 January 1871, and died in 1900 in Lamar, Texas. She was born in May 1850 in Cherokee County and died 30 May 1930 in Hidalgo, Texas.

Their seven children were:

> Harry Whitten
> Laura Fern Whitten
> Laurella Whitten
> Mary Leala Whitten
> Ora Whitten
> Brode Hamilton Whitten
> John Lawrence Whitten

2. **Charles Mack Whitten** was born 5 December 1849 in Cherokee, Alabama, and married about 1874, Mary M. Allen, who was born 22 June 1855 in Alabama. Both died in Lamar County, Texas, and were buried in Antioch Cemetery there: he, 25 May 1943; she, 31 August 1896. After the death of Mary he married, about 1904, Martha E., born in Texas in 1861. Martha died before 1920.

The six children of Charles Mack Whitten and Mary M. Allen were:

Charles William Whitten
Nena Whitten
Luther M. Whitten
Ernest Garrett Whitten
Ukler W. Whitten
Carl Mack Whitten

2. **George Whitten** was born 5 January 1852 in Cherokee, Alabama.

2. **Silas L. Whitten** was born in January 1853 in Cherokee, Alabama, married Ruth Allen in 1878, and died 17 April 1926 in Lamar, Texas. Ruth was born in Alabama in 1861 and died about 1892 in Cherokee County. He married a Mrs. Carpenter in 1894. She died before 1900. They had no children. He was buried in Antioch Cemetery.

The seven children of Silas L. Whitten and Ruth Allen were:

Dorothy Whitten
Leota Whitten
Benjamin Washington Whitten
Joe Garrett Whitten
Jessie Lamar Whitten
Cora Whitten
May Whitten

2. **William F. Whitten**, born in 1854, died before 1860.

2. **Martha Sharlotta Whitten** was born 8 March 1856 in Pollard's Bend, Cherokee, Alabama, where she married Rev. Arlando Harris Jolly 14 March 1898. He was born in Dekalb County, Alabama, 9 November 1855, and became a Baptist preacher, pastor of Mount Vernon Church in Cherokee County. They died in that county: he, 21 February 1930; she, 14 March 1943.

Their seven children were:

Elbert L. Jolly
Rena L. Jolly
William Albert Jolly
Milton J. Jolly
Jesse G. Jolly
Alvis G. Jolly
Raymond Grady Jolly

2. **Laura Permelia Whitten** was born in February 1860 in Cherokee, Alabama, married Byram McHam in 1903, and died 29 April 1944 in Lamar County, Texas.

2. **Willie Ann Whitten**, born about 1861, died after 1880.

2. **Jessie Thomas Whitten** was born 19 February 1868 Cherokee County, Alabama, and married about 1892 there, Alma A. Higgins, born 8 August 1878 in Alabama. They died in Cherokee, and were buried in the Shiloh/Bothwell Cemetery there: he, 17 March 1920; she, 26 March 1927. Alma A. also married William Archer. Their daughter, Lillie May Archer, was later adopted by Erby Judson Whitten. In 1895 Jessie Thomas and Alma sold land that had been part of that originally granted his grandfather, Charles Whitten Jr.

Their five children were:

Erby Judson Whitten
Nora A. Whitten
Mamie P. Whitten
Homer Whitten
Rev. John Clint Whitten

FIFTH GENERATION
Children of Duett Gordon Whitten and Georgia Allen

3. **Harry Whitten**

3. **Laura Fern Whitten**

3. **Laurella Whitten**, who was born in 1872 in Cherokee County, Alabama.

3. **Mary Leala Whitten** was born 15 December 1875 in Centre, Cherokee, Alabama, and on 27 July 1891 in Paris, Lamar, Texas married Perry Mack Miller, born 18 April 1866 in Cherokee. They died in Hidalgo County, Texas: she, 6 September 1932, in Mercedes; he, 23 January 1951 in Weslaco.

Their six children were:

Colia Miller
Raymond Herman Miller
Arthur Milburn Miller
Morris Shepard Miller
Nina Bernice Miller
Oris Whitten Miller

3. **Ora Whitten** was born in 1877 in Cherokee County, Alabama, and married a Mr. Radliff. Their child was:

Robert Radliff

3. **Brode Hamilton Whitten** was born 3 August 1881 in Cherokee County, and married Kate Kaley. In 1917 he married Pearl Ellington, who was born in Mt. Pleasant, Texas. Brode was injured in 1929 while working on a railroad and died 24 June 1934 in San Benito, Cameron, Texas.

The four children of Brode Hamilton Whitten and Pearl Ellington were:

James Albert Whitten
Helen Whitten
Billy Jean Whitten
Robert Whitten

3. **John Lawrence Whitten** was born in September 1883 and died in 1931 in Paris, Texas, where he was buried in Evergreen Cemetery.

Children of Charles Mack Whitten and Mary M. Allen

3. **Charles William Whitten** was born 7 February 1875 in Cherokee, Alabama, died 27 October 1919 in Lamar County, Texas, and was buried in Antioch Cemetery there.

3. **Nena Whitten** was born in February 1877 in Cherokee County, Alabama, married Thomas Benham, and was buried in Evergreen Cemetery, Lamar County, Texas.

Their six children were:

Grady Benham
Mignon Benham
Horace Benham
Russell Benham
Eunice Benham
Dorothy Benham

3. **Luther M. Whitten** was born 5 February 1881 in Cherokee County, Alabama, and married about 1914, there, Bell Laura Norrell, born 10 March 1893 in Alabama. They died in Lamar County, Texas, and are buried in Evergreen Cemetery: he, 18 February 1955; she, 18 November 1967.

Their two children were:

Mary Whitten
Jack Whitten

3. **Ernest Garrett Whitten** was born in March 1885 in Cherokee County, and married 26 November 1908 in Lamar, Texas, Mattie Ervin, who was born 18 April 1887 in Biardstown, Texas. They died in Lamar County and were buried in Evergreen Cemetery: he, 26 December 1943; she, 25 January 1971.

Their seven children, all born in Lamar County, Texas, were:

Gladys Whitten
Carl M. Whitten
Lewis G. Whitten
Lou Nell Whitten
Alfred D. Whitten
Harold E. Whitten
Frank E. Whitten

3. **Ukler W. Whitten** was born 18 October 1886 in Cherokee, Alabama, and married about 1912, Rosa L., born 1 September 1889 in Texas. Ukler died 28 December 1932; Rosa, 17 June 1963 in Lamar County. They were buried in Evergreen Cemetery.

Their four children, all born in Lamar County, Texas, were:

Royce Whitten
Mary Louise Whitten

Ralph Ukler Whitten
Charles Mack Whitten

3. **Carl Mack Whitten** was born 3 November 1892 in Lamar County, died 17 March 1910 there, and was buried in Antioch Cemetery.

Children of Silas L. Whitten and Ruth Allen

3. **Dorothy Whitten**, born in 1879 in Cedar Bluff, Cherokee County, Alabama.
3. **Leota Whitten**, born in May 1881 in Cedar Bluff.
3. **Benjamin Washington Whitten** was born 25 February 1883 in Cedar Bluff, and married 6 July 1906 in Paris, Lamar, Texas, Gertrude Elizabeth Meeks, who was born 17 July 1892 in Shady Grove, Lamar, Texas. They died in Lamar County, and are buried in Evergreen Cemetery: Benjamin Washington, 25 February 1965; Gertrude Elizabeth, 29 September 1954. He also married 28 December 1959 in Paris, Texas, Josie Elizabeth Miller McGee, born 28 May 1895 in Biardstown, Lamar, Texas. Her first husband was Booker McGee, and her father was P. Reese Miller, brother of Perry Mack Miller, who married Mary Leala Whitten. Josie Elizabeth died 18 June 1981 in Paris, Texas.

The fourteen children of Benjamin Washington Whitten and Gertrude Elizabeth Meeks, all born in Lamar County, Texas were:

Bernard Ivy Whitten
Clifford Ausburn Whitten
Earnest Cecil Whitten
Roscoe Earl Whitten
Unnamed son
Leroy Whitten
Leota Mae Whitten
Erma Faye Whitten
Haskell Howard Whitten
Wilma Marie Whitten
Recile Whitten
Neva Maude Whitten
Margie Myrtle Whitten
Janice Ardith Whitten

3. **Joe Garrett Whitten** was born in November 1885 in Cherokee County, Alabama, and married about 1913, Laura Isabell Gates, who was born in 1892 in Louisiana. Joe Garrett died 26 December 1943 in Paris, Texas.

Their five children were:
Shirley Joe Whitten
Ruth Mignon Whitten
James Gates Whitten
John Paul Whitten
Rebecca Isabel Whitten

3. **Jessie Lamar Whitten** was born 28 September 1890 in Cedar Bluff, Cherokee, Alabama, and married about 1913 in Biardstown, Lamar, Texas, Ella Maude Ingram, born 4 June 1896 in Brookston, Lamar. Jessie L. died 7 December 1918 and was buried in Antioch Cemetery. Ella Maude died September 1976 in Lamar County, and was buried in Evergreen Cemetery.

Their two children were:
Alice Ruth Whitten
Clara Mae Whitten

3. **Cora Whitten** was born in 1890 in Cedar Bluff, Cherokee, Alabama.
3. **May Whitten** was born in May 1892 in Cedar Bluff.

Children of Rev. Arlando Harris Jolly and Martha Sharlotta Whitten
Born in Cherokee County, Alabama

3. **Elbert L. Jolly**
3. **Rena L. Jolly**, who married a Mr. Jones.
3. **William Albert Jolly**
3. **Milton J. Jolly**
3. **Jesse G. Jolly**

3. **Alvis G. Jolly**

3. **Raymond Grady Jolly** was born 14 August 1895, and married Burma Hicks in Pollard's Bend, Alabama, on 21 March 1918. She was born 16 July 1894 there. They died in Cherokee County: he, 10 November 1968; she, 23 May 1979.

Their nine children were:

> Thomas Hollis Jolly
> Raymond Troy Jolly
> Fannie Mae Jolly
> Alvis Chester Jolly
> Harold Jolly
> Barbara Lynn Jolly
> Julia Jolly
> Jeanette Jolly
> Bonnie Jolly

Louis Herman Jolly was born 16 August 1904, married Estelle Golden on 27 September 1924, and died 17 November 1966 in Charlotte, North Carolina.

Children of Jessie Thomas Whitten and Alma A. Higgins
Born in Cherokee County, Alabama

3. **Erby Judson Whitten** was born 5 July 1893, and married 23 November 1913 in Cherokee County, Darth Lou Davis, born 26 November 1892 in Alabama. Erby Judson died 26 September 1976; Darth Lou, 18 January 1968, in Cherokee. They were buried in Cherokee Memory Garden. He was called Early Joe.

Their two children, born in Cherokee County, were:

> Ralph Asbury Whitten
> Hobart Judson Whitten

3. **Nora A. Whitten** was born in June 1898, and married 9 May 1914 in Cherokee County, Lige Fortenberry. Both had died by 1994.

Seven of their children were:

> Jim Fortenberry
> Clyde Fortenberry
> Ollie Fortenberry
> Lloyd Fortenberry
> Ruby Fortenberry
> Jack Fortenberry
> Joyce Fortenberry

3. **Mamie P. Whitten** was born in 1904, and married 18 February 1923 in Cherokee, Alabama, Jessie Ragan. They died before 1994.

Their four children were:

> Bonnie Ragan
> Evelyn Ragan
> Clifford Ragan
> Tracy Ragan

3. **Homer Whitten** married 1 June 1929 in Cherokee, Alabama, Anna Mae Smith. He died in prison in the 1980s. They had a son, who died in Chattanooga, Tennessee.

3. **Rev. John Clint Whitten** was born in 1915, and married Lucille Dykes. He died in 1992 in Gadsden, Alabama. She was living there in 1994.

Their two children were:

> Thomas Whitten
> Frances Whitten

SIXTH GENERATION
Children of Perry Mack Miller and Mary Leala Whitten

4. **Colia Miller** was born 20 January 1894 in Paris, Texas, and married there Lloyd Lowman Hill, born 18 February 1895 in Paris. They died in 1984 in Texas: he, 22 May in Corpus Christi; she, 24 September in Alice, Texas.

Their two children were:

> Harold Lloyd Hill

Mary Francis Hill

4. **Raymond Herman Miller** was born 19 November 1898 in Lamar County, Texas, and, on 5 January 1924, married Esther Elizabeth Scheideman in LaCrosse, Rush, Kansas, where she was born 28 March 1907. She died in Edenburg 6 October 1938, after which he married Lillian and died 18 August 1972 in Weslaco.

The six children of Raymond Herman Miller and Esther Elizabeth Schneideman were:

Raymond LeRoy Miller
Perry Jo Miller
Delores Ray Miller
Sue LaVoyce Miller
Jakie Dell Miller
James Hugh Eugene Miller

4. **Arthur Milburn Miller** was born 16 November 1901 in Paris, Texas, and, on 1 August 1924, married Pearl Evelyn Benbow, born 10 August 1905 in LaCrosse, Kansas. They died in Weslaco, Hidalgo, Texas: he, 3 January 1977; she, 12 October 1982.

4. **Morris Shepard Miller** was born in 1903 in Paris, Texas, and, in 1930, married Laura Adeline Smith, who was born in 1902 in Paducah, Kentucky, and died in 1946 in Weslaco. In 1953 he married Mary Pansy Huff, born 10 June 1902 and died in 1978.

The six children of Morris Shepard Miller and Laura Adeline Smith were:

Donald Morris Miller
Robert Mack Miller
David Smith Miller
Charles Edgar Miller
Kenneth Miller
Judith Ann Miller

4. **Nina Bernice Miller** was born 10 August 1908 in Paris, Texas, and married, 18 April 1930 in Raymondville, Willacy, Texas, Howell Newby, who was born 11 June 1902 in Cabot, Arkansas, and died 4 March 1964 in Weslaco, Texas. In 1970 Nina Bernice married Charles Ellis Dewey.

The three children of Howell Newby and Nina Bernice Miller were:

Barbara Yvonne Newby
Glenn Howell Newby
Glenda Hal Newby

4. **Oris Whitten Miller** was born 25 September 1910, and married Marie Reynolds, born in 1910 in Paris, Texas. She died in 1947 in Corpus Christi, and he married, in Nacogdoches, Texas, in 1943, Thelma, born in Palestine, Texas. Thelma died in 1976; he, in 1963, in Harlingen.

The child of Oris Whitten Miller and Marie Reynolds was:

Clifton Mack Miller

Child of Mr. Radliff and Ora Whitten

4. **Robert Radliff**

Children of Brode Hamilton Whitten and Pearl Ellington

4. **James Albert Whitten** was born 25 July 1918 in Cameron County, Texas, and married Nellie Geneva Worlow in 1940.

Their two children were:

James A. Whitten Jr.
Dale Wayne Whitten

4. **Helen Whitten** was born in Cameron County in 1920, and married J. W. Trimble and Ashley L. Stephenson.

The child of J. W. Trimble and Helen Whitten was:

Betty Jo Trimble

The child of Ashley L. Stephenson and Helen Whitten was:

Judy Stephenson

4. **Billy Jean Whitten** was born in 1920 in Cameron County, and married a Mr. Bolton.

Their two children were:

Gloria Bolton
Karen Bolton

William B. Moore Jr.

4. **Robert Whitten** was born in San Benito, Cameron, Texas, in 1926.
His child was:
>Robert Whitten Jr.

Children of Thomas Benham and Nena Whitten
4. **Grady Benham**
4. **Mignon Benham**
4. **Horace Benham**, who married Opal Hood.
4. **Russell Benham**
4. **Eunice Benham**, who married Dudley Rogers.
4. **Dorothy Benham**

Children of Luther M. Whitten and Bell Laura Norrell
4. **Mary Whitten** was born 1915 in Lamar, Texas, married Morris Haynes, died before 1994, and was buried in Evergreen Cemetery.
4. **Jack Charles Whitten** was born August 1918 in Lamar, Texas, died 31 July 1941 there, and was buried in Evergreen Cemetery.

Children of Ernest Garrett Whitten and Mattie Ervin
4. **Gladys Whitten** was born 1911, and married a Mr. Hutchinson. They lived in Waco, but she was buried in Dallas, Texas.
4. **Carl M. Whitten** was born 25 August 1912 and married 29 July 1956, in Lamar County, Iva S. Reagan. They died in Paris, Lamar, Texas, and were buried in Evergreen Cemetery: Carl M., 9 December 1992; Iva S., 3 September 1989.
4. **Lewis G. Whitten**, born May 1919, lived in Houston.
4. **Lou Nell Whitten** married Scott Perrine, who died before 1994. They lived in Vancouver, Washington.
4. **Alfred D. Whitten** married Candy Perrine. He was buried in Australia.
4. **Harold E. Whitten** lived in El Paso, Texas.
4. **Frank E. Whitten** married Evelyn and lived in Paris, Texas.

Children of Ukler W. Whitten and Rosa L.
4. **Royce Whitten** was born in 1913, and married in Paris, Texas, Gladys Miears. He died in 1969 and was buried in Denton, Texas.
4. **Mary Louise Whitten** was born in 1916, and married Lloyd Sterling. Both are buried in Evergreen Cemetery, Lamar County, Texas.
4. **Ralph Ukler Whitten** was born in Biardstown, Texas, and married Alice Kalinec. He died 14 May 1963 in Tyler, Texas, and was buried in Evergreen Cemetery, Lamar, Texas.
4. **Charles Mack Whitten**, born in 1926, married Mary Louise Cowley.

Children of Benjamin Washington Whitten and Gertrude Elizabeth Meeks
4. **Bernard Ivy Whitten** was born 4 August 1909, and married 13 September 1945 in Dallas, Floy Haney. He died 18 October 1982 in Dallas.
4. **Clifford Ausburn Whitten** was born 16 May 1911, and married 27 April 1932, Myrle Kirkham. He died 8 August 1932 in Roxton, and was buried in Restland Cemetery, Lamar, Texas.
4. **Earnest Cecil Whitten**, born 26 August 1912 in Biardstown, Lamar, Texas.
4. **Roscoe Earl Whitten** was born 25 November 1914 in Howland, Texas, and married 19 September 1942 in Colorado Springs, Colorado, Jessie Capp. He died 16 January 1985 in St. Louis, Missouri.
4. **An unnamed son** was born and died 17 December 1916 in Howland.
4. **LeRoy Whitten** was born 20 May 1918 in Howland, and married 3 August 1940 in Paris, Texas, Yvetta Virginia Sibert, who died 2 November 1983 and was buried in Evergreen Cemetery.
4. **Leota Mae Whitten** was born 13 February 1920 in Howland, and married 14 May 1938, LeRoy Loggins. After his death she married a Mr. Bailey, died 11 January 1993 in Paris, and was buried in Evergreen Cemetery.
4. **Erma Faye Whitten** was born 25 March 1922 in Howland, and married 17 October 1947 in Paris, Clyde Jim Rhoades.
4. **Haskell Howard Whitten** was born 6 January 1924 in Howland, and married 6 August 1943 in Faught, Texas, Margaret Virginia Thweatt. He died 17 June 1989 in Dallas.

226

4. **Wilma Marie Whitten** was born 6 June 1925 in Howland, and married 28 April 1943, in Paris, Robert Lee Shugart.

4. **Recile Whitten** was born in 1926 in Howland and died there, 19 February 1927.

4. **Neva Maude Whitten** was born 8 December 1927 in Howland, and died 2 February 1930 in Lamar County, Texas.

4. **Margie Myrtle Whitten** was born 10 April 1931 in Howland, and married 27 October 1950 in Pampa, Texas, Wallace Junior McPeak.

4. **Janice Ardith Whitten** was born 17 May 1932 in Howland, and married 11 September 1952 in Dallas, Eugene Leslie McDonald Jr.

Children of Joe Garrett Whitten and Laura Isabel Gates

4. **Shirley Joe Whitten**, who married Eldon Miller.

4. **Ruth Mignon Whitten** was born in 1914 in Lamar, Texas, died 10 February 1917 there, and was buried in Evergreen Cemetery.

4. **James Gates Whitten** was born in 1916, died 4 February 1986 in Lamar County, and was buried in Evergreen Cemetery.

4. **John Paul Whitten** was born 6 October 1922 in Biardstown, and married 14 December 1945, Opal Morgan. On 4 June 1960, in Dallas, he married Margaret Alexander, died 30 April 1986 in Paris, and was buried in Evergreen Cemetery.

The child of John Paul Whitten and Opal Morgan was:

Thomas Joe Whitten

4. **Rebecca Isabel Whitten** was born 14 December 1926 in Brookston, Lamar, Texas, and married 25 September 1949 in Paris, Floyd Edward Malone.

Children of Jessie Lamar Whitten and Ella Maude Ingram

4. **Alice Ruth Whitten**, born in 1915 in Lamar County, married Robert Leigh about 1940 in Paris.

4. **Clara Mae Whitten** was born 25 November 1916 in Lamar, and married 27 June 1937 in Hugo, Choctaw, Oklahoma, Joseph Bailey McCommon, born 14 October 1914 in Grant, Oklahoma. Clara Mae died 10 September 1951 in Lamar, Texas; he, 31 January 1972 in San Francisco, California.

Their child was:

William Vernon McCommon

Children of Raymond Grady Jolly and Burma Hicks

4. **Thomas Hollis Jolly**

4. **Raymond Troy Jolly** was born 3 December 1924 in Cherokee, Alabama, and was killed 17 September 1944 at Radschied, Germany, while fighting in WWII.

4. **Fannie Mae Jolly**, who married a Mr. Mallet.

4. **Alvis Chester Jolly** was born 31 May 1927 in Cherokee, and married Josephine Acker 29 April 1930.

Their two children were:

Troy Lee Jolly

Alvis Steven Jolly

4. **Rev. Harold Jolly**, who became a Baptist preacher.

4. **Barbara Lynn Jolly**, who was born 13 July 1930 in Cherokee and died 12 January 1982. She married Messrs. Strawbridge and Jahns.

4. **Julia Jolly** was born 13 September 1934, and married Mr. Bishop and Mr. Whaley.

4. **Jeanette Jolly**, twin of Bonnie Jolly, was born 13 September 1934 in Cherokee, and married Mr. Hogan.

4. **Bonnie Jolly** married a Mr. Ingram.

Children of Erby Judson Whitten and Darth Lou Davis

4. **Ralph Asbury Whitten** was born 24 March 1919, and married Evelyn Vaughn, born about 1925 in Cherokee County. He died 24 March 1984 in Centre, Alabama, and was buried in Cherokee Memory Garden. She was living in 1995. While visiting Cherokee County, Alabama, many years ago, author William C. Whitten Jr. met this man who pointed from Centre northwest across Lake Weiss toward Leesburg and said, "My great grandparents are buried over there in unmarked graves." He was referring to William S. and Hariet Honet (or Howard) Whitten, son and daughter-in-law of Charles Whitten Jr. We now know that the land they lived on and later inherited from Charles Whitten Jr. lies where Ralph Whitten

was pointing.

Their four children were:

Lowelle Gene Whitten

LaVaughn Whitten

Dianne Whitten

Charlene Whitten

4. **Hobart Judson Whitten** was born 13 August 1914, and married Sybil Helms. After her death he married Sybil Richardson. Hobart Judson died in January 1992 in Gadsden, Alabama, and was buried in Union Hill Cemetery there.

The two children of Hobart Judson Whitten and Syble Helms were:

Hobart Judson Whitten Jr.

Mary Lynn Whitten

Children of Lige Fortenberry and Nora A. Whitten
Born in Cherokee County, Alabama

4. **Jim Fortenberry**

4. **Clyde Fortenberry**

4. **Ollie Fortenberry**

4. **Lloyd Fortenberry**

4. **Ruby Fortenberry**, who married a Mr. Haynie.

Their two children were:

Hoyt Haynie

Jerry Haynie

4. **Jack Fortenberry** was living in Centre, Alabama, in 1995. He was president of a local bank.

4. **Joyce Fortenberry**

Children of Jessie Ragan and Mamie P. Whitten

4. **Bonnie Ragan**

4. **Evelyn Ragan**

4. **Clifford Ragan**

4. **Tracy Ragan**

Children of Rev. John Clint Whitten and Lucille Dykes

4. **Thomas Whitten**, who lived in Gadsden with his mother in 1994.

4. **Frances Whitten**, who married Gene.

SEVENTH GENERATION

Children of Lloyd Lowman Hill and Colia Miller

5. **Harold Lloyd Hill**, who was born 24 July 1925 in Mercedes, Texas, and married 28 February 1950 in New Iberia, Louisiana, Gladys Ann Nunnelly, born 5 October 1925 in Gatesville, Texas.

Their three children were:

Charles Edward Hill

Caroline Ann Hill

Evelyn Lee Hill

5. **Mary Frances Hill** was born 27 July 1929 in Edcouch, Texas; and, in Alice, Texas, on 15 June 1957, married George F. Center, who was born in Winslow, Oklahoma, and died 17 July 1973.

Children of Raymond Herman Miller and Esther Elizabeth Scheideman

5. **Raymond LeRoy Miller**, born in 1924.

5. **Perry Jo Miller** was born 30 December 1925 in Mercedes, and married Melvin Don Gilmore, who was born 19 March 1923 and died in December 1966. On October 15 1952 in Grand Prairie, Texas, she married Paul Hare, who was born 5 October 1923 in Dodge City, Kansas.

The two children of Melvin Don Gilmore and Perry Jo Miller were:

Laura Sue Gilmore

Pamella Reigh Gilmore

The three children of Paul Hare and Perry Jo Miller were:

228

Michael Paul Hare

James Edward Hare

Virginia Eileen Hare

5. **Dolores Ray Miller** was born 22 November 1928 in Mercedes, Hidalgo, Texas, and married William Wood, after which on 12 April 1947 she married Joseph Bruce Savage, born 18 March 1928 in Alma, Crawford, Arkansas.

The two children of Joseph Bruce Savage and Delores Ray Miller were:

Joseph Dwight Savage

Stephan Dane Savage

5. **Sue LaVoyce Miller** was born 4 September 1931 in Edcouch, Hidalgo, Texas, and on 1 June 1949 in Raymondville married Earl Edward Madden, born 6 August 1927 in San Antonio.

Their three children were:

Esther Earlene Madden

Brenda Sue Madden

Earl Edward Madden II

5. **Jakie Dell Miller** was born 2 July 1934 in Edcouch, Hidalgo, Texas, and in Raymondville, Willacy County, married Cecil Bert Shields on 22 September 1951. He was born 14 December 1934 in Lambert, Quitman, Mississippi.

Their four children were:

Elizabeth Gail Shields

Kay Lugene Shields

Aaron Lawrence Shields

Bruce Gordon Shields

5. **James Hugh Eugene Miller** was born 17 September 1938 in Edenburg, and married Virginia Lee Polvado 27 October 1962 in Weslaco. She was born 11 August 1941 in San Antonio. On 6 January 1984 he married Doris Ann Burkholder, born 20 March 1935 in Monte Vista, Rio Grande, Texas.

The two children of James Hugh Eugene Miller and Virginia Lee Polvado were:

Janine Denise Miller

James Hugh Elwood Miller

Children of Morris Shepard Miller and Laura Adeline Smith

5. **Donald Morris Miller** was born in 1931 in Weslaco, where he married, 5 August 1956, Jo Ellen Phippeny, who was born 16 February 1936.

Their three children were:

Patricia Lynne Miller

Lisa Gayle Miller

Rebecca Mae Miller

5. **Robert Mack Miller** was born 31 October 1933 in Weslaco and in Los Fresnos, Texas, 23 August 1962, married Mary Martha Amayo, born 13 December 1938 in Bayview, Texas.

Their three children were:

Mark Maurice Miller

Myliss Marie Miller

Michael Mack Miller

5. **David Smith Miller** was born 18 January 1936 in Weslaco, and in Rio Hondo 18 August 1959 married Dolores Jean Kilgore, born 21 July 1941 in San Benito.

Their three children were:

Melinda Jean Miller

Lea Christine Miller

Deana Joane Miller

5. **Charles Edgar Miller** was born 7 November 1937 in Weslaco, and married Nancy Susannah Nuchols 10 October 1959 in Santa Rosa. She was born 10 December 1940 in Mercedes.

Their two children were:

Raymond Charles Miller

Steven Duane Miller

5. **Kenneth Miller** was born 25 October 1939 in Weslaco, and, in Raymondville 4 June 1969, married Marion Hellman, born 31 October 1947.

Their five children were:

        Kevin Lowell Miller
        Richard Douglas Miller
        Matthew Henry Miller
        Laura Delaine Miller
        Freida Christine Miller

5. **Judith Ann Miller** was born 1 December 1941 in Mercedes, and married Robert Steven Slovak there, 25 June 1960. He was born in December 1930 in Wichita Falls, Texas.

Their four children were:
        Sharon Ann Slovak
        Barbara Lorraine Slovak
        Marilyn Hope Slovak
        Laura Stephanie Slovak

Children of Howell Newby and Nina Bernice Miller
Born in Mercedes, Texas

5. **Barbara Yvonne Newby** was born 27 March 1936, and in Elsa, Texas, on 20 May 1956, married Jacob DeWitt Hausenfluck, born 20 November 1934 in Pharr, Texas.

Their three children were:
        Terry Lee Hausenfluck
        Beverly Ann Hausenfluck
        Glynda Kay Hausenfluck

5. **Glenn Howell Newby** was born 10 April 1939, and married there on 25 March 1961 Willie Jean Armstrong, born 20 August 1943 in Weslaco. In Harlingen, Texas, 17 July 1986 he married Cynthia Ann Hudson LaFond, who was born 4 November 1946 in Houston.

The three children of Glenn Howell Newby and Willie Jean Armstrong were:
        Perry Glenn Newby
        Jay Howell Newby
        Deborah Kay Newby

5. **Glenda Hal Newby** was born 10 April 1939 in Mercedes, and 13 April 1960 in Donna, Texas, married Joe Clifford Peters, born 22 February 1937 there.

Their three children were:
        Susan Marie Peters
        Clifford Wayne Peters
        Kathy Jo Peters

Child of Oris Whitten Miller and Marie Reynolds

5. **Clifton Mack Miller** was born 28 May 1937 in Mercedes, and married Dorothy Ann Affolter 20 November 1959 in Rio Hondo. She was born 11 November 1941 in Harlingen.

Their three children were:
        Terrell Mack Miller
        James Lee Miller
        Rhonda Ann Miller

Children of James Albert Whitten and Nellie Geneva Worlow

5. **James Albert Whitten Jr.** was a son of his mother by a previous marriage to Burl Wortham. James Albert adopted him and changed his name.

5. **Dale Wayne Whitten** was born 13 October 1942 in Cameron County, Texas, served with the police in Miami, Florida, for twenty-four years before retiring. In 1997 he lived near Rome, Georgia.

Child of J. B. Trimble and Helen Whitten
5. **Betty Jo Trimble** was born in San Benito, Texas.

Child of Ashley L. Stephenson and Helen Whitten
5. **Judy Stephenson** was born in San Benito.

Two Sons of Charles Whitten

Children of Mr. Bolton and Billy Jean Whitten
5. **Gloria Bolton** was born in California.
5. **Karen Bolton** was born in California.

Child of Robert Whitten
5. **Robert Whitten Jr.**

Child of John Paul Whitten and Opal Morgan
5. **Thomas Joe Whitten**

Child of Joseph Bailey McCommon and Clara Mae Whitten
5. **William Vernon McCommon** was born 30 January 1938 in Paris, Texas, and married 13 November 1959 in Redding, Shasta, California, Irene Dwade Martin, born 10 June 1938 in Modesto, California.

Children of Alvis Chester Jolly and Josephine Acker
Born in Cherokee County, Alabama
5. **Troy Lee Jolly** was born 16 April 1948, and married Edna Brannan 10 May 1969. She was born 27 November 1949.
Their two children were:
> David Lee Jolly
> Michael Brian Jolly
5. **Alvis Steven Jolly** was born on 5 April 1949, and married Debra Ferguson.
Their five children were:
> Steven Shane Jolly
> Melissa Ann Jolly
> Raymond Harvey Jolly
> Roy Glenn Jolly
> Gregory Dale Jolly

Children of Ralph Asbury Whitten and Evelyn Vaughn
5. **Lowelle Gene Whitten**, who married Katie.
Their two children were:
> Timothy Gene Whitten
> Tammi Sue Whitten
5. **LaVaughn Whitten**, who married Jan. They also have a son and daughter.
5. **Dianne Whitten**
5. **Charlene Whitten**, who married Richard Money.

Children of Hobart Judson Whitten and Sybil Helms
5. **Hobart Judson Whitten Jr.** was born in Alabama, and married Gloria Shaw. On February 4 1983 he married Carol Tillery. They were divorced in 1994.
The child of Hobart Jr. and Gloria Shaw Whitten was:
> Tyler Wade Whitten
5. **Mary Lynn Whitten**, who married Comer Ellis.

Children of Mr. Haynie and Ruby Fortenberry
5. **Hoyt Haynie**
5. **Jerry Haynie**

EIGHTH GENERATION
Children of Harold Lloyd Hill and Gladys Ann Nunnelly
6. **Charles Edward Hill** was born 12 December 1946 in Pasadena, Texas, and married Marilyn Smith.
Their four children were:
> Betty Jo Hill
> Connie Hill

Gladys Angel Hill

Michael Hill

6. **Caroline Ann Hill** was born 19 June 1953 in Gatesville, Texas, and married in Pasadena, Texas, 1 July 1978 David Allen Bridgforth, born 25 June 1951 in Kansas City.

Their two children were:

Kimberly Bridgeforth

David Bridgeforth

6. **Evelyn Lee Hill** was born 11 January 1995 in Pasadena, Texas, and married Jerry Johnson.

Children of Melvin Don Gilmore and Perry Jo Miller

6. **Laura Sue Gilmore**, who was born 5 February 1946 in Baird, Texas, and married Bruce Milton Thomas.

Their two children were:

Bruce Milton Thomas Jr.

James Johnathon Newall Thomas

6. **Pamella Reigh Gilmore** was born 17 February 1948 in Abilene, Texas, and 2 September 1967, in Monterey, Mexico, married Steven Ross Dunn, born 19 June 1947 in Dallas. On 8 September 1984 in Duncanville, Texas, she married James Robert Bazet, born 4 March 1948 in Morgan City, Louisiana.

The child of Steven Ross Dunn and Pamella Reigh Gilmore was:

Sharon Glen Dunn

Children of Paul Hare and Perry Jo Miller

6. **Michael Paul Hare**, who was born 19 November 1956 in Dallas, and married there on 29 September 1978 Jennie Lynn O'Pry, born 19 March 1959.

Their two children were:

Michael David Hare

Meghan Reigh Hare

6. **James Edward Hare**, born 11 July 1960 in Dallas.

6. **Virginia Eileen Hare** was born 11 July 1960 in Dallas.

Children of Joseph Bruce Savage and Delores Ray Miller

6. **Joseph Dwight Savage** was born 18 March 1948 in Raymondville, Willacy, Texas, and married Barbara Kay Willett, born 3 August 1947 in Dallas.

Their two children were:

Katherine Dean Savage

John David Savage

6. **Steven Dane Savage** was born 12 August 1952 in Raymondville, and on 1 April 1978 married Tammy Lyn Shew, born 4 August 1958 in Akron, Ohio.

Their child was:

Rainey Ray Savage

Children of Earl Edward Madden and Sue LaVoyce Miller

6. **Esther Earlene Madden**, who was born 7 November 1950 in Raymondville, Texas. On 5 October 1976 she married Wilber Stanley Dixon; and in April 1977, James Eugene Lax. On 13 September 1980 in College Station, Texas, she married Stanley Ray Pantel, born 9 December 1950 in Victoria, Texas. This couple lived in Atlanta in 1996, and she furnished many records of the descendants of Duett Gordon Whitten.

The child of Stanley Ray Pantel and Esther Earlene Madden was:

Sarah Colete Pantel

6. **Brenda Sue Madden** was born 17 April 1953 in Raymondville, and, in Austin, 3 November 1973, married Thomas Lloyd Harper, born 31 May 1949 in Mineral Wells, Texas.

Their three children were:

Nathan Shea Harper

Amber Leigh Harper

Joshua Thomas Harper

6. **Earl Edward Madden II** was born 12 December 1955 in Austin, and married there 26 June 1982 Janice Marie Gossell, born 8 February 1955 in Bertha, Minnesota.

Their two children were:
> Emily Sue-Ann Madden
> Earl Edward Madden III

Children of Cecil Bert Shields and Jakie Dell Miller
6. **Elizabeth Gayle Shields** was born 11 November 1952 in Raymondville, Texas and, in Edcouch, Texas on 14 April 1972 married George Allen Younger, who was born 7 August 1951 in Brownsville, Texas.
Their two children were:
> Kelly Mari Younger
> Brian Allen Younger

6. **Kay Lugene Shields** was born 22 September 1955 in Raymondville, and 13 August 1976 married Gary Wayne Todd in Edinburg. He was born 21 December 1954 in Thompsonville, Illinois.
Their two children were:
> Gina Rae Todd
> Jason Michael Todd

6. **Aaron Lawrence Shields** was born 29 November 1957 in Raymondville, Texas, and 24 October 1975, in Corpus Christi, married Peggey Aylene DuBose, who was born 4 January 1957 in Kerrville, Texas.

6. **Bruce Gordon Shields** was born 11 September 1962 in Weslaco, and, in Edinburg 5 June 1982, married Vera Leanne Richards, born 14 July 1964 in Memphis, Tennessee.
Their child was:
> Bruce Gordon Shields II

Children of James Hugh Eugene Miller and Virginia Lee Polvado
6. **Janine Denise Miller** was born 10 September 1963 in Weslaco, where she married 17 October 1992 Thomas Pruski, born 14 February 1963 there.
Their child was:
> Lauren Alexis Pruski

6. **James Hugh Elwood Miller** was born 24 August 1964 in Weslaco, and was married 28 December 1990.
His child was:
> Conner James Miller

Children of Donald Morris Miller and Jo Ellen Phippeny
6. **Patricia Lynne Miller** was born 9 October 1958 in Mercedes, and married Walter Wiegel.
Their two children were:
> Curtis Page Wiegel
> Bradley Morris Wiegel

6. **Lisa Gayle Miller**, born 24 November 1961 in San Benito, Texas.

6. **Rebecca Mae Miller**, born 18 April 1964 in San Benito.

Children of Robert Mack Miller and Mary Martha Amayo
6. **Mark Maurice Miller**, born 14 June 1963 in San Benito.

6. **Myliss Marie Miller** was born 28 July 1964 in San Benito, and 28 June 1988 married Jack Kyle Stephens, born 28 December 1949 in Edenburg.

6. **Michael Mack Miller**, born 11 January 1968 in San Benito.

Children of David Smith Miller and Dolores Jean Kilgore
6. **Melinda Jean Miller** was born 21 July 1963 in Borger, Texas, and married, in Houston on 21 May 1986, Alfred Vail Springer, born 26 February 1963.

6. **Lea Cristine Miller** was born 4 September 1965 in Harlingen, and married Stephen Edward Wright 4 June 1983 in Rio Hondo. He was born in Marion, Indiana, 15 December 1963.
Their two children were:
> Jason Stephen Wright
> Kyle Edward Wright

6. **Deana Joane Miller**, born 12 July 1971 in Conroe, Texas.

William B. Moore Jr.

Children of Charles Edgar Miller and Nancy Susannah Nuchols
6. **Raymond Charles Miller** was born 28 January 1962 in Weslaco, and married Laura Simons Magers 7 April 1985 in San Antonio. She was born 10 December 1965 in Mercedes.
Their child was:
    Megan Elisa Miller
6. **Steven Duane Miller**, born 26 June 1963 in Weslaco.

Children of Kenneth Miller and Marion Hellman
Born in Harlingen, Texas
6. **Kevin Lowell Miller**, born 27 July 1970.
6. **Richard Douglas Miller**, born 11 July 1972.
6. **Matthew Henry Miller**, born 6 February 1975.
6. **Laura Delaine Miller**, born 27 July 1977.
6. **Freida Christine Miller**, born 6 March 1979.

Children of Robert Steven Slovak and Judith Ann Miller
6. **Sharon Ann Slovak** was born 4 January 1961 in Corpus Christi, and, in Houston 13 June 1987, married Robert Douglas Terrill, born 12 September 1956.
6. **Barbara Lorraine Slovak** was born 20 May 1962 in Corpus Christi, and married Richard Keith Harrell there, 28 July 1984. He was born 19 September 1958 in Bay City, Texas.
Their child was:
    Preston Lane Harrell
6. **Marilyn Hope Slovak** was born 28 May 1963 in Corpus Christi, and 19 July 1986, there, married John Wesley Cornelius, born 25 September 1962.
6. **Laura Stephanie Slovak**, born 1 December 1965 in Robstown, Texas.

Children of Jacob DeWitt Hausenfluck and Barbara Yvonne Newby
6. **Terry Lee Hausenfluck** was born 26 April 1957 in Marcedes, and married, in Katy, Texas, Dolleen Anita Froehlich, born September 28 1957 in La Grange, Texas.
Their two children were:
    Lance Jacob Hausenfluck
    Heath Albert Hausenfluck
6. **Beverly Ann Hausenfluck**, born 4 October 1958 in Bad Kreuznach, Germany.
6. **Glynda Kay Hausenfluck** was born 11 September 1959 in Mercedas, Texas, and in Harlingen, Texas, on 14 March 1987, married Martin Duane Johnson, born 28 June 1963 in Ottawa, Kansas.
Their child was:
    Jason Allen Johnson

Children of Glenn Howell Newby and Willie Jean Armstrong
6. **Perry Glenn Newby** was born 27 November 1961 in Mercedes, and married Phyllis Enita George in Weslaco 11 February 1984. She was born 13 July 1961 in Indianapolis, Indiana.
Their two children were:
    Heather Marie Newby
    Tiffany Nichole Newby
6. **Jay Howell Newby**, born 12 March 1963 in Weslaco.
6. **Deborah Kay Newby** was born 21 October 1967 in Weslaco, and married Jim Buck Fulcher, born 11 November 1962.
Their child was:
    Ashley Marie Fulcher

Children of Joe Clifford Peters and Glenda Hal Newby
6. **Susan Marie Peters**, born 6 August 1961 in Mercedes.
6. **Clifford Wayne Peters** was born 14 February 1964 in Weslaco, and in Grand Prairie, Texas, on 14 September 1985, married Linda Sue Callahan, born 10 January 1966 in Cocoa Beach, Florida.
Their child was:

234

Samantha Jo Peters
6. **Kathy Jo Peters**, born 4 March 1966 in Weslaco, Texas.

Children of Clifton Mack Miller and Dorothy Ann Affolter
6. **Terrell Mack Miller** was born 28 October 1964 in Harlingen, and married Martha Eugenia Galindo there, 22 December 1982. She was born in Mexico City 10 November 1954.
Their child was:
Freda Marie Miller
6. **James Lee Miller** was born 22 May 1962 in Harlingen, and on 16 August 1988, there, married Rebecca Sue Stacy Hicks, who was born 13 June 1967.
6. **Rhonda Ann Miller**, born 17 October 1967 in San Antonio.

Child of Hobart Judson Whitten Jr. and Gloria Shaw
6. **Tyler Wade Whitten**, born 22 July 1974 in Gadsden, Alabama.

NINTH GENERATION
Children of Charles Edward Hill and Marilyn Smith
7. **Betty Jo Hill**
7. **Connie Hill**
7. **Gladys Angel Hill**
7. **Michael Hill**

Children of David Allen Bridgeforth and Caroline Ann Hill
7. **Kimberly Bridgforth**, born 31 July 1981 in Tyler, Texas.
7. **David Bridgforth**, born 24 February 1987 in San Antonio.

Children of Bruce Milton Thomas and Laura Sue Gilmore
7. **Bruce Milton Thomas Jr.**, born 20 June 1968 in Dallas, Texas.
7. **James Johnathon Newall Thomas**, born 21 November 1970 in Dallas.

Child of Steven Ross Dunn and Pamella Reigh Gilmore
7. **Sharon Glynn Dunn**, who was born 1 October 1967 in Dallas, and married, in September 1989, Darrin Tyrrell.
Their child was:
Alex Tyrrell

Children of Michael Paul Hare and Jennie Lynn O'Pry
7. **Michael David Hare**, born 20 May 1979 in Dallas.
7. **Meghan Reigh Hare**, born 10 December 1985 in Dallas.

Children of Joseph Dwight Savage and Barbara Kay Willett
7. **Katherine Dean Savage** was born 23 January 1969 in Longview, Texas, and married Terry Darzy 5 June 1990.
7. **John David Savage**, born 8 March 1974 in Dallas.

Child of Steven Dane Savage and Tammy Lyn Shew
7. **Rainey Ray Savage**, born 29 November 1978 in Grand Prairie, Texas.

Child of Stanley Ray Pantel and Esther Earlene Madden
7. **Sarah Colete Pantel**, born 31 January 1982 in San Marcos, Hays, Texas.

Children of Thomas Lloyd Harper and Brenda Sue Madden
7. **Nathan Shea Harper** was born 5 February 1976 and died 17 February that same year in Austin, Texas.
7. **Amber Leigh Harper**, born 3 March 1980 in San Antonio, Texas.
7. **Joshua Thomas Harper**, born 8 March 1984 in San Antonio.
Children of Earl Edward Madden II and Janice Marie Gossell
7. **Emily Sue-Ann Madden**, born 6 November 1984 in Austin, Texas.

7. **Earl Edward Madden III**, born 1 May 1986 in Austin.

Children of George Allen Younger and Elizabeth Gail Shields
7. **Kelly Mari Younger**, born 20 May 1979 in Odessa, Texas.
7. **Brian Allen Younger**, born 4 February 1984 in Colorado City, Texas.

Children of Gary Wayne Todd and Kay Lugene Shields
7. **Gina Rae Todd**, born 30 November 1978 in DuQuoin, Illinois.
7. **Jason Michael Todd**, born 7 May 1982 in DuQuoin.

Child of Bruce Gordon Shields and Vera Leanna Richards
7. **Bruce Gordon Shields II**, born 20 May 1987 in McAllen.

Child of Thomas Pruski and Janine Denise Miller
7. **Lauren Alexis Pruski**, born 22 November 1995 in Abilene.

Child of James Hugh Elwood Miller
7. **Conner James Miller**, born 5 June 1994 in Chicago.

Children of Walter Wiegel and Patricia Lynne Miller
7. **Curtis Page Wiegel**, born 9 December 1981.
7. **Bradley Morris Wiegel**, born 6 November 1983.

Children of Stephen Edward Wright and Lea Christine Miller
7. **Jason Stephen Wright**, born 4 September 1984 in San Antonio, Texas.
7. **Kyle Edward Wright**, born 10 February 1986 in San Antonio.

Child of Raymond Charles Miller and Laura Simons Magers
7. **Megan Elisa Miller**, born 6 September 1985 in Bryan, Texas.

Child of Richard Keith Harrell and Barbara Lorraine Slovak
7. **Preston Lane Harrell**, born 30 June 1987 in San Antonio.

Children of Terry Lee Hausenfluck and Dolleen Anita Froelich
7. **Lance Jacob Hausenfluck**, born 8 June 1984 in Bryan, Texas.
7. **Heath Albert Hausenfluck**, born 2 February 1988 in Bryan.

Child of Martin Duane Johnson and Glynda Kay Hausenfluck
7. **Jason Alan Johnson**, born 25 May 1988 in Weslaco, Texas.

Children of Perry Glenn Newby and Phyllis Enita George
7. **Heather Marie Newby**, born 29 November 1984 in Weslaco.
7. **Tiffany Nocole Newby**, born 28 March 1988 in Weslaco.

Child of Jim Buck Fulcher and Deborah Kay Newby
7. **Ashley Marie Fulcher**, born 20 July 1986 in McAllen, Texas.

Child of Clifford Wayne Peters and Linda Sue Callahan
7. **Samantha Jo Peters**, born 20 December 1987 in Arlington, Texas.

Child of Terrell Mack Miller and Martha Eugenia Galindo
7. **Freda Marie Miller**, born 5 April 1983 in Harlingen.

TENTH GENERATION
Child of Darrin Tyrrell and Sharon Glynn Dunn

8. **Alex Tyrrell**

THIRD GENERATION
SILAS REAGAN WHITTEN

1. **Silas Reagan Whitten**, eighth child of Charles Whitten Jr., was born in 1815 in Pendleton District, South Carolina, and married 20 October 1851 in Louisville, Winston, Mississippi, Martha Caroline Yarbrough, who was born 10 February 1832 in South Carolina. Silas Reagan and Martha Caroline died in Dallas, Texas, and were buried in Greenwood Cemetery there: he, 16 August 1889; she, 16 November 1919. In 1850 he was living unmarried in the home of Dr. J. C. Hughes in Louisville. The couple moved to Ellis County, Texas, in 1873 with daughter Mary Amelia, her two small children, and "numerous aunts uncles and cousins," then to Dallas County, in 1883. He had lost a leg, probably from some genetic defect. From 1819 to 1849 he was a member of the Free and Accepted Masons Lodge in Louisville, Winston, Mississippi. A Silas R. Whitten, in 1837, served as constable in Cherokee County, Alabama, the home of his father. After the death of her husband, Martha Caroline operated grocery stores in Dallas. The first, from 1902 to 1904, was on Akard Street. The second, opened in 1905, was located at 365 Grand Street.

Their seven children were:

Mary Amelia Whitten
Charles Everette Whitten
Elizabeth M. Whitten
James J. Whitten
John William S. Whitten
Sarah Nannie Whitten
Unnamed child Whitten

FOURTH GENERATION
Children of Silas Reagan Whitten and Martha Caroline Yarbrough
Born in Louisville, Winston, Mississippi

2. **Mary Amelia Whitten**, twin of Charles Everette, was born 7 December 1852, and married 24 December 1867, Henry William Holsomback, born in May 1845 in South Carolina. She died 16 April 1910 in Dallas. He died in 1911 in Wills Point, Van Zandt, Texas, and was buried in White Rose Cemetery, in that county. They divorced in 1873 in Mississippi, after which he married Julia. Mary Amelia married a second husband 30 April 1876 in Ellis County, Texas. He was Albert Michael Greenlun, who was born in Ohio in December 1846 and died after 1910 in Dallas.

The two children of Henry William Holsomback and Mary Amelia Whitten were:

John Henry Holsomback
George Everette Holsomback

The two children of Albert Michael Greenlun and Mary Amelia Whitten were:

Thomas S. Greenlun
Lillian Greenlun

2. **Charles Everette Whitten** was born 7 December 1852 and married Carrie about 1884. She was born in August 1860 in Tennessee. Charles Everette died 14 December 1945 in Houston, Texas, and was buried in Rest Haven Cemetery there. Carrie died before Charles. Twin of Mary Amelia, Charles left home at age seventeen and was not seen by his family until 1943. He had been a Texas Ranger, called Charles White, a name he used for most of his life. In 1910 he and his family were in El Paso, and, in 1900, Dallas. Charles mined for gold in California and worked on railroads in Mexico.

Two of their children were:

Beatrice Whitten
A son Whitten

2. **Elizabeth M. Whitten** was born in December 1854, and married, about 1879, in Ellis County, Texas, Jesse James Whitten, born about 1857 in Louisville Winston, Mississippi. Elizabeth M. died 13 February 1911 in Dallas, and was buried in Greenwood Cemetery there. Jesse James died about 1880 in Waxahatchie, Ellis, Texas, and is buried there. She was widowed, with her parents in Ellis County in 1880, and working as a dressmaker and bookkeeper.

Their child was:

Thomas Lee Whitten

2. **James J. Whitten** was born about 1857 and died before 1880 in Waxahatchie, Ellis, Texas.

2. **John William S. Whitten** was born in November 1858 and married about 1890 in Texas, Lillie D. O'Brien, born in May 1870 in that state. Lillie died 3 April 1920; he, later in Dallas. They divorced 21 March 1904 in Dallas, after which she married Harry E. Dossett and Samuel D. John William S. Whitten was a carpenter.

The two children of John William S. Whitten and Lillie O'Brien were:
> Hattie G. Whitten
> Earle R. Whitten

2. **Sarah Nannie Whitten** was born in 1861, and married about 1884 in Dallas. Her husband's name is not known. She had at least one child who died before 1900.

FIFTH GENERATION
Children of Henry William Holsomback and Mary Amelia Whitten

3. **John Henry Holsomback** was born in October 1868, and married about 1893, Jenny Cox, born in September 1876 in Texas. John Henry died 22 December 1916 in Dallas, and was buried in Greenwood Cemetery. Jenny died after 1918. He was a typesetter.

3. **George Everette Holsomback** was born 15 April 1870, and married 24 December 1895 in McComb, Mississippi, Nanny Elizabeth Parker, born 5 April 1881. He died 3 April 1957 in Meridian, Mississippi; she, 12 December 1934.

Their ten children were:
> Hazel D. Holsomback
> Elizabeth George Holsomback
> James Arista Holsomback
> Joseph Oscar Holsomback
> Robert Lee Holsomback
> Mable Clair Holsomback
> Hubert William Holsomback
> George Samuel Holsomback
> Daisy Ruth Holsomback
> Penny M. Holsomback

Children of Albert Michael Greenlun and Mary Amelia Whitten

3. **Thomas S. Greenlun** was born in 1877 in Dallas, Texas, and married Grace about 1902 and Maude in 1923 in Dallas. He died after 1930.

3. **Lillian Greenlun** was born in 1879 in Dallas, and died before 1900 in Texas.

Children of Charles Everette Whitten and Carrie

3. **Beatrice Whitten** was born in January 1888 in Texas, and married John F. Dittmar, born in 1876 in Germany. They lived in Los Angeles, California, in 1945.

Their five children were:
> Lorena Dittmar
> Caroline Dittmar
> LaDean Dittmar
> John Dittmar
> Gordon Dittmar

3. **A son Whitten**
His child was:
> Lewis E. White

Child of Jesse James Whitten and Elizabeth M. Whitten

3. **Thomas Lee Whitten** was born in August 1880 in Ellis County, Texas, died in 1904 in Dallas, and was buried in Greenwood Cemetery there. He lived with his mother at 112 Carter Street in Dallas from 1896 to 1902.

Children of John William S. Whitten and Lillie D. O'Brien

3. **Hattie G. Whitten** was born in March 1891 in Dallas, and married about 1913, Guy M. Tune, born in December 1888 in Arkansas. Hattie G. died after 1920; Guy M., after 23 September 1927 in San Antonio, Texas.

3. **Earl R. Whitten** was born in January 1893 in Dallas, and married about 1920 there, Willie Marguerite. Earl R. died after 1930. He paid his parents' Greenwood Cemetery dues until 1930 from his home at 618 North Lancaster Street in Dallas.

SIXTH GENERATION
Children of George Everette Holsomback and Nanny Elizabeth Parker

4. **Hazel D. Holsomback** was born 22 November 1898 in Texas, and married John Jacob Fitzgerald, born in 1892. Hazel D. died 7 April 1984 in California; he, 20 February 1928 in Meridian, Mississippi.

Their two children were:
Hazel Anna Fitzgerald
John Everette Fitzgerald

4. **Elizabeth George Holsomback** was born 5 December 1900 in Tennessee, and married Lowis E. Hale, born 28 January 1892. She died 13 March 1975; he, 14 September 1922 in Meridian, Mississippi. After the death of Lowis, she married Frank A. Tittle.

The child of Lowis E. Hale and Elizabeth George Holsomback was:
Mary Elizabeth Hale

The child of Frank A. Tittle and Elizabeth George Holsomback was:
John Wilson Tittle

4. **James Arista Holsomback** was born 28 September 1902 and died 16 June 1904 in Tennessee.

4. **Joseph Oscar Holsomback** was born 24 September 1904 in Tennessee, and married Lois Giles. His second wife was Mary Lee Webb, born 4 June 1915 in Mississippi. Joseph Oscar died 23 March 1983 in Mississippi.

The child of Joseph Oscar Holsomback and Lois Giles was:
Emily Clair Holsomback

The child of Joseph Oscar Holsomback and Mary Lee Webb was:
Joseph Webb Holsomback

4. **Robert Lee Holsomback** was born 12 October 1908 in Mississippi, and married Mary Smith, born 1 December 1908. He died 27 April 1983 in Texas.

4. **Mable Clair Holsomback** was born and died 20 August 1910 in Mississippi.

4. **Hubert William Holsomback** was born 6 April 1912 and died 12 August 1918 in Mississippi.

4. **George Samuel Holsomback** was born 21 September 1914, and married Myrtle Irene Bounds, born about 1914. They divorced, and he married Estell Gammage. George and Myrtle died in Texas: he, 4 September 1980; she, in 1986.

The four children of George Samuel Holsomback and Myrtle Irene Bounds were:
Nancy Burnett Holsomback
Jane Elizabeth Holsomback
George Samuel Holsomback Jr.
Mary Catherine Holsomback

4. **Daisy Ruth Holsomback** was born 5 August 1916 in Mississippi, and married Otha Eugene Hall, born 17 June 1914. They died in Mississippi: she, 6 April 1983; he, 4 February 1947.

Their two children were:
Daisy Jean Hall
George Meyer Hall

4. **Penny M. Holsomback** was born 8 December 1921 in Mississippi, and married James Earl Williams, who was born 25 January 1922 and died in 1972. After his death, she married John Gerome Stanley Rupel. Her third husband was Gerald Patrick McNair, born 25 August 1918 in Mississippi. They lived in Meridian, Mississippi, in 1993 when Penny supplied much of this information on the Silas Reagan Whitten family. She died there 5 January 1995 after a long battle with cancer.

The child of James Earl Williams and Penny M. Holsomback was:
John Frederick Williams

Children of John F. Dittmar and Beatrice Whitten

4. **Lorena Dittmar** married a Mr. Tincup and lived in Los Angeles, California, in 1945.

4. **Caroline Dittmar** married a Mr. Hill. They also lived in Los Angeles in 1945.

4. **LaDean Dittmar** married a Mr. Richardson. They lived in Muskogee, Oklahoma, in 1945.

4. **John Dittmar**

4. **Gordon Dittmar**

Child of a son of Charles Everette Whitten

4. **Lewis E. White**, who lived in Houston in 1945.

SEVENTH GENERATION
Children of John Jacob Fitzgerald and Hazel D. Holsomback
5. **Hazel Anna Fitzgerald** was born 3 December 1918 and died 16 August 1982 in California.
5. **John Everette Fitzgerald** was born 1 January 1921 in California, and married Frances Payne, born 19 August 1918.

Their three children were:
John Everette Fitzgerald Jr.
Ronald Francis Fitzgerald
Kathryn Dianne Fitzgerald

Child of Lowis E. Hale and Elizabeth George Holsomback
5. **Mary Elizabeth Hale** was born 9 August 1920 in Mississippi, and married V. G. Priester. She died 2 February 1971 there.
Their child was:
Palelam Priester

Child of Frank A. Tittle and Elizabeth George Holsomback
5. **John Wilson Tittle** was born 25 August 1926 and died 25 August 1991.

Child of Joseph Oscar Holsomback and Lois Giles
5. **Emily Clair Holsomback** was born 23 February 1928, married William McDaniel, and died 14 July 1982 in Mississippi.

Child of Joseph Oscar Holsomback and Mary Lee Webb
5. **Joseph Webb Holsomback** was born 1 June 1944, and married Virginia Altman, born 11 November 1931.

Children of George Samuel Holsomback and Myrtle Irene Bounds
5. **Nancy Burnett Holsomback** was born 11 February 1943 in Texas, and married John Shanks. Her second husband was William Harrison Branson Jr., born 6 January 1932.
The two children of John Shanks and Nancy Burnett Holsomback were:
John Preston Shanks
Andrew Christopher Shanks
The child of William Harrison Branson Jr. and Nancy Burnett Holsomback was:
Allison Elizabeth Branson
5. **Jane Elizabeth Holsomback** was born 25 May 1944, and married John Bruce Huckeba, born 17 September 1952.
Their child was:
Jonathon George Huckeba
5. **George Samuel Holsomback Jr.** was born 5 April 1947 in Texas, and married Judith Ann, born 21 October 1947.
Their four children were:
Jeffrey Payton Holsomback
Amy Renae Holsomback
Emily Jon Holsomback
Colby Andrew Holsomback
5. **Mary Catherine Holsomback** was born 27 May 1948, and married Richard Earl Blunk, born 15 August 1947.
Their three children were:
Richard Brett Blunk
R. Everett Blunk
Allen Clifford Blunk

Children of Otha Eugene Hall and Daisy Ruth Holsomback
5. **Daisy Jean Hall** was born 30 August 1933 in Texas, and married Stanley Edward Hollingsworth, born 25 September 1932 in Alabama.
Their five children, born in Alabama, were:

Martha Jean Hollingsworth
Carol Beth Hollingsworth
Cynthia Ann Hollingsworth
Steven Arthur Hollingsworth
Sandra Ellen Hollingsworth
5. **George Meyer Hall** was born 15 November 1935 in Mississippi.

Child of James Earl Williams and Penny M. Holsomback
5. **John Frederick Williams**, born 1 May 1947 in Texas.

EIGHTH GENERATION
Children of John Everette Fitzgerald and Frances Payne
6. **John Everette Fitzgerald Jr.** was born 27 August 1939 in California, and married 7 August 1960, Phyllis Lynn.
Their two children were:
Phyllis Fitzgerald
John Everette Fitzgerald III
6. **Ronald Francis Fitzgerald**, born 19 January 1941 in California.
6. **Kathryn Dianne Fitzgerald** was born 27 February 1948 in California, and married Larry Grimm. Later she married Daniel Eller.
The two children of Larry Grimm and Kathryn Dianne Fitzgerald were:
Larry Grimm Jr.
Kenneth Grimm
The two children of Daniel Eller and Kathryn Dianne Fitzgerald were:
Robert Joseph Eller
Dennis Michael Eller

Child of V. G. Priester and Mary Elizabeth Hale
6. **Palelam Priester** was born 1947 and died 4 April 1985 in Mississippi.

Children of John Shanks and Nancy Burnett Holsomback
6. **John Preston Shanks** was born 5 August 1966, and married Kristi Beth Becker, born 10 April 1969.
6. **Andrew Christopher Shanks** was born 15 July 1968, and married Macy Metzger, born 24 April 1969.
Their two children were:
Margaret Louise Shanks
Andrew Christopher Shanks Jr.

Child of William Harrison Branson Jr. and Nancy Burnett Holsomback
6. **Allison Elizabeth Branson**, born 5 February 1974.

Child of John Bruce Huckeba and Jane Elizabeth Holsomback
6. **Jonathan George Huckeba**, born 9 August 1983.

Children of George Samuel Holsomback Jr. and Judith Ann
6. **Jeffrey Payton Holsomback**, born 14 February 1972.
6. **Amy Renae Holsomback**, born 20 January 1976.
6. **Emily Jon Holsomback**, born 21 December 1978.
6. **Colby Andrew Holsomback**, born 24 August 1982.

Children of Richard Earl Blunt and Mary Catherine Holsomback
6. **Richard Brett Blunk**, born 18 August 1969.
6. **R. Everett Blunk**, born 5 July 1972.
6. **Allen Clifford Blunk**, born 29 May 1973.
Children of Stanley Edward Hollingsworth and Daisy Jean Hall
6. **Martha Jean Hollingsworth** was born 17 December 1952, and married Mark Jordan.

6. **Carol Beth Hollingsworth**, born 7 July 1955.
6. **Cynthia Ann Hollingsworth**, born 2 January 1957.
6. **Steven Arthur Hollingsworth**, born 23 February 1959.
6. **Sandra Ellen Hollingsworth**, born 1 April 1967.

NINTH GENERATION
Children of John Everette Fitzgerald Jr. and Phyllis Lynn
7. **Phyllis Fitzgerald**, born in 1960 in California.
7. **John Everette Fitzgerald III**, born in 1962 in California.

Children of Larry Grimm and Kathryn Dianne Fitzgerald
7. **Larry Grimm Jr.**, born September 1967 in California.
7. **Kenneth Grimm**, born June 1969 in California.

Children of Daniel Eller and Kathryn Dianne Fitzgerald
7. **Robert Joseph Eller**
7. **Dennis Michael Eller**, born 5 April 1982.

Children of Andrew Christopher Shanks and Macy Metzger
7. **Margaret Louise Shanks**, born 13 July 1989.
7. **Andrew Christopher Shanks Jr.**, born 5 October 1991.

Book IV
TEXAS PIONEERS

The southern sections of our country were settled primarily by English, Scotch-Irish, German, French, and African immigrants and their descendants. Arriving by ship they traveled south and west, stopping along the way, until the boldest and most adventuresome reached east and south-central Texas. The journeys were generally neither continuous nor completed in a single generation. Couples traveled a few hundred miles, built a cabin, cleared land, planted crops, raised a family, then bid sons and daughters farewell as they set out to repeat the process. Usually, at each stop, some family members put down roots, vestiges of which can still be found.

Our Reagans, Earles, Whittens, and their relatives traveled these routes. Members of each family made it all the way to Texas. Of the Reagans, William arrived in Nacogdoches, capital of the Mexican state of Tejas, in 1835. Many of his descendants remain in the area. His cousin Ahimas died in Cass County, Republic of Texas, in 1842. It is probable that he, too, reached the area before Sam Houston's Texans defeated Santa Anna at San Jacinto in 1836.

Many Earles settled in Texas. Of those close to our Whittens, Harriet Harrison Earle Roddy may have been the first. During the period from 1851 through 1855, she wrote to her sister, Eleanor Kee Earl Whitten, the lonely, homesick letters contained in *Letters to Rebecca*. Those were mailed from Prospect, String Prairie, and Lexington in Burleson and Lee Counties. However, according to her grandson, Baylis John Fletcher, who grew up in her home, the Roddys reached Tejas in September of 1830. Their adventures are recounted in a paper written by Baylis John and published in the book *Lee County History*.

Married in 1810 at her home in old Rutherford County, North Carolina, to Ephriam Roddy, a lawyer of nearby Spartanburg District, South Carolina, Harriet Earle had four children by 1828, when the family moved by wagon train to western Tennessee. The Roddys lived there about two years, during which a fifth child was born. Attempts to farm were unsuccessful, so the couple determined to move to the Stephen Austin colony in Tejas. The trip was long, hard, and nearly disastrous. After constructing a flatboat, the family used it to float down the Mississippi River to the port of New Orleans, where they boarded ship and set sail for the Brazos River in what was then the Mexican state of Tejas. While still in the Gulf of Mexico, a hurricane drove the ship aground. As the winds and high seas pounded it to pieces, the passengers launched small boats in which they were able to reach beaches near Quintana at the mouth of the Brazos River. The family first settled at San Felipe de Austin near the present town of Sealy, where Ephriam began to practice law and the last child was born.

Baylis John Fletcher records that Major Roddy, on a trip through Washington City (D.C.) had met Thomas Jefferson, and while living in Tennessee knew Sam Houston. He tells of Ephriam's friendship in Tejas with Davy Crockett, William Barrett Travis, and James Bowie, who later were martyred at the Alamo; the flight from San Felipe to avoid Santa Anna; and yet another move, this time to the capital of the new Republic of Texas, Washington on the Brazos. When the Texas capital was transferred to Austin, the Roddys moved to nearby Gayhill and, in 1850, to Tanglewood. In 1869 they settled at Liberty Hill, where both died and are buried, having lived under four of the six flags that flew over Texas.

The number of Charles Whitten Sr. descendants who reached and settled in Texas during the nineteenth century is, I think, remarkable. It is the purpose of this chapter to record what we know of those, to explore their interaction, and to speculate about what they knew of each other.

Of the children of Charles Whitten Jr. and Millicent Reagan, Alvin Earle reached Matagorda County, Texas, in 1847, settling in an area that became Wharton County two years later; and Silas Reagan (b. 1815) moved into Ellis County in 1873, transferring ten years later to Dallas. His son, Charles Everett, preceded him, leaving Winston County, Mississippi, at age seventeen in 1869, mining gold in California, working on a Mexican railroad, and serving with the Texas Rangers. He apparently lived most of his life in Texas. At least four children of William S. Whitten, son of Charles Jr., moved from Leesburg, Cherokee County, Alabama, to Lamar County, Texas, after 1895 and before 1900. They were Permelia Laura, Silas L., Charles Mack, and Duett Gordon. Many Alvin Earle descendants live in south Texas today; and, around Paris, in Lamar County, most of the numerous Whittens descended from William S. and his wife, Hariet A. Honet (Howard?). A branch of Duett Gordon Whitten's family reached and settled in the Rio Grande Valley, where several of his descendants still make their homes.

John Whitten and Mary Reagan had nine children, three of whom ended their lives in the Lone Star State. Elizabeth Whitten, with husband David Barrett and their children, became Texans in 1840 during the days of the Republic. Arriving in Houston County from Fayette County, Tennessee, they settled between Crockett and Madisonville. Next came

Alfred, who entered Montgomery County, Texas, from Fayette County, Tennessee, late in 1849, soon settling in nearby Madison County. Sister Mariam, with several of her children, transferred from Pontotoc County, Mississippi, to Texas after the death of her husband in 1862. These three siblings lived north of the present city of Houston. Their descendants can still be found spread over south Texas.

The grandchildren and great-grandchildren of John and Mary Whitten contributed liberally to the growing Texas population. First to reach the area, traveling by wagon train in 1836, was John Whitten Barrett, son of Elizabeth Whitten and David Barrett. His sister Mariam Hannah, with her husband, Hansell Coburn, arrived in Houston County prior to 1840; and brother Albert Gallatin with wife, Elizabeth D. Seaton, came with his parents in 1840, while sister Mary with her second husband, John R. Parker, was in Texas by 1843.

Traveling with their father, Alfred, in 1849 were children Sarah Elanor, John D. G., James Frank, Martha, Harriett Louise, Alice Anderson, and Helen Josephine. Alfred's daughter Mary Jane came to Texas from Tennessee with her husband, Edward Americus Anderson, in 1853.

The only child of Rev. James Whitten to reach Texas, Calvin Thompson Whitten, followed his daughter Mary Clifford to Bell County at about the time she married a Texan, Capt. 1, in 1871. Reverend James contributed grandchildren in addition to Mary Clifford. Talitha Emily and Mary Didema, daughters of son Rev. Arphax Whitten and his first wife, settled in Texas about 1872 following their marriages. After his death in that same year, the second wife of the reverend, Aurelia Priddy, with children Joanna, James, and Harriett, moved into Smith County and lived near Tyler.

Harriet Earle Lankford, daughter of Silas Reagan and Eleanor Kee Whitten and grandchild of John and Mary Whitten, moved to Belton, Bell, Texas, after the death of her husband, Nathan Alexander Lankford, in 1872. She wrote to Mississippi relatives from there in 1884. The following year she was in nearby Cameron. Several of her children made the move at about the same time. These included: William Henry, who lived in Sherman; Anna C., who lived with her mother; Charles Alexander, who later moved into Indian Territory in what is now Oklahoma; Mary Kee, who lived in Waco; and Dr. John Silas, who lived in San Antonio. Her descendants can still be found nearby.

Several members of later Whitten generations moved into Texas. A reunion of the extended Texas family would be a large and noisy one. I have met, spoken to, or exchanged letters with many Texas Whittens. Although a few have discovered their roots, most cannot trace their ancestry back to John or brother Charles Jr., much less Charles and Nancy Smith Whitten.

It appears to me that ancestor recognition generally dims by the third generation and dies thereafter. Most of us have little knowledge of great-grandparents and their siblings, and have lost sight of those who went before. John and Charles Whitten Jr. went separate ways early in their adult lives. Their sons and daughters moved, many times, settling far from their parents and each other, losing contact while succeeding generations continued to disperse.

During much of the nineteenth and early twentieth centuries, Whitten generations moved to Texas, and some lived in fairly close proximity. Were the various families aware of the others? What did they know of relationships, family history? Was there interaction, friendship, animosity, even curiosity? We have insufficient knowledge to formulate complete answers, but old letters, published reports, and memories of some still living allow us to reach some interesting conclusions. In the following paragraphs I will try to interpret some of what I have learned from these sources:

The Paris, Lamar County, Whittens have no knowledge of related Whittens other than those who descended from William S. and Hariet A. Honet (Howard?) Whitten. I have only found one William S. descendant who even suspected himself to be a son of Charles Whitten Jr. William S. descendants who remain in or near Cherokee County, Alabama, where Charles Jr. lived from about 1830 until he died before 1860, know nothing of him and very little of William S.

Of Charles Jr.'s son, Silas Reagan Whitten (b. 1815) and his family, who moved in 1873 to Ellis County and later Dallas, there is no record to indicate they knew where their relatives were, but there is this with which to speculate: Brothers Alvin Earle, John R., and Silas Reagan (b. 1815) had lived in adjacent Mississippi counties, Winston, Choctaw, and Holmes. Surely Silas knew that brother Alvin's family was in Wharton, Texas, when he left for Ellis County.

In Bell County, Capt. Rufus Young King, after the death of his second wife, Mary Clifford Whitten, married Amaryllis Woodlief, granddaughter of a sister of Eleanor Kee Earle Whitten. Mary Clifford's father, Calvin Thompson Whitten, lived in Bell County. He knew Eleanor Kee personally. She was the wife of his uncle. They must have known that a reconnection of sorts was consummated by that marriage. Captain King and Calvin Thompson were alive and in Bell County when Harriet Earle Whitten Lankford moved to Belton. Perhaps that is why she chose to settle there. She had known Cousin Calvin when both lived in Mississippi: she in Pontotoc; he in Guntown, Lee, County, less than a day's journey away. We can be assured that the Bell County contingent, comprised of descendants of two brothers, Silas Reagan and James, sons of John Whitten, were well within the Texas loop.

Elizabeth Whitten Barrett and her family were early settlers of Houston County. Brother Alfred arrived about ten years later and settled in Madison, which adjoins Houston. Both migrated from Fayette County, Tennessee. Each branch was well known and produced large families that quickly expanded into surrounding counties. They knew each other, and recognized their kinship; some living descendants still do.

There is evidence in *Letters to Rebecca* that the Wharton County Whittens knew of the others. Alvin Earle's daughter, Julia Foster, visited Reverend James and Dr. Isaac Smith Whitten in Georgia in 1851. I have talked with several members of this line. Few retain knowledge of their ancestry.

There was traffic between Whitten branches in Texas, and grandchildren of Reverend James recorded some of it. The daughters and granddaughters of Rev. Arphax Whitten and his first wife, Matilda Allen, were interested in family history. They talked of it, wrote each other letters on the subject, contacted other relatives seeking information, and kept up with their Whittens as best they could. Two especially—daughter Doleska Fitzallen "Dolly" and her niece, Annie Ard—kept the cauldron boiling, writing, collecting, and asking questions.

The sisters in Texas—Talitha Emily Bell, who lived in Caldwell, and Mary Didema Tarver, who lived in nearby Cameron—sought their kin and reported findings to the folks at home. They returned on visits to Alabama and Georgia, and were visited by sisters, nieces, and nephews from "back home." Melicent Mazelle, who married Nathan Harbin Goss and moved to Phelps County, Missouri, wrote and probably visited. Some of these letters survive. Annie Ard inherited those saved by her Aunt "Dolly," collected more, and left the enlarged collection to her nephew, George Walter Ward, of Smyrna, Georgia. Copies of letters, Bible pages, and notes she saved have been widely distributed. I have received some of these from Whitten researchers Arthur Reagan, Eugene Perry of California, and Jim Ward of Copper Hill, Tennessee. Some original letters written by "Dolly" and Anne were saved by Rebecca Berry Whitten and published in *Letters to Rebecca.*

The following letter, sent me by James Ward, contains an appraisal by grandchildren of Reverend James of descendants of Alvin Earle Whitten of Wharton County and of Silas Reagan (b. 1815), who had reached Texas from Mississippi. It is undated, unsigned, and inaccurate, but indicates they were aware of each other and not too happy about the relationship.

I send you a list of mine, (which you can return) that you can get something from. There are some mistakes. The Aunt Eliza Thompson is entirely of the Bennett side. Aunt E. Whitten never married but was a cheery happy maiden lady, died at 35 years.

I think Uncle Ranson had a son Charles who died several years ago in Selma, also Julia Foster, your mother remembers her.

Mrs. Lee Blanchard once lived here, who think was another one. I will try to find out about her, as she never rested until she got in the DAR. She was so haughty I never sought her company though I know she was a Whitten of Mississippi or Texas. It is characteristic of those to be very proud and aristocratic.

Mrs. Davis was Mariam Whitten. While in Cameron, Texas, I visited her daughter who was a Mrs. Elizabeth Lankford; very nice people. I will write Cousin Charles Lankford and see if he can find more about them in Cameron.

Uncle Calvin's family
Clifford King, Belton, Texas
Sallie Ritchie, Guntown, Mississippi

Clif had four children, Florrie, Whitten, Sayers, and another I have forgotten. Sallie's were Lela who married Smith, Robert Ritchie. I used to get letters from cousin Sallie, but if she lives in Guntown, Mississippi, she is an invalid. Cousin E.S.G. sent me those letters and I sent them to Mrs. Crow.

A few years ago I wrote to a Dr. John Charles Whitten of Louisville, Kentucky, connected with the college there. He said there were two brothers came over from England. His grandfather went to Maine and others drifted to Virginia so he knew little of them, but I am sure they are the ones we seek, our grandfather, 3rd. removed. He wrote me a nice letter. I think I sent it to but the name is sure.

Auntie, Mrs. E.T. Bell

Who wrote this letter?
Minnie

This letter, though filled with mistakes, illustrates not only the hunger for family history felt by these descendants of Reverend James Whitten, but also that various Whitten branches in Texas were well aware of each other.

It was apparently written by Talitha Emily Whitten Bell, daughter of Reverend Arphax, who lived after her marriage, in Caldwell, Burleson, Texas. If it was written before Anne Ard had died in 1915, I would be convinced she had solicited and received it, as was her lifetime practice. It was found in Anne's collection. If written after 1915, the most likely recipient was Anne's mother, Sarah Mitchell Whitten Ard, who lived in Stewart County, Georgia.

The following sheds all the light I have on her various references.

Aunt Eliza Thompson: Talitha Emily's mother was a Bennett; her father's mother was Elizabeth Ann Thompson.

Surely she knew that "Aunt" Eliza Thompson was neither an aunt nor a Bennett. Or, could her mother have had Thompson relatives?

Aunt E. Whitten was "Eliza" Elizabeth Ann Whitten, her father's sister and daughter of Reverend James. Letters to Rebecca *contains many of her letters to the Silas Reagan Whitten family. She died early and unmarried.*

"Uncle Ranson" was either Ranson Edwin Whitten, son of Silas Reagan; or Ranson, Silas Reagan's brother. Both were known to the James Whitten clan. Neither had a son who fits the description in her letter. Ranson Edwin had a son, Joseph Earle, who lived near Selma, Alabama. He, however, lived well beyond any possible date for this letter. I cannot find a match for this claim, though, like most family traditions, it is likely to contain a grain of truth, badly garbled.

Julia Foster was most likely Alvin Earle's daughter, Julia, who married W. C. C. Foster and was murdered in Memphis, where they lived, in 1879. This couple visited Reverend James in 1851, so the family would have remembered her. The visit was long before this letter was written. Could she have been referring to Julia F. Whitten, a granddaughter of Alvin Earle, who died after 1880? I think not.

Mrs. Lee Blanchard was Corinne T. Whitten, daughter of James Drayton, son of Alvin Earle Whitten. In 1917, while living in Caldwell, she applied for membership in the DAR, claiming her grandfather, Alvin Earle Whitten, was a son of Silas Reagan Whitten, son of John, veteran of the Revolution. She lists John's children in the application. Their birth dates are correctly recorded, as are other dates used in the application. She cites as her source family records and a Bible. Silas Reagan was not the father of Alvin Earle. Surely she knew that. He was not even married when Alvin Earle was born. Whitten researcher Arthur Reagan believes Mrs. Blanchard had access to the Bible of John Whitten, and well she might, for John died in Fayette County, Tennessee, and son Alfred was his executor. In 1850 Alfred moved to Texas and lived quite close to Caldwell. However, Harriett Earle Lankford, daughter of Silas Reagan, also lived close by. She was a student of Whitten history and the earliest of that line known to have become interested in the DAR. John's daughter, Mariam Whitten Davis, who came to Texas after the death of her husband in Pontotoc County, Mississippi, also lived close by and was probably known to Mrs. Blanchard. Either of them could have supplied the information used in this application. DAR membership number 78278 was granted Mrs. Blanchard 4 January 1918, by which time she lived in the city of Houston.

Talitha Emily was confused concerning the relationship of Mariam Whitten Davis and the Lankford family. She also had the name wrong. Harriet (not Elizabeth) Earle Whitten, daughter of Silas Reagan, married Nathan Alexander Lankford in South Carolina and moved to Pontotoc County, Mississippi, in 1845. When Nathan died, she moved to Texas and lived among several of her children. For a time she was with her daughter Anne C. Sample in Cameron. Talitha Emily wrote the letter she promised. Here is the reply:

Charles A. Lankford to Mrs. E. Alonzo Bell (*Talitha Emily Whitten, daughter of Rev. Arphax Whitten*)—Indian Territory, Oklahoma, to Columbus, Georgia, 25 March 1909

My grandfather Whitten's name was Silas. He was of revolutionary fame. He had a son named Ranson (Ranson Edwin Whitten). My mother's name was Harriet Earle Whitten. She died only a few months ago. She was with my sister in Waco, Texas. If you will write Mrs. Thomas Marion Dilworth (*his sister, Mary Kee*), 521 N. 13th St., Waco, Texas, she can tell you all about the history of the family. I moved to this place about two years ago. We have three children. Our oldest girl, Ethel, Mrs. J. F. Coffield, is in Waco. Our boy, Milton is living in Dallas, not married. Florence, the youngest girl, is not married.

Charles A. Lankford, President

This letter was written on stationery of the J. D. (James Dwight, his brother) Lankford Lumber Company, Indian Territory. It is the only record we have that places James Dwight there. He was probably alive at the time. Needless to say, the grandfather was not old enough to have participated in the Revolution. Silas Reagan Whitten was a veteran of the War of 1812.

The dates of Charles Lankford's letter and those of the application and acceptance of Corinne T. Whitten Blanchard for DAR membership render it impossible for me to accurately deduce the year of Talitha Emily Bell's letter. She spoke of writing Charles Lankford, and obviously did so before March 1909. The DAR application was received by that organization in February 1917 and approved in January 1918. And yet Talitha Emily says, "and never rested until she got in the DAR." Perhaps there was a second letter to Charles Lankford written after the 1918 approval. If so, it came to naught as he had died in 1915. The most likely date for the letter of our study is about 1908 with Talitha Emily mistaken or misinformed about Mrs. Blanchard's earlier acceptance by the DAR.

Next, the letter refers to Uncle Calvin Thompson Whitten's family.

His two daughters were Mary Clifford Whitten King, who had lived in Belton in Bell, the adjoining county, and *Sarah Rebecca "Sallie" Whitten Ritchie, who lived in Guntown, Mississippi, until her death in 1908. The Kings' four children were: Sallie Florence, Joseph Sayers, Rufus Whitten, and Hugh Clarence. The Ritchie children were: Jettie Clifford, Robert Calvin, and Linda Rilla, who married David Edward Smith.*

Cousin E. S. G. very probably was a member of the large Goss family, descendants of Talitha Emily's Aunt Melicent Mazelle Whitten, who married Nathaniel Harbin Goss and moved to Phelps County, Missouri. Members of the Goss clan wrote often and were much interested in Whitten history. Mrs. Crow was her sister, Matilda Allen Whitten, who married Ira Crow and lived in Lee County, Alabama.

The paragraph describing correspondence with Dr. Whitten of Louisville seems to be a shot in the dark. I can find nothing to connect our Whittens to the two brothers, although the search goes on. Another of Reverend James Whitten's daughters wrote that our earliest Whitten, Charles, came into Virginia from Pennsylvania. Research in that state and in Maryland may yet lead us to his origins.

Several branches of our family produced Texas pioneers. The Roddy family seems to have led the pack, arriving in 1830. William and Ahimas Reagan reached Tejas before 1836. John Whitten Barrett and his parents arrived during the days of the Republic. The Alvin Earle and Alfred Whittens settled there shortly after Texas became one of the United States. Within a few short years following the Civil War came these families: the Calvin Thompson Whittens, Rufus Young and Mary Clifford King, the Lankfords, the Davises, four children of William S. Whitten, the Silas Reagan (b. 1815) Whittens, married daughters of Rev. Arphax and Matilda Bennett Whitten, plus the Reverend's second wife, Aurelia Priddy, with their children. Their graves are scattered over east and south Texas. Records of their presence abound. Living descendants can be easily located.

There surely must be other Whittens, Earles, and Reagans whose trails we have not yet discovered who helped build the Lone Star State. We can only hope someone finds and records the stories of their lives.

Index

Armistead, Cassidy Clark, 80, 98
Armistead, Emily Murray, 98
Armistead, Eugene Francis, 80, 98
Armistead, Jack Murray, 59, 80, 98
Armistead, Jane Theresa Barber (wife of
Jack), 80, 98
Armistead, Marianne Ferris (wife of
Willis Jr.), 80, 98
Armistead, Martha Sidney Clark (wife of
Willis), 44, 59, 80
Armistead, Sidney Merrill. See Dixey,
Sidney Merrill Armistead (wife of
Robert)
Armistead, Willis William, 59, 80
Armistead, Willis William Jr., 59, 80, 98
Armstrong, Willie Jean. See Newby,
Willie Jean Armstrong (wife of
Glenn)
Aronson, Charles A., 28
Aronson, Cora Elvira Elizabeth Grogan
(wife of Charles), 25, 28
Arrington, Alice Estelle. See Mason,
Alice Estelle Arrington (wife of
Edwin)
Arthur, Tomie Elizabeth Grogan (wife of
William), 25, 28
Arthur, William Andrew, 28
Atkinson, Lillian. See Ard, Lillian
Atkinson (wife of Thomas)
Attebug, Johnnie Joyce. See Grimes,
Johnnie Joyce Attebug (wife of
Randall)
Autry, Dustin Eugene, 173, 174
Avera, Mary Earle Lankford (wife of
Thomas), 105, 111
Avera, Thomas Jefferson, 111
Avert, Rachel Grace Carter, 152, 157
Avery, Needham, 7
Avery, Sarah Elizabeth Reagan (wife of
Needham), 5
Aviani, Judith. See Turnbow, Judith
Aviani (wife of William)
Axen, Evans, 32
Axen, Mary Patricia Floyd (wife of
Evans), 32
Ayers, Julia A., 16, 24
Ayers, Loucinda E. See Rogers,
Loucinda E. Ayers (wife of Timon)
Ayers, Louvicie Caroline, 16, 24
Ayers, Malinda C. See Redmond,
Malinda C. Ayers (wife of Manuel)
Ayers, Martha Elizabeth Goss (wife of
Nathaniel), 14, 16, 24
Ayers, Mary Melicent, 16, 24
Ayers, Nathaniel Jackson, 16, 24, 28
Ayers, Reuben, 16
Ayers, Sarah E. See Clay, Sarah E. Ayers
(wife of Eleazer)
Ayers, Sarah Frances Manly (wife of
Nathaniel), 28
Ayres, Harriet Turrell (wife of
Nathaniel), 24
Ayres, Lucinda Ellen. See Slagle,
Lucinda Ellen Ayres (wife of James)
Ayres, Nathaniel Jackson Jr., 24

Ayres, Reuben C., 24
Ayres, Sarah Frances Manley (wife of
Nathaniel), 24

B

Bagley, Caroline Matilda "Carrie" (wife
of James J.), 6, 8, 9
Bagley, James J., 8, 9
Bagley, James Robert, 8, 9
Bagley, Noble Reagan, 8, 9
Bailey, Freeda Yvonne. See Martin,
Freeda Yvonne Bailey (wife of
Glenn)
Baily, Sarah. See Holt, Sarah Baily (wife
of Creed)
Bainer, Gregory, 138, 145
Bainer, Madeline Jane, 138, 145
Bainer, Martha Laurie McCallen (wife of
Gregory), 128, 138, 145
Bainer, Whiteney Ann, 137, 147
Bainer, Whitney Ann, 138, 145
Baines, Berta. See Morgan, Berta Baines
(wife of Norman)
Baker, Alberta Collins (wife of Shelby),
214, 215, 217
Baker, Connie. See Tabler, Connie Baker
(wife of Russell)
Baker, Dawn Ann Pittman (wife of
Joseph), 217, 218
Baker, Delbert, 29
Baker, Elizabeth Claire, 215, 217
Baker, Elizabeth Gaye McCann (wife of
Richard), 54, 75
Baker, Joseph Shelby, 217, 218
Baker, Joseph Wiley, 217, 218
Baker, Julia Irene Simmons (wife of
Delbert), 25, 29
Baker, Richard, 75
Baker, Shelby Harold, 215, 217
Banks, Dallas Alaina, 88
Banks, Dohn, 88
Banks, Maya Elaine Dixon (wife of
Dohn), 67, 88
Barber, Ida S. See Whitten, Ida S. Barber
(wife of Albert)
Barber, Jane Theresa. See Armistead,
Jane Theresa Barber (wife of Jack)
Barber, Nora. See Whitten, Nora Barber
(wife of Albert)
Barett, Julie. See McDonald, Julie
Barrett
Barker, Leonard, 4, 6
Barker, Sarah Reagan (wife of Leonard),
3, 4, 6
Barker, Thomas, 4, 6
Barley, Annie Barnett Roten (wife of
Claude), 148, 152, 157
Barley, Beatrice Carlton (wife of
Thomas), 157
Barley, Claude L., 152, 157
Barley, Pauline Ross. See Salmon,
Pauline Ross Barley (wife of James)
Barley, Thomas Luther, 152, 157
Barmore, Bunyan B., 165

Barmore, Mary Ellen Davis (wife of
Bunyan), 164, 165
Barnes, Angela Tabler (wife of Paul), 75,
94
Barnes, Derek Michael, 94
Barnes, Paul, 94
Barnwell, James Foster, 216, 217
Barnwell, Laura, 175
Barnwell, Laura Ann Holmes (wife of
James), 214, 216, 217
Barnwell, Patricia Ann. See Richardson,
Patricia Ann Barnwell (wife of
Kenneth)
Barret, John Marion, 57, 78, 97
Barrett, Ada Mae. See Shuck, Ada Mae
Barrett (wife of Tom)
Barrett, Albert Gallatin, 34, 35, 244
Barrett, Alice Lynch (wife of Joseph),
44, 58
Barrett, Alice Mae Gerston (wife of
Louise), 62, 83
Barrett, Alma Crystal, 42, 56
Barrett, Altha Mae, 57
Barrett, Alvis C., 40, 49
Barrett, Alyse Caroline, 79, 97
Barrett, Amanda, 36, 43
Barrett, Amanda Annis, 37, 44
Barrett, Amanda Catherine. See McCan,
Amanda Catherine Barrett (wife of
James)
Barrett, Amy Elizabeth, 66, 88
Barrett, Andre, 58, 78
Barrett, Andrea, 84
Barrett, Andrienne Louise. See Rabe,
Andrienne Louise Barrett (wife of
Richard)
Barrett, Ann (wife of Lee), 78, 97
Barrett, Ann Elizabeth "Nancy". See
Jenkins, Ann Elizabeth Barrett (wife
of John)
Barrett, Ann Louise, 79, 97
Barrett, Anne Mae Brazelton (wife of
William), 50, 67
Barrett, Anne Seales (wife of William),
42, 56
Barrett, Annevieve Fraser (wife of Ottie),
49, 66
Barrett, Annie Laura, 42
Barrett, Ariah Carolyn Adams (wife of
Johnston), 39, 48
Barrett, Arie Lena. See Floyd, Arie Lena
Barrett (wife of Jason)

Barrett, Ariebeth Alma. See Bott,
Ariebeth Alma Barrett (wife of
Ronald), See Stanley, Ariebeth Alma
Barrett (wife of Harry)
Barrett, Ava Rae, 43, 57
Barrett, Avalon Bennett, 49, 66
Barrett, Barbara (daughter of Henry), 57,
78

Barrett, Barbara (daughter of William), 50, 78

Barrett, Barbara Ann Craig (wife of John Louis), 63, 84

Barrett, Barbara Cunningham (wife of James Jr.), 79, 97

Barrett, Beatrice Little (wife of Roland), 56, 76

Barrett, Bernice. See Powers, Bernice Barrett

Barrett, Bertha Ohlenberger (wife of Samuel), 43, 57

Barrett, Bessie, 42, 56

Barrett, Bessie Lee Wells (wife of Marion), 58, 79

Barrett, Betty Jean, 56, 76

Barrett, Betty Spake (wife of Robert), 96

Barrett, Beulah, 39, 48

Barrett, Billie, 62

Barrett, Billie Jean. See Heck, Billie Jean Barrett (wife of Maurice)

Barrett, Billie Joe. See Gray, Billie Joe Barrett (wife of James)

Barrett, Billio Joe. See McDonald, Billie Jo Barrett (wife of Mason)

Barrett, Billy Ray Barrett Jr., 83

Barrett, Blanche, 44, 58

Barrett, Bobbie Jean. See Lowe, Bobbie Jean Barret (wife of Henry)

Barrett, Bobbie Marigold (wife of Henry), 57, 78

Barrett, Bobbie O'Nell. See Jolly, Bobbie O'Nell Barrett (wife of Winston)

Barrett, Bracil C., 87

Barrett, Brenda Ann. See Thompson, Brenda Ann Barrett (wife of Mark)

Barrett, Bruce O'Neal, 79, 97

Barrett, Carol Ann Klapperich (wife of Ottie), 66, 88

Barrett, Carolyn. See Nelson, Carolyn Barrett (wife of Morris)

Barrett, Carolyn Louise. See Guedry, Carolyn Louise Barrett (wife of Joel)

Barrett, Catherine Delbert Haley (wife of Floyd), 59, 79

Barrett, Celil, 39

Barrett, Charlene, 50, 67

Barrett, Charles Robert, 56, 76

Barrett, Cherie (wife of Lee), 78

Barrett, Christine, 62

Barrett, Christy Ann, 79, 97

Barrett, Clarence Brooks, 45, 60, 81

Barrett, Clarence Randall, 63, 84

Barrett, Clemmons Carmon, 39, 48, 64

Barrett, Cleo Ferrell (wife of John William), 47, 62

Barrett, Connard W., 36, 42

Barrett, Dana Lynn. See Fincher, Dana Lynn Barrett (wife of Jeff)

Barrett, Dana Renee. See Grant, Dana Renee Barrett (wife of William)

Barrett, Daniel Alton, 39, 47

Barrett, Daniel Eugene, 66, 88

Barrett, Daniel Louie, 83

Barrett, Daniel William, 84

Barrett, Darla Sue, 77, 96

Barrett, Darla Tiel (wife of Robert), 96

Barrett, David, 11–12, 12, 34, 243

Barrett, David (son of John Daniel), 39, 46

Barrett, David Albert, 34, 36, 42

Barrett, David Earl, 56, 76

Barrett, David Lee, 59, 79

Barrett, David Roscoe, 62, 83

Barrett, David Russell, 83

Barrett, David William, 34, 35, 38

Barrett, Deborah Kay, 77, 96

Barrett, Della, 39, 48

Barrett, Della Ilene Lloyd (wife of James David), 44, 58

Barrett, Delma Lee Walls (wife of Marion), 57

Barrett, Denise Orlean, 77, 96

Barrett, Devin, 83

Barrett, Diana (wife of Patrick), 66

Barrett, Donald J., 57

Barrett, Donald Louis, 58

Barrett, Donald Ray, 76

Barrett, Donna Jean, 79, 97

Barrett, Doris. See Frings, Doris Barret (wife of Gerhard)

Barrett, Dorothy Elaine, 48, 64

Barrett, Earl M., 47, 62

Barrett, Eddie C., 40, 48

Barrett, Edgar Lee, 39, 47, 61

Barrett, Edith Hill Davis (wife of Samuel), 43, 57

Barrett, Edna Hines (wife of Guy), 43, 58

Barrett, Edna Pearl Carroll (wife of Jake), 49, 65

Barrett, Effie Hale (wife of Jonathon), 38

Barrett, Eldra. See Telotte, Eldra Barrett (wife of Ira)

Barrett, Eldra Randolph (wife of James Walter), 43, 56

Barrett, Elizabeth Ann Comer (wife of James Bruce), 79, 98

Barrett, Elizabeth D. Seaton (wife of Albert), 34, 244

Barrett, Elizabeth E. Walters (wife of William), 35, 39

Barrett, Elizabeth Hannah. See Coburn, Mariam Hannah Barrett (wife of Hansell)

Barrett, Elizabeth Hill (wife of David), 35, 38

Barrett, Elizabeth Mariam, 34, 35

Barrett, Elizabeth Skelton (wife of Joseph), 35, 38

Barrett, Elizabeth Whitten (wife of David), 12, 33, 34, 243, 244

Barrett, Ellen Johnson (wife of Julius), 47, 62

Barrett, Ellie Marie. See Smith, Ellie Marie Barrett (wife of Wendall)

Barrett, Ellwood Talmage, 48, 65, 86

Barrett, Elma Blanche (wife of William Robert), 48, 65

Barrett, Elma Blanche Henry (wife of William Robert), 48, 65

Barrett, Elwood Talmage Jr., 65

Barrett, Emma Ardel (wife of James), 58, 79

Barrett, Ennis Marie Whitley (wife of Ellwood), 65, 86

Barrett, Ercel. See Straley, Ercel Barrett (wife of Carl)

Barrett, Ernest, 42, 56

Barrett, Essie Eula, 43, 56

Barrett, Essie Marcum (wife Jonathon), 38

Barrett, Etta Maud, 39, 47

Barrett, Evelyn Marie. See Nichols, Evelyn Marie Barrett (wife of Edward)

Barrett, Evelyn Roland (wife of Roy), 58

Barrett, Fannie Florence May. See Henderson, Fannie Florence May Barrett (wife of Leon)

Barrett, Fannie May Johnson (wife of Robert), 62, 83

Barrett, Finias, 39, 46

Barrett, Florence. See Jones, Florence Barrett (wife of Jim)

Barrett, Florence (daughter of Samuel), 43

Barrett, Frankie Lucille. See Vetuski, Frankie Lucille Barrett (wife of Mitchell)

Barrett, Freida. See Cummings, Freida Barrett (wife of Troy), See Weidel, Frieda Adel Barrett (wife of Roy)

Barrett, Gayle, 44, 58

Barrett, Gayle Gordon Rhea (wife of Melvin), 65, 86

Barrett, George (son of David), 36, 43

Barrett, George (son of Luther), 37, 44

Barrett, George T., 40, 49

Barrett, Georgianna Rose Redcan (wife of Ronald), 79, 97

Barrett, Gerald Elmer, 57, 77, 96

Barrett, Gerald Mark, 77, 96

Barrett, Glen Law, 56, 76

Barrett, Glenda Ann. See Spate, Glenda Ann Barrett (wife of Ronald)

Barrett, Glenda Gail. See Bierschwale, Glenda Gail Barrett (wife of William)

Barrett, Glenda Jo Ward (wife of Bracil), 49, 66, 87

Barrett, Glenda Ruth, 76

Barrett, Glenn Andrew, 42, 56, 76

Barrett, Glenne Ruth, 56, 76

Barrett, Guy Roland, 37, 43, 58

Barrett, Guy Roland Jr., 44, 59

Barrett, H. Richard, 40, 50

Barrett, Harriett Reggio (wife of William), 49, 67

Barrett, Hattie Lee. See William, Hattie Lee Barrett (wife of John)

Barrett, Hattie Louise Furlow (wife of Louise), 56, 78

Barrett, Helen, 62

Boyd, John J., 99
Boyd, Martha E., 99
Boyd, Mary E. Dalton (wife of John), 99
Boyles, Carol Teresa. See Whitten, Carol
    Teresa Boyles (wife of Joseph)
Bradley, Bertha. See Morgan, Bertha
    Bradley (wife of Silas)
Bradley, Donna Ellen. See Johnson,
    Donna Ellen Bradley (wife of Bert)
Bradley, Ed Farmer, 107, 116
Bradley, Elliott Elizabeth, 107, 116
Bradley, Faye Whitten (wife of J. L.),
    153, 158
Bradley, Frank Herman, 107, 116
Bradley, Frank Hudson, 107, 116
Bradley, J. L., 158
Bradley, Lina Mae Davis (wife of Ed),
    116
Bradley, Louise Elverta, 107, 116
Bradley, Maude Elliott Whitten (wife of
    Frank), 102, 107, 116
Bradley, Naomi. See Karch, Naomi
    Bradley (wife of Hamilton)
Branson, Allison Elizabeth, 240, 241
Brawner, Nancy. See Reagan, Nancy
    Brawner
Brazeal, Harley Elizabeth, 131, 141
Brazeal, Kayla Marie, 131, 141
Brazeal, Lawrence Mitchell, 131, 141
Brazeal, Nancy Ann Gillespie (wife of
    Lawrence), 120, 131, 141
Brazelton, Anne Mae. See Barrett, Anne
    Mae Brazelton (wife of William)
Brewer, Frances Marion, 118
Brewer, Mariam Elinor Whitten (wife of
    Frances), 118
Bridgeforth, Caroline Ann Hill (wife of
    David), 232, 235
Bridgeforth, David, 232
Bridgeforth, David Allen, 232, 235
Bridgeforth, Kimberly, 232
Bridges, Richie. See Whitten, Richie
    Bridges (wife of Lester)
Briggs, Helen. See Hale, Helen Briggs
    (wife of Jack)

Brimer, Trenie Diane. See Malone,
    Trenie Diane Brimer (wife of Larry)
Britt, Omazelia. See Thomason,
    Omazelia Britt (wife of James)
Brooks, Beverly Samsa (wife of John
    III), 68
Brooks, Ford Lamar, 51, 68, 90
Brooks, Harris Wycoff, 90
Brooks, Harry Ford, 51, 68
Brooks, Jeffrey August, 90
Brooks, John Redding II, 68, 90
Brooks, John Redding III, 90
Brooks, Leslie. See Suskin, Leslie
    Brooks (wife of Marc)
Brooks, Lucy Elizabeth. See Barrett,
    Lucy Elizabeth Brooks (wife of
    Silas)

Brooks, Mildred Ellena. See Hull,
    Mildred Ellena (wife of Carl)
Brooks, Minnie Gladys Winborn (wife of
    Harry), 41, 51, 68
Brooks, Norene Janice Franzer (wife of
    Ford), 68, 90
Brooks, Owen, 30, 32
Brooks, Rubye Dell Floyd (wife of
    Owen), 27, 30, 32
Brooks, Samuel Young II, 68, 90
Brooks, Samuel Young III, 90
Brooks, Sandra Sue Harris (wife of
    Samuel), 90
Brown, Alta May. See Hamilton, Alta
    May Brown (wife of Boyd)
Brown, Fred, 46
Brown, Irene (wife of Terry), 86
Brown, James Henry, 28
Brown, Jane Ann. See Yarbough, Jane
    Ann Brown (wife of Michael)
Brown, Julia May Grogan (wife of
    James), 25, 28
Brown, Lingo, 67, 88
Brown, Patricia. See Young, Patricia
    Brown (wife of Loren)
Brown, Shirley Jane Dixon (wife of
    Lingo), 50, 67, 88
Brown, Terry Lee, 67, 88
Brown, Zetha Roberta Holcomb (wife of
    James), 38, 46
Brownfield, Lester, 25
Brownfield, Lillian Myrtle Louise
    Morgan (wife of Lester), 18, 25
Brownlee, Emily C. See Whitten, Emily
    C. Brownlee (wife of Edd)
Bruce, Orville Glenn, 29
Bruce, Shirley Ruth Simmons (wife of
    Orville), 25, 29
Brudnick, Blythe Loreen. See Allen,
    Blythe Loreen Brudnick (wife of
    Larry)
Bryan, Ima Osamae Barrett (wife of
    Jim), 40
Bryan, Jim, 40
Bryant, Jeanette. See Whitten, Jeanette
    Bryant (wife of James)

Bryd, Ruby Kathryn McGaughey (wife
    of Sylvestor), 155, 160
Bryd, Sylvestor, 160
Buchan, Dorothy. See Turnbow, Dorothy
    Buchan (wife of William)
Burch, Harry Allen, 29
Burch, Patricia Jean Simmons (wife of
    Harry), 25, 29
Burgess, Dink, 61
Burgess, Rose Lee Morgan (wife of
    Dink), 46, 61
Burke, Carlton Clark, 125, 136
Burke, Celia Kay Davis (wife of
    Carlton), 136
Burke, Coda. See Roten, Coda Burke
    (wife of Earnest)

Burke, Corrine Whitten (wife of
    William), 107, 115, 125
Burke, Crystal Lynne, 136, 144
Burke, Deborah Lynne. See Bay,
    Deborah Lynne Burke (wife of
    Kevin)
Burke, DeeVonne Clark (wife of Leslie),
    125, 136
Burke, Ethan Luke, 136
Burke, J. W., 12
Burke, Laura. See Barrett, Laura Burke
    (wife of Jonathon)
Burke, Leslie Carlton, 115, 125, 136
Burke, Sarah Lorinne, 125, 136
Burke, Steven Dean, 125, 136
Burke, Tiffany Lynne, 136, 144
Burke, William Leslie, 115, 125
Burkett, Lee Anne, 129
Burkitt, Evelyn Kay Whitten (wife of
    Frank), 128, 138
Burkitt, Frank, 128, 138
Burnett, Amanda, 89
Burnett, John, 89
Burnett, Justin Cain, 89
Burnett, Le Anne Turner (wife of John),
    89
Burnett, May, 89
Burnich, Louise Kathryn. See Barrett,
    Louise Kathryn Burnich (wife of
    Clarence)
Burns, Rebeckah Reagan (wife of
    William), 3, 5
Burns, William, 5
Burr, Marie. See Whitten, Marie Burr
    (wife of Sherod)
Burt, H. H. (Mrs.), 22
Burzynski, Michael, 133–34
Burzynski, Patricia Anne Marceau (wife
    of Michael), 123, 133–34
Byers, Lessie May. See Whitten, Lessie
    May Byers (wife of Harvey)
Byrd, Larry, 159
Byrd, Paula Kay Kelton (wife of Larry),
    155, 159
Byrnes, Alena Victoria. See Whitten,
    Alena Victoria Byrnes (wife of
    Leon)

C

Cain, Kay McCallen (wife of Robert),
    128, 138, 145
Cain, Robert Bruce, 138, 145
Cain, Robert Neil, 138, 145
Caldwell, Amelia, 22
Caldwell, Elizabeth. See Young,
    Elizabeth Caldwell (wife of Lester)
Calef, Anna Myrtle Grimes (wife of
    Mahlon), 179, 192, 193, 197
Calef, Elizabeth. See Howells, Elizabeth
    Calef (wife of Mansfield)
Calef, Gladys. See Hanson, Gladys Calef
    (wife of Albert)
Calef, Lucie. See Walp, Lucie Calef
    (wife of James)

256

Davis, Horace A., 91
Davis, Isaac Alvin, 164, 165
Davis, J. T., 111
Davis, James, 194, 198
Davis, James (son of James), 194, 198
Davis, James Addison, 164, 166
Davis, James Alvin, 165, 166
Davis, Jewell Celeste, 165
Davis, Joan Kathleen Barrett (wife of Robert), 49, 66, 88
Davis, Joanna Lee, 66, 88
Davis, John Alexander, 165
Davis, Joseph Alexander, 164, 165
Davis, Josephine Rebecca. See Cunningham, Josephine Rebecca Davis (wife of W. M.)
Davis, Joyce Walker (wife of Bobby), 167
Davis, Kay Lynn, 66, 88
Davis, Lina Mae. See Bradley, Lina Mae Davis (wife of Ed)
Davis, Lucille. See Odom, Lucille Davis (wife of Bert)
Davis, Marianna Johnson (wife of Addison Jr.), 166, 167
Davis, Martha Ann. See Reagan, Martha Ann (wife of Joseph)
Davis, Martha Caroline. See Porter, Martha Caroline Davis (wife of Hosea)
Davis, Mary Ellen. See Barmore, Mary Ellen Davis (wife of Bunyan)
Davis, Mary Ethel Sharp (wife of Addison), 166
Davis, Mary Jean, 166
Davis, Mary Lynne, 167
Davis, Mary Shufford. See Moore, Mary Shufford Davis (wife of William III)
Davis, Nancy Ellen. See Handley, Nancy Ellen Davis (wife of S. Finis)
Davis, Nancy M. See Dupree, Nancy M. Davis (wife of Tom)
Davis, Olive, 166
Davis, Olive (wife of James), 165
Davis, Robert Earl, 66, 88
Davis, Robert Scott, 167
Davis, Ruth (wife of David), 166
Davis, Stanley, 166
Davis, Susan Leigh, 167
Davis, Thomas, 165, 166
Davis, Walter Wood, 194, 198
Davis, Wanda. See Forrester, Wanda Davis (wife of Leroy)
Davis, Zeena Holt (wife of James), 192, 194, 198
Dean, Laura Delia, 216, 218
Dean, Sheila Ann. See Grimes, Sheila Ann Dean (wife of David)
Deburger, Sandra Arlene. See Vetuski, Sandra Arlene Deburger (wife of Michael)
DeForge, Laura Katharine Holt (wife of Michael), 200, 205
DeForge, Michael James, 205

Delgado, Keri Gloria. See Lee, Keri Gloria Delgado (wife of Robert)
Densmore, Mary Ann. See Goss, Mary Ann Densmore (wife of Calvin)
Densmore, Melicent Elvira (wife of Samuel), 14, 17
Densmore, Melicent Rhoda. See Grogan, Melicent Rhoda Densmore (wife of Richard)
Densmore, Samuel Mercer, 17
Dent, Anna. See Cook, Anna Dent (wife of Francis)
Desantis, Andrew William, 144, 146
Desantis, Drew Anthony, 146
Desantis, Kyle Anthony, 144
Deshough, Martha, 147, 149
Deshough, Rebecca Ann M. Whitten (wife of Sam), 147
Deshough, Sam Louis, 147
Deshough, William, 147, 149
Desmore, Melicent Elvira (wife of Samuel), 25
Desmore, Samuel Mercer, 16, 25
DeWald, Henry, 29
DeWald, Jessie Lucille Simmons (wife of Henry), 25, 29
DeWitt, Jay C. Lane (wife of John), 82
DeWitt, John, 82
Dickey, Alice Blanche. See McCan, Alice Blanche Dickey (wife of Samuel)
Dickey, Donald, 80
Dickey, Matisa Ann (wife of Donald), 59, 80
Dickey, Sarah Ida. See McCan, Sarah Ida Dickey (wife of James)
Dikeman, Alice. See Golden, Alice Dikeman (wife of Joseph)
Dilworth, Celia Kee. See Morgan, Celia Kee Dilworth (wife of Edward)
Dilworth, Evelyn Elsie Jay (wife of Thomas II), 121, 132
Dilworth, Gara Katherine Wheelock (wife of Thomas), 112, 121
Dilworth, Kathryn Earle. See Hemphill, Katherine Earle Dilworth (wife of Meredith)
Dilworth, Margaret Scott. See Cooper, Margaret Scott Dilworth (wife of William)
Dilworth, Margaret Scott (wife of Thomas). See Dilworth, Margaret Scott (wife of Thomas)
Dilworth, Marion Adair. See Lucenay, Marion Adair Dilworth (wife of Henri)
Dilworth, Mary Kee Lankford (wife of Thomas), 102, 105, 244
Dilworth, Thomas Gordon, 105, 112, 121
Dilworth, Thomas Gordon II, 112, 121, 132
Dilworth, Thomas Gordon III, 121, 132
Dilworth, Thomas Marion, 105, 112
DiSantes, Damon, 144, 146

DiSantes, Karen Wells Dannels (wife of Damon), 136, 144, 146
Disharoon, J. R., 157
Dissmeyer, Felice, 164
Dissmeyer, George Edward, 31
Dissmeyer, Jewel Felice Floyd (wife of George), 30, 31
Dissmeyer, Sharon Beth, 32
Dissmeyer, Stacy Leann, 32
Dittmar, Beatrice Whitten (wife of John), 237, 238, 239
Dittmar, Caroline. See Hill, Caroline Dittmar
Dittmar, George, 238, 239
Dittmar, John, 238, 239
Dittmar, John F., 238, 239
Dittmar, LaDean. See Richardson, LaDean Dittmar
Dittmar, Lorena. See Tincup, Lorena Dittmar
Ditzman, Cary Lynn, 99
Ditzman, Lisa Louise Jordy (wife of Cary), 81, 99
Dix, Cecil V., 121, 133
Dix, Dorothy Ann, 121, 133
Dix, John Lankford, 121, 133
Dix, Lettie Belle Crebau (wife of Cecil), 112, 121, 133
Dixey, Robert Livingston, 80
Dixey, Sidney Merrill Armistead (wife of Robert), 59, 80
Dixon, Carl Cranfield, 67
Dixon, Dawn Ione. See Gaston, Dawn Ione Dixon (wife of Billy)
Dixon, James Ray, 50, 67, 88
Dixon, James Ray Jr., 67, 88
Dixon, Lanore Mannon Johnson (wife of James), 88
Dixon, Lauren Camille, 88
Dixon, Mary Ellen Finley (wife of James), 67, 88
Dixon, Maya Elaine. See Banks, Maya Elaine Dixon (wife of Dohn)
Dixon, Shirley Jane. See Brown, Shirley Jane Dixon (wife of Lingo), See Turner, Shirley Jane Dixon (wife of Mac)
Dixon, Tana Arlene. See Harrington, Tana Arlene Dixon (wife of Jack), See Stewart, Tana Arlene Dixon (wife of Daniel)
Dixon, Toby, 67, 89
Doane, May. See Grimes, May Doane (wife of Richard)
Dobbs, Avarilla Thoresa. See Perry, Avarilla Thoresa Dobbs (wife of Benjamin)
Doctor, Katherine Conant Francis (wife of Kenneth), 200, 205
Doctor, Kenneth, 205
Dodd, Pam. See Castle, Pam Dodd (wife of Ronald)

Gless, Earl William, 214, 216
Gless, Earl William Jr., 214, 216
Gless, Kelly Christopher, 216
Gless, Mattie Jo Turner (wife of Earl), 213, 214, 216
Gless, Sydney Ann. See Stadnicki, Sydney Ann Gless (wife of Richard)
Godwin, Brian Frank, 133, 142, 146
Godwin, Eileen, 142, 146
Godwin, Jennifer Curington (wife of John), 142, 146
Godwin, Jessica Mauree, 142, 146
Godwin, John Scott, 133, 142, 146
Godwin, Joshua Tyree, 142, 146
Godwin, Margaret Ann Cooper (wife of Robbie), 121, 133, 142
Godwin, Mary Aline, 142, 146
Godwin, Robbie Don, 133, 142
Godwin, Romy Klein (wife of Brian), 142, 146
Golden, Alice Dikeman (wife of Joseph), 52, 70
Golden, Allie Angeline McCan (wife of Eugene), 36, 41, 52
Golden, Anna Bell. See Simmons, Anna Bell Golden (wife of Alton)
Golden, Byron Ethyl, 52, 70
Golden, Connie Ola. See McGee, Connie Ola Golden (wife of Charlie)

Golden, Edward, 52, 70
Golden, Effie Wyonia. See Vacula, Effie Wyonia Golden (wife of Ernie)
Golden, Ethel Cronnin (wife of Virgil), 52, 70
Golden, Eugene Henry, 41, 52
Golden, George Woodburn, 41, 53
Golden, Hulden Eugene. See Blair, Hulda Eugene Golden (wife of R. D.)
Golden, James, 52, 71
Golden, James Joseph, 41, 52, 70
Golden, Marie, 52, 71
Golden, Maxine, 52, 71
Golden, Minnie Lucille, 41, 53
Golden, Olen, 52, 70
Golden, Sadie Mae. See Harper, Sadie Mae Golden (wife of George)
Golden, Talitha Amanda. See Harris, Talitha Amanda Golden (wife of William), See Stowe, Talitha Amanda Golden (wife of William)
Golden, Verla, 52, 71
Golden, Virgil, 52, 70
Golden, Virgil Littleton, 41, 52, 70
Golden, Winnie Viola. See Mason, Winnie Viola Golden (wife of Williad)
Goodwin, Adonna Rose Vetuski (wife of Albert), 64, 85
Goodwin, Albert Glenn, 85
Goodwin, Martha Lynn. See McCann, Martha Lynn Goodwin (wife of Gary)

Gordon, Clyde Hearne Whitten (wife of Frank), 212, 213
Gordon, Frank, 213
Gosnell, Charles, 11
Goss, Alfred Webb, 14, 17
Goss, Benjamin Franklin, 14, 16
Goss, Calvin Benson, 14, 17
Goss, Catherine Ellen Shelton (wife of Silas), 17
Goss, Eunice West (wife of James), 17
Goss, Hannah Mancencella (wife of Robert), 17
Goss, Hulda Jane Wilkins (wife of William), 17
Goss, James Whitten, 14, 17
Goss, Juliann Melissa Irene. See Morgan, Juliann Melissa Irene Goss (wife of John)
Goss, Louisa Caroline. See West, Louisa Caroline Goss (wife of James)
Goss, Louisa Perry (wife of Benjamin), 16
Goss, Malinda Caroline Payne (wife of James), 17
Goss, Malinda Eleanor. See Perry, Malinda Eleanor Goss (wife of Evan)
Goss, Martha Elizabeth. See Ayers, Martha Elizabeth Goss (wife of Nathaniel)

Goss, Mary Ann Densmore (wife of Calvin), 17
Goss, Mary Elizabeth Roe (wife of Nathaniel), 17
Goss, Mary Irene, 14, 17
Goss, Melicent Elvira. See Densmore, Melicent Elvira (wife of Samuel)
Goss, Melicent Mazelle Whitten (wife of Nathaniel), 13, 14, 15, 16, 22, 245–47
Goss, Nathaniel Harbin, 14, 15, 16, 22, 245–47
Goss, Nathaniel Jackson, 14, 17
Goss, Orpha Louisa, 14, 18
Goss, Robert Lewis, 14, 17
Goss, Silas Washington, 14, 17, 22
Goss, Wilson Lumpkin, 14, 17
Gossell, Janice Marie. See Madden, Janice Marie Gossell (wife of Edward)
Gowensville Baptist Church. See Tygar Baptist Church
Grabow, Sally Mae. See Turpin, Sally Mae Grabow (wife of James)
Grady, Clyde Frederick, 77, 96
Grady, Dennis Leon, 77, 96
Grady, Hazel Louise Starns (wife of Clyde), 57, 77, 96
Graham, Bridget. See Whitten, Bridget Graham (wife of Alfred)
Graham, Howard Marvin, 128, 139
Graham, Howard Marvin Jr., 128, 139
Graham, John, 146
Graham, Kathryn Martin, 128, 139

Graham, Martha Ann. See Mask, Martha Ann Graham (wife of Howard)
Graham, Ruby Elizabeth Henderson (wife of Howard), 118, 125, 139
Grant, Brooklyn Renee, 96
Grant, Dana Renee Barrett (wife of William), 77, 96
Grant, Ryann Nichole, 96
Grant, William Kyle, 96
Grantham, Arthur Ross, 80
Grantham, Joyce Rae Manning (wife of Arthur), 59, 80
Graves, Bennie Forest. See Whitten, Bennie Forest Graves (wife of Hulbert)
Graves, Bessie Bell, 38, 46
Graves, Ida Lou, 38, 46
Graves, Katie Emma, 38, 46
Graves, Margaret Coburn (wife of T. J.), 35, 38, 46
Graves, T. J., 38, 46
Gray, Billie Joe Barrett (wife of James), 58
Gray, James H., 58
Gray, James Robert Alexander, 58
Gray, John Peter, 29
Gray, Marjory Estel Simmons (wife of John), 25, 29
Gray, Patricia Ann. See Baust, Patricia Ann Gray (wife of Michael)
Graybeal, Betty Holt (wife of Jay), 194, 198, 203
Graybeal, Danielle, 204, 208
Graybeal, Jason, 204, 208
Graybeal, Jay, 198, 203
Graybeal, Kylee, 203, 208
Graybeal, Travis, 203, 208
Green, Bettie Louise, 216, 217
Green, Carlene Ramage. See Langley, Carlene Ramage Green (wife of Judson)
Green, Carline Ramage, 216
Green, Ethel Irene Whitby, 214, 215
Green, Mark, 217, 218
Green, Ripley P., 215, 217
Green, Ripley P. Jr., 216, 217, 218
Green, W. T., 101
Green, Whitten, 217, 218
Green, Yvonne Sweat (wife of Ripley Jr.), 217, 218
Greenlum, Grace (wife of Thomas S.), 238
Greenlum, Lillian, 237, 238
Greenlum, Thomas S., 237, 238
Greenlun, Albert Michael, 237, 238
Greenlun, Mary Amelia Whitten (wife of Albert), 237, 238
Gregory, Brenda. See Whitten, Brenda Gregory (wife of George)
Griffin, David Barrett, 66, 87
Griffin, Harold Dean, 66, 87
Griffin, Rebecca Lynn Curry (wife of David), 87
Griffin, Stephen Anthony, 87
Griffin, Walter Lewis, 66

Griffith, Alice Melinda Grogan (wife of Lawrence), 25, 28
Griffith, Charles Emmity, 28
Griffith, Eva Lucinda Matilda Grogan (wife of Charles), 25, 28
Griffith, Lawrence, 28
Griffon, Mary Jo Bennett (wife of Harold), 49, 66, 87
Grimes, Alfred Holt, 193, 197, 202
Grimes, Amelia Sorenson (wife of Henry), 193, 196
Grimes, Angela Maire, 201, 206
Grimes, Angelica Crystal, 201, 206
Grimes, Anna Myrtle. See Calef, Anna Myrtle Grimes (wife of Mahlon)
Grimes, Annalee Marie Glennen (wife of Lee), 201, 206
Grimes, Betty. See Kaluzok, Betty Grimes (wife of Lawrence)
Grimes, Bevin, 202
Grimes, Brandon Patrick, 201, 206
Grimes, Bruce Bell, 133, 196, 206
Grimes, Bryan Kelly, 201, 206
Grimes, Carolyn Kay. See Neff, Carolyn Kay Grimes (wife of Carroll)
Grimes, Cindy Christine, 196
Grimes, Daniel Allen, 201, 206
Grimes, Darby Clark. See Wyatt, Darby Clark Grimes (wife of Richard)
Grimes, David John, 196, 201, 206
Grimes, Dena Marie, 196, 201
Grimes, Derrick, 201, 206
Grimes, Diane Kein (wife of William), 202, 207
Grimes, Donald Frank, 196, 201
Grimes, Donovan, 201, 206
Grimes, Douglas, 200, 202, 206
Grimes, Douglas (son of William), 202
Grimes, Dustin Chancellor, 201, 206
Grimes, Edgar, 193, 196, 200
Grimes, Edna May Grimes. See Osbourne, Edna May Grimes (wife of Peter)
Grimes, Eileen. See Haney, Eileen Grimes (wife of John)
Grimes, Elmer, 193, 196, 201
Grimes, Emily Cramer (wife of Elmer), 196, 201
Grimes, Frances Adella Holt (wife of John), 178, 179, 180, 181–91, 191, 193
Grimes, Glenda Joyce, 196, 201
Grimes, Gwen Lamson (wife of Lyle), 197, 202
Grimes, Heidi Hrung (wife of Bruce), 201, 206
Grimes, Helen June Murphy (wife of John), 196, 201
Grimes, Henry Loring, 192, 193, 196
Grimes, Ida Helen Reese (wife of Lloyd), 196, 200
Grimes, James, 196, 201
Grimes, Jason Adam, 200, 206
Grimes, Jeffrey Neil, 201, 206
Grimes, Jenifer, 202, 207

Grimes, Jennifer Michele, 201, 206
Grimes, Joanne McEwen (wife of Michael), 201, 206
Grimes, Jocile Norene. See Coate, Jocile Norene Grimes (wife of Larry)
Grimes, John, 193, 196, 201
Grimes, John William, 191, 193
Grimes, Johnnie Joyce Attebug (wife of Randall), 196, 201
Grimes, Karen Jeanelle, 200, 206
Grimes, Kevin, 201, 207
Grimes, Leanne Kaye, 200, 206
Grimes, Lee Allen, 196, 201, 206
Grimes, Lenore Lynn, 200, 206
Grimes, Linda Zito (wife of Steven), 201, 206
Grimes, Lloyd, 193, 196, 200
Grimes, Lloyd Harold, 196, 200, 206
Grimes, Lyle Clark, 193, 197, 202
Grimes, Mahlon Henry, 196, 200
Grimes, Marian Shelmau (wife of Edgar), 196, 200
Grimes, Marsha Henslee (wife of Lloyd), 200, 206
Grimes, Mary Leanne Grimes (wife of Douglas), 196, 200, 206
Grimes, May Doane (wife of Richard), 201
Grimes, Megan, 202, 207
Grimes, Melanie Norlund (wife of Robert), 201, 206
Grimes, Melissa Elliot (wife of Mahlon Henry), 200
Grimes, Michael, 202, 207
Grimes, Michael Clinton, 196, 201, 206
Grimes, Myrtle Hubbell (wife of Alfred), 197, 202
Grimes, Ollie Adella, 192, 193
Grimes, Randall, 193, 201
Grimes, Richard (son of Alfred), 197, 202, 207
Grimes, Richard (son of Elmer), 196, 201, 207
Grimes, Robert Randall, 196, 201, 206, 207
Grimes, Rodney Lee, 196, 200
Grimes, Roy Edgar, 196, 201
Grimes, Sharyl Gentry (wife of Richard), 202, 207
Grimes, Sheila Ann Dean (wife of David), 201, 206
Grimes, Sherri, 201, 207
Grimes, Stephen Randall, 201, 206
Grimes, Steven, 196, 201
Grimes, Steven Patrick, 196, 201, 206
Grimes, Tracy Travis, 200, 206
Grimes, Vici Christena, 200
Grimes, William Alfred Randal, 192, 193
Grimes, William Edward, 196, 201
Grimes, William Ralph, 197, 202, 207
Grimes, Zena, 193, 196
Grimes, Zola Ena. See Sorenson, Zola Ena Grimes (wife of Bernard)

Grimm, Kathryn Dianne Fitzgerald (wife of Larry), 240, 241, 242
Grimm, Kenneth, 241, 242
Grimm, Larry, 241, 242
Grimm, Larry Jr., 241, 242
Grogan, Alice Melinda. See Dragicerie, Alice Melinda Grogan (wife of Mile), See Griffith, Alice Melinda Grogan (wife of Lawrence)
Grogan, Cora Elvira Elizabeth. See Aronson, Cora Elvira Elizabeth Grogan (wife of Charles), See Holt, Cora Elvira Elizabeth Grogan (wife of Alfred)
Grogan, Dewey Grady, 25
Grogan, Dewie Grady, 29
Grogan, Eva Lucinda Matilda Grogan. See Griffith, Eva Lucinda Matilda Grogan (wife of Charles)
Grogan, Homer Calvin, 25, 28
Grogan, Julia May See Brown, Julia May Grogan (wife of James)
Grogan, Melicent Rhoda Densmore (wife of Richard), 17, 25, 28
Grogan, Oscar William, 25, 28
Grogan, Osha Viola. See Frazier, Osha Viola Grogan (wife of Solomon)
Grogan, Richard Wilson, 25, 28
Grogan, Tomie Elizabeth. See Arthur, Tomie Elizabeth Grogan (wife of William), See Phelps, Tomie Elizabeth Grogan (wife of Andrew)
Groover, Margaret Ann. See Malone, Margaret Ann Groover (wife of Lawrence)
Groth, Hazel. See Simmons, Hazel Groth (wife of Laurence)
Guedry, Carolyn Louise Barrett (wife of Joel), 48, 65, 86
Guedry, Joel D., 65, 86
Guedry, Mark Dean, 65, 86
Guidry, Ava Danielle. See Clubb, Ava Danielle Guidry (wife of Paul)
Guidry, Dana Ann. See Eckles, Dana Ann Guidry (wife of Milton)
Guidry, Pauline Suzanne. See West, Pauline Suzanne Guidry (wife of James)
Guidry, Roland Edmond, 160, 162
Guidry, Shirley Ann Roten (wife of Roland), 157, 160, 162
Guinn, Lucy Vining (wife of Paul), 151, 156
Guinn, Paul, 156
Gundy, Maxine Venable (wife of Melvin), 150, 154
Gundy, Melvin Ray, 154
Gunn, Ora Gertrude Barrett (wife of Zaney), 42, 56
Gunn, Zaney, 56
Gurley, Peggy Ann. See Whitten, Peggy Ann Gurley (wife of Taylor)
Guttierrez, Donald, 163
Guttierrez, Patti Gayle Reed (wife of Donald), 161, 163

265

Gutzman, Jeanie Ray. See McCann, Jeanie Ray Gutzman (wife of Donald)

Guyes, Timothy, 83

Guynes, Janet Hutchinson (wife of Larry), 84

Guynes, John, 63, 84

Guynes, Larry Wayne, 63, 84

Guynes, Linda. See Kellerman, Linda Guynes, See Tim, Linda Guynes (wife of Kenneth)

Guynes, Lottie Mae Barrett (wife of Robert), 47, 62, 83

Guynes, Robert, 62, 83

Guynes, Robert Earl, 62, 83

Guynes, Shannon, 83

Guynes, Shirley Jones (wife of Robert), 83

Gyetvay, Janice. See McCallen, Janice Gyetvay (wife of William)

H

Habib, Billie June Vetuski, 63, 85

Haggard, Doris Ann Whitten (wife of Ralph), 110, 120

Haggard, Ralph, 120

Hahamura, Tomo. See Holt, Tomo Hahamura (wife of John)

Hale, Annie, 42

Hale, Effie. See Barrett, Effie Hale (wife of Jonathon)

Hale, Elizabeth Ann, 69, 90

Hale, Elizabeth George Holsomback (wife of Lowis), 238, 239, 240

Hale, Hartwell, 42, 55

Hale, Helen Briggs (wife of Jack), 56

Hale, Hettie M. McCan (wife of Hartwell), 36, 42, 55

Hale, Jack Carl, 42, 56, 76

Hale, James, 69, 90

Hale, James Jr., 69, 90

Hale, Lowis E., 239, 240

Hale, Margaret Winter (wife of Jack), 56, 76

Hale, Marvin, 42, 55

Hale, Mary Elizabeth. See Priester, Mary Elizabeth Hale (wife of V. G.)

Hale, Robin Arnold, 56, 76

Hale, Ruby Jewel, 42, 56

Hale, Shirley Jean, 56, 76

Hale, Stacie Aliene McCann (wife of James), 51, 69, 90

Hale, Virginia. See Farber, Virginia Hale (wife of James)

Haley, Catherine Delbert. See Barrett, Catherine Delbert Haley (wife of Floyd)

Haley, Mary Ellen Belote (wife of Mitchell), 104, 110

Haley, Mitchell, 104, 110

Hall, Billie Earlene Manning (wife of Loys), 59, 80

Hall, Daisy Ruth Holsomback (wife of Otha), 238, 239, 240

Hall, George Meyer, 239, 241

Hall, Glenda. See Floyd, Glenda Hall (wife of Jackson Jr.)

Hall, Loys Lyle, 80

Hall, Otha Eugene, 239, 240

Hall, Winnie. See Reagan, Winnie Hall (wife of Charles III)

Halm, Karen. See Howells, Karen Halm (wife of Robert)

Halsell, Margaret Josephine. See Whitten, Margaret Josephine Halsell (wife of Alfred)

Hamilton, Alta May Brown (wife of Boyd), 195

Hamilton, Boyd, 192, 195

Hamilton, Earl, 192, 195

Hamilton, Mary Savage (wife of Otis), 194

Hamilton, Norma. See Stuht, Norma Hamilton (wife of Albert)

Hamilton, Ortis, 192, 194

Hamilton, Tallulah Tecoa Holt (wife of William), 178, 182, 192, 194

Hamilton, William, 192, 194

Hamlin, Anna Reagan (wife of Eliakim), 3, 5, 175

Hamlin, Dudley J., 175

Hamlin, Eliakim, 5, 175

Hamlink, Betty. See Holt, Betty Hamlink (wife of Raymond)

Hammelman, James Edward, 162, 163

Hammelman, James Robert, 162, 163

Hammelman, Lauren Elizabeth, 162, 163

Hammelman, Patricia Dianne Roten (wife of James), 160, 162, 163

Hand, Nettie Mae. See Whitten, Nettie Mae Hand (wife of Ellis)

Handley, Nancy Ellen Davis (wife of S. Finis), 164, 165, 166

Handley, Robert D., 165, 166

Handley, S. Finis, 165, 166

Haney, Bernard Ivy Whitten (wife of Floy), 223, 226

Haney, Eileen Grimes (wife of John), 196, 201

Haney, Floy, 226

Haney, John, 201

Hannaford, Charlotte Lorene McCann (wife of Jimmie), 54, 74, 94

Hannaford, Jimmie Lee, 74, 94

Hannaford, Teresa Jane, 74

Hanniford, Teresa Jane. See Keen, Teresa Jane Hanniford (wife of Ralph)

Hannon, William, 100, 101

Hansen, Katherine Marie "Kate" Whitten (wife of William), 210, 211

Hansen, William A., 211

Hanson, Albert, 197

Hanson, Gladys Calef (wife of Albert), 193, 197

Hanson, Hope Natalie Sloan (wife of M. D.), 153, 158, 161

Hanson, Joseph Warren, 158, 161

Hanson, M. D., 158, 161

Hanson, Wilma. See Walp, Wilma Hanson (wife of James)

Hanusch, Laura Lynette Jordy (wife of Phil), 81, 99

Hanusch, Phil Erstz, 99

Hardin, Sarah Reagan (wife of Thomas), 2, 3

Hardin, Thomas, 3

Hardy, John, 160

Hardy, Toni Kay Morgan (wife of John), 155, 160

Hare, James Edward, 229, 232

Hare, Jennie Lynn O'Pry (wife of Michael), 232, 235

Hare, Meghan Reigh, 232, 235

Hare, Michael David, 232, 235

Hare, Michael Paul, 229, 232, 235

Hare, Paul, 228

Hare, Perry Jo Miller (wife of Paul), 225, 228, 232

Hare, Virginia Eileen, 229, 232

Harmon, Anise Lindsay (wife of Thomas), 45

Harmon, Benjamin Franklin, 45

Harmon, Edward Francis, 45

Harmon, Ethel Gorden (wife of Edward), 45

Harmon, Lila Kate. See Farber, Lila Kate Harmon (wife of Joseph)

Harmon, Louise Parker (wife of Benjamin), 35, 37, 45

Harmon, Lydia Lovella. See Teel, Lydia Lovella Harmon (wife of Enos)

Harmon, Mary Lee Barrett (wife of Edward), 45

Harmon, Mary, Nancy. See Thigpen, Mary Nancy Harmon (wife of Tom)

Harmon, Thomas Franklin, 45

Harper, Allie Sonoma, 52, 71

Harper, Amber Leigh, 232, 235

Harper, Brenda Sue Madden (wife of Thomas), 27, 229, 232

Harper, Cole Patrick, 71, 92

Harper, Colin Dean, 71, 92

Harper, Dolores Clara Morton (wife of George Jr.), 71, 91

Harper, Donald Raymond, 52, 71, 92

Harper, Dorothy Lee, 52, 71

Harper, Elizabeth Elaine. See Gillespie, Elizabeth Elaine Harper (wife of Jeffry)

Harper, Fatima Ann Stroud (wife of Donald), 71, 92

Harper, George Hartford, 52

Harper, George Hartford Jr., 52, 71, 91

Harper, George Hatford, 71

Harper, Joshua Thomas, 232, 235

Harper, Mark Edward, 71, 92

Harper, Michael Neal, 71, 92

Harper, Nathan Shea, 232, 235

Harper, Nile Raymond, 71, 92

Harper, Sadie Inez. See Allen, Sadie Inez Harper (wife of Clarence)

Hicks, Audrey Faye. See McCan, Audrey Faye Hicks (wife of Kenneth)

Hicks, Burma. See Jolly, Burma Hicks (wife of Raymond)

Hiffner, Susie. See Barrett, Susie Hiffner (wife of Jonathon)

Higgins, Alma A. See Whitten, Alma A. Higgins (wife of Jessie)

Higgins, Anna Turner. See Holmes, Anna Turner Higgins (wife of William)

Higgins, Carline Whitten. See Ramage, Carline Whitten Higgins (wife of Alfred)

Higgins, Carlinne Whitten (wife of John), 210, 212

Higgins, Harry, 220, 221

Higgins, Hulit Elizabeth. See Jenkins, Hulit Elizabeth Higgins (wife of James)

Higgins, John Hubert, 212

Higgins, Julia Clara. See Collins, Julia Clara Higgins (wife of Albert)

Higgs, Millie Lorrine. See Vetuski, Millie Lorrine Higgs (wife of Woodrow)

Hilderbrant, Ruby Marie (wife of Glenn). See Barrett, Ruby Marie Hilderbrant (wife of Glenn)

Hill, Betty Jo, 232, 235

Hill, Caroline Ann. See Bridgeforth, Caroline Ann Hill (wife of David)

Hill, Caroline Dittmar, 239, 246

Hill, Charles Edward, 228, 231, 235

Hill, Colia Miller (wife of Lloyd), 222, 224, 228

Hill, Connie, 232, 235

Hill, Elizabeth. See Barrett, Elizabeth Hill (wife of David)

Hill, Evelyn Lee. See Johnson, Evelyn Lee Hill (wife of Jerry)

Hill, Gladys Angel, 232, 235

Hill, Gladys Ann Nunnelly (wife of Harold), 228, 231

Hill, Harold Lloyd, 225, 228, 231

Hill, Lloyd Lowman, 224, 228

Hill, Marilyn Smith (wife of Charles), 231, 235

Hill, Mary Francis, 225

Hill, Michael, 232, 235

Hilton, Patricia Ann. See Vetuski, Patricia Ann Hilton (wife of Mitchell Jr.)

Hines, Carl Sidney, 110, 120

Hines, Chester Olen, 110, 120

Hines, Harriet Beulah Whitten (wife of Carl), 104, 110, 120

Hines, Joseph Steen, 110, 120

Hines, Mary Laura, 110, 120

Hines, Thelma Elaine, 110, 120

Hinton, Catherine Farrow Richey (wife of James), 26, 29, 31

Hinton, James Karr, 29, 31

Hinton, Robert Richey, 29, 31, 33

Hipp, Daniel Lawrence, 200, 205

Hipp, David Leonard, 200, 205

Hipp, Sally Ann Kendall, 195, 200, 205

Hitch, Jane Joyce. See Willingham, Jane Joyce Hitch (wife of Clark)

Hix, J. D., 73

Hix, Shirley Jean McCann (wife of J. D.), 53, 73

Hobson, Sarah Frances. See Whitten, Sarah Frances Hobson (wife of Henry Lee)

Hoffman, Andrea, 204, 209

Hoffman, Annie Louis. See Lankford, Annie Louis Hoffman (wife of Earle)

Hoffman, Brad, 204, 208

Hoffman, Brett, 204, 208

Hoffman, David, 204, 208

Hoffman, Gail Leach (wife of Jack), 204, 208

Hoffman, Heidi, 204, 209

Hoffman, Jack Jay, 199, 204, 208

Hoffman, Janice May Boone (wife of John), 195, 199, 204

Hoffman, John Jay, 199, 204

Hoffman, Nicholis, 204

Hoffman, Ronald B., 199, 204, 208

Hoffman, Teresa Monahan (wife of Ronald), 204, 208

Hogan, Annie, 14, 18

Hogan, Belle Wilson (wife of James), 18

Hogan, Eliza. See Yortson, Eliza Hogan (wife of Charles)

Hogan, Emily, 14, 18

Hogan, James, 14, 18

Hogan, Jeanette Jolly, 224, 227

Hogan, John L., 14

Hogan, Mary E., 14, 18

Hogan, Orpha Judson Whitten (wife of Thomas), 13, 14, 18

Hogan, Rebecca, 14, 18

Hogan, Sarah Little. See Whitten, Sarah Little Hogan (wife of James)

Hogan, Susan E. See Moore, Susan E. Hogan (wife of Peyton)

Hogan, Thomas, M., 14, 18

Hogan, Thomas, M. (son of Thomas M.), 14

Hogan, James, 14

Hoke, Danny Lynn, 81, 98

Hoke, David Lee, 81, 98

Hoke, Dennis Lloyd, 81

Hoke, Dennis Loyd, 98

Hoke, Donald Lee, 60, 81, 98

Hoke, Jana Lynn Creighton (wife of Jana), 98

Hoke, Louise Donna, 81, 98

Hoke, Mildred Arlene Jordy (wife of Donald), 60, 81, 98

Hoke, Sandra Joyce McLemore (wife of David), 98

Holcolmb, Thomas William, 45

Holcomb, Anna Miller (wife of William Coburn), 46

Holcomb, Barney, 38, 46

Holcomb, Benton Rogers, 38, 46

Holcomb, Charles Andrew, 38, 46

Holcomb, Dana Andrew, 130, 140

Holcomb, Donald Ray, 119, 130, 140

Holcomb, Dorothy Mary Cole (wife of Donald), 130, 140

Holcomb, Eva. See Reynolds, Eva Holcomb (wife of William)

Holcomb, George, 138

Holcomb, Hannah Jane Coburn (wife of Thomas), 35, 38, 45

Holcomb, Jacob Loy, 131, 141

Holcomb, Jenifer Clair, 131, 141

Holcomb, Jimmy Adams, 119, 131, 140

Holcomb, Jodie Marie, 130, 140

Holcomb, Julie Ann, 131, 140

Holcomb, Julie Erin, 131, 141

Holcomb, Linda Kravanger (wife of Jimmy), 131, 140

Holcomb, Lucinda Jane Cooley (wife of George), 128, 138, 145

Holcomb, Marilyn. See Dohr, Marilyn Holcomb (wife of Raymond)

Holcomb, Mary Elliott Whitten (wife of Roy), 110, 119, 130

Holcomb, Mary James (wife of William Alfred), 49

Holcomb, Mary Shannon, 138, 145

Holcomb, Mary Willa. See Mitchell, Mary Willa Holcomb (wife of Perry)

Holcomb, Mayme Locke (wife of Benton), 46

Holcomb, Meghan, 131, 140

Holcomb, Minnie Lou Puckett (wife of Charles Andrew), 46

Holcomb, Patricia Yvonne Gillespie (wife of Timothy), 120, 131, 141

Holcomb, Robert Charles, 119, 130, 140

Holcomb, Robert Charles Jr., 130, 139

Holcomb, Roy DeWitt, 119, 130

Holcomb, Shannon Lee, 130, 140

Holcomb, Sherry Lynn Kreusher (wife of Robert), 130, 140

Holcomb, Stephanie Leigh, 138, 145

Holcomb, Thomas Wayne, 119, 130

Holcomb, Thomas William, 38

Holcomb, Timothy DeLane, 131, 141

Holcomb, Tracy Marie, 131, 140

Holcomb, William Alfred III, 38, 46

Holcomb, William Coburn, 38, 46

Holcomb, Zetha Roberta. See Brown, Zetha Roberta Holcomb (wife of James)

Holcombe, Elias, 101, 102, 107

Holcombe, Isabelle Tominson "Bell", 102

Holcombe, Narcissa Amaryllis, 164

Holcombe, Narcissa Amaryllis Whitten (wife of Elias), 21, 101, 102, 107

Holden, John Stephen, 19

Holden, Millicent Louisa Malinda Perry (wife of John), 19

Holdford, David Jarrod, 173, 174

Holley, Beverly Ann Whitten (wife of George), 115, 125, 136

268

Manning, Melvin Iredell, 44

Manning, Mozelle. See Whitten, Mozelle Manning (wife of Leven Jr.)

Manning, Nugent B., 37, 45

Manning, Peggy Lee Nabb (wife of Harold), 75

Manning, Prudence Polk (wife of John), 44, 59

Manning, Robbie Orine Rhodes (wife of Billy), 59, 80

Manning, Ruby Aileen. See Nesmith, Ruby Aileen Manning (wife of Bobbie Jones)

Manning, Ruby Elizabeth. See Jordy, Ruby Elizabeth Manning (wife of Archie)

Manning, Sadie Augusta. See Skains, Sadie Augusta Manning (wife of Currie)

Manning, Sarah Alice Iantha Barrett (wife of James), 34, 37, 44

Manning, Tommy Jo Tinkle (wife of Joe), 158, 161

Manning, Wanda Stuts (wife of Lloyd), 59, 80

Mansfield, Julia Ann Holt (wife of William), 180–91, 193

Mansfield, Luna, 191, 193

Mansfield, William, 190, 191, 193

Marceau, André Julien, 143

Marceau, Audrey Judith Meyer (wife of Julien), 134, 143

Marceau, Chantel (wife of John), 132

Marceau, Daniel Joseph, 123, 134, 143

Marceau, Debra Jean Marie. See Craig, Debra Jean Marie Marceau (wife of Ken), See McLaughlin, Debra Jean Marie Marceau (wife of Hugh)

Marceau, Diane Marie. See Leveque, Diane Marie Marceau (wife of Rino)

Marceau, Jean Paul Etienne, 123, 132

Marceau, Joseph Michael Sylvair, 123, 134

Marceau, Joseph Patrice, 123, 133

Marceau, Julien Pierre Joseph, 123, 134, 143

Marceau, Juliette Elida Marie. See McLeod, Juliette Elida Marie Marceau (wife of Robert)

Marceau, Justin Patrice Albert, 134

Marceau, Lorraine (wife of Daniel), 134, 143

Marceau, Louis Joseph Gabriel, 123, 134

Marceau, Louis Medgar Silas, 123, 134

Marceau, Margaret Helen Cunningham (wife of Joseph), 114, 123, 133

Marceau, Patricia Anne. See Burzynski, Patricia Anne Marceau (wife of Michael)

Marceau, Sopie Deanie, 134

Marceau, Sylvia Maire Yolanda, 123, 134

Marcum, Essie. See Barrett, Elizabeth Whitten (wife of David)

Marigold, Bobbie. See Barrett, Bobbie Marigold

Markey, Andrew William, 142, 146

Markey, Mary Katherine Hemphill (wife of Andrew), 132, 142, 146

Markey, Sarah Katherine, 142, 146

Martin, August Leo, 8, 53

Martin, Barbara Elaine. See Stone, Barbara Elaine Martin (wife of Oscar)

Martin, Bonnie Jean, 53, 72

Martin, Donna Jones (wife of Otis), 72, 92

Martin, Edna Louise, 72, 93

Martin, Frances Dorene. See Rhyner, Frances Dorene Martin (wife of Gerald), See Tapp, Frances Dorene Martin (wife of Walter)

Martin, Francis Virginia. See King, Francis Virginia Martin (wife of Rufus)

Martin, Freeda Yvonne Bailey (wife of Glenn), 72, 92

Martin, Glenda Joyce, 72, 92

Martin, Glenn Dale, 53, 72, 92

Martin, Glenn Dale Jr., 72, 92

Martin, Homer, 110, 119

Martin, Irene Dwade. See McCommon, Irene Dwade Martin (wife of William)

Martin, James Lowry, 120, 134

Martin, Johnie Mae McCann (wife of August), 42, 53, 72

Martin, Karen Elaine, 72, 92

Martin, Karla Dorene, 72, 92

Martin, Marcus Leo, 53, 72, 92

Martin, Marcus Leo Jr., 72, 92

Martin, Marjory Estel Simmons (wife of Robert), 25, 29

Martin, Mavis Louise Thompson (wife of Marcus), 72, 91

Martin, Otis Carl, 53, 72, 92

Martin, Robert, 29

Martin, Roy Rudolph, 111, 120

Martin, Ruth Lowry (wife of Homer), 105, 110, 120

Martin, Sarah Louise, 111, 120

Martsch, William Lee Gibson, 74, 94

Mary, Rebecca. See Reagan, Rebecca Mary (wife of John)

Mask, Martha Ann Graham (wife of Howard), 128, 139

Mason, Alice Estelle Arrington (wife of Edwin), 72

Mason, Dolores Willets (wife of Kenneth Jr.), 72

Mason, Edwin Earl, 53, 72

Mason, Ja Kay Warren (wife of Raymond), 51

Mason, Josephine Ruth. See Prebble, Josephine Ruth Mason (wife of Harry)

Mason, Kenneth Gale Jr., 53, 72

Mason, Marguerite Ann. See Morris, Marguerite Ann Mason (wife of Charles)

Mason, Raymond Leon, 53, 72

Mason, Robin Johnson (wife of Kenneth Jr.), 72

Mason, Tracy Lynn, 72, 92

Mason, Wilford, 53, 71

Mason, Winnie Viola Golden (wife of Wilford), 6, 41, 71

Massa, Lois Norene Barrett, 84

Massa, Louis Anthony, 84

Massey, Bettie Ann. See Casey, Bettie Ann Massey (wife of Jefferson)

Masso, Carolyn. See Jordy, Carolyn Masso (wife of Bennie)

Mathewson, Bradley, 87

Mathewson, Kay Wakefield (wife of Bradley), 66, 87

Matusiewicz, Grace. See Peatross, Grace Matusiewicz (wife of Bradley)

Mauldin, Charles, 111

Mauldin, Fannie Lula Lynn Sample (wife of Charles), 105, 111

Maxey, Lucinda Jane Cooley (wife of Russell), 128, 138, 145

Maxey, Russell Allen, 138, 145

Maxey, Russell Allen Jr., 138, 145

May, Betty Jo Whitten, 171, 172, 174

Mayes, Nancy Moorehead. See Hopkins, Nancy Moorehead Mayes (wife of William)

Mayo, Vivian Dale Whitten (wife of William), 130, 140

Mayo, William Vance, 130, 140

Mayo, William Whitten, 130, 140

Mc. Davis, David, 19, 164

Mc. Davis, Mariam Whitten (wife of David), 12, 19, 164, 245, 246

McAlister, Linda Eggleston (wife of Robert), 160

McAlister, Lucy Geraldine Morgan (wife of William), 150, 155, 160

McAlister, Robert Otis, 155, 160

McAlister, William Ray, 155, 160

McAlister, William Ray Jr., 155, 160

McBride, Charles William, 111, 121

McBride, Florence Kee Lankford (wife of Joseph), 105, 111, 120

McBride, Joseph Murrow, 111, 120

McBride, Joseph Murrow Jr., 111, 121

McCafferty, Bob, 62, 83

McCafferty, Earl, 62

McCafferty, Earl Jr., 62, 83

McCafferty, Maddie Barrett (wife of Earl), 47, 62

McCafferty, Polly (Earl), 62

McCaffety, Eugene, 62, 83

McCaffety, Johnnie Mae. See Bishop, Johnnie Mae McCaffety

McCaffety, Marie. See Tumlinson, Marie McCaffety

McCaffety, Mary Beth, 62, 83

McCaffety, Shirley, 83

McCallen, Janice Gyetvay (wife of William), 139, 145

McCallen, John Thomas, 128, 138

McCallen, John Thomas II, 139, 145

McCallen, Kay. See Cain, Kay McCallen (wife of Robert)

McCallen, Martha Ann Henderson (wife of John), 118, 128, 138

McCallen, Martha Laurie. See Bainer, Martha Laurie McCallen (wife of Gregory)

McCallen, Mary Elizabeth. See Spurlock, Mary Elizabeth McCallen (wife of Michael)

McCallen, William Thomas, 128, 139, 145

McCan, Agnes (wife of James), 50

McCan, Alice Blanche Dickey (wife of Samuel), 41, 51

McCan, Allie Angeline. See Golden, Allie Angeline McCan (wife of Eugene)

McCan, Alma Mcree Rhodes (wife of William), 41, 53

McCan, Amanda Catherine Barrett (wife of James), 34, 36, 40

McCan, Andrew Buron, 41, 50

McCan, Annie Bell Duncan (wife of Kenneth), 41, 51

McCan, Audrey Faye Hicks (wife of Kenneth), 50, 67

McCan, Benjamin Monroe, 36, 42, 54

McCan, Carroll, 41, 50

McCan, Charles Edward, 42, 54

McCan, Clemmie. See Frazier, Clemmie McCan (wife of Dan)

McCan, Connie Ford, 41, 50, 67

McCan, Debra June Stowe (wife of John), 41

McCan, Franklin, 42, 54

McCan, Georgia, 41, 50

McCan, Hallie, 41, 50

McCan, Hettie M. See Hale, Hettie M. McCan (wife of Hartwell)

McCan, Hulda. See Winborn, Hulda McCan (wife of James)

McCan, James Earl, 42

McCan, James Littleton, 36, 40, 50

McCan, James Marion, 36, 40

McCan, James Matthew, 41, 50

McCan, John Reuban, 41, 54

McCan, John Reuben, 36

McCan, Kenneth Kyle, 41, 50, 67

McCan, Kenneth Nathan, 36, 41, 51

McCan, Laverne Palen (wife of James), 50

McCan, Leona Ellen Wilbeck (wife of Connie), 50, 67

McCan, Lottie Bell. See Knight, Lottie Bell McCan (wife of Wiley)

McCan, Mae Bell Newton (wife of Charles Edward), 54

McCan, Maggie E. Stowe (wife of Benjamin), 42, 54

McCan, Maggie L., 40, 50

McCan, Minnie Ola, 36, 41

McCan, Paul, 42, 54

McCan, Rosa Lynch (wife of John), 41, 54

McCan, Samuel Wooldridge, 36, 41, 51

McCan, Sarah Ida Dickey (wife of James), 40, 50

McCan, William Walter, 36, 41, 53

McCann, Alice Jean Williams (wife of Larry), 69, 91

McCann, Amanda Elizabeth. See Tabler, Amanda Elizabeth McCann (wife of Jesse)

McCann, Ana Caso (wife of Connie), 67, 89

McCann, Ann Mary Pohoresky (wife of Ed), 51, 69

McCann, Ann Ruth Turner (wife of Kenneth), 53, 72

McCann, Anna Celeste Caso, 67

McCann, Anne Willis (wife of Miner), 51, 69

McCann, Annie Nora Collins (wife of Donnell), 51

McCann, Bell Field, 41, 51, 69

McCann, Bell Field Jr., 51, 69

McCann, Benjamin Monroe, 55, 76

McCann, Benny Star, 42, 55, 76

McCann, Betty Lou, 53, 73

McCann, Billy Eugene, 54, 73

McCann, Bluford Wesley, 42, 55, 76

McCann, Bobby Gene, 42, 55

McCann, Bonnie Minnie (wife of Bluford), 55, 76

McCann, Brandy Marie, 69, 91

McCann, Brenda Wilson (wife of Thomas), 90

McCann, Buena Lorene Hayhurst (wife of Charles Keith), 54, 74

McCann, Carl Preston, 51, 69, 90

McCann, Carl Steven, 69, 90

McCann, Carol Joyce Sharp (wife of Charles Keith), 54, 74

McCann, Carole Owens (wife of Michael), 72, 92

McCann, Catherine Hayes (wife of Connie), 89

McCann, Catherine Susanna, 8, 90

McCann, Celeste, 89

McCann, Charles Edgar, 42, 55, 75

McCann, Charles Keith, 42, 54, 74

McCann, Charlotte Lorene. See Hannaford, Charlotte Lorene McCann (wife of Jimmie)

McCann, Cheryl Ann, 55, 76

McCann, Connie Michael, 50, 51, 67, 89

McCann, Danny Floyd, 74

McCann, Darrell Lloyd, 42, 54, 75

McCann, Darrell Wayne, 55, 76

McCann, David Earl, 55, 76

McCann, David Gregory, 88

McCann, Deborah Lynn. See Muckenthaler, Deborah McCann Lynn (wife of Tom)

McCann, Debra Lois. See Platts, Debra Lois McCann (wife of David)

McCann, Delyse, 72, 92

McCann, Dixie Nadine Whisenant (wife of Darrell), 54, 75

McCann, Dolores Willets (wife of Kenneth Jr.), 72

McCann, Donald Wayne, 53, 73, 93

McCann, Donnell Earl, 41, 51

McCann, Donnell Wayne, 51, 68, 91

McCann, Dorothy Landers (wife of Walter Stanley), 53, 72

McCann, Douglas Glenn, 50, 67, 88

McCann, Douglas Glenn III, 88

McCann, Douglas Glenn Jr., 67, 88

McCann, Doyle Ray, 55, 76

McCann, Earl David, 42, 55

McCann, Ed Sloan, 41, 51, 69

McCann, Edgar Kahle, 42

McCann, Edward Lee, 55

McCann, Elizabeth Gaye. See Baker, Elizabeth Gaye McCann (wife of Richard)

McCann, Elsie Mae Bennett (wife of Charles Keith), 54, 74

McCann, Evelyn Francis (wife of Bell), 51, 69

McCann, Frances Earl. See Ray, Frances Earl McCann (wife of Delbert)

McCann, Gary Lee, 51, 69, 91

McCann, Gerald Wayne, 53, 72, 92

McCann, Harold Floyd, 42, 54, 74

McCann, Heather Norene, 69, 91

McCann, Hettie Vernal. See Gibson, Hettie Vernal McCann (wife of Charles)

McCann, Icely Aline. See Travis, Icely Aline McCann (wife of Leonard)

McCann, James Earl, 54

McCann, James Elmer, 42, 55

McCann, Jane Kate, 41

McCann, Janet Marie, 69, 90

McCann, Janice Patton (wife of Douglas Jr.), 88

McCann, Jeanie Ray Gutzman (wife of Donald), 73, 93

McCann, Jennifer Mechell, 69, 91

McCann, Jodie Harrell (wife of Pat), 74

McCann, John Douglas, 53, 72

McCann, John Fitzgerald, 55, 76

McCann, Josephine, 41

McCann, Joyce Smith (wife of Benny), 55, 76

McCann, Judith Inez Froelich (wife Donnell), 69, 91

McCann, Judy, 55, 76

McCann, Karen Penelope. See Hett, Karen Penelope McCann (wife of Arthur)

McCann, Katherin Gale, 72

McCann, Kathy Jean, 54, 74

McCann, Kelly, 72, 92

McCann, Kenneth Gale, 41, 53, 72

McCann, Kenneth Gale Jr., 53, 72

Nuchols, Nancy Susannah. See Miller, Nancy Susannah Nuchols (wife of Charles)

Nunnally, Carrie Estella, 8, 10

Nunnally, Charles Lewis, 8, 10

Nunnally, Charles Lewis Jr., 8, 10

Nunnally, Daisy, 8, 10

Nunnally, Edmund Lee, 8, 11

Nunnally, Guy Reagan, 8, 10

Nunnally, Harriet Albina Reagan (wife of Charles), 6, 8, 10

Nunnally, Lawrence, 9, 11

Nunnally, Percy, 8, 10

Nunnally, Robert Bruce, 8, 10

Nunnelly, Gladys Ann. See Hill, Gladys Ann Nunnelly (wife of Harold)

O

O'Brien Lillie D. See Whitten, Lillie D. O'Brien (wife of John William)

Odam, Glenn, 166, 167

Odam, Peggy, 166, 167

Odell, Marguerite. See Whitten, Marguerite Odell (wife of William)

Odom, Bert, 166, 167

Odom, Geraldine, 166, 167

Odom, Lucille Davis (wife of Bert), 166, 167

Odom, Lucy. See Roten, Lucy Odom (wife of Edward)

Ogg, Mary Catherine Janicke, 77, 95

O'Grady, Peggy Ann, 200, 205

O'Grady, Sally Ann Kendall, 195, 205

O'Grady, Timothy Kendall, 200, 205

Ohlenberger, Bertha. See Barrett, Bertha Ohlenberger (wife of Samuel)

Olbrich, Laurentia Marie. See Holt, Laurentia Marie Olbrich (wife of Alfred)

Oliver, Charles, 3, 4

Oliver, Elijah, 3

Oliver, Elizabeth Edging (wife of William), 6

Oliver, George, 2–3

Oliver, George Jr., 3, 4

Oliver, George R., 4, 6

Oliver, James, 1, 3, 4

Oliver, Jemima Reagan (wife of George), 2–3

Oliver, John, 4, 6

Oliver, John Sr., 3, 4

Oliver, Lurena Frazier (wife of John), 6

Oliver, Martha Whitworth (wife of George), 2

Oliver, Mary, 4

Oliver, Mary (daughter of John Sr.), 4, 6

Oliver, Mary White (wife of James), 6

Oliver, Nancy Agnes, 4, 6

Oliver, Nancy Painter (wife of William), 6

Oliver, Peter, 3

Oliver, Rebecca. See Cunningham, Rebecca Oliver (wife of William)

Oliver, Susannah White (wife of George Jr.), 4

Oliver, William, 4

Oliver, William (son of George), 3

Oliver, William (son of John), 6

O'Neal, Linda. See Barrett, Linda O'Neal (wife of Joe)

O'Neill, Kathleen May. See Whitten, Kathleen May O'Neill (wife of Nathaniel Carter II)

O'Pry Jennie Lynn. See Hare, Michael Paul

Ormsbee, Helen Holt (wife of Lyle), 192, 193, 198

Ormsbee, Lyle, 194, 198

Ormsbee, Nancy. See Simmons, Nancy Ormsbee (wife of Horace)

Osbourne, Carroll, 156, 160

Osbourne, Clark, 156, 160

Osbourne, Edna May Grimes (wife of Peter), 196, 206, 207

Osbourne, Peggy Morgan (wife of Wallace), 151, 156, 160

Osbourne, Peter Robert, 200, 206

Osbourne, Wallace, 156, 160

Osburn, Dinah K. See Wright, Dinah K. Osburn (wife of Philip)

Oster, Arlie Day, 25

Oster, Mary Ellen Elizabeth Morgan (wife of Arlie), 18, 25

Oster, Ruby. See Morgan, Ruby Oster (wife of John)

Owen, Hazel Ophelia. See Knight, Hazel Ophelia Owen (wife of Frank)

Ownes, Carole. See McCann, Carole Owens (wife of Michael)

Oxspring, Wrenda Wray. See Barrett, Wrenda Wray Oxspring (wife of Lloyd)

P

Padilla, Pearl. See Barrett, Pearl Padilla (wife of Lloyd Jr.)

Painter, Nancy. See Oliver, Nancy Painter (wife of William)

Palen, Laverne. See McCan, Laverne Palen (wife of James)

Palmer, Marilyn Gwen Zimmerman (wife of Ronnie), 161, 163

Palmer, Ronnie Joe, 163

Pantel, Esther Earlene Madden (wife of Stanley), 229, 232, 235

Pantel, Sarah Colete, 232, 235

Pantel, Stanley Ray, 232, 235

Parchment, Linda. See Bova, Linda Parchment (wife of Donald)

Parish, Eric, 126, 137

Parish, Gayla Marie Whitten (wife of Eric), 116, 127, 137

Park, Annie Lemons (wife of Thomas), 157

Park, Billy Gordon, 157, 161, 163

Park, Daisy Cook (wife of William), 157, 161

Park, David Gordon, 161, 163

Park, Dora Melvina. See Morgan, Dora Melvina Park (wife of Thomas)

Park, Hallye. See Crabb, Hallye Park (wife of Columbus)

Park, Helen Beatrice. See Reed, Helen Beatrice Park (wife of Edward)

Park, James William, 152, 157

Park, Laura Sue, 161, 163

Park, Martha E. See Whitten, Martha E. Park (wife of Alfred W.)

Park, Mary Helen Stewart (wife of James), 148, 152, 157

Park, Patsy J. Reeves (wife of Billy), 161, 163

Park, Sarah Ellen, 151, 163

Park, Thomas Henry, 152, 157

Park, William Hiram, 152, 157, 161

Parker, David Henry, 34, 37

Parker, Iola Faulkner (wife of Lawrence), 44, 58, 79

Parker, James, 34, 37

Parker, Jim, 99

Parker, John R., 34, 244

Parker, Lavina, 35, 37

Parker, Louise. See Harmon, Louise Parker (wife of Benjamin)

Parker, Lulu Barret (wife of W. T.), 62

Parker, Marion, 34, 37

Parker, Mary, 35, 37

Parker, Mary "Polly" Barrett (wife of John), 34, 37, 244

Parker, Nanny Elizabeth. See Holsomback, Nanny Elizabeth Parker (wife of George)

Parker, Rebecca Elizabeth, 34, 37

Parker, Richard, 35, 37

Parker, Sarah, 35, 37

Parker, Tina Lynette Gamblin (wife of Jim), 81, 99

Parker, W. T., 62

Parker, William, 35, 38

Parkman, Lois. See Whitby, Lois Parkman (wife of Thomas)

Patterson, William, 190

Patton, Eola Lexa Boone (wife of Roy), 195, 199

Patton, Gerald Mark, 96

Patton, Jacqueline Ruth Barrett (wife of Larry), 77, 98

Patton, Larry Wayne, 96

Patton, Lindsey Michelle, 96

Patton, Matthew Roland, 96

Patton, Roy, 195, 199

Patton, Terrie Kay, 96

Payne, Malinea Caroline. See Goss, Malinda Caroline Payne (wife of James)

Pearson, Carol Jean Heck (wife of Jerry), 65, 86

Pearson, Jerry, 86

Pearson, Laura, 86

Pearson, Michele, 85

Peatross, Betty Jean Boone (wife of Edwin), 199, 204

Peatross, Bradley Boone, 199, 205

Peatross, Catherine Whitesell, 205

Peatross, Christine Susan, 199, 204
Peatross, Edwin Lamson, 199, 204
Peatross, Grace Matusiewicz (wife of
    Bradley), 205
Peatross, Scott Lamson, 199, 205
Pedrosa, Christine. See Whitten,
    Christine Pedrosa (wife of Ronaldo)
Peebles, Jane. See Whitten, Jane Peebles
    (wife of William)
Perkins, Effie Berry Whitten (wife of
    John), 103, 108, 117
Perkins, Estilla, 108, 117
Perkins, John Caswell, 108, 117
Perrin, Lou Nell Whitten (wife of Scott),
    222, 226
Perrine, Candy. See Whitten, Candy
    Perrine (wife of Alfred D.)
Perry, Alexis. See Kone, Alexis Perry
    (wife of James), See Woods, Alexis
    Perry (wife of Robert)
Perry, Alice Mille. See Johnson, Alice
    Mille Perry (wife of William)
Perry, Alma Edge. See Worley, Alma
    Edge Perry (wife of Walter)
Perry, Amy, 19, 26
Perry, Angeline Anderson (wife of
    Thomas), 19, 26
Perry, Artamissa Millicent. See Miller,
    Artamissa Millicent Perry (wife of
    Benjamin)
Perry, Artimissa Edgel A., 15, 19
Perry, Avarilla Theresa Dobbs (wife of
    Benjamin), 19, 26
Perry, Beatrice Katherine Meehan (wife
    of Eugene), 28, 30
Perry, Benjamin Arphax, 15, 19, 22, 26
Perry, Benjamin Franklin, 17, 24
Perry, Beulah Mae. See Blankenship,
    Beulah Mae Perry (wife of
    Spurgeon)
Perry, Clarence Bell, 19, 27, 30
Perry, Doris Ann. See Stam, Doris Ann
    Perry (wife of Carl)
Perry, Elvira Edgel Whitten (wife of
    James), 13, 14, 16, 19, 22
Perry, Emment Stephens, 27
Perry, Emmet Stephens, 19
Perry, Eugene, 245
Perry, Eugene R., 24, 28, 30
Perry, Eugene R. Jr., 28, 29, 31, 33
Perry, Eva Lou McGowen (wife of
    Clarence), 27, 30
Perry, Evan Pierson, 16, 22, 24
Perry, George Dewey, 24, 28
Perry, Gertrude Thacker (wife of James),
    27
Perry, Henry Clay, 19, 27
Perry, Ina Ethel. See Floyd, Ina Ethel
    Perry (wife of Roy)
Perry, James Green, 14, 19

Perry, James Roy, 17, 25
Perry, James Vance, 19, 26
Perry, James Whitten, 15, 19, 26
Perry, John Evans Green, 15, 19

282

Perry, John Hamilton, 17, 24, 28
Perry, John Preston, 24, 28
Perry, Karen Lynn Richmond (wife of
    Eugen Jr.), 31
Perry, Karen Lynn Richmond (wife of
    Eugene Jr.), 31
Perry, Karen Usher (wife of Lewis), 31,
    33
Perry, Lance Adam, 31, 33
Perry, Laura Winifred, 24, 28
Perry, Leah Jane Fricks (wife of James),
    19, 26
Perry, Lewis Devillo, 17, 24
Perry, Linda Jean Shull (wife of Eugene
    Jr.), 30
Perry, Lisa Jean, 31, 33
Perry, Lisa Jeanne, 31, 33
Perry, Lorinda Caroline. See Spencer,
    Lorinda Caroline Perry (wife of
    Robert)
Perry, Louisa. See Goss, Louisa Perry
    (wife of Benjamin)
Perry, Louisa Lowman (wife of
    William), 19
Perry, Lula Thompson, 19, 26
Perry, Lydia Emily, 24, 28
Perry, Malinda Eleanor Goss (wife of
    Evan), 14, 16, 22, 24
Perry, Martha L. Darnell (wife of
    Benjamin), 19, 26
Perry, Mary Cochran "Sis" Thomas
    (wife of John), 19
Perry, Mary Jane Spencer Crow (wife of
    William), 24
Perry, Mary Josephine. See Schrum,
    Mary Josephine Perry (wife of
    Henry)
Perry, May, 19, 26
Perry, Millard Arphax, 19, 27
Perry, Millicent Louisa Malinda. See
    Holden, Millicent Louisa Malinda
    Perry (wife of John)
Perry, Mineola Allen (wife of Millard),
    27
Perry, Missouri Angeline Anderson (wife
    of Thomas), 19
Perry, Missouri Angleline Anderson
    (wife of Thomas), 26
Perry, Nancy. See Young, Nancy Perry
    (wife of James)
Perry, Nathan Alan, 31, 32, 33
Perry, Nathaniel Lewis, 15, 19
Perry, Orpha Elvira, 15, 19
Perry, Rebecca Anderson (wife of
    Thomas), 19
Perry, Sadie Carmack (wife of John), 19
Perry, Sarah Elvira Elizabeth. See
    Mearse, Sarah Elvira Elizabeth Perry
    (wife of Benjamin)

Perry, Sarah Jane Weaver (wife of
    Willaim), 24
Perry, Stephen Lewis, 28, 31, 33
Perry, Thomas Jackson, 15, 19, 26

Perry, Walter, 24, 28
Perry, William Nathaniel, 17, 24
Perry, William Washington, 15, 19
Perry, Winnie Lucille Langston (wife of
    Emment), 27
Perryman, Julia Bennett Crowe, 16, 23
Persman, James, 140
Persman, Linda Carol Dohr (wife of
    James), 130, 140
Peters, Clifford Wayne, 230, 234, 236
Peters, Glenda Hal Newby (wife of Joe),
    225, 230, 234
Peters, Joe Clifford, 230, 234
Peters, Kathy Jo, 230, 235
Peters, Linda Sue Callahan (wife of
    Clifford), 234, 236
Peters, Lois Diana. See Whitten, Lois
    Diana Peters (wife of Leonard)
Peters, Samantha Jo, 235, 236
Peters, Samatha Jo, 235, 236
Peters, Susan Marie, 230, 234
Peterson, Lillian Myrtle Louise Morgan
    (wife of Ray), 25
Peterson, Ray, 25
Phelps, Andrew, 28
Phelps, Tomie Elizabeth Grogan (wife of
    Andrew), 25, 28
Phillips, Laura. See Whitten, Laura
    Sydney Phillips (wife of Hamilton)
Phillips, Ora May. See Whitten, Ora May
    Phillips (wife of Benjamin)
Phips, Mary. See Whitten, Mary Phips
    (wife of John R.)
Pickens, James John, 139, 145
Pickens, James Joshua, 140, 145
Pickens, Nicole Lynn Whitten (wife of
    James), 129, 139, 145
Pior, Alice Marie. See Turpin, Alice
    Marie Pior (wife of James)
Pittman, Dawn Ann. See Baker, Dawn
    Ann Pittman (wife of Joseph)
Pitts J. J., 154
Pitts, Gwendolyn. See Koska,
    Gwendolyn Pitts (wife of LeRoy)
Pitts, Milton Eugene, 60, 81
Pitts, Ruby Ethel Moody (wife of J. J.),
    150, 154
Pitts, Wanda Jarnell. See Rice, Wanda
    Janell Pitts (wife of Robert)
Platts, David B., 73, 93
Platts, Debra Lois McCann (wife of
    David), 53, 73, 93
Platts, Michael David, 73, 93
Plumley, Bud, 46, 61
Plumley, Ida Lee Barrett (wife of Bud),
    39, 46, 61
Plumley, Lee, 61, 82
Poe, Harry, 126
Poe, Harry Lee, 126
Poe, Julia May, 126
Poe, Mary Anne Whitten (wife of
    Harry), 116, 126
Poe, Mary Ellen, 126, 137
Poe, Rebecca, 126, 137

Reagan, Elizabeth Henry (wife of Charles Jr.), 2
Reagan, Elizabeth Holt (wife of James Hayes), 6, 9
Reagan, Elizabeth Larrimore (wife of William), 7
Reagan, Eugenia Octavia, 7, 9
Reagan, Frances. See Narramore, Frances Reagan (wife of Eli W.)
Reagan, Francis Washington, 5, 7, 9
Reagan, Helen Jane, 6, 8
Reagan, Henry, 2, 3, 5
Reagan, James, 1
Reagan, James (son of James R. Jr.), 5, 7
Reagan, James H., 6, 7–8, 9
Reagan, James Hayes, 6, 9
Reagan, James Jr., 2
Reagan, James R. Jr., 3, 5
Reagan, James Sr., 2, 3, 4
Reagan, Jane. See Evans, Jane Reagan (wife of Samuel)
Reagan, Jemima. See Oliver, Jemima Reagan (wife of George)
Reagan, Joan, 1
Reagan, John (son of Charles Jr.), 2
Reagan, John (son of Charles), 2, 3
Reagan, John (son of James R.), 5, 7
Reagan, John (son of James Sr.), 3, 5
Reagan, John (son of James), 2
Reagan, Joseph, 5, 7, 9
Reagan, Julia, 7, 9
Reagan, Julia Neely. See Whitfield, Julia Neely Reagan (wife of Matthew)
Reagan, Katherine, 2
Reagan, Keziah (wife of William), 2
Reagan, Leah, 3
Reagan, M. E., 8, 9
Reagan, Margaret. See Cochran, Margaret (wife of Hugh)
Reagan, Margaret Johnson. See Johnson, Margaret Reagan (wife of Jacob)
Reagan, Martha, 5, 7
Reagan, Martha Ann (wife of Joseph), 7
Reagan, Martha Ann Davis (wife of Joseph), 9
Reagan, Martha Black (wife of John), 3
Reagan, Martha H., 8, 9
Reagan, Mary. See Whitten, Mary Reagan (wife of John)
Reagan, Mary Dandridge. See Hull, Mary Dandridge Reagan (wife of Reuban)
Reagan, Mary Elizabeth. See Jordan, Mary Elizabeth (wife of Joseph)
Reagan, Mary Emily. See Cater, Mary Emily Reagan (wife of Douglas)
Reagan, Matilda Caroline (wife of William), 7
Reagan, Matthew, 2
Reagan, Millicent. See Whitten, Millicent Reagan (wife of Charles Jr.)
Reagan, Mira Ann Lenoir (wife of James Hayes), 6, 9

Reagan, Nancy A. See Abbott, Nancy A. Reagan
Reagan, Nancy Brawner (wife of John), 7
Reagan, Nancy Cook (wife of James Sr.), 3, 4
Reagan, Nancy Cunnyngham (wife of Peter), 5, 7
Reagan, Noble Marion, 6, 8
Reagan, Peter, 3, 5, 7
Reagan, Phoebe Harrison (wife of Henry), 3
Reagan, Rebecca. See Berry, Rebecca Reagan (wife of James)
Reagan, Rebecca Black (wife of Ahimas), 3
Reagan, Rebecca DeLona Stanton-Neeley (wife of Thomas), 7, 9
Reagan, Rebecca Mary (wife of John), 3
Reagan, Rebeckah. See Burns, Rebeckah Reagan (wife of William)
Reagan, Rebeckah (wife of James Sr.), 3
Reagan, Robert William, 6, 8, 9
Reagan, Robert William (son of James H.), 8
Reagan, Sara Elizabeth Frances Dodson (wife of James H.), 7–8
Reagan, Sarah. See Hardin, Sarah Reagan (wife of Thomas), See McMillan, Sarah Reagan (wife of Thomas)
Reagan, Sarah Cecelia Refo (wife of Francis Washington), 7, 9
Reagan, Sarah E., 7, 9
Reagan, Sarah Elizabeth. See Avery, Sarah Elizabeth Reagan (wife of Needham)
Reagan, Sarah Elizabeth Frances Dodson (wife of James H.), 7, 9
Reagan, Silas, 243
Reagan, Sophia, 3
Reagan, Thomas Jefferson, 5, 7, 9
Reagan, William, 2, 3, 243, 247
Reagan, William (Judge), 5, 7
Reagan, William Morrison, 5, 7
Reagan, Winnie Hall (wife of Charles III), 3
Rector, Brandy, 95
Rector, David Lee, 95
Rector, George, 95
Rector, Louanna Jane Malone (wife of George), 77, 95
Redcan, Gerogianna Rose. See Barrett, Georgianna Rose Redcan (wife of Ronald)
Redding, Hulda. See Barrett, Hulda Redding (wife of John)

Redmond, Malinda C. Ayers (wife of Manuel), 16, 24
Redmond, Manuel C., 24
Reed, Edward Ellsworth, 157, 161
Reed, Helen Beatrice Park (wife of Edward), 152, 157, 161

Reed, James Edward, 157, 161, 163
Reed, Louise Watson (wife of James), 161, 163
Reed, Mary Kathryn. See Hice, Mary Kathryn Reed (wife of Donald)
Reed, Mary Maxine. See Zimmerman, Mary Maxine Reed (wife of Luther)
Reed, Patti Gayle. See Guttierrez, Patti Gayle Reed (wife of Donald)
Reese, Ida Helen. See Grimes, Ida Helen Reese (wife of Lloyd)
Reeves, Patsy J. See Park, Patsy J. Reeves (wife of Billy)
Refo, Sarah Cecelia. See Reagan, Sarah Cecelia Refo (wife of Francis Washington)
Reggio, Harriet. See Barrett, Harriett Reggio (wife of William)
Reid, Andrea, 133, 143
Reid, Katherine Ann Cunningham (wife of Paul), 123, 133, 143
Reid, Paul, 133, 143
Reisiger, Sigrid. See Richey, Sigrid Reisiger (wife of Robert)
Reynolds, Eva Holcomb (wife of William), 38, 46
Reynolds, Jacqueline Rhea, 128, 139
Reynolds, Marie. See Miller, Marie Reynolds (wife of Oris)
Reynolds, William Jack, 129, 139
Reynolds, William Raymond, 128
Reynolds, William Raymond Jr., 141
Reynolds, William Z., 46
Rhea, Gayle Gordon. See Barrett, Gayle Gordon Rhea (wife of Melvin)
Rhimer, Robert Ellis, 29
Rhimer, Shirley Ruth Simmons (wife of Robert), 25, 29
Rhoades, Clyde Jim, 226
Rhoades, Erma Faye Whitten (wife of Clyde), 223, 226
Rhodes, Alma Mcree. See McCan, Alma Mcree Rhodes (wife of William)
Rhodes, Beatrice. See Whitten, Beatrice Rhodes (wife of Harold)
Rhodes, Jewell Ona Manning (wife of William), 44, 59
Rhodes, Robbie Orine. See Manning, Robbie Orine Rhodes (wife of Billy)
Rhodes, William Hayes, 59
Rhyner, Frances Dorene Martin (wife of Gerald), 72
Rhyner, Gerald William, 72
Rice, Christopher David, 131, 140
Rice, David Hay, 131, 140
Rice, Dora Mae Whitten (wife of Thomas), 110, 120

Rice, Judy Dianne Vinson (wife of David), 119, 131, 140
Rice, Melody Dianne, 131, 140
Rice, Paula Ann, 81, 99
Rice, Robert Ernest, 81, 99
Rice, Thomas Allen, 120

284

Roten, Howard Macon, 148, 151, 156
Roten, Irvin Tabor, 148, 152, 156
Roten, James Whitten, 152, 157
Roten, Jessie McDowell (wife of Irvin), 152, 156
Roten, Jo Bess. See Casey, Jo Bess Roten (wife of William)
Roten, Karen Leigh. See Crawford, Karen Leigh Roten (wife of George)
Roten, Laura Ann, 160, 162
Roten, Leola. See Metts, Leola Roten (wife of James)
Roten, Loyce Marie. See LaCombe, Loyce Marie Roten (wife of Eugene)
Roten, Lucy Odom (wife of Edward), 151, 156
Roten, Lucy Victoria. See Duty, Lucy Victoria Roten (wife of Emmitt)
Roten, Luray, 151, 156
Roten, Martha Ellen Evans (wife of Howard), 151, 156
Roten, Marvinal, 152, 156
Roten, May J. Laughter (wife of Edward), 151, 156
Roten, Neil, 151, 156
Roten, Nellie Grace Wilson (wife of Wallace), 156, 160
Roten, Nena. See McDonald, Nena Roten (wife of Joseph)
Roten, Oran, 151, 156
Roten, Patricia Dianne. See Hammelman, Patricia Dianne Roten (wife of James)
Roten, Patrick Robert, 160, 162
Roten, Pleasant, 151, 156
Roten, Robert Wallace, 157, 160, 162
Roten, Ruba Lee. See Vining, Ruba Lee Roten (wife of George)
Roten, Ruby Lee. See Jackson, Ruby Lee Roten (wife of J. C.)
Roten, Shirley Ann. See Guidry, Shirley Ann Roten (wife of Roland)
Roten, Travis, 152, 156
Roten, Wallace Wesley, 152, 156, 160
Roten, Walter, 152, 156
Roten, William Marvin, 142, 148, 156
Rousculp, Carole Lynne. See Roten, Carole Lynne Rousculp (wife of Robert)
Rowlett, Floi Slater Landrum (wife of James), 211, 217
Rowlett, James Benjamin, 217
Roy, Adams Hughes, 127, 138
Roy, Charlotte Ann Hughes (wife of Vance Jr.), 127, 137
Roy, Hazel Marie Whitten (wife of Vance), 108, 117, 127
Roy, Vance Cyril, 117, 127
Roy, Vance Cyril Jr., 117, 127, 137
Roy, Vanessa Lyn. See Morse, Vanessa Lyn Roy (wife of Richard)
Rucker, Carol Jefferson, 117, 127
Rucker, Clyde Lafayette, 117, 127
Rucker, Eleanor Kee Whitten (wife of Thomas), 108, 117, 244

Rucker, Eleanor Kee Whitten (wife Thomas), 103
Rucker, Eleanor Maxine, 117, 127
Rucker, Emmaline Medora. See Rucker, Eleanor Kee Whitten (wife of Thomas)
Rucker, Ernest, 108, 117, 127
Rucker, Ernestine, 117, 127
Rucker, Evelyn Kee. See Harris, Evelyn Kee Rucker
Rucker, Garnier Gill (wife of Ernest), 117, 127
Rucker, Jesse Rogers, 117, 127
Rucker, Joe Rogers, 108, 117
Rucker, Lloyd Jackson, 117, 127
Rucker, Mary Elaine, 117, 127
Rucker, Rufus Lee, 117, 127
Rucker, Rupert Clyde, 108, 117, 127
Rucker, Sarah Lou, 117, 127
Rucker, Thomas Counsielle, 108, 117
Rucker, Troy Ellis, 117, 127
Rucker, William Harrell, 117, 127
Rucker, Willie Leaty Spencer (wife of Rupert), 117, 127
Rudicil, Brenda Diane. See Siverston, Brenda Diane Rudicil (wife of George)
Rudicil, Lonzo Quitman, 64, 86
Rudicil, Margaret Faye Barrett (wife on Lonzo), 48, 64, 86
Rudicil, Margaret Kay. See Smith, Margaret Kay Rudicil (wife of Charles)
Rudicil, Wanda Carol, 64
Runnells, Virginia Isabel. See Barrett, Virginia Isabel Runnels (wife of Hugh)
Rush, Matteel. See Crowe, Matteel Rush (wife of William)
Russell, Ema Miller (wife of H. H.), 24, 28
Russell, Emma Goss, 22
Russell, H. H., 22, 28
Rust, Albert, 9
Rust, Alberta, 7, 9
Rust, Eliza Adaline Reagan (wife of Francis), 6, 7, 9
Rust, Elizabeth Alice, 7, 9
Rust, Francis Marion, 7
Rust, James Edwin, 7
Rust, Matilda E., 7, 9
Rust, Noble Marion, 7, 9
Rust, Robert William, 9

S

Salmon, James, 157
Salmon, Pauline Ross Barley (wife of James), 152, 157
Sample, Anna C. Lankford (wife of James), 102, 105, 111, 244
Sample, Anna Margaret, 111, 120
Sample, Dora Eugenia. See Davis, Dora Eugenia Sample (wife of J. T.)
Sample, Dwight Edward, 111, 120

Sample, Fannie Lula Lynn. See Mauldin, Fannie Lula Lynn Sample (wife of Charles)
Sample, James, 105, 111
Sample, James Dwight, 111, 120
Sample, Jeanne, 111, 120
Sample, Jessie Dwight, 105, 111, 120
Sample, Josephine, 111, 120
Sample, Lulyn Dorothy, 120, 134
Sample, Margaret Rosanna Kimmons (wife of Jesse), 111, 120
Sample, Maurine Earle. See Jackson, Maurine Earle Sample (wife of J. T.)
Sample, Mollie Juanita. See Yarbrough, Mollie Juanita Sample (wife of D. M.)
Sample, Pauline McCullough (wife of James), 120
Samsa, Beverly. See Brooks, Beverly Samsa (wife of John III)
Sands, Madel. See Barrett, Madel Sandes (wife of Edgar)
Satterwhite, Norma Mae. See Forrester, Norma Mae Satterwhite (wife of Leroy)
Savage, Barbara Kay Willet (wife of Joseph), 232, 235
Savage, Delores Ray Miller (wife of Joseph), 225, 229, 232
Savage, John David, 232, 235
Savage, Joseph Bruce, 229, 232
Savage, Joseph Dwight, 229, 232, 235
Savage, Katherine Dean. See Danzy, Katherine Dean Savage (wife of Terry)
Savage, Mary. See Hamilton, Mary Savage (wife of Otis)
Savage, Rainey Ray, 232, 235
Savage, Stephen Dane, 229
Sawyer, Mary Patricia Floyd (wife of Thomas), 30, 32
Sawyer, Ruth. See Whitten, Ruth Sawyer (wife of Silas Ray)
Sawyer, Thomas M., 32
Sawyer, Thomas Vincent, 32
Schatte, Lucille. See Barrett, Lucille Schatte (wife of George T.)
Schneiderman, Ester Elizabeth. See Miller, Ester Elizabeth Schneiderman (wife of Raymond)
Schofield, Emily. See Cook, Emily Schofield (wife of Fenton)
Schrum, Henry, 24
Schrum, Mary Josephine Perry (wife of Henry), 17, 24
Schulenberg, Joanne. See Kendall, Joanne Schulenberg (wife of Robert)
Schuler, George, 193, 196
Schuler, Lola (wife of George), 191, 193, 196
Schuler, Ruth, 193, 196
Schultz, Kimberly Kay. See Jessup, Kimberly Kay Schultz (wife of Benjamin)

Stansel, Ellizabeth Farrow. See Duke, Elizabeth Farrow Stansel (wife of Shelby)
Stansel, Eugene Augustus, 29, 31
Stansel, Eugene Augustus Jr., 29, 31, 33
Stansel, Jane Gilbert (wife of Eugene Jr.), 31, 33
Stansel, Martha Alford, 29, 31
Stanton-Neeley, Rebecca DeLona. See Reagan, Rebecca DeLona Stanton-Neeley (wife of Thomas)
Staples, George A., 158, 161
Staples, George A. Jr., 158, 162
Staples, Harriet Louise Whitten (wife of George), 153, 158, 161
Staples, Leven, 158, 162
Stapp, Mattie Bobo (wife of W. M.), 36, 40
Stapp, W. M., 40
Starns, Hazel Louise. See Grady, Hazel Louise Starns (wife of Clyde), See Malone, Hazel Louise Starns (wife of Billy)
Starns, Louis B., 57, 76
Starns, Margaret Ann. See Villars, Margaret Ann Starns (wife of Vernon)
Starns, Mary Alice. See Janicke, Mary Alice Starns (wife of Raymond), See Robertson, Mary Alice Starns (wife of Donald)
Starns, Mattie Addie Barrett (wife of Louis), 43, 57, 76
Stearns, Christianna. See Dohman, Christianna Stearns (wife of Henrik)
Stein, Charles, 126, 137
Stein, Grace Jasmine, 126, 137
Stein, Merri Lynn Whitten (wife of Charles), 116, 126, 137
Stenzel, Jeanne Ardell. See Skains, Jeannne Ardell Stenzel (wife of Billie)
Stephens, Alma. See Gilbert, Alma Stephens
Stephens, Annie, 23, 27
Stephens, Frances. See Hatlford, Francis Stephens
Stephens, George, 23, 27
Stephens, Jack Kyle, 233
Stephens, Mary Jane Ard (wife of Wesley), 16, 23, 27
Stephens, Myliss Marie Miller (wife of Jack), 229, 233
Stephens, Wesley W., 23, 27
Stephenson, Ashley L., 225, 230
Stephenson, Helen Whitten (wife of Ashley), 225, 230
Stephenson, Judy, 225, 230
Sterling, Jack, 85
Sterling, Lloyd, 226
Sterling, Mary Louise Whitten (wife of Lloyd), 223, 226
Sterling, Sandra Anna Vetuski (wife of Jack), 63, 85
Stevens, Alex David, 208, 209

Stevens, Carrie Sisson (wife of David), 203, 209
Stevens, David Simmons, 203, 208, 209
Stevers, Kyle Vincent, 208, 209
Stevers, Martha Jean Simmons (wife of Vernon), 198, 203, 208
Stevens, Vernon Edward, 203, 208
Stevens, Vernon Edward (son), 203
Stevenson, Alan, 77, 97
Stevenson, Scott, 77, 97
Stevenson, Theda Rae Barrett (wife of Wayne), 57, 77, 97
Stevenson, Wayne, 77, 97
Stewart, Dan Jr., 148, 152
Stewart, Daniel, 88
Stewart, Dylan Anthony, 88
Stewart, Helen Josephine Whitten (wife of James), 147, 148, 152
Stewart, James A., 148, 152
Stewart, Jim, 148, 152
Stewart, Lillie Stephens, 23, 30
Stewart, Mary Helen. See Park, Mary Helen Stewart (wife of James)
Stewart, Norman, 148, 152
Stewart, Tana Arlene Dixon (wife of Daniel), 67, 88
Stocker, Marjorie. See Moreland, Marjorie Stocker (wife of Rembert)
Stone, Barbara Elaine Martin (wife of Oscar), 53, 72, 92
Stone, David Bryne, 72, 93
Stone, Jonathon Martin, 72, 93
Stone, Oscar Bryne Jr., 73, 92
Stovall, Bonna Fay Whitten (wife of Richard), 118, 128
Stovall, Richard Frank, 118, 128
Stowe, Clyde, 52, 70
Stowe, Debra June. See McCan, Debra June Stowe (wife of John)
Stowe, George W., 52, 70
Stowe, Harold, 52, 70
Stowe, Maggie E. See McCan, Maggie E. Stowe (wife of Benjamin)
Stowe, Oddis, 52, 70
Stowe, Talitha Amanda Golden (wife of William), 52, 70
Straley, A. Carl, 48, 64
Straley, A. Carl Jr., 48, 65
Straley, Ercel Barrett (wife of Carl), 39, 48, 64
Strange, Susan. See Turner, Susan Strange (wife of James)
Street, Anita. See Horton, Anita Street (wife of James)
Street, Effie Whitten (wife of Vibrait), 169, 170, 172
Street, Hazel Franklin (wife of John), 172, 173
Street, John Whitten, 170, 172, 173
Street, Mary Rogers (wife of Robert), 172, 173
Street, Mavis Miller (wife of Vernon), 172, 173
Street, Robert, 170, 172, 173
Street, Vernon, 170, 172, 173

Street, Vibrait L., 170, 172
Strickland, Dick, 63
Strickland, Dolly Mae William (wife of John), 47, 63
Strickland, Vivian. See Lowry, Vivian Strickland (wife of Mark)
Stringer, Mary Jeanette. See McCann, Mary Jeanette Stringer (wife of Carl)
Stroud, Fatima Ann. See Harper, Fatima Ann Stroud (wife of Donald)
Stubblefield, Sarah Holt Lee (wife of William), 198, 203
Stubblefield, William, 198, 203
Stuht, Albert, 194, 196
Stuht, Albert (son), 195, 198
Stuht, Earnest, 195, 198
Stuht, Norma Hamilton (wife of Albert), 192, 194, 198
Stuht, William Boyd, 195, 198
Stuts, Wanda. See Manning, Wanda Stuts (wife of Lloyd)
Sullivan, Arthur A., 62, 83
Sullivan, Dan Arthur, 62, 83
Sullivan, James Vick, 62, 83
Sullivan, Janet (wife of Dan), 83
Sullivan, Jenny Morlen (wife of James), 83
Sullivan, Mary Evelyn Barrett (wife of Arthur A.), 47, 62, 83
Sump, William Ray, 87
Suskin, Leslie Brooks (wife of Marc), 30, 32
Suskin, Marc, 32
Suskin, Marc (son of Marc), 32
Suskin, Sam, 32
Suttles, Elsie Dell Clark (wife of Paul), 44, 59, 80
Suttles, Paul, 59, 80
Swann, Harriette V. Whitten (wife of William), 14, 16
Swann, William H., 16
Sweat, Yvonne. See Green, Yvonne Sweat (wife of Ripley Jr.)

T

Tabler, Amanda Elizabeth McCann (wife of Jesse), 42, 55, 75
Tabler, Angela. See Barnes, Angela Tabler (wife of Paul)
Tabler, Annie. See Spiginer, Annie Tabler (wife of Glenn)
Tabler, Barbara B., 75, 94
Tabler, Barbara Elaine. See Beaver, Barbara Elaine Tabler (wife of Carl), See Dyer, Barbara Elaine Tabler (wife of Louis)
Tabler, Charles Morroe, 55, 75, 94
Tabler, Christopher, 94
Tabler, Connie Baker (wife of Russell), 75, 94
Tabler, Diedra, 75, 94
Tabler, Jesse, 94
Tabler, Jesse Benjamin, 55, 75
Tabler, Jessie, 75
Tabler, Judy (wife of Richard), 75

Whitten, Cardelia Capehart (wife of Benjamin), 126, 137
Whitten, Carl M., 222, 226
Whitten, Carl Mack, 221, 223
Whitten, Carla Wardenburg (wife of Andrew), 135, 144
Whitten, Carlinne. See Higgins, Carlinne Whitten (wife of John)
Whitten, Carol Margaret Gifford (wife of William), 129, 139
Whitten, Carol Teresa Boyles (wife of Joseph), 107, 126
Whitten, Caroline Matilda Prince (wife of Alfred), 147
Whitten, Carrie (wife of Charles), 237, 238, 239
Whitten, Carrie Isabel. See Richardson, Carrie Isabel Whitten (wife of Mark)
Whitten, Carrie Lynn, 130, 140
Whitten, Cary Langston, 130, 140
Whitten, Catharine Whiting Jones (wife of Alvin), 209, 210
Whitten, Cecile Boyd Young (wife of Nathaniel), 129
Whitten, Charlene. See Money, Charlene Whitten (Richard)
Whitten, Charles, 4, 11–12, 12, 13, 26, 175, 244–47
Whitten, Charles (son of John), 1, 33
Whitten, Charles II, 167
Whitten, Charles Jr., 1, 15, 175–76, 243
Whitten, Charles Alvin, 210, 212, 213
Whitten, Charles Alvin Jr., 212, 213
Whitten, Charles Everette, 237, 238, 239, 243
Whitten, Charles Mack, 220, 222, 243
Whitten, Charles Mack (son of Ukler), 223, 226
Whitten, Charles William, 221, 222
Whitten, Christine Pedrosa (wife of Ronaldo), 139, 145

Whitten, Christopher, 139, 145
Whitten, Christopher Mark, 137
Whitten, Clara Mae. See McCommon, Clara Mae Whitten (wife of Joseph)
Whitten, Clifford Ausbun, 223, 226
Whitten, Climmie Twanda, 110, 120
Whitten, Clyde Hearne. See Gordon, Clyde Hearne Whitten (wife of Frank), See McCart, Clyde Hearne Whitten (wife of J. B.)
Whitten, Connie T. See Blanchard, Connie T. Whitten (wife of Burton)
Whitten, Cora, 221, 223
Whitten, Cora Mae, 104, 110
Whitten, Cordia D. Savell (wife of Robert Lee), 149, 153
Whitten, Corinne Eahi, 210, 211
Whitten, Corinne Levinia Thomas (wife of James), 210, 211
Whitten, Corrine. See Burke, Corrine Whitten (wife of Wiliam)
Whitten, Dale Wayne, 225, 230
Whitten, Daniel Lee, 124, 135

Whitten, Darth Lou Davis (wife of Erby), 224, 227
Whitten, David Milton, 166, 171, 174
Whitten, Deborah Ann, 119, 130
Whitten, Della Kee. See Williams, Della Kee Whitten (wife of Thomas)
Whitten, Dianne, 228, 231
Whitten, Doleska Fitzallen "Dolly", 13, 14, 15, 20, 245–47
Whitten, Donald Homer, 113, 122
Whitten, Donna Alice Ruby, 113, 122
Whitten, Donna Kaye, 158, 162
Whitten, Dora Mae. See Rice, Dora Mae Whitten (wife of Thomas)
Whitten, Doris Ann. See Haggard, Doris Ann Whitten (wife of Ralph)
Whitten, Dorothy, 221, 223
Whitten, Dorothy (wife of Dudley E.), 213
Whitten, Dorothy Iola Jordan (wife of John Graves Jr.), 113
Whitten, Dorothy Louise, 113, 122
Whitten, Dortha Estell Kirland (wife of Bonner), 118, 128
Whitten, Dudley E., 211, 213
Whitten, Dudley J., 175, 209
Whitten, Dudley V., 210, 211, 212
Whitten, Duett Gordon, 220, 221, 232, 243
Whitten, Earle R., 238
Whitten, Earnest Cecil, 223, 226
Whitten, Edd, 149, 153, 158
Whitten, Ediwn, 167, 168
Whitten, Edward, 153, 158
Whitten, Edward Earle, 106, 113, 122
Whitten, Edward Earle Jr., 113, 122
Whitten, Edward Lee, 170, 171, 173
Whitten, Edward Lee III, 173, 174
Whitten, Effie. See Street, Effie Whitten (wife of Vibrait)

Whitten, Effie Berry. See Perkins, Effie Berry Whitten (wife of John)
Whitten, Eileen Aubrey, 211, 212
Whitten, Eleanor Kee. See Rucker, Eleanor Kee Whitten (wife of Thomas)
Whitten, Eleanor Kee Earle (wife of Silas), 18, 21, 100, 101, 244
Whitten, Elena Hunter, 135, 144
Whitten, Eliza. See Whitten, Elizabeth Ann
Whitten, Elizabeth. See Barrett, Elizabeth Whitten (wife of David)
Whitten, Elizabeth (daughter of Alfred), 169, 171
Whitten, Elizabeth Ann "Liza" (Eliza), 12, 14, 15, 22, 245–46
Whitten, Elizabeth Ann Thompson (wife of James), 12, 21
Whitten, Elizabeth M. (wife of Jesse), 237, 238
Whitten, Elizabeth Sullivan (wife of Ranson), 167

Whitten, Ella Maude Ingram (wife of Jessie), 223, 227
Whitten, Ellen Floyd (wife of Berry), 153
Whitten, Elliot Kee. See Belote, Elliot Kee Whitten (wife of James)
Whitten, Elliott Ann Ray (wife of Alfred W.), 102
Whitten, Elliott Ann Ray (wife of Alfred), 102, 105, 106
Whitten, Ellis H., 168, 170, 171
Whitten, Elton B., 169, 170, 172
Whitten, Elvira Edgel. See Perry, Elvira Edgel Whitten (wife of James)
Whitten, Elwanda Kniffin (wife of Woodrow), 116, 126
Whitten, Emily, 13, 14
Whitten, Emily C. Brownlee (wife of Edd), 149, 153, 158
Whitten, Emily Inez Wade (wife of William), 110, 120
Whitten, Emma Landusky, 148
Whitten, Erby Judson, 219, 221, 227
Whitten, Eric Matthew, 130, 140
Whitten, Erma Faye. See Rhoades, Erma Faye Whitten (wife of Clyde)
Whitten, Ernest Garrett, 221, 222, 226
Whitten, Ervin Dunaway, 147, 148
Whitten, Estelle Meacham (wife of Joseph), 115, 125
Whitten, Ester Riggs (wife of Leslie III), 135
Whitten, Ethel Duckworth (wife of Elton), 170, 172
Whitten, Ethyl W., 168, 169
Whitten, Eugene Grimes, 147, 148
Whitten, Evelyn (wife of Frank), 226
Whitten, Evelyn Kay. See Burkitt, Evelyn Kay Whitten (wife of Frank)
Whitten, Evelyn Vaughn (wife of Ralph), 227, 231
Whitten, Fannie Carter (wife of Leven), 153, 158
Whitten, Fannie Eugenie, 211
Whitten, Faye. See Bradley, Faye Whitten (wife of J. L.)
Whitten, Faye B. See Moore, Faye B. Whitten (wife of Edgar)
Whitten, Flora Lee Bennett (wife of Bedford), 107, 115
Whitten, Florence Lee, 110, 119
Whitten, Florence Williams (wife of Leon), 110
Whitten, Frances Ann Yates (wife of Edward), 170, 171, 173, 224, 228
Whitten, Frances Medora Ray (wife of Silas Jr.), 101
Whitten, Frank Adams, 20, 101, 103, 106, 109
Whitten, Frank Adams Jr., 104, 109
Whitten, Frank Alma. See Tate, Frank Alma Whitten (wife of Charles)
Whitten, Frank E., 222, 226
Whitten, Frank Harvey, 114, 124
Whitten, Gary, 158, 162

Whitten, Mary Ellen Tate (wife of
William), 104, 110
Whitten, Mary Elliott. See Holcomb,
Mary Elliott Whitten (wife of Roy)
Whitten, Mary H., 169, 170
Whitten, Mary Jane. See Anderson,
Mary Jane Whitten (wife of Edward)
Whitten, Mary Jane (daughter of John D.
G.), 148, 149
Whitten, Mary Leala. See Miller, Mary
Leala Whitten (wife of Leala)
Whitten, Mary Louise. See Sterling,
Mary Louise Whitten (wife of Lloyd)
Whitten, Mary Lynn. See Ellis, Mary
Lynn Whitten (wife of Comer)
Whitten, Mary M. Allen (wife of
Charles), 220, 222
Whitten, Mary M. E., 220
Whitten, Mary Phips (wife of John R.),
218, 219
Whitten, Mary Reagan (wife of John), 1,
2, 4, 11, 15, 33, 167
Whitten, Masina Deborah Adams (wife
of Joseph), 101, 104, 106
Whitten, Mason, 13
Whitten, Matilda Allen. See Crowe,
Matilda Allen Whitten (wife of Ira)
Whitten, Matilda Allen Bennett (wife of
Arphax), 13, 15, 21, 244–47
Whitten, Mattie E. Bell (wife of Dudley),
211, 212
Whitten, Mattie Ervin (wife of Ernest),
222, 226
Whitten, Maude Elliott, 20
Whitten, Maude Elliott. See Bradley,
Maude Elliott Whitten (wife of
Frank)
Whitten, Maureen Margaret Foster (wife
of Kenneth), 129, 140
Whitten, Maxine, 115, 125
Whitten, May, 221, 223
Whitten, May Isom. See Moore, May
Isom Whitten (wife of William)
Whitten, Melba. See Bowman, Melba
Whitten (wife of R. V.)
Whitten, Melicent Mazelle. See Goss,
Melicent Mazelle Whitten (wife of
Nathaniel)
Whitten, Melissa Ann. See Crenshaw,
Melissa Ann Whitten (wife of Joe)
Whitten, Merri Lynn. See Stein, Merri
Lynn Whitten (wife of Charles)
Whitten, Mesina Elliot. See Smith,
Mesina Elliot Whitten (wife of
Varda)
Whitten, Mildred Pauline Darwin (wife
of Jessie), 119
Whitten, Millicent Reagan (wife of
Charles Jr.), 1, 3, 4, 15, 175, 243
Whitten, Milly, 11
Whitten, Milton Clay, 169, 170
Whitten, Minnie Irene Shannon (wife of
James), 211, 213
Whitten, Miriam Bonner Lesley (wife of
Nathaniel), 118, 129

Whitten, Mirian Elinor, 109
Whitten, Montine Taylor (wife of
William), 119, 129
Whitten, Moses L., 13
Whitten, Mozelle Manning (wife of
Leven Jr.), 158, 162
Whitten, Myra Jean Prather (wife of
Jerry), 129, 139
Whitten, Myrle Kirkham (wife of
Clifford), 223, 226
Whitten, Myrtle Anna Wiseman (wife of
Nathaniel), 109, 118
Whitten, Nancy, 13
Whitten, Nancy (daughter of John). See
Dalton, Nancy Whitten (wife of John
Bradley)
Whitten, Nancy Ann Lewis Malone
(wife of Alfred), 147, 148
Whitten, Nancy Hollan. See Thomason,
Nancy Hollan Whitten (wife of
James)
Whitten, Nancy Smith (wife of Charles),
1, 4, 11, 175, 244
Whitten, Narcissa Amaryllis. See
Holcombe, Narcissa Amaryllis
Whitten (wife of Elias)
Whitten, Nathaniel Carter, 104, 109, 118
Whitten, Nathaniel Carter II, 128, 138
Whitten, Nathaniel Craig, 118, 129
Whitten, Nathaniel Harbin, 22
Whitten, Nathaniel Murry, 109, 118, 129
Whitten, Neil Durwood, 115, 124
Whitten, Nellie Geneva Worlow (wife of
James Albert), 225, 230
Whitten, Nena. See Benham, Nena
Whitten (wife of Thomas)
Whitten, Nettie D. See Moody, Nettie D.
Whitten (wife of Augustus)
Whitten, Nettie Mae Hand (wife of
Ellis), 170, 171
Whitten, Neva Maude, 223, 227
Whitten, Nicholas Boone, 173, 174
Whitten, Nicole Lynn. See Pickens,
Nicole Lynn Whitten (wife of James)
Whitten, Nora A. See Fortenberry, Nora
A. Whitten (wife of Lige)
Whitten, Nora Barber (wife of Albert),
170
Whitten, Olivia Linnore, 135, 144
Whitten, Opal. See Carter, Opal Whitten
(wife of Henry)
Whitten, Opal Morgan (wife of John),
227, 231
Whitten, Ora May Phillips (wife of
Benjamin), 113
Whitten, Orpha Judson. See Hogan,
Orpha Judson Whitten (wife of
Thomas), See Lamb, Orpha Judson
Whitten (wife of Alexander)
Whitten, Patience Stone, 126, 137
Whitten, Patricia Odell, 115, 124
Whitten, Paula Laeta, 107, 114
Whitten, Paulene Earle. See
Cunningham, Paulene Earle Whitten
(wife of Gilbert)

Whitten, Pauline Wakeland (wife of
Abb), 153
Whitten, Pearl, 147, 150, 176
Whitten, Pearly Gladys. See Crews,
Pearl Gladys Whitten (wife of
William)
Whitten, Peggy Ann Gurley (wife of
Taylor), 130, 140
Whitten, Permelia Laura, 243
Whitten, Phyllis Webber (wife of Leslie),
123, 135
Whitten, Pochontas Medora Rogers (wife
of Ranson), 103, 108
Whitten, Ralph Asbury, 224, 227, 231
Whitten, Ralph Ukler, 223, 226
Whitten, Ranson, 12, 103, 108
Whitten, Ranson Edwin, 14, 15, 20, 21,
99, 101, 108, 109, 177, 191, 244–47
Whitten, Ranson Hosea, 103, 108
Whitten, Rebecca "Becca" Berry, 11, 20,
21, 101, 102, 175, 237
Whitten, Rebecca Ann M. See
Deshough, Rebecca Ann M. Whitten
(wife of Sam)
Whitten, Rebecca Isabel. See Malone,
Rebecca Isabel Whitten (wife of
Floyd)
Whitten, Rebecca Joyce. See Jackson,
Rebecca Joyce Whitten (wife of
John)
Whitten, Recile, 223, 227
Whitten, Richardson, 212, 213
Whitten, Richie Bridges (wife of Lester),
115
Whitten, Robbie Estelle Smothers (wife
of Howard), 116, 126
Whitten, Robert, 155, 158, 222, 226

Whitten, Robert Bailey, 170, 171, 172
Whitten, Robert Bailey Jr., 171, 173
Whitten, Robert Jr., 225, 231
Whitten, Robert Lee, 147, 149, 153
Whitten, Ronaldo, 129, 139, 145
Whitten, Rosa L., 222, 226
Whitten, Roscoe Earl, 223, 226
Whitten, Rose Marie McNerney (wife of
Stanley), 124, 135
Whitten, Royce, 223, 226
Whitten, Ruby, 170
Whitten, Ruby Farris (wife of Sam), 153,
158
Whitten, Ruth. See Landers, Ruth
Whitten (wife of Harry)
Whitten, Ruth Allen (wife of Silas), 221,
223
Whitten, Ruth Christine. See Levring,
Ruth Christine Whitten (wife of
Carl)
Whitten, Ruth Mignon, 223, 227
Whitten, Ruth Sawyer (wife of Silas
Ray), 106, 113
Whitten, Sallie Griffin Worsham (wife of
John), 105, 112
Whitten, Sam, 168, 169

Young, Marsha Lee, 125, 136
Young, Mary Grace. See Malone, Mary
 Grace Young (wife of James)
Young, Nancy Elizabeth. See Smith,
 Nancy Elizabeth Young (wife of
 Scott)
Young, Nancy Lynn, 125
Young, Nancy Perry (wife of James), 27,
 30, 32

Young, Patricia Brown (wife of Loren),
 125, 136
Young, Rufus, 247
Young, Ticer, 115, 125
Younger, Brian Allen, 233, 236
Younger, Elizabeth Gail Shields (wife of
 George), 229, 236
Younger, George Allen, 236
Younger, Kelly Mari, 27, 236

Z

Zimmerman, Joan, 161, 163
Zimmerman, Luther Miles, 161, 163
Zimmerman, Marilyn Gwen. See Palmer,
 Marilyn Gwen Zimmerman (wife of
 Ronnie)
Zimmerman, Mary Maxine Reed (wife
 of Luther), 157, 161, 163

www.ingramcontent.com/pod-product-compliance
Lightning Source LLC
Chambersburg PA
CBHW080413270326
41929CB00018B/3014